The Chinese

The Chinese

Portrait of a People

by
Alain Peyrefitte

Translated from the French by
Graham Webb

The Bobbs-Merrill Company, Inc.
Indianapolis/New York

Designed by Jerry Byers
Manufactured in the United States of America

Library of Congress Cataloging in Publication Data

Peyrefitte, Roger Alain, 1925–
   The Chinese.
   Includes index.
   1. China—Civilization—1949–   I. Title.
DS724.P48   951.05   76–11620
ISBN 0–672–52005–2

ACKNOWLEDGMENTS

I would like to thank the Chinese authorities, who made all the facilities we wanted available to our study mission and gave us a very warm welcome: Their Excellencies the late Prime Minister, Chou En-lai; the President of the Academy of Sciences, Kuo Mo-jo; the Minister of Foreign Affairs, Chi Peng-fei; and Ambassador Huang Chen;

the Chinese people—workers, peasants, soldiers, intellectuals, cadres, officials of revolutionary committees, students, school children and Red Guards—whose conversations were of great value to us;

the French Ambassador in Peking, Étienne Manach, and his colleagues, experienced China hands whom he permitted to accompany us;

the French Consul-General in Hong Kong, Gérard de la Villèsbrunne, who arranged some useful contacts for me; and the officials of the Assemblée Nationale who traveled with us and were patient enough to make notes of our conversations and keep an hour-by-hour diary of the trip;

the journalists whose curious minds contributed a great deal to making our trip so rewarding: Jean Carlier, Maurice Delarue, Jean-François Kahn, Georges Menant, André Pavolini, Jean-Claude Turjmann, Bernard Volker, and especially Robert Guillain, for whom this was the sixth trip to China since 1937, and Max Olivier-Lacamp and Marc Riboud, who made some useful comparisons between our trip and others they had made to China;

and the sinologists who were very willing to instruct me in their science—Lucien Bianco, Professor of the History of China at the École Pratique des Hautes Études; Jacques Guillermaz, Director of Studies and Director of the Centre de Documentation sur l'Extrême-Orient at the École Pratique des Hautes Études; and my old friend Robert Ruhlmann, Professor of Chinese at the Institut National des Langues et Civilisations Orientales.

CONTENTS

PART FOUR
THE PRICE OF SUCCESS

"Quand la Chine s'eveillera,
le monde tremblera . . ."

("When China rises, the world
will tremble . . .")

—NAPOLEON

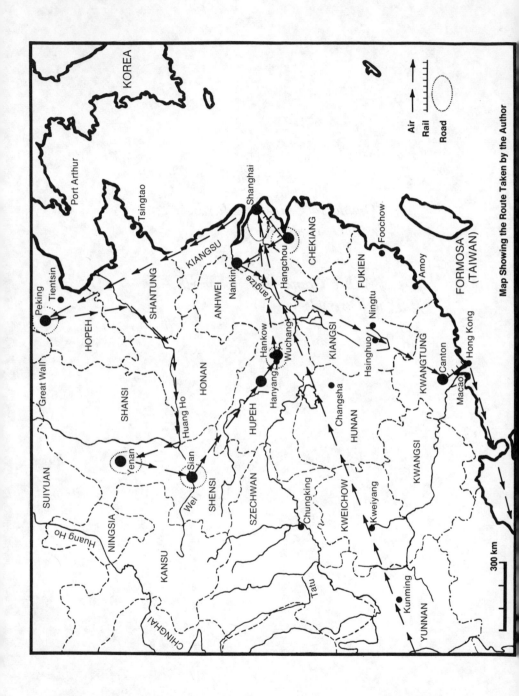

Map Showing the Route Taken by the Author

Part I

Some Secrets

of the

Chinese Way

The Chinese Way is the Way of man. The Chinese Way will last as long as mankind.

Wang Tao (1870)

The civilization of Europe and America is completely materialistic. There is nothing more vulgar, more brutal, more evil. We Chinese call that barbarism. Our inferiority as a power derives from the fact that we have always scorned and avoided it. The Chinese Way is the way of mankind and morals. Our ancient books call this system the royal Way.

Sun Yat-sen (1925)

Contemporary China has grown out of the China of the past; we are Marxist in our historical approach and must not lop off our history. We should sum up our history from Confucius to Sun Yat-sen and take over this valuable legacy. This is important for guiding the great movement of today. . . . We can put Marxism into practice only when it is integrated with the specific characteristics of our country and acquires a definite national form.

Mao Tse-tung (1938)

We must tell the people and tell our comrades that there will be twists and turns in our road. There are still many obstacles and difficulties along the road of revolution. We must be prepared to follow a road which twists and turns.

Mao Tse-tung (1945)

1

Introduction: A Model, a Fashion and a System

A few days before I left for the People's Republic of China, the President of the West Berlin Polytechnic Students' Union told me with considerable passion: "My comrades and I aren't here to study. We're here to make the revolution. And we intend to stick together until we've founded the socialist society." I asked: "What's a socialist society?" He replied: "A truly egalitarian society in which there are no classes and where men live not for themselves but for others, not for profit but for justice." My friend Fritz Stern* asked: "Has such a society ever existed? Can it exist?" The student leader replied: "We've seen that the Soviet model has failed. But the society we want does exist—in China. We'll adapt the Chinese model to conditions in Germany."

"The Chinese Model"—the same phrase kept cropping up in Bremen, in Hamburg and in Stuttgart, and we heard similar statements from student leaders, lecturers and even professors. We had heard them in France, and we were hearing them again in Germany. But wasn't this less a "model" than a fashion?

With China, the fashion is produced by an enigma—Too much mystery discourages curiosity; a little less intensifies it. During the Cultural Revolution, when the country was in a state of frenzy, the information that came out was either too paltry for interest or merely unconvincing. After five years, during which the country withdrew into itself, a few visas were granted and

---

*Professor of the History of Ideas at Columbia University and a member of an O.E.C.D. study delegation I led to various German universities.

the dialogue with the West was resumed—and this was enough to create the same kind of infatuation with China that there had been with the Soviet Union after the death of Stalin. On my way home from China, I took a few days off in Jerusalem, and as I was climbing up to the Qumran caves, I was joined by some Israeli journalists. They wanted to know if my stopover meant I had been secretly negotiating the establishment of diplomatic relations between Peking and Tel-Aviv. And at Orly airport, a huge crowd had gathered; I was asked if I was carrying a message from Chairman Mao to President Pompidou.

In the most famous travel book ever written, *Description of the World*,* Marco Polo talks of the intermingling of two civilizations, one of great refinement, scented with jasmine, and the other savage and brutal, stinking of the droppings of Tartar horses. Whenever his story bordered on the incredible, Marco Polo stamped it with his personal seal: "And at the time when all this happened, Messer Marco was there." He assured his reader that he was telling only a small fraction of what he could relate. When called upon to confess that he had been lying, he retracted nothing, even on his death-bed. There was a general refusal to believe that on the other side of the globe there could live a people so different. But are we any better at accepting this today?

In subsequent centuries, the Western world built other defenses against its fear of the Occident. The dragon was kept at bay by drinking tea, importing lacquered screens, reproducing porcelain,** and painting coolie hats, mandarins in long robes and palankeens on walls.

Caricature and parody are the best ways to make a frightening phenom-enon harmless. Reducing the "Yellow Peril" to a passing fashion is nothing but a propitiatory rite. At the time of the French Revolution the children of the aristocracy used to amuse themselves in the gardens of the Jeu de Paume by watching puppets putting their heads on the block. A country bigger than Europe, which has twice the people and is so backward that many have to live on a bowl of rice a day, and yet is sufficiently advanced to have exploded thermonuclear devices before France, arouses a similar anxious fascination. But the monster is tamed by the craze for Chinoiseries—albeit nowadays political Chinoiseries. As an object of fashion, the Chinese model becomes a *scale model* reduced in size to fit within the confines of our intelligence and imagination, an exotic miniature which can take its place easily within our world.

In applying the term "model" to the social system in China, one is using the word in two senses—as an analytical schema and as an example to be followed. Both interpretations are valid.

---

*Better known to English readers as *The Travels* (TRANSLATOR'S NOTE).
**The "Chinese model" of Sèvres: the *Chinesisches Muster* of Meissen.

China is and aspires to remain a system. If a model is really, in the scientific sense of the term, "the simplified but complete representation of the main characteristics of a society,"* no society has ever sought with more determination to conform to the "representation" it makes of itself. The model becomes a vision. It is not an *a posteriori* explanation, but an *a priori* principle of action. The Maoist regime is trying to build a piece of precision engineering in which all the parts serve as keys to one another and are driven by a common source of energy—the revolutionary ideal.

As China gradually becomes the model she has chosen for herself, she also quite naturally becomes a model in the current sense of the word—a prototype to be imitated. Men have always been attracted by strong individuals who take control of their destiny, and the attraction when an entire people is involved is ten times greater.

This book sets out—through personal experience and reflection—to analyze this model which is shaping an entire society. It attempts to take it apart like a clock and to reveal the central idea from which each and every detail is defined. I should like to help the reader understand how the oldest civilization in the world is striving—by passing through a period of great turmoil—to become the newest.

Just as the Russian revolution remains the most important consequence of the First World War, the Chinese revolution is the most important consequence of the Second. These two revolutions have without doubt given rise to the greatest historical phenomena of the twentieth century. Were the two Chinese revolutions—the one culminating in 1949 and the Cultural Revolution—caused by the inability of traditional forces to adapt themselves to new conditions, or were they epic events heralding a world revolution? Were they a hope for the oppressed and injured everywhere or destructive convulsions? Did they represent the regeneration of the Third World, or the incarnation of Great Power chauvinism? And what chances does this model have, compared with the Soviet model, which although somewhat dated is still highly respected?

The fact that I made a study trip to China one summer does not in any way make me a Pekinologist, still less a sinologist. It would seem presumptuous of anyone to write about a country on such slight acquaintance. But how often can one say: "If I hadn't seen it, I wouldn't have believed it"? This happened in China. So the visitor is driven to write about what he has seen. You have to be there, on the spot, before you realize how much short-sightedness there is in the West; it is caused by prejudice, ideologies and, more than anything else, ignorance. People in the West lurch from fear to enthusiasm and back again, hardly ever managing to reach a balanced

---

*According to the classic definition given in A. Vincent, *Initiation à la conjoncture économique*, 1947.

judgment. Many of the books that have been written about China since 1949 do no more than present the hasty and unconsidered judgments of the passionate admirer and the crabby tourist. Even in the best of them—those I took with me—there are astonishing misconceptions.

A frog at the bottom of the well says: "The sky is no bigger than the mouth of the well." You should see the whole as well as the parts. There is no substitute for direct experience. "If you want to know the taste of a pear," Mao says, "you must change the pear by eating it yourself." Or, as Valéry might have put it, "As the fruit melts in acquaintance, as it changes its absence into knowledge . . ."

Time changes both the onlooker and the object at one and the same time. As I was strolling along the sun-baked streets of Hong Kong, like a "Westerner" returning to his planet, I was unable to shake off a feeling of alienation. Hong Kong had *changed*. I was shocked more than I had ever been before by the contrast between the luxury in its shop windows and the begging, scrounging street urchins, between the skyscrapers which are springing up all over the city and the misery of families packed into sampans and crammed into shanty-towns, between the city's convents and its prostitutes. China, too, had *changed* for me. It was not at all what I had imagined from the reports I had read by both admirers and critics. Still more mysterious, China had also become more familiar. Had *I changed*, perhaps? There is possibly no journey that makes the traveler feel more like a fish out of water than a journey to China. Teilhard de Chardin was told by a friend in Shanghai: "Quick, write about China before you've been there too long. If you leave it, you'll break your pen trying to write about it, because you'll have become incapable of understanding those fleeting, enigmatic people, whose values are not ours."*

This book covers our journey, in which we visited six of China's eighteen provinces. We stayed in Peking and Shanghai, but instead of visiting the third autonomous town, Tientsin, which they were prepared to take us to, we decided to go to Yenan. In addition to this, we visited five other towns, each with over a million inhabitants—Sian, for a long time the emperors' capital; Wuhan, a big center of heavy industry; Hangchow, a town with textile and silk industry and surrounded by lakes, green spaces and pagodas; Nanking, where the building of the great bridge over the Yangtse-kiang assumed the epic proportions of a challenge to the Soviet Union, foreigners and fate; and Canton (Kwangchow), which is renowned for its cooking, its jasmine tea, its biennial international fair and its revolutionary associations—from the 1911 uprising to the breach between the Communists and the Kuomintang, which was the signal for the civil war in 1927. We were received with great

---

*As a matter of fact, the travelers who have written the most vivid accounts of China since 1949—Simone de Beauvoir, Alberto Moravia, Tibor Mende and Klaus Mehnert—were all there for a few weeks or, in some cases, less.

splendor—and I will make no attempt to hide how pleased I was by this welcome. We covered four thousand miles in a special aircraft, in private railway carriages, in a VIP boat and in limousines. It sounds like a lot—and yet it was tantalizingly little.

There were innumerable conversations, and some of them were of great interest. The late Prime Minister, Chou En-lai, honored me with three, and I had several with the writer Kuo Mo-jo, President of the Academy of Sciences and Vice-Chairman of the Standing Committee of the National People's Congress. I had other talks with the Minister of Foreign Affairs, Chi Peng-fei,* and the Deputy Minister of Foreign Trade, Li Chiang, a close colleague of the Prime Minister. We also met a fairly large number of senior officials, teachers (from university professors to village schoolmasters), research workers, astronomers, archaeologists, physicists, chemists, biologists, doctors, surgeons, journalists, engineers, technical experts, agronomists, actors, dancers, artists, trade unionists and heads of people's communes. We had working sessions and meals with the leaders of the revolutionary committees in the towns and the provinces. When we asked them straight questions, almost all of them readily consented to answer.

Some will say that the presence of interpreters took away all the spontaneity from our experience of China. In fact, they did not foist themselves on us—we needed them. We heard through their ears and spoke through their mouths—without them we would have been deaf and dumb. But we also saw through our own eyes and remained alert to what was happening. They did not restrict our freedom of movement.** We would go out for walks whenever the program allowed for a moment's respite, although we took the precaution of having the name and telephone number of our hotel written on a visiting card in Chinese characters. Perhaps you could say that our Chinese couriers surrounded the delegation with a mobile bamboo curtain. They were exceedingly attentive to our needs. It must be admitted that it comes to much the same thing: their ability to influence our view of things was equal to their finesse, and was therefore very considerable.

An enormous amount of what happens and what is thought in China remains obscure. The three people's communes we visited were not communes but "brigades"—three villages, each about half the size of a French *arrondissement,* *** which belonged to people's communes. All the Westerners living in Peking and all those who have been in China in the past few years

---

*When we met, Chi Peng-fei had the title "Minister of Foreign Affairs ad interim," although he had effectively been Minister for a year. He had taken the place of Marshal Chen Yi, who was seriously ill, and was confirmed in the post on the latter's death.

**Far from it; contrary to the widely held belief, they increased it. A much closer watch is always kept on the movements of Western sinologists and Westerners who take their own interpreters.

***A French administrative district, rather like a New York postal district (TRANSLATOR'S NOTE).

have visited only a few dozen of the 750,000 different brigades in China—and foreigners are often shown the same ones.

Extrapolations on the subject of China should be made with care. If some Japanese journalist states categorically that the Chinese are not managing to get high rice yields or that cattle- and pig-breeding have stopped, we can reply equally categorically that this is not so, but if he alleges that millions of Chinese have been deported to concentration camps, how can one contradict him? The visible face of China is minuscule compared with her invisible one.

What is the situation in Szechwan, Yunnan, Sinkiang and Tibet, where no foreigner has been for a long time? Why were hundreds of Chinese bodies washed up on the beaches of Kowloon in 1968 and 1970? One can only put forward hypotheses. We simply do not know.

No one is more aware than I am of the shortcomings of this book. The information we gathered is in some respects too copious, in others too fragmentary. The notes that were taken on conversations and working sessions cover a thousand or so pages, and only a small fraction of them will be used here. Some it is wiser not to use, while others have to be left out for reasons of space. China's international relations and the struggle for power, which have already been the subjects of many studies, will only be touched on in passing. The information we came back with is too fragmentary. It would be rash to make any synthesis; it could only be done with a great deal of humility. Let us simply say that this book interweaves different points of view, which—although incomplete—may make China, a country which is so often misunderstood, a little clearer.

There were two situations in which the strict and meticulous plans of the organizers were regularly upset. Working sessions and tête-à-tête conversations would often develop, suddenly and quite spontaneously, into genuine exchanges. And several times a day—at meals, during chats over tea, in the car, on the train, on the boat or on the airplane—there would be opportunities to gather information. Whenever we arrived at enterprises or banquets, the local leaders would be lined up to shake hands with us, but gradually this formal welcome gave way to a more relaxed atmosphere. The ice was broken during roundtable discussions, on long journeys and at cocktail parties. If he keeps his eyes and ears open, a Westerner can learn a great deal from almost anyone he meets, whether a leader, an intellectual, a worker or a peasant—about his past, his experience of the old order, his contribution to the revolution, his view of the Leftists and his family situation. When you eat rice and drink tea with a Chinese, the link that is established lasts a long time.

However stubborn the Chinese—and communist—obsession with mystery, in the long run it does not prevail over the irrefutable experience of the senses, and of the group. What Lincoln said about fooling people applies to secrecy too: You can hide everything from some of the people; you can hide some things from all the people; but you cannot hide everything from all the people. You do not have to get your guides drunk to see the evidence. In China, appearances don't lie.

When he was conducting Catherine the Great on her tours of Russia, Potemkin used to arrange for villagers in their Sunday best to dance all along her route in front of a moving theatre set. The empress was delighted by the happiness of her people. She was not a very curious person and hardly ever got out of her carriage; she would sleep from one stop to the next. There is no doubt that the Chinese are tempted, like the Russians, to "do a Potemkin." But you can't deceive an alert observer forever. You can't fake four thousand miles of roads, countryside and villages. Not for a minute did anyone attempt to hide or disguise whatever chance—the best investigator's aid—brought before us. We were not prevented from entering houses unannounced. We were not kept away from the densely populated, poor areas. Above all, no attempt was made to interfere with the continual checking and cross-checking which is such a vital part of a study mission's work.

It is axiomatic that a group of researchers will gather more information than an individual working on his own. The speeches and the proclamations on hoardings begin to fall into perspective when set in the context of material collected by others. This is especially important in a country where the only acceptable point of view is an official one.

Some of us had associations with China that went back a long time; some had even lived there under the old regime, and several had been there during the Cultural Revolution. But there was one in our party who had never been to Asia, although he had visited countries under Communist control, another had seen Asia but never a Communist country, a third knew neither. As a result, we all formed vastly differing opinions. It was a never-ending debate. Since we were all so different, our views often conflicted and our experiences were complementary.* Even in questions of minutest details having such a wide variety of opinions made for lively debate. "Have you noticed that there aren't any dogs?" someone asked. "They must have been eaten during a famine." When we made an enquiry, we learned that the dogs had been put down for reasons of hygiene.

To get a balanced judgment, it was important to know something of China's history.

In Wuhan, Nanking and Canton, tens of thousands of men and women,

---

*It is hardly necessary for me to add that my impressions and opinions, which are purely personal, are solely my responsibility. Only the official text of the mission, which was drawn up by the members collectively, contains the feelings of the delegation I led.

young and old alike, were herded together to sleep in the streets. They
blocked the sidewalks and spilled over into the road. They were lying so close
together that it looked like an enormous open-air barracks. A similar sight in
Calcutta would bring forth the conclusion that these were the city's homeless.
But in China everyone has his appointed home, whether a communal
residence, a dormitory for a single person or a tiny place with shared
bathroom and kitchen for a family. So why did they bed down on the ground?
Various theories were bandied about. Perhaps their houses were uncomfortable. Perhaps they had not been city-dwellers for long and they had gone back
to their rural habits, sleeping out under the stars. Perhaps they looked for
reassurance in sensing their own number. Perhaps the Party encouraged them
to seek brotherhood in this way. Perhaps they had been ordered to do so by
Mao.

On my return from China I reread the account of the journey made in
1793 by the delegation led by Lord Macartney.* According to the narrator,
people who lived in towns and villages would unroll their mats on the ground
and sleep in the open air during the summer; they would "squeeze up against
one another like cattle." The revolution was in no way responsible for this; it
is in large part due to the climate of the Chinese summer.

In order to understand the patterns of Chinese behavior, one must
constantly turn to the history books. One can only evaluate successes and
failures by comparing the achievements of the present with the situation that
existed before. You cannot be objective without absorbing other views,
especially those of witnesses to China's past. It is stimulating too to read on
the subject before setting out on a study trip—without that reading, the trip
would be merely an excursion. This combination of preliminary reading and
on-the-spot observation makes research afterwards far more valuable, and
likewise discussions with specialists. A kind of "cross-fertilization" is
brought about with these continual exchanges of views.

I have said all this to throw light on certain fundamental principles of this
book.

The first is *historical relativity*. Present-day China makes sense to us only
if we see it in perspective, in the light of yesterday's China. If a traveler notes

---

*This account, which unfortunately is no longer available, is only rarely quoted in books on
China past and present. It is in twelve volumes, five of them the work of Sir George Staunton,
the Minister-Counselor, and the other seven of John Barrow, the Ambassador's Private
Secretary. I discovered the work by chance twenty years ago in a second-hand bookshop in
Cracow. The more I become acquainted with it, the more I am convinced that it is as useful for
an understanding of present-day China as Tocqueville's *De la démocratie en Amérique*—which
describes the America of 1831—is for an understanding of the United States today, or as the
Marquis de Custine's *La Russie en 1839* is for an understanding of the Soviet Union. If one is to
believe Emmanuel de las Cases's *Mémorial de Sainte-Hélène,* Napoleon read it with enormous
interest and spoke at length about it to his companions.

that food and textiles are strictly rationed and compares this with the situation in our consumer societies, he is tempted to conclude that there is no point in imposing a dictatorship on a people when this is the miserable result. But if he compares it with the situation in China before 1949, he will realize that a high proportion of the population formerly inadequately fed and clothed now enjoys a decent standard of living. Travelers' impressions must be measured against history and Marxist ideology; otherwise, they would tell the reader as little as photographs without captions. So direct narrative and historical flashbacks will be interwoven throughout this book.

The second basic principle—*ethnological relativity*—derives from this continual interaction between immediate observation and historical reflection. A reading of Marco Polo, Father du Halde, Father Huc and especially Lord Macartney brings out the constant factors about China, its civilization and its imperishable cultural heritage (a reading of de Tocqueville and the Marquis de Custine does likewise for the United States and the Soviet Union). What one often ascribes to Peking, Washington and Moscow regimes are in fact the achievements of the Chinese, American or Soviet people themselves. Many political, economic and sociological analyses of contemporary China tend to emphasize the ideological factors and to minimize the decisive ethnic factors. While acknowledging the part Marxist-Leninist writings have played in the intellectual formation of the Chinese leaders, one should render unto Marx the things which are Marx's and unto China the things which are China's. The Chinese model hides its roots well, because they go deep.

The third basic principle is *relativity in judgment*. How wrong foreigners are when they continually explain and evaluate things that don't fit into their views of life! In order to know and understand the Chinese, one must stop trying to reduce the unknown to the known, and one must put oneself in the position of the Chinese as they really are. Let us beware of being Europe-centered—non-Chinese should as far as possible see China through the eyes of the Chinese. Even the experts best acquainted with China have felt the same sense of bewilderment in the face of this people, which seems to become more impenetrably closed the more one explores. In any case, let us not judge the Maoist regime as if China were an industrialized society.

But at the same time let us not refrain altogether from passing judgment. People's China has come of age. The Liberation and the Cultural Revolution are now behind us, and it is time to draw up a balance sheet, however fragmentary our information may be. There is a positive and a negative side to any balance. Some people have unreserved admiration for the regime's successes and forget at what cost they have been achieved. Others, obsessed by the cost, deny the successes. We must try to avoid both these pitfalls. The first part of this book reveals certain little-known aspects of the Chinese way to socialism. The second part presents the "New Man" to which the revolution intends to give birth. The third part describes the successes that have been achieved, and the fourth part evaluates the human price which has been and still is being paid for these successes. The concluding section tries to answer the question: Does the reawakening of China provide a model which other countries can follow? It should come as no surprise to the reader that the first three parts—especially the third—are sunny in tone, the fourth is dark, and the conclusion is full of question marks. Maybe he will feel he is passing from one extreme to the other. Just let him remember that, as General de Gaulle once said, "In China things had come to the point where everything was excluded except the extremes."

It is a tricky task for an observer to keep an independent and critical eye while maintaining friendly relations with his hosts. We were the guests of the Chinese government, and we certainly would not have accepted the invitation if we had felt hostile toward China. But we made no agreement to keep quiet or to change our views. Our hosts were taking their own chances. The only moral obligation we had toward them was complete sincerity and good faith.

As we went along, we acquired another obligation. However monolithic the regime's apparatus may seem to a foreigner, it is not possible to spend several weeks with Chinese of all professions without spotting the chinks in their official ideological armor—a smile caught here, a hesitant reply there, a contradiction, a moment's silence and the occasional confidence. This was where the most valuable part of our investigation and the most demanding of our duties began.

The Chinese are not as hard as one imagines them to be—even those who hold posts in the administration, the army, the Party and revolutionary committees. They have hidden resources of genuine modesty, kindness, intellectual honesty and sympathy. One wants to avoid repeating anything which might compromise them. After his journey to America, de Tocqueville warned: "The reader must necessarily take my word for that [the fact that he did not rely on the testimony of only one witness but based his opinions on that of several]. . . . A stranger often hears important truths at his host's fireside; it is a relief to break a constrained silence with a stranger whose short stay guarantees his discretion. I noted down all such confidences as soon as I heard them, but they will never leave my notebooks; I would rather let my comments suffer than add my name to the list of those travelers who repay generous hospitality with worries and embarrassments."* And that concerned a country founded on liberal principles.

As the Prime Minister, the late Chou En-lai, was seeing me off on the steps of the Palace of the People, I asked him if I was to regard what he told me as

---

*From the introduction to Volume One of De la démocratie en Amérique.

confidential. He smiled and said: "Things move quickly. . . . The confidential nature of a conversation rarely lasts more than a few months." Although a considerable amount of time has passed, I still do not feel I have the right to reveal everything he told me. With even more reason, I shall not reveal the identities of less famous people with whom I spoke and who, on rare occasions, were frank or indiscreet.

"Things move quickly. . . ." Or, to be more accurate, although the deep-seated truths about a people take a long while to evolve, the events, personalities and trends of their political life change rapidly; this is especially true of a country which is waking up from a thousand-year sleep. The Chinese, who have always lived in an eternal present, have abruptly become aware of change. The dialectics and the objectives of the revolution have accustomed them to constant activity aimed at transforming man and society. They have embarked on permanent revolution. Caution in passing judgment and in making predictions is imperative. Any look at China has to be loaded with questions.

Our idea of the Chinese will change as they change. In any event, Western thought needs to keep up with them. This book does not claim to do more than make a very modest contribution to reflections on China. For anyone interested in such grand-scale human adventure, it will raise plenty of questions.

2

The Worship of the Sage, the Hero
and the Saint

The Omnipresent Absentee

We wondered whether we would get to see him. But while we were waiting, he was omnipresent.

He had gone into one of his periodic retreats.* For several months at a time he would disappear into obscurity. It was said that he never stayed in Peking for more than four months a year. We pondered the reasons for his withdrawal from the world. Perhaps he was meditating or needed to revitalize himself in some hiding place, in some image of Mother Earth, like the old Taoist sages who sought refuge in caves. He might simply have been

---

*Mao had made several public appearances in 1970 and had frequently talked with foreign delegations. In 1971 he failed to appear in public, even on October first (China's National Day). He received Maurice Couve de Murville (the French Foreign Minister at the time) in October 1970 and Edgar Snow (the American writer on China) in December, but then during the entire following year he granted only three audiences, and those to national leaders—the Romanian President, the Burmese Prime Minister and Emperor Haile Selassie of Ethiopia. He was not seen again until January 1972, when he attended the funeral of Marshal Chen Yi. In February he had a brief talk with President Nixon. Then, after disappearing again for a time, he granted only occasional audiences—to the Prime Minister of Ceylon in June, Maurice Schumann in July, the Japanese Prime Minister in September, the Nepalese Prime Minister in November, representatives of the Vietcong in December, and the President of Zaïre in January 1973. His last audience was with Pakistan's Prime Minister Bhutto early in 1976. On September 9, 1976, he died at the age of 82.

making tours of inspection and investigation in the provinces. Whatever the reason, his way of life was an art, both in living and in government.

Mao's disappearances seemed quite natural to the Chinese with whom we spoke. They believed them to be regenerative—Mao would emerge invigorated and rejuvenated, to give the people new impetus. One man even assured me that the efficiency of the regime depended on Mao's disappearing every so often.

In this connection a leader of the Kiangsu Provincial Revolutionary Committee recounted the ancient legend of the giver of rain. The inhabitants of a drought-stricken region had come to implore a hermit to make it rain. He shut himself up for three days in a temple "to purify himself." After three days had passed, it started to rain. In the same way, he added, Mao needed to create his own inner harmony so that the harmony of his people might then follow.

This is why silence was so necessary to him. During his retreats he reached those states so precious to traditional Chinese wisdom (after which the gates of the Forbidden City are named), Earthly Tranquillity, Heavenly Purity, Majestic Peace, Supreme Harmony. This was no mere superstitious belief; it was more an instinctive understanding of the uniqueness of his position as leader—as the mediator between the masses and their future. Under his guidance, there was a harmony in Chinese society which would otherwise have been impossible. Mao stood aloof from the world in order to keep more closely in touch with his people and with events.

Western observers did not understand this. They needed a rational explanation for Mao's disappearances. It had to be a political crisis, or Mao must have been ill, or already dead. Each disappearance from the scene gave rise to the same unverifiable rumors. Shortly after we returned to France, the decision to cancel the October first parade caused a flurry of excitement in the chancelleries and in the world's press. In the middle of the night the director of a major Paris daily asked me to dictate on the spot, over the telephone, a hundred lines of comment on the death of Mao, which a news agency had just reported. Ever since 1930 Mao's death had frequently been "reliably" reported.

But the sleuths were constantly finding all sorts of clues. American heart specialists were in Peking (but was it conceivable that Chinese leaders would have called on "capitalist" doctors to attend Mao if he had been on the point of dying?). Air links were suspended for three days (this did happen from time to time for unknown reasons, but there were so few routes that their closure hardly paralyzed the country). Portraits of Mao were reported to have been taken down in some streets in Peking (but many had been taken down since the end of the Cultural Revolution). Chinese soldiers were reported to have been recalled urgently to their units (but dispositions like these were frequently made). Nine members of a Chinese delegation visiting

France under the leadership of Minister Pai Hsiang-kuo were not wearing their Mao badges (but the staff of the Chinese Embassy in Paris were still wearing theirs).*

It was often pointed out that when Stalin and Khrushchev died, it was a long time before the Soviet people knew about it. This was not only a Russian tradition; it had been a Chinese tradition long before. The founder of the Chin dynasty in the third century B.C., Shih Huang-ti, died, just as secretly as he had lived, while making a tour of the provinces. He had directed the affairs of state more often than not by staying out of sight. When his remains were brought back to the Imperial Palace it was to all appearances a normal return journey, but to hide the smell of the corpse the imperial chariot was surrounded by wagons carrying fish. The news of Shih Huang-ti's death was not made public until all the arrangements had been made for the succession. Fifteen hundred years later Genghis Khan, the founder of the Yuan dynasty, died while fighting in Kansu province, near Yenan. He continued to pacify the province, although he was dead. His lance remained planted in the ground in front of his white tent and the senior officers, who were the only ones allowed to enter, appeared to the troops to be coming and going as usual to receive their orders and to make their reports. It was only after the victory had been won that Genghis Khan's death was made known.

There was no reason to suppose the tradition might not have been revived. Some people went so far as to say that Mao had been dead for a long time and that a double stood in for him at his rare audiences. He may have been dead politically—or perhaps nothing at all was going on. Most likely, though, these fantastic pieces of guesswork were based on a common source—total lack of information. All these "Mao is dead" stories revolved like a danse macabre around the fact that so little was known of his private life, which was half the time the life of a semi-recluse.

When we were in China Mao had not yet "died" on the pages of the world's press, but he was certainly "ill." Western circles in Peking and China watchers in Hong Kong were explaining his absence from the scene by saying that he had had to be put on a strict diet and was resting in the country, possibly at his home in Hangchow. He was surrounded by doctors and nurses. He could eat only vegetables. He was on a cure which meant he had to drink the juice of a plant which could be found in North Korea and nowhere else. And so on. On other occasions he was said to have had tuberculosis, or Parkinson's Disease, or to be suffering from "an incurable illness." However, on the sixteenth of July, 1966 he swam ten miles down the Yangtse.**

---

*It has since become known that some of these "clues" were connected with the disappearance not of Mao but of Lin Piao.
**Most observers will admit that this was a genuine achievement, even if he was carried along by the current; but there are some who have their doubts about it.

No matter how often his death, recent or imminent, had been announced—and it was almost half a century since Chiang Kai-shek had put a price on his head—Mao remained immovable. His many deaths had not prevented him from keeping, or regaining, control of a revolution which has not ceased.*Although often involved in fighting and even taken prisoner, he had never been wounded or seriously ill. His family had had a hard time, but he had passed through all his troubles unharmed. He seemed to have been protected by some magical charm.

Portraits Everywhere

Why should he have bothered to show himself in public, since his presence was felt everywhere? People sport his medallion on their chests. His likeness is displayed at crossroads, on walls, along the roadside, in the houses into which we peered; it is painted vividly in oils by some latter-day David, woven in black and white silk (we saw the factory that makes these in Hangchow), in tapestries, and fashioned in hulking white plaster statues. He is depicted full-length or bust-size, sometimes looking like a monk in a long gray teacher's gown, facing a crowd of Cantonese hanging on his every word; other times as Chairman, his coat blowing in the wind; still other times with a halo of clouds or a crown of lightning. He is always recognizable, in spite of increasing age, by the wart on his chin and the visionary glint in his eyes.**

Before the Cultural Revolution he was often shown surrounded by the six important figures who with him made up the Standing Committee of the Party Political Bureau. Since, he has been shown alone.***

In former times official iconography spread the worship of the emperor throughout the country. Sculptures and tapestries filled public buildings not with his face—which they were forbidden to show—but with his symbol, a dragon surrounded by clouds. From time to time, although rarely, public audiences or the reception of foreign visitors showed the emperor to be indeed alive, in spite of rumors of his death.

These ancient traditions had degenerated into empty ritual. Mao gave these traditions meaning again by bringing to them the realism of the sage, the epic dimension of a hero and the mysticism of a saint.

---

*Mao acknowledged that he was partially ousted from power in the years preceding the Cultural Revolution, and he also implied in his last conversation with Edgar Snow that the Cultural Revolution at times got out of his control.

**To us from the West the number of pictures seemed excessive, but in fact the popularity of pictures was on the decline—and this trend has continued.

***The pictures of Chou En-lai are always separate from those of Mao. Between 1969 and 1971 Lin Piao sometimes appeared at his side, slightly in the background; these pictures completely disappeared at the end of September 1971 and the sequel is now well known.

The Peasant Sage

More than anything else, *The Complete Works of Mao Tse-tung* is a collection of peasant wisdom.* In order to measure the extent to which Mao imposed his rural realism on the Chinese revolution we must return to the two sources of his ethics and his deeds—Canton and Yenan, at opposite ends of the country.

The Institute of the Peasant Movement in Canton is an old Confucian temple; cloisters surround a garden of exotic plants. Built under the Ming dynasty and destroyed during the civil war, the buildings have been restored to their original state.

Between 1925 and 1927 this Institute, which had been founded in 1923 by the Third Congress of the Communist Party and supported by Sun Yat-sen, was under the direction of Mao. In the course of one session during one of the first stages of the peasant rising in 1926 he trained 327 rural cadres. However, this did not survive the 1927 break between the Kuomintang and the communists. It was only a transitory phase in the revolution, although our guides presented it as being of prime importance.**

Mao's room at the Institute contains a bed without springs or mattress, just a mat on boards, plus a chair and a desk of walnut-stained white wood. In the classrooms a table and chair are perched on a dais, with the pupils' desks set out in neat rows below. Beds are stacked upon one another in the dormitories. It looks like a bivouac which has just been abandoned—but not before someone had taken the trouble to lock up the guns in their racks, fold the uniforms, line up the sandals and hang up the bags. Every morning there was bayonet practice in the garden. Then it was time to sit down and listen to the young master. A big oil painting shows his disciples listening to him speak.***

It was in this atmosphere of alertness, physical training and eagerness for learning that Mao went deeper into his class analysis of Chinese society. He made it the central and guiding idea of his teaching from that time on: "The peasants constitute eighty or ninety percent of the population. The peasant problem is therefore the first problem of the Chinese revolution. The peasant forces constitute the principal revolutionary force."

In the two galleries, which open onto the garden, dramatic mementoes were on exhibit. One bas-relief depicted the arched back of a Chinese peasant.

---

*Let me add that it is also a transposition, into the Chinese context, of Marx, Lenin and military thinking.

**Some Western historians feel that Mao played only a minor role in Canton, but the official Chinese view is quite the reverse. Whatever the truth of the matter, it seems that the years in Canton did play an important role in the formation of Mao's ideas. The emphasis which the regime places on the Institute of the Peasant Movement is therefore legitimate.

***Mao's actual influence seems to have been more modest than this painting suggests.

A map used savage caricatures of landlords and pictures of vultures to symbolize the dismemberment of the rural population. The curator who showed me over the Institute stood for a long time in front of two horrifying photographs, either overcome by emotion herself or hoping to arouse mine. One photograph was of a poor peasant in blood-stained rags who had had his fingers cut off and his eyes put out by a landlord; the other showed a peasant woman who had found her husband lying in the garden—he was holding his severed head in his hands.

This important place, which has been transformed into a museum, sets out not only to teach visitors about the miseries of the past and the early days of the revolution; it also seeks to re-create a past which has been reconstituted as a projection of the present—for the benefit of the school children, factory workers and peasants who are marched through it behind their guides. The peasant movement—who knew of its existence at the time? And the teaching of Mao Tse-tung—who had heard of it? But on the other hand, the Canton Institute would have its visitors believe that Sun Yat-sen's two favorite disciples, who at one time were very prominent on the scene, never even existed. Of course one of them, Chiang Kai-shek, was to become Mao's main adversary, and the other, Wang Ching-wei, was to be China's Laval* in the hands of the Japanese. There is no Borodin at Sun Yat-sen's side, just as Trotsky is never seen beside Lenin. Only Chou En-lai, the political commissar of the Whampoa Military Academy, figures in the photographs of the riots—although he in fact played no larger part in the Canton Commune than did Mao himself. At that time, when the majority of the revolutionaries, whether communist or not, were proclaiming that the revolution could only come from the urban proletariat, Mao would appear to have been alone in saying that it could come only from the peasantry.**

Son of the Earth

One doesn't have to dig very far into his life to discover the source of the basic conviction that Mao was a son of the earth. He grew up on the legends, ethics and folklore of his native Hunan. He had a peasant soul.

Ten years after the Southeast, it was the Northwest and Yenan. Troglodyte dwellings in the yellow loess of the mountains. From December 1936 to 1947 Mao lived in four different places, and three of them were grottoes. They all look like the vaulted, whitewashed cells of a Cistercian monastery.

---

*Pierre Laval (1883–1945), head of the Vichy government in 1940, and again from 1942 to 1944, was condemned to death and shot after the war (TRANSLATOR'S NOTE).

**But in fact he did not have a monopoly on this idea. History seems to have been somewhat rewritten to meet the needs of the cause. The first peasant communist movements—those of the "East River" (in Kwangtung) led by Peng Pai—predate Mao.

They are still there to this day, with their simple peasant furniture such as Mao had used in Canton—hideouts dug deep into the fertile soil like wombs in Mother Earth. Mao would be out of sight behind grayish windowpanes of packing paper, but a skylight over his desk would open just far enough for him to see without being seen—as he lay in wait.

Down in front of the caves lies the field which Mao tended every day with the diligence and devotion of a Carthusian monk cultivating his garden. He immersed himself in manual labor—the daily drudgery of watering soy beans and weeding. An analogy can be made with his later rule of China—he cultivated many flowers, and weeded out the poisonous ones.*

Mao described how his own family represented for him the class struggle.** His father, who had once been a soldier but had become a "poor peasant" again, had saved every penny and piled up quite a tidy sum in savings, become a "middle peasant" and then a "rich middle peasant" and then a "small landlord," owning two and a half acres of land. He also bought mortgages on other people's land. He bought grain cheap at harvest time and sold it very dear in times of scarcity. His father represented to Mao the tyranny of those landowners who robbed, speculated and demanded unquestioning obedience from their servants. In face of this paternal despotism, the young Mao, his mother, his brother and their farm laborer formed themselves into an Opposition. His mother, an illiterate, pious and kindly woman, would give the "poor peasants" rice when they came to ask for it during times of famine, but she would never do so when his father was present.

Mao went a long way in his revolt against his father, seeing in him everything he was later to hate—the landlord and rich peasant class,

---

*It is said that Mao grew vegetables for many years in the little garden of his villa in the center of the Forbidden City.

**Present-day Chinese historians dispute this story, although it was confirmed by Edgar Snow in 1936. The American writer tells in detail in *Red Star over China* how at the end of the Long March he got Mao to spend a dozen nights in his cell in Paoan, telling of his childhood, youth and early revolutionary days. Snow took notes by candlelight, put them together and submitted them to Mao for his approval. Mao then handed them back with corrections, and here a few dozen pages of Snow's book is the only autobiography of Mao we have.

It seems unlikely that the tale is apocryphal, since Mao had a loyal friendship with Snow which lasted from 1936 to 1972, a friendship closer than any foreigner and almost any Chinese could claim. If Snow had been guilty of a literary hoax, especially in a country and in a field of study in which one is so careful about the accuracy of quotations, would Mao have received him every time he visited China and told him things which he confided to no one else? Would he have had Snow on his right hand as he stood on Tien An Men Square on October 1, 1970? In December of the same year he apologized for the fact that he had not been able to get Snow a visa during the Cultural Revolution—"It was wicked people wanting to stop you coming." He even sent his personal doctors to Snow when he lay ill in Switzerland. These gestures would seem to affirm Snow's biography. I consider it authentic and refer to the stories in it because they are astonishingly valuable from a psychological point of view.

profiteering, fraud, greed, contempt for the poor, and betrayal of one's origins.

One day, when he was thirteen, his father accused him in front of others of being a good-for-nothing. Mao cursed him and ran off, crying that he was going to kill himself; he ran to the edge of a pond and threatened to jump in. His mother ran after him, begging him to return. His father also pushed him and insisted that Mao *kowtow** as a sign of submission. Mao argued the toss on the edge of the pond, and agreed to give a one-knee *kowtow* if his father would promise not to beat him. He learned a lesson from this "civil war"—when the weak submit, the strong hit them even more; when they defend their rights in public and are ready to face anything, even death, the strong give way. They are paper tigers.

Psychoanalysts would probably see this episode as a foreshadowing of Mao's ambivalent behavior when he became the nation's leader. He was both revolutionary and traditionalist at the same time. He broke violently with a past symbolized by his father—exploitation of misery, weakness and ignorance—but identified with a past symbolized by his mother—fidelity to the soil—and this he sought to restore. Mao's hatred of the feudal and patriarchal system and of everything that contributed to it, his passion for giving equal opportunity to "poor peasants" and women, and for defending the interests of the humble against the powerful grew out of his adolescent years in family conflict.

When he left his village, his poverty went with him. He became an assistant librarian in Peking and shared a small room with seven friends. He could hardly breathe at night and had to warn the people sleeping on each side of him when he wanted to turn over. Among the eight of them they had only one winter overcoat, and they took turns wearing it when they went out. In later years, Mao never forgot his poor peasant origins. The images of his childhood and youth dominated his life.

"Is That a Marxist Talking?"

From 1921 on, details of Mao's personal life are lost in the history of the Party with which he found hard-won liberty, strict equality and a warm fraternity.

Almost from the start he was a peasant chief, and so he remained. Undoubtedly the most important of his numerous writings is the "Report on an Investigation of the Peasant Movement in Hunan" written in February 1927, which suggested a change of strategy to the Political Bureau. If the dogma that one could achieve the revolution only through the workers was

---

*Bowing down so the forehead makes contact with the ground three times.

indeed true, then, he argued, China should renounce the idea of revolution altogether.

He tried to convince the then Communist Party Secretary, Chen Tu-hsiu. He had just made a thirty-two day trip to the Hunan of his childhood, and he reported that the peasants were ready to rise "like a mighty storm, like a hurricane, a force so swift and violent that no power, however great, will be able to hold it back." He added that "the poor peasants comprise seventy percent, the middle peasants twenty percent, and the landlords and the rich peasants ten percent of the population in the rural areas" and that "being the most revolutionary, the poor peasants must take the leadership. Without the poor peasants there would be no revolution. They have never been wrong on the general direction of the revolution."

Even if he did not manage to persuade Chen Tu-hsiu, he did at any rate strengthen his own belief that he was right, and this confidence never left him. He was to embody an agrarian revolution of which the peasants were to form the core. This was utter heresy in the eyes of the orthodox Marxists like Marx and Engels, Lenin and Trotsky,* Stalin and Khrushchev—for whom only the industrial proletariat could form the vanguard of the revolution.

Of course, Mao later admitted that collaboration with the worker proletariat was necessary. He did not disregard the potential help of a Liu Shao-chi, controller of workers' organizations in urban China; and when he was in opposition to Liu in the 1960s, far from reproaching him for having given too much support to the workers, he accused him of having betrayed their interests. But for him the core of the revolution was always the peasantry, and it was there that he placed his trust.

As he saw it, neither Stalin nor his envoy to Canton, Mikhail Borodin, understood anything about the peasants. Mao refused to accept the comparison the Soviets made between China's small landowners, bound to their patch of soil, and Russia's kulaks. He thought that by pushing the Chinese communists to take the towns in order to ensure the success of the workers' revolt, Moscow was leading them into a fiasco. In November 1927 Mao was dropped from the Political Bureau as a heretic; in June 1930 his views were again condemned by the Central Committee. Chinese communism was still the obedient tool of the Comintern, which—with its out-and-out urban strategy—dragged it into some bloody defeats. When one thinks of the subsequent difficulties between the Soviet Union and China, one should keep these details in mind.

Nonetheless, Mao launched a temporary experiment in agrarian radicalism which allowed him, after much research and exploration, to find

---

*Lenin firmly believed in the possibility of a peasant revolt but thought it would be a kind of "national" revolution and not a truly "socialist" or "internationalist" one. Like Mao, Trotsky said that China had no alternative to reliance on the peasants, but he agreed with Lenin that they could never be true revolutionaries because of their *petit-bourgeois* mentality.

the Chinese way of revolution, namely the rural way. Even though his "Kiangsi Republic"* was soon annihilated, it did give the Red Army the impetus it needed for the Long March.

Mao developed his hold on the Chinese people by simply turning his back on directives from Stalin and his emissaries, the resolutions of the Comintern, and the Chinese Communist Party line, which stubbornly followed the Kremlin. He remained in the minority from 1927 to 1935, but refused to abandon his position, even when the Party leadership was taken over by a group of young Moscow-trained Marxists who were dubbed, with some irony, "the twenty-eight Bolsheviks." He had no doubt that he was right and the majority wrong. So he kept quiet and bided his time. This was his tactic later, between 1959 and 1965, when he was secretly preparing the Cultural Revolution as a way of crushing the majority of the Party's leadership, which was no longer following him.

In China's revolutionary museums today, they pass lightly over this early period. Emphasis is put on the fact that Mao was elected to the Central Committee at the Sixth Congress in the summer of 1928 and that he became Chairman of the Provisional Government of the Chinese Soviet Republic upon its creation in November 1931. His removal for eight years from the top echelons of the Party is passed over in silence. Also ignored is the reversal of fortune which took place at Tsunyi in January 1935, in the middle of the Long March, when an expanded meeting of the Political Bureau gave Mao a majority after acknowledging the bloody failure of the previous one. Of course the intention is that the masses believe the Party never wavered in its support for Mao—that the "Red Sun has never been in eclipse." But this also reflects Mao's continual reluctance to engage in personal polemics with other communists, whether in China or anywhere else. He never challenged Stalin. He confined himself to contesting openly Marxist-Leninist dogma—which all the world's communist parties continued, despite the crushing of the insurrections in China's towns, to espouse without a flicker of doubt. He practiced the ancient Chinese art of "seeming to move in a straight line, while actually following a curve." This practice led Henri Michaux to write—and he was not exaggerating—that "everything that is straight puts the Chinese ill at ease and gives them the painful impression of being false."

Under the very nose of the Stalinists, the Chinese Party came to consist almost entirely of landless peasants. Khrushchev himself was under no illusions about this deviation. Even after Mao's triumph, he condemned Mao's orientation in very direct terms: "When Mao's victorious revolutionary

---

*In spite of the fact that Mao was opposed to the views of Moscow, or perhaps as a way of compensating for this, he called his first "peasant" republic, of which its Kiangsi base was the principal element, "Soviet." The Kiangsi Republic survived for three years (1931–34); before its foundation Mao held out for almost four years in the mountains of Chingkangshan, on the border between Kiangsi and Hunan.

army was approaching Shanghai,* he halted their march and refused to capture the city. Stalin asked Mao, 'Why didn't you take Shanghai?' 'There's a population of six million,' answered Mao. 'If we take the city, then we'll have to feed all those people. And where do we find food to do it?' This hardly sounds like a Marxist talking. Mao Tse-tung has always relied on the peasants, not on the working class. That is why he didn't take Shanghai. He didn't want responsibility for the welfare of the workers. Stalin properly criticized Mao for this deviation from true Marxism. But the fact remains that Mao, relying on the peasants and ignoring the working class, achieved victory. Not that his victory was some sort of miracle, but it was certainly a new twist to Marxist philosophy, since it was achieved without the proletariat."

Khrushchev, who was completely Stalinist in this respect, felt categorically that Mao had not played the game. The proletariat is the workers. He would rather have seen the Chinese revolution fail than a principle abandoned.

The Old Man of the Mountain

Of all the parables Mao used so superbly to illustrate peasant wisdom, the one the Chinese quote most often is the one he told the Party School at Yenan,** that of the *old man of the mountain*. Yu Kung—"The Foolish Old Man of North Mountain"—irritated by a mountain which blocked the way to his house, called his sons and set about attacking it with pick and shovel. The neighbors made fun of them. "When I die, my sons will carry on," the old man replied, "and when they die, there will be my grandsons, and then their sons and grandsons. High as they may be, the mountains cannot grow any higher, and with every bit we dig, they will be that much lower."

Mao applied this fable to the Chinese people, the point being that through their unceasing labor they could rid themselves of imperialism and feudalism.*** For the Chinese the parable evokes Mao himself—the Wise Man detached from day-to-day tasks but who stubbornly pursued the same long-term objective.

Mao took this role upon himself. He did not devote himself to everyday matters, although he did keep in touch with everything that was going on. He did not—or at least did not appear to—make the decisions which are required for the administration of such a vast country. He saw in terms of

---

*In 1949.
**Mao did not invent it himself; it is an old legend borrowed from the ancient philosopher Lie-tzu, one of the fathers of Taoism, but the majority of Chinese seem convinced the story is Mao's.
***See "The Foolish Old Man who Removed the Mountains" in Mao Tse-tung, *Selected Works*, Vol. 3, p. 272 (TRANSLATOR'S NOTE).

history. In his fifty years of fighting and subsequent power, he never once abandoned the pursuit of his objective—the revolutionary transformation of China along the lines he had laid down. He knew only too well that the secret of secrets, the peasant's secret, is to hold out. You wait either until the situation reverses or until developments point up the mistake of those who too quickly thought their way was the right one. The Chinese proverb "With patience, the leaves of the mulberry tree become a satin dress" must have been often on his mind.

Through him, Marxism-Leninism changed not merely in appearance, but in its very nature. Mao rewrote the Marxist Scriptures with a Confucian pen, using the language of a small farmer in Hunan.

Mao's approach, colored by his ties with the soil, may seem a little romantic, primitive or moralistic to the Westerner. But his simple, common-sense ideas reflect the deep-seated and vague aspirations of the peasants in whom he had already sensed the dynamic that would regenerate China.

In the heart of the Shensi mountains there is a pagoda, the Pagoda of the Treasure, which has been sitting like a lump of sugar on a mountain peak for a thousand years and is almost as famous in China as the Gate of Heavenly Peace. Beneath this pagoda a quotation from Mao is inscribed in enormous gold letters on a red background. It says: "Spread the spirit of revolutionary tradition in order to achieve still greater successes." Since its grottoes and barren lands gave a decade of shelter to a handful of outlaws, Yenan has become the trustee of this tradition.

The annals of Mao—from Canton to Yenan, from 1925 to 1947—are the annals of Chinese communism, but they are also the annals of China herself since time immemorial, as if the whole of Chinese history has been directed toward the sole aim of achieving an indigenous form of communism. This is no ideology imported from abroad and imposed in an authoritarian way from above. It is an authentic product of China, growing out of her culture and her people, and gradually perfected with infinite care over a quarter of a century.

But between Canton and Yenan there was the Long March.

The Hero of the Long March

In Yenan, in the heart of the highlands where the survivors gathered, the vestiges of the Long March take on flesh and blood.

From the time of the break between the Kuomintang and the Communist Party in 1927, Mao asserted himself as the leader of the revolt. Not that he instigated the revolt—it already existed in embryo. He organized it as a guerrilla struggle. His strategy, set out in his article "Problems of Strategy in China's Revolutionary War," can be summarized with the formula: Win over the villages for the Party and then encircle the towns.

A Barefoot Army

Chiang Kai-shek believed in the towns, modern arms and American aid. Mao believed in villagers armed with picks and relying on no one but themselves. A peasant himself, he never once doubted that a peasant army could take power. The secret of his victory lies in this unshakeable faith.*

The rurally based Party had a membership of only a few hundred peasants on the eve of the Canton defeat, but swung the entire countryside behind it in twenty-two years. The towns then fell like nine-pins. The Long March—one of the cruelest setbacks at the time, but one of the greatest of triumphs from a long-term historical perspective—was the triumph of Mao's peasant wisdom.**

The first "peasants' revolt" led by Mao had begun with success in the province of Kiangsi. During seven years of struggle, he perfected—from skirmish to skirmish and rout to rout—the tactic which led him to final victory: concentrate your forces in the attack, then disperse them to evade the counter-attack; destroy the enemy by surprising him, and never let yourself be taken by surprise. "When the enemy advances, we retreat. When the enemy camps, we harass. When the enemy tires, we attack. When the enemy retreats, we pursue." In this way he held out against forces ten times greater in number. All this time, he was organizing *peasant power* by handing out the land of the fleeing landowners.

But at the beginning of the 1930s Chiang Kai-shek unleashed his war of extermination against the Red Army of Kiangsi. On the insistence of his German advisers, led by Generals von Seeckt and von Falkenhausen, the Generalissimo changed his tactics. He avoided falling into traps, built a ring of blockhouses and deported people who had been indoctrinated by guerrillas. In 1934 the Red Army was on the point of being caught in a pincer movement.

---

*There were certainly many other factors—the Second World War, the defeat of Japan, the occupation of Manchuria by the Soviet Union, etc., but they only acted in Mao's favor because he was prepared and had bided his time.

**In October of 1934, over 90,000 men and women of the Red Army broke through an encirclement by Chiang Kai-shek's forces in Kiangsi, and commenced a strategic withdrawal that would continue for a full year, incurring disastrous losses but ending in political triumph. Their march would cover more than 8,000 miles, and during it they would escape or defeat more than 300,000 Kuomintang troops, break through the enveloping armies of ten different provincial warlords, pass through twelve major provinces, each one about the size of Texas, and cross eighteen mountain ranges and twenty-four rivers. Only 7,000 of the original marchers would be alive by the time they reached Shensi province 368 days later. This became known as the Long March, from the Chinese *Ch'ang Ch'eng. Ch'ang* in the historical sense also invokes immortality (EDITOR'S NOTE).

So the dramatic decision had to be made: the defense of the "Kiangsi Soviet Republic," which Mao had been at such pains to set up, and where the population thought it was firmly established, had to be relinquished. On October 16, 1934, the main body of the Red Army, the First Front Army, began the great retreat, which was to lead it twelve months later to Shensi, where it was to be joined another year later by the remnants of the other armies.

The Fortified Castle of Shensi

Shensi is only a thousand miles northwest of Kiangsi as the crow flies, but for the Red Army it was a tortuous route of eight thousand miles which curved around the Tibetan border, was frequently buried beneath snowfalls and wound its way through the heights of Sikang. A forced march on a Chinese scale.

Mao decided to seek refuge in Shensi because this virtually inaccessible plateau was safe ground for him. The province first came to prominence in 1000 B.C. when it was the cradle and capital of imperial power. Then, at the beginning of the seventeenth century, it was the scene of a serfs' revolt under the Ming. And finally, in 1911, at the time of the overthrow of the Manchu Empire, it carried on its revolutionary traditions by rising up once again. At the heart of the old China—far from the towns, the coast, the West, Japan, industrial areas and international commerce, and also far from all those sectors of society from which Chiang Kai-shek could seek support—the people of Shensi were ready for revolution.* Mao could not have found a more protected place or a better base from which to conquer the whole country. All that was necessary was to get to the fortress. But this was not so simple.

In October 1934 the First Front Army set off on foot, accompanied by peasants, women and children—several hundred thousand people in all. Mules carried enormous loads of luggage. "A stampede" Mao was to call it; he was also to accuse the "twenty-eight Bolsheviks" of "lacking initiative and mobility" and of having passed "from military adventurism to military conservatism." The Long March began as a disorderly flight and only later became a great exploit to be celebrated.** The Red soldiers marched day and night along mountain paths, through jungles and cols. They were constantly

---

*While Mao was organizing the "Autumn Harvest Movement" in Hunan in 1927, Liu Chih-tan and Kao Kang—who was to commit suicide in 1954—were organizing the peasant movement in Shensi.
**The character of the Long March changed when Tsunyi was taken in January 1935. At a mysterious meeting there of the Political Bureau Mao gained a majority in the Party after eight years in the minority. Talks soon collapsed, and there was bitter fighting. The Red Army was determined to rebuild the Kiangsi Soviet Peasant Republic in Shensi and seized the initiative. The most difficult phase was over; they had broken through the blockade, and the soldiers who did not want to leave their native region had deserted, leaving only diehard supporters.

delayed by battles and compelled to make long detours to cross rivers; they ventured into territory where they had to depend on a hostile people in order to survive. They spent their entire time marching, fighting and trying to convince others of their views, never knowing where they might eat or sleep that night.

The Long March as such ended after a year, on October 20, 1935, when seven thousand men of the First Front Army (less than a tenth of those who had set out) met up with the rebels of Shensi under the Great Wall. The Second and Fourth Armies did not finish their Long Marches until October 1936. Twenty-five thousand men were all that was left. The majority of these had been recruited during the March. The rest had either been killed in action or had died of hunger, disease or cold. Some had dropped dead from fatigue, others had deserted or been captured. "The air was thick with their absence." Mao wrote about the march in two poems*:

> The sky is high, the clouds are pale,
> We watch the wild geese vanish southward.
> If we fail to reach the Great Wall, we are not men,
> We who have already measured twenty thousand li . . .

> The Red Army fears not the trials of the Long March,
> Holding light ten thousand crags and torrents . . .
> Mimshan's thousand li of snow joyously crossed,
> The three Armies march on, each face glowing.

A Veteran of the Long March

We met a veteran of the Long March in Canton; he is now leader of the Kwangtung Provincial Revolutionary Committee. He was reticent about this brave venture, as was the Chinese Ambassador in Paris, General Huang Chen, who is another one of the few survivors. When I pressed him, he answered in monosyllables and seemed irritated. Yes, eight thousand miles on foot was tiring. Yes, they had often gone hungry. Yes, there were better times when their daily ration of millet appeared—just enough to keep them going—but often it didn't. Yes, they used to eat leaves off trees. Yes, they

---

*The first excerpt is the opening two verses of Mao's poem "Mount Liupan" written in October 1935, which concerns the capture of a mountain range on October 7, 1935 by the First Front Army under Mao. The second is from "The Long March," also written in October 1935. The translation is from the Foreign Languages Press edition of Mao's poems in English, Peking, 1976. Translations of these and others of Mao's poems can also be found in Jerome Ch'en, *Mao and the Chinese Revolution*, Oxford University Press, 1965, and *The Poems of Mao Tse-tung*, translated and with an introduction and notes by Willis Barnstone in collaboration with Ko Ching-po, Barrie & Jenkins, London, and Bantam Books, New York, 1972. Barnstone's collection is a parallel text, and the notes are very helpful (TRANSLATOR'S NOTE).

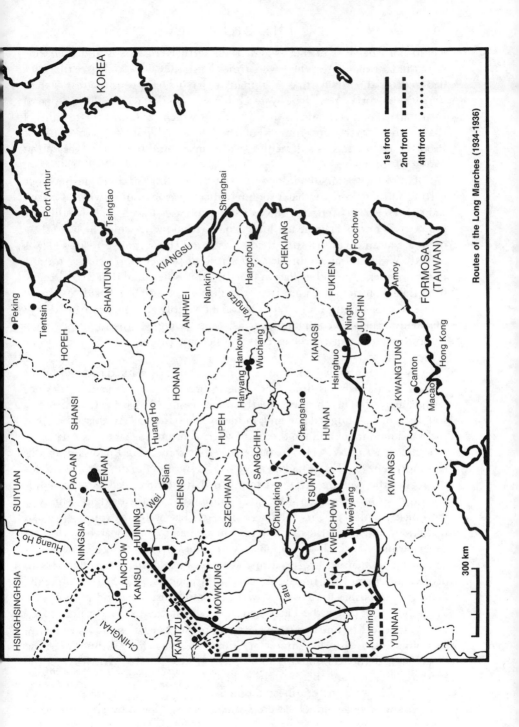

Routes of the Long Marches (1934-1936)

1st front

2nd front

4th front

would boil the soles of their shoes, their leather cross-belts and their rifle slings and eat them. Yes, there were times when they were so thirsty that they had to drink their own urine. Yes, many survivors had spent the rest of their lives in sanatoria. Yes, there were children and adolescents along—one of them carried on his shoulders the iron casket which contained the remains of the archives of the government of the "Soviet Republic of the Chinese People." Yes, there was a detachment of women, and they were every bit as strong as the men.

Up to this point I had done most of the talking, asking questions but getting so little in reply that I soon felt that I was intruding where I wasn't wanted. He simply repeated the words and phrases I used, merely adding a grumpy yes or no. Then he used the exquisite food with which he was filling my plate as an excuse to turn the conversation to Cantonese recipes. I was baffled. Was he afraid of breaking the rule of secrecy (top priority for any Party member, especially a Party official)? Or was he afraid that his colleague from the revolutionary committee or the interpreter sitting beside us would accuse him of having broken it? Or was he simply reticent from modesty? Mao had warned his comrades-in-arms: "You have given distinguished service, but guard against arrogance; if you become proud you will cease to be heroes."

I was about to give up, when without warning he walked to a podium to read a speech which was almost the same as those we had heard every day since we had arrived. Then he gave me the microphone. When I returned to my seat, he got up, hugged me and suddenly announced: "At this moment a thousand mountains and ten thousand rivers could not separate us." Then he brought me a *kan-pei*.* Had he been moved by something I had said, or was he simply relieved that he had no more public speaking to do? In any case, for the rest of the evening he talked so much that I didn't need to say a word, except to set him off again. "We would often destroy the bridges behind us with picks, with the help of the peasants—we had so little explosive we had to economize. . . . As the march went on, we had to make matches, clothes, paper, arms or makeshift weapons. We printed money with a block. . . . Sometimes, when we had no arms, we gave the soldiers dummy rifles to deceive the enemy. . . . In wild regions of the country, warlike tribes like the Lolos laid ambushes for us. They were set against us. They did not know of the policy of equality the Party had adopted for the national minorities."

A lot could be said about this last statement. The Lolos had for centuries been disaffected with the Chinese of China, the Han. They did not need the propaganda of the Kuomintang to set them against the Red Army. As for the Party's policy toward the minorities . . .

"Which were the deadliest moments?"

"Many of our comrades were sucked down in swampy steppe land or

---

*A drink (literally, "bottoms-up") usually made of *mao-tai* (very strong rice alcohol).

succumbed to the cold on mountains over twenty thousand feet high. Some died while holding back Chiang Kai-shek's armies or while securing the last bridge on the river Tatu."

He fell silent. Then slowly, as if he had created a picture in his mind's eye, he started speaking again: "Our ranks got thinner every day. Men lay down on the glacis to die. But the dead men were replaced by boys from the provinces we crossed. In the poor regions famine was our best recruiting officer; people felt that if they were going to starve they might as well suffer for a cause. We took prisoners after each clash with the regular units. We would keep them a few days, and then let them go. Many chose to remain with us.

"There was no need for lengthy brainwashing—the prisoners understood quite quickly what the Red Army was fighting for. . . ."* As he was talking, his emotions were getting the better of him. I remembered the exhibits in the Yenan museum: a bowl of millet, straw sandals, belts that had been half nibbled away. There were arms, some of which had been taken from the Kuomintang and some from the Japanese, although our guide seemed to confuse the two; he blamed both enemies equally—as if they were still accomplices. Other arms, more rudimentary, had been made with whatever came to hand—hunting guns, hand-made grenades, dummy arms. The people had been ready for the fight. Victory came "out of the barrel of a gun" even if the barrel was made of wood, because the people had the courage to go on forced marches almost as badly shod as the *va-nu-pieds* (the barefoot fighters) of Year 11.**

A year later the survivors were able to assess the achievements of the march. The entire exodus took 368 days; 235 days and eighteen nights had been spent actually marching. Out of the hundred or so days of rest, more than half had been taken up with skirmishes; only forty-four were genuine rest days. An average of twenty-five miles was covered every day—a rate which is barely credible for some of the steepest terrain in the world. One squad once covered eighty miles in twenty-four hours; this was during the Tatu episode when they crossed eighteen mountain ranges and twenty-four rivers.

The Long March began as a heavy defeat—a strategic defeat in Kiangsi in which the Red Army narrowly escaped being wiped out. It was a defeat for the tactic which Mao had been so sure of. It was also a defeat in terms of a retreat—barely seven out of a hundred made it, and maybe five of those had been recruited on the way. It was a political defeat, since the support it gathered did not make up for the technical inferiority of the Red Army. Some historians say that the discontent of a section of the population, as a result of

---

*This process, which seems to have been fairly rare during the Long March in spite of what my friend said, was used frequently in the last period of the civil war (1947–49).
**That is, Year 11 of the French Revolution: 1793.

the extreme agrarian measures taken by Mao's Soviet, may have contributed to the loss of Kiangsi.

But Mao held out long enough to turn this defeat into victory. It was a military victory, because it enabled the Red Army to keep its nucleus, its morale and its nerve. It was a strategic victory, since the occupation of this region gave the communists a key position in the war with Japan, flanking their army as it advanced south. It was a political victory, because Yenan— deep in the heart of Chinese China—enabled Mao to take the initiative again, to develop his views and apply his theories under real conditions and for long enough to show that they could succeed.

Of course, one must clear away the myth which clouds the memory of the Long March. It certainly had aspects which were lamentable rather than heroic, especially in the first few months. Only Mao can admit that it began with a rout. The episode of the crossing of the Tatu River, which has been glorified by the revolutionary ballet and iconography, was only a small engagement on a batallion or company scale. What is perhaps most strange is that notice is taken only of the Long March of the First Front Army—in which Mao took part—and not of the other Long Marches that preceded and followed it, which were just as heroic. Here the Westerner senses a tendency toward hagiography. At times one feels one is witnessing the making of an epic poem in thirty years, a task which, in the cases of Charlemagne, Roland, Achilles and Ulysses, required some three centuries.

Anyway, no one can dispute the historical reality of the Long Marches, even if one of them is presented, perhaps a little wrongly, as the only one. Guillaumet in *Terre des Hommes* could have been writing of such an adventure when he said, "What I have done, I swear to you, no fool would have done." This armed exodus compares with the journey of Moses and the Jews through the desert to the Promised Land or the march of the Ten Thousand whom Xenophon led across the Anatolian plateau to the Black Sea (but this feat involved much weaker forces and much more modest distances and altitudes; as Napoleon said, it owed its fame to the pen of its author) or the retreat from Moscow—a retreat which would have launched the Grand Army on a reconquest of Europe.

The Long March Opened the Chinese Way

How were these straggling armies, exhausted, frozen and hungry—in desperate straits and still pursued by Chiang Kai-shek, whose strength was intact—able to reverse their situation in only twelve years?

Helped by the "Sian incident"* in December 1938, the revolutionary movement prepared for its future battles in the austere splendor of Yenan.

---

*See Chapter 16.

In the village there were over twenty cadre schools. The guns and agricultural implements were bundled up together: *ense et aratro*. Soldiers' manuals were corrected in Mao's own hand. Possessing no watches, they used a makeshift sundial. There was neither paper nor ink, so they wrote in the sand. Yellowing photographs taken near Mao's first cell in 1936 show troops assembled in the yard of the building which is now the museum; others show Mao and Chou En-lai* and Mao and Lin Piao. Others show plenary sessions of the Chinese Communist Party: Mao sharing out the land: Mao burning the leases, which were evidence of the former oppression; Mao organizing agricultural and craft production on cooperative lines.

It took eleven years for the army of liberation to build itself up again.** It worked out its doctrine and its technique for implementing it, and built up its stock of arms. In 1947, confronted by Chiang Kai-shek's 230,000 men, the 30,000 men of the Red Army were forced to abandon Yenan. Mao called his top commanders together in the room where tourist guides now lower their voice in reverence. " 'We must,' he told them—he was standing near the window at the time—'draw the enemy first this way and then that way in order to tire him out. We'll come back in a year's time. *To lose Yenan is to save Yenan.*' " As Mao predicted, it was a year before they took the region again. On the evening of the retreat, with the Kuomintang troops just a few miles away, Mao calmly invited his principle associates to dinner. At the end of the meal he asked them to go home, put everything there in order and make their men do the same. "So that everything is perfectly clean—then the enemy will understand what communism is." Chiang Kai-shek's troops arrived in the night, but for them it was the beginning of the end. In twelve years Mao had learned to turn failure into success.

It is important to remember that Maoism grew out of a long and hard war, and that it took over at a time of much suffering. Mao and his people won their autonomy together. Because communism is their conquest, it is also *their* communism. They are accountable only to themselves and their dead. This is why Mao was unafraid of breaks with his allies.

Like Tito and Ho Chi Minh, he was a resistance hero. The leaders of communist parties supported, dictated to and directed by Moscow have no alternative to obeying the Soviet model. The possibility of a schism or of being accused of heresy is enough to fill them with terror: Gomulka in 1956 and Dubček in 1968 could only retreat when faced with these prospects. A guerrilla chief who knows his victory comes from partisans at home is not

---

*These are genuine photographs. In official paintings however, Mao and Chou En-lai are never together. Only Lin Piao had the privilege of appearing beside Mao—and then only for a short period.
**Between the end of 1935 and the end of 1936 the remnants of the First Army had regrouped at Paoan, a short distance from Yenan. They transferred to Yenan at the time of the Sian incident.

afraid to disobey outside orders. He can and should proceed to govern in accordance with the particular spirit of his people. He has no need for foreign ideas.

The Saint of Yenan*

When you visit a place where Mao lived, made speeches or taught, you feel as though you are visiting a shrine. Your guide adopts the tone of the sexton showing you his church.

The Congress halls where the Party held clandestine meetings are preserved like holy places. The building in Yenan where the plenum of the Central Committee used to meet is like a church—spacious and hushed, with a vaulted wooden nave, rows of benches separated by a central aisle leading to an altar-like tribune, and a rapt and ardent congregation, transfixed like primitive religious sculptures, intoning verses from the *Little Red Book* as though they were hymns.

One of our companions wondered if the whole set had been erected for Catholic missions. The theme was the same—meditation, deprivation, help for the oppressed and a desire to spread the teachings of the master and prepare the devout for the Crusade.

The Pilgrimage to the Holy Land

Pilgrims file past one after another of Mao's former abodes, as reverently as though they were following the stations of the Cross.

First station: The grotto where Mao lived from January 1937 to November 1938. Once while writing an article, he sat with his feet on his brazier, deep in thought, unaware that his shoes were burning. Like Saint Martin, he shared his blanket with one of his guards; half of it is on display there under glass.

Second station: The grotto where Mao lived from November 1938 to the beginning of 1943. One can touch the relics: his ping-pong bat and the stone table at which he gave an interview to Anna Louise Strong and made the famous statement "All reactionaries are paper tigers," which has been applied ever since to the United States but which was not aimed at that country.

Third station: The grotto hidden among clumps of jujube trees, called the Garden of Jujubes. (As with the *Garden of Olives*, sometimes they say *Garden*, sometimes *Mount*.) Mao wrote more articles here—between 1943

---

*Naturally, I do not mean to suggest Mao was a saint—only that he was revered as one. If one does not take this into account, the Chinese revolution remains incomprehensible.

and 1945—than anywhere else. They have preserved the iron bar he used to cool his writing hand when he got a cramp.

Fourth station: The Troglodyte house where he lived from January 1946 until 1947. It was here that he decided to abandon Yenan, with the prophecy: "We will be back next year."

Westerners expect to be told of the birth of socialism and the history of the resistance. They are rather taken aback when they hear a chapter from *The Lives of the Saints*.

Yang Chen-fou was brought to meet us; the old district chief had a pimply face and eyes reddened by the dust of the loess. He had been a member of the Party since 1941, and had known Mao in 1943 on the *Mount of Jujubes*. He told us the following: "When Mao was living among the jujube trees, he was very worried about the life of the people. When he was free he would go around the countryside finding out what the masses were thinking.

"At New Year 1943, the district chiefs came with loaves of maize and millet to present their good wishes. He shook hands with us, invited us to sit down and gave us a drink of water. He asked us if we could produce four years' food in three years. All the village chiefs answered: 'We will even be able to grow three years' food in two. If we use more manure on the land and plow it several times, we'll make it.' Then Mao said: 'That's good, but it's not enough. The people must organize themselves in mutual aid groups.'

"During the 1945 spring holiday, Chairman Mao brought the heads of families together and asked them if they had had a good year. They replied: 'This year, between the twenty-four of us we've killed eighteen pigs for the spring festival.' Then Mao said: 'That's not enough. Next year you will kill twenty-four.'

"At all our festivals the soldiers helped the masses. They carried water and helped in the cleaning up, and those who could write taught the others . . ."

There was not a trace of the commercialization a Westerner would have expected—no souvenirs; no one was making a fortune selling the chairs Mao had sat on, the brushes he had used to write his articles, the hair his barber had surreptitiously kept. The visitors were quite content merely to stand and stare humbly at these religious caves, this basic furniture, these objects once touched by the Chairman.

Workers and young people flock to Yenan. The workers and peasants come from their factory or people's commune in trucks or buses. The young people come on foot, often from several hundred miles away, camping at farms or sleeping beside the road. They come in groups of twenty or thirty—school children shepherded by their masters, Red Guards who are recognizable by their red armbands, and troops on exercise. These little "Long Marches" are regularly organized—I was assured by a high Party official—in response to the Chairman's express wish that the memory of the

Long March be perpetuated. They train the young in the art of war, so they will become good militiamen and militiawomen—sound minds in sound bodies. And they inspire them, by mass pilgrimages like those of Santiago-de-Compostella and Chartres, with the strength to withstand physical exhaustion. They teach the young communal living and self-denial and encourage fervent participation in society. It appears that these aims are being achieved, judging from the general attitude of the young. They visit the relics with an air of reverence; they sing revolutionary songs as they march behind their flag and the portrait of Mao Tse-tung, which is carried by a chosen few, just as the banner of Corpus Christi and the portrait of the Virgin of Czestochowa are carried by the faithful in Poland.

A Basket of Mangoes

None of our Chinese companions had forgotten the story of the mangoes, and they told it easily; only one of them gave the impression of feeling somewhat uncomfortable about it.

On August 5, 1968 Mao sent a basket of mangoes—a gift from a Pakistani delegation—to the workers and peasants of Tsinghua University's "Mao Tse-tung thought propaganda group."* This gift, which was immediately seen as a tangible sign of the Chairman's blessing, aroused intense feelings. A Peking paper described it some days later: "When this happy news was known, a single cry rang out in all corners of Tsinghua University—*Long Live Chairman Mao!* The air echoed with cries of joy. People gathered immediately around the gift. They shouted with joy and sang. With tears welling up in their eyes, they shouted from the depths of their hearts: *Long live, long live our beloved great leader, our most respected Chairman Mao!* In the evening, public rejoicings of all kinds were organized. In spite of the rain, people went along to the Central Committee of the Chinese Communist Party to express their loyalty to our great leader."

The "good news" was immediately telephoned to all the factories where the members of the propaganda team worked. "Young revolutionary fighters of the Red Guards, teachers, students, workers and craftsmen of Tsinghua University were overjoyed at this happy event. A number of young Red Guards announced, enraptured: 'We love what Chairman Mao loves. We shall stand for what he stands for. We unite in serried ranks under his farsighted leadership.' "

In their turn, the workers in the units to which the members of the propaganda team belonged expressed the desire to obtain at least one of these precious fruits. So the mangoes were distributed among the various factories and rural communes, and even to the crew of a boat. According to another journal, a meeting was organized in a Peking print works in honor of the

---

*This gesture takes on a political significance in the context of the Cultural Revolution.

mango that had been awarded to it. At about eleven o'clock at night the workers unanimously decided that the precious fruit could not be allowed to go bad. A way must be found of preserving it, no matter what the cost. This way, it could be passed on to future generations so that they would "remain eternally loyal to Chairman Mao." The following day they searched feverishly for a chemical process with which to treat the mangoes. The Peking Institute of Agronomy and the Natural History Museum, which had been called in to help, confessed that they were unable to suggest anything except a bottle of formalin. So straightaway—"forgetting even to eat"—the carpenters at the print works set to making a casket for the bottle containing the mango. Photographs of the casket and the bottle with the mango were published throughout the country. The workers were standing around the fruit which had brought them Mao's blessing and announcing with pride: "The preservation of these mangoes is of utmost importance. This way the revolutionary line of Chairman Mao will be forever imprinted on our minds."

There was no stopping now—teachers and students held meetings around the mangoes. "Overjoyed, the revolutionary fighters of the group cried out: 'We shall carry out all the latest instructions from Chairman Mao in all fields and we shall turn the universities into Red colleges of Mao Tse-tung thought.' " The whole country became involved. A peasant woman from the province of Hopeh decided to defy the harsh climate of Northern China and plant a mango tree "so that each time they see mangoes, peasants will think of our dear Chairman Mao, and so that these mangoes will remain in the hearts of the peasants for future generations." *Et in saecula saeculorum* . . .

Durkheim and Freud would probably have been keenly interested in the significance of such behavior. Maybe they would have been tempted to add chapters to *Formes élémentaires de la vie religieuse* and *Totem and Taboo* on the basis of this story of the totemized mangoes—the refusal to eat them and the concern with immortalizing a sacred object, the tangible sign of divine benevolence.

The Worship of the Red Emperor

Marxist theories may be of less assistance in understanding the Chinese regime, the way it works and its achievements than modern research on the prelogical mind. Observing the power Mao had over the masses was disconcerting, but it was also illuminating. He would shake someone's hand, and people would rush forward to touch the hand he had shaken. The good that has come of this contact is then passed from one person to another, so that thirty years later "the man who shook Mao's hand" is shown off to pilgrims. He speaks to a crowd. They hang on his words and are inspired by them.

Toward these heights of deification, akin to worship of the old emperors, Mao proceeded in the array of grandeur but of poverty.

He usually went about on foot, like his men, although when he was ill for a short time he went on horseback.* People told us that it was a historical fact that Mao had marched barefoot when his soldiers did not have any shoes and that when they were crossing a snow-covered mountain he had given his jacket to a wounded man. Although he was Chairman of the "Chinese Soviet Republic," he was, they said, no different from his men. On the collar of his rather austere jacket, made fashionable by Sun Yat-sen, he wore only the two red stripes of the Red soldier. In Yenan his kit and equipment—even including his mosquito net—were no different from those of his officers. Mao, who had been in command of whole regions for ten years and had confiscated so much property from landowners, had in his personal possession only his blankets and two cotton uniforms; one he wore and the other was slung over the back of a chair. Everyone at Yenan knew that, if he had agreed on an alliance with the Kuomintang, he could have immediately stepped into a top position which would have brought plenty of money. His austere way of life was especially surprising when compared with that of others who had become powerful leaders. He encouraged self-denial in his colleagues too.

Mao was constantly exhorting the Chinese to return to the "spirit of Yenan," in other words, poverty and equality. It is the spirit of soldiers who form a strange kind of Salvation Army. The spirit of leaders who demand more from themselves than from their men and who continually provide an example of unselfishness. The spirit of humble peasants struggling to find fulfillment in a united China. A highly demanding patriotism which implies severe restriction on personal needs, which restores and maintains national unity, and which both opposes the abuses of the past and maintains popular traditions.

Mao understood that theory was not enough. He established a relationship of simplicity between himself and his men which took on a religious force. Can one believe in people who promise others a better life but begin by making sure they get one themselves? By the same token, can one mistrust those who refuse it for themselves until it has been secured for others? The Chinese revolution was based not on reason but on faith.

Two Angels That Move Mountains

The parable of the *Old Man of the Mountain* ends with divine intervention: "Yu Kung, the Old Man of the Mountain, went on digging every day, undaunted. God was moved by this, and he sent down two angels, who carried the mountain away on their backs." The miraculous intervention is

---

*No doubt one could get along without the stuffed remains of the horse Mao is reputed to have ridden. As a notice at the Yenan museum says that he almost always went on foot with his men, this stuffed animal adds nothing to the other relics, at least in a Westerner's eyes. But this horse does have greater claim to contact with Mao than a basket of mangoes.

necessary so that the absurd becomes reasonable; the Old Man could not fail. At this point Mao revealed the act of faith that justified his work: "Today, two big mountains lie like a dead weight on the Chinese people—one is imperialism, the other is feudalism. The Chinese Communist Party has long made up its mind to dig them up. We must persevere and work unceasingly, and we, too, will touch God's heart. Our God is none other than the Chinese people. If they stand up and dig together with us, why can't these two mountains be cleared away?"

So the people were God and Mao was the prophet. Chinese Marxism is a people's religion. Mao, the Moses of the Long March, was the inspired interpreter, the priest, at one and the same time the servant and the leader—the leader of the God-people, the servant of the people-God. Mao was the mediator.

Before 1911, the emperor, who was known as the Son of Heaven, was the intermediary between Heaven and Earth. People prayed to the emperor to intercede with God to spare them trials and afflictions, plagues and other natural disasters. The last empress, Tzu-hsi, wrote public prayers intended to put an end to a drought. "The rains have come," her Prime Minister told her. "Your Majesty is great. See how God answers your prayers. It is almost as if you were God." To the people it is clear that Mao interceded on behalf of China, and that God answered his prayers.

The Tai-ping Emperor Hong expressed the Chinese tradition in Biblical language. In a note in the margin of the First Epistle of John, he wrote that he was the third person of the Trinity: "There is only one Supreme God. Christ is the first son of God. Hong is also the son of God, born, like Christ, of the same mother." The emperor of the Tai-ping had invented a Chinese transposition of the Bible. Mao found a Chinese transposition of Marxism.

One of the most persistent misconceptions about China is that the Chinese people are not religious. Some sinologists—especially those who have not been able to visit China—refuse to believe that their revolutionary ardor is religious in nature, because, they say, it is well known that the Chinese are nonreligious.

The Romans of the Lower Empire were unquestionably irreligious; using a similar argument, one would have had to conclude that it would be impossible for a new religion to take root among them. In the first half of the twentieth century, when their society was well on the way to breaking up, the Chinese no longer believed in anything much other than ancestor worship. Does this mean that they were no longer able to believe in anything? Mao has, so to speak, collectivized ancestor worship, the only religion of the masses—the Chinese people is the collectivity of all its ancestors, living and dead. Today the Son of Heaven has been replaced by the Son of the People. Mao, who is the object and subject of the worship of the people, has come to symbolize the national bond. The people worship themselves—in him.

A Hymn to the Great Helmsman

"Thanks to Chairman Mao"—everything one hears in China about what is good on this earth begins with these words. Even if, in the beginning, this formula did not always express the sentiments of those who used it, might it not end up—by being reverentially repeated by hundreds of millions of people—having the force of a truth? A large proportion of the Chinese people give the impression of believing that any event that is good for China is due to Mao and that any national reverse or affront can be attributed to those who have betrayed his thought. It is not Mao who made the "Hundred Flowers" campaign end so suddenly,* who was responsible for the "Great Leap Forward" not fulfilling its promises, who caused the Cultural Revolution to get out of control and go further than its organizer intended; it is always the fault of others—the "renegades," the "deviationists," the "evil elements," the "Leftists."

All plays, films, folk evenings and acrobatic displays begin and end— or, at any rate, begin *or* end—with a song of praise to the "Great Helmsman," the "Great Teacher," the "Red Sun." These displays of devotion may seem irrational or puerile to Westerners, but they forget that, had it not been for a certain cult of Mao, the Maoist system could never have prevailed and could probably not have survived the difficult phases of construction. The self-denial that is demanded of everyone is too painful for the people to bear unless at the same time they are able to feel optimism about the future. "The East Is Red" and "The East Wind" and other revolutionary songs have the same ability to move people to action as the canticles.

When one of Mao's recent Western visitors got back to his Peking hotel he was greeted by one of the staff who had been waiting for him. Knowing where he had been, she came out to ask him, in a state of some excitement: "Well, did you see him? Was he well?" When he told her, she shook his hand with tears in her eyes.

---

*In January of 1956, only a month before Khrushchev's denunciation of Stalin at the Twentieth Communist Party Congress of the Soviet Union, Mao discussed "contradictions among the people" in his annual address to the Supreme State Conference of the National Congress of party and nonparty representatives. Taking his thought from the classic texts of *I Ching* and *Chuang-tzu*, which evoke the principles of Yin and Yang and the "unity of opposites," Mao characterized the existing contradictions between the state and its critics as mainly "nonantagonistic" or "within the people." Instead of resorting to Stalinist repression to preserve order, he recommended a policy of "letting a hundred flowers bloom and a hundred schools of thought contend," in order to resolve differences. The result was what became known as the Hundred Flowers campaign, encouraging self-criticism and relaxing press censorship and other controls on freedom of expression. What followed was a flood of complaints about the dogmatism and sectarianism of party members and officials, and virulent denunciations of the party bureaucracy. The depth and extent of dissension had been totally unexpected. Soon the more outspoken critics were themselves denounced as "Rightists," and within eighteen months, by June of 1957, press controls had been restored and the Hundred Flowers campaign was over (EDITOR'S NOTE).

Only skeptics ridicule the sublime. Almost anything is possible for those who believe. Belief is the essence of the Chinese model.

What Is Behind the Cult of Personality

"What does Chairman Mao think of the cult that surrounds him?" Each time we asked a Chinese this, back came the same answer like a record: "Chairman Mao is a modest man who has always lived a simple life. He would wish to be spoken of as little as possible. He is always giving orders to this effect. But it is impossible to curb the enthusiasm of the masses, who know how much they owe him."

This may seem difficult to believe, but the explanation is certainly at least partly true.*

The Tradition of the Infallibility of the Leader

Once he took over the position formerly held by the infallible Emperor Son of Heaven, Mao was considered infallible. When I asked a young Chinese if Mao could ever make a mistake, she smiled and shook her head: "Impossible. He has never misled us." She added, or maybe the interpreter added for her: "He has never made a mistake." This young woman was repeating the Roman Catholic catechism: "I firmly believe all the truths Thy Church teaches, because it is Thou who revealest them to it and Thou canst not be mistaken or mislead us."

It is one of the basic principles of Confucian philosophy that the Leader must be a virtuous person if the nation is to progress. "The Master says: If the prince is virtuous himself, the people will do their duties without having to be ordered; if the prince is not virtuous himself, he will have to give orders, and the people will not obey them." The imagery which likens Mao to the Red Star, the Red Sun, the Red East, the Red Light, which are everyone's guides, goes straight back to the teachings of Confucius. "The Master says: He who governs a people by setting it good examples is like the Pole Star which hangs motionless in the sky while all the other stars revolve around it."

Mao was almost always above the mêlée, like the Pole Star above the horizon. Whatever troubles were brewing—even those he had caused himself—he was hardly ever attacked in public after he emerged from the clandestine struggle. He knew how to present himself as personally unassailable, even at the worst moments of the "Hundred Flowers" campaign and the Cultural Revolution.

---

*Manifestations of this cult became much less frequent after 1970, which leads one to believe that popular enthusiasm had to be worked up when the revolution was in full spate and the regime was in danger.

We know now, though, that he was severely criticized on many occasions, but always in secret. He was criticized not only between 1927 and January 1935, when he was thrust into the background, but also in December 1935 in Paoan at the end of the Long March. There, members of the Political Bureau sharply reproached him for seeking to present the Long March as a success when it was in fact a failure. In 1938 in Yenan—on the occasion of his divorce and remarriage to the young actress Chiang Ching—the old communist leaders were shattered to see him repudiate a woman who had shared the sufferings of the Long March with them. They did all they could to dissuade him from going ahead with something that would harm his image. And again in 1958 and 1959, after the catastrophic halting of the "Hundred Flowers" campaign and the first difficulties of the "Great Leap Forward," Marshal Peng Teh-huai openly attacked Mao for the brutal launching of the people's communes; he paid for his frankness by being publicly disgraced.

It was probably because of these reversals in policy and criticisms that Mao was led to give up the Presidency of the Republic and to find himself for the second time—from 1959 to 1965—in a minority within the Party. But he remained the nominal leader. His status had not changed as far as the masses were concerned. The criticisms barely went beyond the small circle of political officials and intellectuals.* Today they have either been swept away or drowned by the powerful wave of Maolatry generated by the Cultural Revolution.**

Under Mao everything happened as if a consensus had been reached between the members of the Party, whether they were loyal supporters of Mao or not, so as not to tamper—in view of the public—with a symbol they considered vital. The myth of Mao's infallibility—although it was questioned many times and contested by Mao himself—was considered a necessity of government.

The Excesses of the Cult of Personality

One-party states insist that the leaders be presented as infallible, and the supreme leader—generally the First Secretary of the Party—is always the subject of a vast iconography. His picture is everywhere—in the air terminals of Leipzig and Sofia, Conakry and Hanoi—and it is impossible to escape his gaze. But nowhere, except perhaps in the Soviet Union at the end of Stalin's

---

*At various times terrifying allegories have been written against Mao. Wu Han's *Hai Jui Dismissed from Office* clearly refers to the dismissal from office of Marshal Peng Teh-huai after he spoke out against Mao; the violent attacks later made on this play even raised the curtain on the Cultural Revolution.

**In a conversation with Lucien Paye, France's first Ambassador to Peking from 1964 to 1969, and in his last conversation with Edgar Snow, Mao explained that he had to put his weight behind the intensification of the cult of personality in order to incite the masses to demolish the bureaucratic apparatus that was hostile to his teaching.

rule, has the personality cult reached the level it did in China during the Cultural Revolution; even Lenin did not become a cult figure until after his death.

This phenomenon can be explained. Stalin was the only leader in modern times who did as much for his country as Mao. Stalin molded a society that was threatened with break-up and extended an empire that Lenin—naively believing that the world revolution was near—had deliberately sacrificed. But Stalin was merely a great Head of State, a successor to the czars. No one took him for a *starets*.* His literary genius was not remarkable.

Mao appeared as a complete man. He founded a new philosophy but at the same time he was skillful enough to pass himself off as the true successor of Marx and Lenin, whom the Moscow revisionists had betrayed. His contribution to ideology, his radical views on permanent revolution, on anti-bureaucratism, and on the creative strength of the masses, his actual implementation of them, the supreme power he exercised over such a long period—there is nothing to compare with this in any other country. China is possibly the only country in which one man has to such an extent embodied the hope of the people, the revolt of the oppressed, the quintessence of culture, the doctrine of government, the nation in its struggle.

The Virtues of Charismatic Power

But however much Mao deserves the gratitude of his people, that is not the only reason for his popularity. As a phenomenon, the cult of personality is as old as time. All leaders of men have benefited to a greater or less extent from what Max Weber calls "charismatic power"—that mysterious current that passes between a leader and a people determined through him to satisfy its conscious and unconscious aspirations, because he has been able to divine them and embody them. To different degrees and using different methods, Caesar, Napoleon, Roosevelt, Churchill, Nasser, Kennedy, Gandhi and de Gaulle all knew how to enter into this kind of secret resonance with the nation whose destiny they took upon themselves.

The faith of the people is a very valuable thing to have—almost as valuable in a democratic regime as in a despotic one. It makes any self-sacrifice which leaders demand of the people easier to bear, or at least less difficult. It enables obstacles to be overcome which would otherwise have been insurmountable.

The Westerner visiting China has difficulty avoiding a feeling of suffocation. He is appalled by the magnitude of the sacrifices demanded of the Chinese people. He realizes that the harsh measures are the only way to shake an enormous mass of illiterate and superstitious people out of their inertia, to wake them up and get them moving, to force them to jump from the

---

*Russian: a wise and respected elder (TRANSLATOR'S NOTE).

sixteenth century to the twenty-first in a few decades. But the Chinese would not have steeled themselves for such enormous effort and would not have accepted so much suffering if they had not been hypnotized by their faith in an infallible and invincible man.

"O Lord," said Saint Augustine, "it is when I obey Thy wishes more that I feel more free." A Westerner may think quite sincerely that the Chinese are enslaved—in their place he would feel so. The Chinese communists seem not to feel their chains because they believe in communism; they would only become slaves if they ceased to believe in it. Their faith feeds on itself. By all appearances, such constraint upon men might be expected to end up provoking revolt and hatred. But no one is allowed to express his private thoughts—who knows what risks a man would run if he did. But psychology shows that repressed resentment gradually gives way to an intense identification with the object of one's fear. Oppression becomes an intense sensual pleasure. Obeying the idol is a joy; indeed, it gives you a chance to become a party of history. The individual is too weak to rebel against this mirage, which is lived by an entire people.

The strength of charismatic power is that it raises the threshold of perception of collective suffering.

Mao Face to Face with Maolatry

"But, I assure you, our Great Leader has nothing to do with the proliferation of pictures of himself. He frequently asks that his pictures be removed. It's one of his main worries. He struggles against a personality cult."

"Why doesn't he manage to get his orders obeyed?"

"He has, to a certain extent. You see far fewer pictures of him now than you did a few years ago . . ."

Our group listened to this with some skepticism. How could a personality cult have been organized against the wishes of the personality? Was Mao then a mere puppet? Was he not very well aware of the fact that his prestige was the most powerful force holding China together? Why would he have called for the Maolatry to be wound down and run the risk of dividing his country, which derives its cohesion from this same Maolatry? Why would he have risked letting the power that derives its strength from the same source become diluted? We felt these questions came close to the heart of the political mystery of China.

There is certainly plenty of evidence that Mao mistrusted too much power. In September 1948, when none of his closest colleagues had any doubt that he would soon gain the leadership, Mao asked the Party Central Committee to vote unequivocally for this resolution: "The system of committees must guarantee collective leadership and prevent power being exercised by a single individual. All important questions must be widely debated by the members present." It would seem he wanted to avoid the temptation to which Lenin succumbed. Having proclaimed until 1917 that authority had to be exercised by the committees, Lenin then hastily thrust them aside in order to concentrate power in his own hands.

In March 1949 the Central Committee decided "at the suggestion of Comrade Mao Tse-tung" to ban "the celebration of Party leaders' birthdays and the naming of streets, squares and enterprises after them."

Edgar Snow mentioned this decision in his last interview with Mao Tse-tung in December 1970. "It has been respected," Mao replied, "but other forms of worship have appeared. There have been so many slogans, pictures and plaster statues . . ." Mao regretted the excesses of this cult and pointed out that those who applauded him most loudly and bore his banner highest fell into three categories—"those who are sincere, those who are opportunists and swim with the tide, shouting *Long Live Mao* because everyone else is doing so, and those who are hypocrites. You mustn't take all these demonstrations at face value."

Mao did not seem to have fallen into megalomania, nor did he appear to believe in his own infallibility. "There is not a man in the world," he would say, "who has never made a mistake."

However, can one possibly believe that the man one has seen standing and taking the salute for hours on end as hundreds and thousands of pictures of himself are marched past did not *want* to establish a personality cult? Obviously he never applied to himself the system of committees he advocated in 1948. The cult of images and the cult of personality remained his monopoly. It is clear that after the dramatic Tsunyi conference in January 1935 he continually forced the Party's hand in various ways; it is also clear that the collegial principle has remained a myth. If he had not wanted a personality cult, he would not have let Lin Piao describe him in the preface to the *Little Red Book* as "the greatest Marxist-Leninist of our era [who] has inherited, defended and developed Marxism-Leninism with genius" and imply that the leadership of the international communist movement was his inalienable right.

After all, no one was humbler, it was always said, than the Emperor of China. Many times Chiang Kai-shek declared that he was "not up to his task" and "resigned." These are rituals in China. Furthermore, in the writings and speeches of Stalin denunciations of the cult of personality are expressed in almost identical terms. Mao scornfully condemned glorification of the individual, but when, at the Eighth Congress in 1959, Peng Teh-huai proposed that all references to Mao Tse-tung thought be removed from the Party Constitution, Mao did not forgive him.

However genuine Mao's modesty may have been, one cannot know the secret thoughts of a man who for at least forty years was convinced that it was his duty to assume the destiny of China. With passing years, the man ended up by becoming identified with the power. How could one hate certain attributes of power without hating oneself? Mao explained this to Edgar Snow by showing him that the cult of personality was the most common thing in the world: "After all, don't the Americans have their own idolatry? How could a State Governor, a President or a Minister get along if no one worshipped him? There has always been the desire to be worshipped and the desire to worship. Would you be happy if no one read your books and articles? It's the same with the cult of personality. This applies to me, too."

There are circumstances in which the well-being of the country gets the better of a statesman's natural modesty, even if that modesty has formed the subject of resolutions passed in public. Many times Mao used his cult to impose his will, whether within the Party, on the public with the support of the Party, or on the Party with the support of the public. He used Maolatry as a powerful means of governing—as both the consequence and the instrument of success.

But the complexity of the human soul does not allow us to accept this explanation. Resignation—whether real or not—can go hand in hand with a secret enjoyment. Mao offered the Chinese an idealized image of themselves which made them abandon their own egos. Why should one assume that he did not relish this identity of his individual ego and the ideal of the collective ego? If the public who idolized him felt, because they had an ideal in common, that they had become one with him, how could he help being fascinated, seeing his own ego being absorbed by hundreds of millions of people, who then reflected back to him an idealized image of it? The Chinese knew the narcissistic joy of loving themselves in him. It is only natural that he should have loved himself through them.

The Children's Crusade

The "Great Proletarian Cultural Revolution" is no doubt the most extraordinary successful *tour de force* in the whole history of revolution: a revolution launched not against a regime by its opponents but by the founder of a regime, the leader of the Party in power, against the cadres of this Party and against the deviation into which this regime was drifting. All Mao needed to do was to release a flight of children in order to attack his old companion-in-arms, the President of the Republic, Liu Shao-chi; the Party apparatus; the intellectuals; the political class; the bureaucracy; the bourgeois spirit; and the love of money. He called on the base to act against the hierarchy. But the hierarchy did not dare to attack him. His adversary Liu Shao-chi never expressed a single reservation about him in public. Although Mao had the majority of the Party and the trade unions against him, no one doubted that he would win in the judgment of the people. The cadres could not hold out in their views for long in the face of the simple faith that drove the masses.

Mao confirmed this interpretation in some remarks that ring true: "During the Cultural Revolution" he had "reckoned that a growing personality cult was vitally necessary to stimulate the masses to dismantle the Party bureaucracy which was composed of anti-Maoists. It is hard for a people to overcome the habits of three thousand years of emperor-worshipping tradition." He added, oddly: "The Red Guards said that if you weren't covered with insignia and slogans of Mao, then you were being anti-Maoist. In the past few years there has been a need for the cult of personality."

As a matter of fact, there is any amount of evidence that the accusation of anti-Maoism gave rise to an upsurge of revolutionary energy in the hearts of the masses. The surest way of getting rid of someone was to accuse him in public of being lukewarm toward the Great Helmsman. The reaction was immediate. "The public began to shout: We'll smash in the head of anyone who opposes Chairman Mao."

Mao's attitude to his own cult is hard to appraise. According to one thesis to which Chinese officials have given their support, his followers, not satisfied with merely insisting on his infallibility, made an idol out of him against his own orders. So the idolatry that surrounded him is not—as in the case of Stalin—a sign of his excessive power, but, on the contrary, shows his inability to get his orders obeyed and implemented, either by leaders who need to glorify him to keep their hold on the masses or by the latter, determined to satisfy their Maoist passion.

This thesis is difficult to accept in this form, but it could be put another way. One might say that Mao allowed his cult to develop because without it he would not have managed either to govern China or to regain power after having practically been ousted. This interpretation may seem to the Westerner to be paradoxical to the point of absurdity. However, it is the most plausible hypothesis. Mao was obliged to be what the Chinese people expected him to be. During the most difficult periods, he felt he was powerless to govern if he did not conform to the image his fellow-countrymen created for themselves, namely a man in whom, without realizing it, they saw not only the leader of the revolution but also the emperors' successor and the guarantor of China's unity. The exercise of power involves these constraints—and these joys.

3

Mao Tse-tung Thought: A "Spiritual Atom Bomb"

The Great Proletarian Cultural Revolution

"Before the Great Proletarian Cultural Revolution . . . After the Great Proletarian Cultural Revolution . . ." We heard this all the time—much more frequently than "before the Liberation" and "after the Liberation." The second Chinese revolution, between 1965 and 1970, seemed to have eclipsed the first one, which took place in 1949. In all areas of thought and in all sectors of economic activity, the Great Proletarian Cultural Revolution appeared as the great watershed, as the reference point for the Chinese.

One wonders whether they will continue to situate their history with reference to it, just as the Muslims date their history from the Hegira. Maybe the trend will reverse—indeed there are more and more signs that this is happening—and the Cultural Revolution will no longer be taken so seriously. Certainly we thought we saw signs of this on more than one occasion. At times it seemed as though the phrase "Cultural Revolution" no longer had any meaning, but was an expression learned by heart and repeated out of habit.

Neither possibility should be ruled out. It is bound to be a long time before we have enough information on this movement, which is still hard to see clearly and to judge. The two opposing camps clashed on an enormous scale, earning this revolution the official titles "great" and "proletarian."*

---

*A chronology in the appendix gives the stages of the Cultural Revolution in detail.

It is perhaps above all what the West has come to call it—*cultural*. But in using this adjective one must give it its full meaning; current usage in the West does not.

In a period of four years the Cultural Revolution provoked a radical change in the way people behaved toward others as well as toward themselves, in their conscious and unconscious motivations, in generally accepted ideas and values, as well as in the organization of society—all this comes under the heading "cultural."* It would be a complete misunderstanding to think that this revolution was aimed simply at making small changes in some aspects of spiritual life. It puts everything in question. Chinese *cultural* activity—in the strict sense of the word—is completely dominated down to the very last detail by—in the broadest sense—imperative *cultural* demands, in other words, by the desire to build a new civilization made up of new men.

Conversely, cultural life in the narrow sense—intellectual life—has been at the center of the Cultural Revolution; indeed, it developed as a battle of ideas, a kind of *bataille d'Hernani*,** which lasted several years and then degenerated into a pitched battle. The Cultural Revolution was certainly a *Querelle des Anciens et des Modernes*,*** but it was also a palace revolution.

The Barriers Smashed to Pieces

"How would you define the Cultural Revolution?" I asked the writer Kuo Mo-jo.

"It is the movement in which Mao Tse-tung thought, that spiritual atom bomb, broke down the barriers that were stopping the course of the revolution—the barriers which the Liberation had left standing and those which revisionism was trying to rebuild."

---

*The word "cultural" is ambiguous. In the West it is most frequently used in connection with "intellectual life"—education, the arts and letters ("cultural relations," "cultural affairs"). The Chinese use it in the anthropological sense, as opposed to *nature*. For them it covers the entire spectrum of acquired behavior—ways and customs, beliefs handed down from one generation to the next, the legacy of individual and collective minds molded by society.

**An all-out fight between "classicists" and "romantics" on the opening night of Victor Hugo's *Hernani* at the Comédie Française on February 25, 1830. To support his play against the habitués of that official playhouse, Hugo gathered some four hundred students and writers—among them Gérard de Nerval and Théophile Gautier—in the audience for the premiere. After the very first line of the drama—which was written in deliberate defiance of the classical tradition—a riot erupted in the theatre and did not subside for the rest of the performance (TRANSLATOR'S NOTE).

***A literary quarrel which broke out in 1674 and again in 1714 between the "Ancients," represented by Boileau, Racine and La Bruyère, and the "Moderns," Quinault, Charles Perrault, Desmarets and Charpentier. The former group held that modern artists and writers should only imitate classic forms; the latter upheld the right to draw on new themes and invent new forms without reference to ancient Greek and Latin models (TRANSLATOR'S NOTE).

Whether it is a soldier or a scholar talking, the words are almost the same. In a speech to the army in 1965, on the eve of the Cultural Revolution, Marshal Lin Piao said: "The best weapon is not the aircraft, heavy artillery, tanks or the atom bomb, it is Mao Tse-tung thought; the greatest fighting force is the man armed with Mao Tse-tung thought."

Isn't it strange, though, that such a cataclysm was needed to put an end to resistance which seventeen years of revolutionary rule had been unable to quash? In November 1967, Mao's own wife, the actress Chiang Ching, passed harsh judgment on this long period of communist rule: "These seventeen years are to be condemned utterly." When Madame Mao—along with the various Leftist movements which the Cultural Revolution thrust into the public eye—stigmatized the "capitalists," the "bureaucrats," the "feudal lords," the "bourgeois state mechanism," "class justice," the "police in the pay of the bureaucracy," one might think she was speaking of China before 1949. Not at all—she was speaking of China just before the Cultural Revolution, after the "seventeen condemned years."

These are the obstacles to the revolution which were kept in existence or re-created by the communist regime, and which the bomb Kuo Mo-jo was telling me about finally blew up.

We were welcomed by Kuo Mo-jo on the first day of our stay in China. A much quoted poet, man of great learning, philosopher, historian, novelist and playwright, Kuo Mo-jo is the regime's most celebrated cultural figure. He is honored as the supreme Chinese in the sciences, in the world of letters and in the arts. For a long time Deputy Prime Minister and Minister of Culture, protocol still gives him precedence over all the ministers except the Prime Minister.

In the early days of the Cultural Revolution it is said he underwent a severe test. Before the Red Guards could jeer at him and put a dunce's cap on his head, he made a spontaneous self-criticism, recognizing in himself the prototype of the "scholar" in the mandarin tradition. He then accused himself of being "baser than dirt" and "more fetid than the dungheap." He reemerged from his ordeal as respected as ever; he is one of those illustrious figures a revolutionary regime likes to bring forward, especially since he does not really appear to be a revolutionary. He is a guarantor. He reassures. As a principal dignitary, Kuo Mo-jo brings intelligence, culture and science to the Maoist regime.

Almost every day we were in Peking we met Kuo Mo-jo in one or another of his roles. This octogenarian is President of the Academy of Sciences and First Vice-Chairman of the Standing Committee of the National People's Congress.* Still fully active as an archaeologist, he had just led a dig

---

*Whose Chairman is Marshal Chu Teh, the hero of the Long March and head of the Red Army for twenty years.

at an imperial burial place of the Han dynasty dating from the second century B.C., which had been discovered by accident. He had translated a text to which no one else had found the key, although he hadn't been able to decipher one character and had put a black square around it. For four evenings he patiently helped me to overcome my awkwardness with chopsticks and at the same time treated me to a conversation which was full of vivid images and expressions but which was also very frank; he was too old to have anything to fear either from the regime or from foreigners.

Night as Well as Day

"Why is Maoism always described as a star and a sun?" I asked him.

"There is no such thing as Maoism," he replied quietly. "There is Mao Tse-tung thought. The sun shines only during the day. The stars twinkle only at night. Mao Tse-tung thought shines at night as well as during the day."

I thought it reasonable enough to use slogans to enable workers and school children to understand Chairman Mao's ideas, but I did find it somewhat surprising that an old man of such accomplishment and refined intellect should take them up and use them himself.

"The essential thing is to *think well*. To grow rice well, to cast good-quality steel, to heal the sick, you must first of all think well. Before the Cultural Revolution, people thought badly—in the schools and universities, in the theatres and newspapers. It was well worth closing them down so as to make them capable of teaching people to think well."

"So, it's 'In the beginning was the Word'? If we think well, *everything will be given unto us in abundance* . . .*"

"If you like. In our country doctrines which sought the best way for men and society have always flourished. The doctrine which once triumphed was that of Confucius—all others revolved around it. China lived on it for 2,500 years. Today, it's Mao Tse-tung thought which lays down the basic principles of reasoning and life."

Revolutionary Thought

"What you call Mao Tse-tung thought—is that the thoughts of Mao Tse-tung?" I asked.

Kuo Mo-jo made me repeat the question.

"The Thought can no more be reduced to 'the thoughts' than a river can be reduced to the drops of water which sparkle and dance in the sun. When individual drops of water fall, they merely form a puddle which soon becomes stagnant. The river is not just a collection of drops; it is movement, energy."

"If all the philosophies that have emerged in China in the past twenty-five centuries are simple variants of the thought of Confucius, isn't this also the case with Mao Tse-tung thought?"

"Certainly not. The thought of Confucius ended by drying up like the silt in the Yellow River which hardens and forms dykes when the current drops."

Since the end of the last century most of China's intellectuals had been trying to breach these dykes. They attacked Confucian traditions and sought a new philosophical direction. They all failed. Mao succeeded.

"Mao Tse-tung thought transforms man, nature and society. It is true revolutionary thought."

But Mao gave the impression of having preserved and consolidated as much as he destroyed—as the cost of transmutation. No doubt, according to one's point of view, one could either say he built with the traditional materials that were on hand or he blew up the building and then used the rubble to build anew.

"What struck me," I said, "was that Mao never destroys all at once."

He proceeded step by step. Before fighting the Kuomintang, he made a common front with them on two occasions. Before eliminating the "national capitalists," he proposed an alliance. He made the intellectuals the magnificent present of the "Hundred Flowers" before sending them off to labor camps. Then he launched the "Great Leap Forward" and the Cultural Revolution: each time, one step further—or rather, "two steps forward, one step back." The Soviet revolution took place all at once, with a great upheaval, and then stopped. The Chinese revolution established itself by degrees, without there ever being a complete break.

"Ours is an uninterrupted revolution," Kuo Mo-jo said. "It's like a forest fire. At one moment it seems to be making no advance and to have lost its force. But then it takes off. Suddenly it shoots up like an explosion. And this time, all of a sudden, the fire has set light to the whole forest. Revisionism is reduced to charred branches."

"What you call 'revisionism' is going back, compromising, isn't it?"

"Revisionism is the fire when it's out. The waters of the river when it subsides."

When we asked in the factories, schools and rural communes what the Cultural Revolution had changed, we always got the same answer: "the level of political consciousness of the workers has risen a lot." And it was explained to us that left to itself the level of political consciousness will fall unless it is raised. Revisionism is this tendency to fall. It is the weight of the past. A lack of confidence in the revolution. A sort of defeatism. For the revolution to triumph, what counts most is not that the masses produce more, but that their level of consciousness rise continually. If one contents oneself with wanting to stabilize it, one throws the revolution back into the past; one loses the ability to hunt down "revisionist ideas," and soon there will be a rout.

China Turned Inside Out like a Glove

"If Mao Tse-tung thought is so revolutionary, how do you explain," I asked, "that we foreigners have the impression of a typically *Chinese* system, as if national character were a permanent factor, present from ancient China right through to People's China, unchanged by time?"

"Chairman Mao has turned China inside out like a glove," Kuo Mo-jo replied. "But it's still the same glove, on the same hand."

"What are the basic values you've preserved?"

"The traditional virtues. After a good sifting, they enable us to reject what is adulterated and assimilate what is living."

Confucius made a portrait of the virtuous man, the *Sheng jen*, trained to live in harmony with others—he practiced courtesy, justice, integrity, self-control, good faith, loyalty, and moderation. This is still the ideal today. Or rather it is the ideal once again, for it had been lost in the meantime.

Courtesy? The Confucian rites have disappeared, but I noticed that, even though it was swelteringly hot, Kuo Mo-jo, Chou En-lai, and Chi Peng-fei always kept their jackets buttoned right up to the neck. The old formalism has been toned down, but there is still a fine sense of etiquette—you do not bore others by telling them your troubles and you compliment them so they feel at ease.

Justice? It really does seem that there is more justice in People's China than there was in classical China.

Integrity? What the people have appreciated most in the new leaders is their total honesty, which contrasts vividly with the corruption of the cadres of the old order.

Self-control? You would think the inscrutable smile came with practice. The Chinese value their inner feelings but feel no need to reveal them to others. One man assured me that his compatriots "had realized how little notice needed to be taken of Khrushchev after he banged his shoe on the desk at the United Nations."

Good faith? When the Chinese make a promise, they keep it. If it is a commercial agreement, they carry out its provisions to the letter.

Loyalty to friends? Before the Chinese invitation to President Nixon was made public, Peking notified the North Korean and North Vietnamese governments. Chou En-lai personally went to see Prince Norodom Sihanouk in the middle of the night. This made me realize that the White House had not behaved in the same way toward its allies, in particular the Japanese, and that it would be wrong to believe that China was ready to abandon Hanoi for Washington.

Moderation? Even if the developments of the Chinese revolution often give the impression of being excessive, it is always the middle way that triumphs in the end. The excesses bring discredit upon themselves. The Chinese travel the path between anarchist Leftism and conservative Right-ism, between utopia and routine, between issuing a challenge to the world and renouncing worldly ambitions. This moderation reconciles "intransigent principle with flexibility in applying it"—Mao's dogged struggle against Chiang Kai-shek and his journey to Chungking, his steadfast conflict with the United States and the invitation to Nixon.*

"So, a century before Socrates, while Heraclitus and Pythagoras were laying the foundations of Greek philosophy, there lived in China a philosopher whose ideal one can say is still yours?"

"It still is . . . well, not entirely. Chairman Mao invites us to preserve what is good in tradition and cast aside what is bad. So we have to take all the stitches out of our ancient clothes, separate the good from the bad and sew them together again with the good cloth."

Thus the new man the Chinese revolution seeks to create is a revival of the Confucian. Like Confucius, Mao worked out a philosophy which rules both personal life and government of society; but it is the life and the society of today. He translated the communist ideal into the language of Confucius: "Communism will be the Great Harmony."

The Tribulations of Marx in China

In China no Marxist theoretician has ever been placed above or even on the same level as Mao. The founding fathers, Marx, Engels, Lenin and Stalin, are respected as ancestors, but one is left in little doubt that these four have not brought as much to China as Mao himself. Besides, it is natural to minimize the importance of influences from abroad and exaggerate native ideas. Lin Piao once wrote: "Ninety percent of the thought which drives us comes from Mao Tse-tung, and ten percent from Marx and Lenin." This statement is not just exaggeration and flattery. The Statutes of the Chinese Communist Party** state quite categorically in the very first chapter: "For half a century now, in leading China's great struggle to accomplish the new

---

*During the anti-Confucius campaign of 1974, moderation was branded a curb to revolution—which *must* be excessive.
**Adopted by the Ninth National Congress on April 14, 1969; they may be invalid, as the Vice-Chairman of the Party, Lin Piao, and several members of the Politburo (Chen Po-ta, Huang Yung-sheng, Wu Fa-hsien, etc.) have since been "purged."

democratic revolution, in leading her great struggle for socialist revolution and socialist construction, and in the great struggle of the contemporary international communist movement against imperialism, modern revisionism and the reactionaries of various countries, Comrade Mao Tse-tung has integrated the universal truth of Marxism-Leninism with the concrete practice of revolution, inherited, defended and developed Marxism-Leninism and has brought it to a higher and completely new stage." Wherever one sees portraits of Marx and Engels, Lenin and Stalin, Mao is there facing them, alone and larger.

The Sino-Soviet split must have had a direct effect on the upsurge of Mao Tse-tung thought. China became free to stress the originality of the Chinese contribution and to contrast the purity of Mao Tse-tung thought with the confused, murky temptations of "Soviet revisionism." The new Constitution* perpetuates this unforeseen result of the parting of the Soviet and Chinese ways. In its Second Article it establishes Mao Tse-tung thought as "the theoretical foundation of The People's Republic of China." An irrevocable, official declaration.

But at the same time, although Marxist ideas are state doctrine in some fifteen countries, is there a single one of them in which they have struck deeper roots than in China? Why has the climate been so good for Marxist ideas?

Kuo Mo-jo explains: "Mao Tse-tung thought exhibits a traditional Chinese approach to the Marxist heritage—it peels away the doctrines, cracks the shell of dogma, and extracts the kernel containing the seed."

China has always borrowed her doctrines from abroad. She has adapted them to her own way of thinking. This is particularly true of Buddhism, which has become so much incorporated into Chinese culture that Indian Buddhists today look to China to find authentic texts, which Chinese scholars had translated after getting them in India itself.

"One day," I said, "the Russian leaders will be coming and asking you how you've managed to preserve the spirit of Marxism-Leninism while at the same time making it Chinese."

Kuo Mo-jo replied: "Mao Tse-tung thought puts Marxism-Leninism in a Chinese form without deforming it. If we were to copy the Soviet model in a servile manner, without taking into account our history and society, we would be unfaithful successors of Marx and Lenin. We would be betraying them."

He went on: "What is the kernel of Marx's philosophy? To arrive at communism by means of a dialectic. Communism existed in ancient China. Our people have always been disposed toward communism. The highest ideal of our whole tradition demands that we renounce egotism in order to blend into the community. The greatest joy for the Chinese is to be together. As for

---

*Adopted by the People's National Assembly in January 1975.

the dialectic, research may in time show that in fact Marx borrowed it from China. He took it straight from Hegel, and Hegel—along with Fichte and Schelling—seems to have derived it from Asiatic thought."

"But at the time of Confucius, Heraclitus and Empedocles were saying that everything moves along in one continuum, that conflict is the father of all things, and that a divine harmony rules the interplay of opposites."

Kuo Mo-jo gave me a long look and smiled. He was in his element. "No doubt. But it was not the Ionian philosophers who left their mark on Western thought; it was Aristotle and your Descartes. Chinese thought has always turned around the Yin and the Yang."

At the Base of Everything—the Yin and the Yang

"One part of Yin, one part of Yang—that is Tao," said the ancient books. Yin and Yang are complementary opposites; the harmony of the opposites is Tao. Tao is the Way—an endless, winding way. Yin is the shady side of the valley. Yang is the sunny side. Yin is humidity, cold, winter, dark, waiting, latent energy, negativity, passivity, femininity. Yang is dryness, heat, summer, arousing desire, conquering energy, positiveness, activity, virility.

The complementariness of the opposites applies in all fields—north and south, high and low, earth and sky, left and right. It even applies to Chinese cooking: stewed (Yin) and crispy (Yang), sweet (Yin) and sour (Yang). These pairs of antithetical rubrics are the source of all fecundity, production and reproduction. For Tao is not the sum of one Yin and one Yang, which would be just its two halves; it is the principle of creative alternation of one Yin and one Yang, which remain two independent entities.

In place of the binary thought of the West—yes and no, lawful and unlawful, true and false—the Chinese have tertiary thought: thesis, antithesis and the effect of their opposition to one another, which is not really their synthesis but the product of their attraction and repulsion.

A child take after his father and mother, but he does not resemble them in all their characteristics as a hermaphrodite would. He is himself an element of a new asymmetric couple, whose opposition will produce another new element independent of the two preceding ones.

"One Divides into Two"

For Mao, as for classical Chinese philosophers, there was no yes and no, no true and false, as Western rationalism demands. Or rather, the yes and no have no absolute meaning. The yes becomes no and the no becomes yes in the continual passage of time. Mao invited the Chinese "to walk on two legs— agriculture, which is the base, and industry, which is the dominant factor." The Cultural Revolution launched the Leftists against the revisionists of the Right, so that the center Right, reconstituted against the excesses of the Left, eliminated the Left, which had become nationalist, and was then itself eliminated. The intellectuals have to recharge themselves by undertaking manual labor, but manual labor is improved by this contact with the intellectuals. The countryside counterbalances the towns; the towns bring fertility to the countryside, etc.

"One divides into two," as we were told so often. This means that two asymmetric elements have come together into apparent unity. The two elements are differentiated by analysis. Artificial synthesis reunites them, but it must not hide the fact that there are two elements in opposition, and that the struggle between them will end with the victory of the one and the elimination of the other.

"Do you think," I asked, "that the revisionism of Liu Shao-chi meant that he didn't subscribe to the theory of the complementariness of opposites?"

"Liu Shao-chi reckoned that 'two unite in one' is more fundamental than 'one divides into two.' He believed in the possible reconciliation of opposites. He did not believe that there is an antagonism between the proletariat and the bourgeoisie which can end only with the victory of the one over the other—either revisionism, which is the *embourgeoisement* of socialism, or the victory of the proletariat, which is the pursuit of the revolution. He wanted to make definitive compromises."

"Does the defeat of Liu Shao-chi mean that the bourgeois must disappear?"

"It means that they must reform themselves in order to draw inspiration from the proletarian spirit. Mao says: *A bad thing can transform itself into a good thing*. One mustn't destroy men. One must change man."

Another Logic

When a philosopher back at home asked me for my impressions of China, I told him that the Chinese did not have the *same* logic we do. He jumped on me. "There isn't a Chinese logic and a Western logic! Logic is *logic*! In the West we've assimilated it, and what you mean is that the Chinese aren't there yet."

No, this is certainly not what I mean. There is a Mao Tse-tung logic which is not like that of Descartes. Western thought is based on certain principles which Chinese thought does not recognize. One is the principle of *causality*. What Chinese thought—Mao Tse-tung thought—reveals is not abstract links between cause and effect but a concrete interdependence between harmonized contrasts, like verso and recto, light and shade. Chinese thought does not record successions of phenomena in which one is the sole and direct cause of the next, but alternations of different aspects linked by their opposition. Others are the principles of *contradiction* and of the *excluded middle*: a thing cannot at one and the same time be itself and its opposite. Of two contradictory propositions, one must be true and the other false; there is no third alternative. Mao, in keeping with Chinese tradition, rejected these fundamental laws. Contradiction is at the heart of all living things; it is the very element that keeps them alive. Instead of the logic of the excluded middle, he substituted a logic of the included middle, which results from the antagonism of the first two terms.

So it follows that reversals were frequent in Mao's actions; alliance leads to a break, success follows failure, as day follows night. "In war," he said, "offense and defense, advance and retreat, victory and defeat are all mutually contradictory phenomena. One cannot exist without the other. The two aspects are at once in conflict and in interdependence, and this constitutes the totality of a war, pushes its development forward, and solves its problems." Creative thought is a contrasted thought. A living society goes from contradiction to contradiction, as a basic—and basically Taoist—text from the Cultural Revolution says: "It is false to state that there are no contradictions in socialist society. How could there not be contradictions? There always will be—in a thousand, ten thousand years. When the earth is destroyed and the sun put out there will still be contradictions in the universe. Each thing is in contradiction, conflict and change." This text is called "A great revolution which touches man in his innermost being."

Yes, Mao Tse-tung thought and the Cultural Revolution reach man's innermost being. But can a Westerner attain that depth? How could men brought up from the cradle on the dichotomic law of Greco-Latin thought adapt themselves to the trichotomic rhythms of Chinese thought?

A Unifying Thought

So many leaders in the past have been misfits, fanatics and madmen; indeed, there are many today and there will always be many. But the Chinese revolution took place under the aegis of a philosopher with the gift of uncommon intuition and powers of assimilation, an indefatigable reader engaged in constant meditation, a clear writer, sensitive poet and elegant calligrapher, driven in all he did by a sense of balance and of what is human.

During his "years in the wilderness" from 1927 to 1935 and from 1959 to 1966, years which are still shrouded in mystery, it was always to the masses that Mao turned. In this too he was acting in accordance with tradition—when a sovereign lost the respect of his subjects, the "mandate of heaven" returned to the people, who then conferred it on a new sovereign in a revolt. The masses "withdrew the mandate" from Chiang Kai-shek, after first withdrawing it from the emperor—in order to grant it to a man in whom they saw themselves. It is in the nature of a leader who has been brought to power by popular revolt that he is in communion with the people. Who would deny Mao this?

But he did not believe that in order for a thought to be profound, it had to be difficult to understand. To be true it must be concrete. The ideological debate of the Cultural Revolution should not be represented as the complacent and excessively abstruse ratiocinations of a few ideologists. It was a confrontation between men who knew that the outcome would decide the daily life of the people and their own survival. Mao Tse-tung thought is no more a theory than is Confucianism or Taoism. It is essentially practical. It cannot be proven; it has to be lived. It cannot be taught; it has to be aroused in each individual. It is a personal statement like art and poetry.

Beyond the institutions, the Party and the State, it is Mao Tse-tung thought which imposes on the country a higher form of organization. China can boldly decentralize at the level of people's communes and factories because she has centralized thought into total uniformity. This is Mao's intellectual triumph. His legitimacy derived from his thought, which has become the source of all legitimacy.

4

Chou En-lai

Would we have a chance to see one of the big three? No light was thrown on this either before we left France or after we arrived in China; mystery was part of the game. Mao? We had been told in advance that there was little hope, and in Peking it was confirmed that he was not in the capital, but "somewhere in the provinces." Lin Piao, his appointed successor, the star of the Cultural Revolution? We soon learned that to speak of him was ill-advised; he was said to be seriously ill.

We wondered if we would meet Chou En-lai, Prime Minister since 1949; the grandson of an imperial mandarin who became the central pivot of Chinese communism; the charmer who told Nasser with a smile how China was growing her best poppies to poison the G.I.'s in Vietnam in memory of the Opium War; the man of sly cunning who had been on the scene at all the important turning-points of Chinese history over the past fifty years. In 1913, as a fifteen-year-old boarder at the secondary school in Nankai, he was already dreaming of ways to change China. At nineteen he went to Tokyo to try to find the answer. He returned to take part in the student revolt of 1919; he was arrested and imprisoned. In 1920 he was one of the little group of progressive students whom Mao enviously saw to the boat in Shanghai when they set sail for the West to discover the secrets of revolution. Along with Chen Yi, he was the moving spirit of the French section of the Chinese Communist Party, whose survivors half a century later still formed—around him—the most influential and most disciplined nucleus in China's top administration. On his return in 1952, he became Political Commissar of the Whampoa Military Academy, alongside Chiang Kai-shek. He tried to prevent the break between the Party and the Kuomintang. When it finally took place in 1927, he hurled himself into the insurrection, first in Shanghai with three hundred workers, then in Nanchang, at the head of the Party of which he had become General Secretary. Both times he was crushed. He rejoined Mao and his army of peasants in Kiangsi. Then he popped up again in Paoan in 1935, among the survivors of the Long March. In December 1936 he was sent from Paoan to Sian. There he obtained from Chiang Kai-shek those years of respite which enabled the communists to acquire national stature in the conflict with the Japanese; this was obtained from Chiang Kai-shek—who had been taken prisoner by his own lieutenants—in exchange for saving his life. He was Mao's representative to the Nationalist Chinese in Chungking for almost ten years.

From the moment of the Liberation he took charge of the government and diplomacy of People's China. He was in the limelight at the Geneva conference of 1954, which put an end to the first Indochina war, and at the Bandung conference of 1955, which gave birth to the Third World. He was on the rostrum at the "Conference of the Seven Thousand" in January 1962, alongside Lin Piao, to defend Mao, who was under attack from all quarters following the failure of the Great Leap Forward; he thereby led Liu Shao-chi to allow Mao at least the semblance of power, a semblance which was to become reality four years later with the Cultural Revolution. When the Cultural Revolution hesitated and lost its sense of direction, as in Wuhan in July 1967, there he was, giving the Red Guards, who had been on the rampage and decimated, the illusion of one last victory, and also giving the traditional military men promises for the future. At the same time, he was saving Mao's face after his first emissaries had been sent to prison by the commandant there, General Chen Tsai-tao. He was there again in February 1972—for talks with President Nixon; it was he in fact whom the American President had come to see. It was he to whom the Japanese Prime Minister Tanaka proposed a reconciliation between their two countries. It was he who remained by Mao's side after the ousting of Lin Piao.

Would we be meeting the diplomat who was able to win battles without waging them—by gaining the time needed for the wind to turn, by moving the one piece that changed the whole game? This man who, without ever representing anything but himself, had been able to steer a course for himself between the various opposing factions, between the "revolutionary rebels" and the administrative cadres, and between the Party and the army. Not only was he able to steer a course, he was also able to steer the Chinese revolution to it, as if he were the focal point of the various forces which at first tore it apart and then, thanks to his subtle gameplay, put it together again.

July Fourteenth at the Embassy

Just as had been the custom in ancient China when foreigners were granted access to the emperor, we were kept in the dark until the very last moment. We found ourselves in Peking on July 14; our embassy was open for the traditional Bastille Day reception.* The year before, the first French government delegation to visit People's China had been in Peking on the same date, and Chou En-lai had come. Would he come this time? The reception began at six-thirty. At this very moment the telephone rang; it was a call to tell our Ambassador, Étienne Manach—who was already busy shaking official hands—that the Prime Minister was coming. He arrived at seven on the dot. In his strange, gliding gait, as if moving on slippers, he proceeded through the crowd of diplomats and Chinese officials. People who were talking stopped in mid-sentence. People who were sitting stood up. People who were drinking put their glasses down. There was a deathly silence. Even Louis XIV could not have produced such an effect among his courtiers when he entered the Galerie des Glaces to the cry of "Gentlemen, the King!"

After everyone had been presented to him, we sat down together on a sofa on the edge of a terrace. The guests were standing in a semicircle on the lawn, their glasses in their hands. They had an air of expectancy—not for what we might be saying to each other, for they could not pick up anything of our conversation, but for the Prime Minister's facial expressions, of which the photographers were taking pictures. An interpreter sitting behind us on a stool was leaning forward and speaking into my ear. We chatted for an hour while the Ambassador entertained the guests, especially the Acting Foreign Minister, Chi Peng-fei.

The essential parts of this conversation and of the two others we had later can be found in various places throughout the book. The talks we had revealed some aspects of the personality of the man who, although inspired from afar by Mao, was the real boss of China.

Behind Chou's questions about the Common Market was a concern for independence. He said: "We are very pleased to see that the negotiations to enlarge the Common Market with the admission of Great Britain and other countries have succeeded. It's a good thing that Europe's power is being strengthened. It's part of the struggle against the hegemony of the two super-Powers."

This reaction is significant. Ten years before, China had seen the European organization as a subterfuge for American hegemony. The image of Europe had changed, and it was largely due to the perseverance of the French. So much so that the Chinese leaders were clearly in advance of the political

*In commemoration of the storming of the Bastille, in 1789, which launched the French Revolution.

climate in Europe. What was also striking was that their judgment was more diplomatic than ideological: the European Community did not appear to them as something to be condemned or to be disregarded as an arrangement between capitalist countries, but as something which was both interesting and worthy of praise as a new pattern on the geo-political chessboard. The journalists to whom I reported this statement were in no doubt as to its importance—they headlined their articles with this very point.

From the Small Steps to the Big Step

"International relations are evolving," I went on to say. "You find yourselves facing a new situation in your relations with the United States. You must be pleased to see the Americans developing their policy with ping-pong balls and other small overtures."

I did not know that Henry Kissinger had been in Peking the week before and that two days later President Nixon's visit was going to be announced; I had no idea I was so close to the truth. The reply was almost brusque: "Small overtures aren't enough. The time is coming when the Americans will have to take a big step."

Four days later, Chou En-lai made it clear to me that in his view long journeys are still only small steps.

Our conversation came to an end, but not before Chou En-lai gave me two nice examples of the traditional humility of the Chinese, both collective and personal. What of China's achievements in the nuclear and space fields? "They're just a few atomic tests and rocket launchings. We're still in an exploratory stage. . . . Yes, we're a backward country. We'll need at least a hundred years to catch up." What of his own reputation as a tireless worker? "I don't know if I work eighteen hours a day, but it's quite true that the Chinese people work hard." When he was pressed, he did confess: "I seldom stop work before five o'clock in the morning; I start again about eleven."

This night work—in the silence of the Forbidden and slumbering City—seems to be a habit of Chinese leaders. Khrushchev said of Mao: "Mao is like an owl; he works all night long." It was the same in Moscow in Stalin's time.

World affairs were always Chou En-lai's favorite subject. He saw the Soviet Union, the United States and Japan revolving around China, and he would spare no effort to prevent their joining up together. Such a liaison would be fatal.

This came about when the American involvement in Vietnam and Formosa brought in the Japanese against China, and the Soviet Union was pressing against China's northern border. The game had reached the point where the players had to be separated—so that the balls could start rolling again across the table. No one could say where they would come to rest, but as far as China was concerned anything was better than the game in which she had been trapped since the beginning of the 1960s.

Chou En-lai did much to prove to the Americans that his only plan was patiently to build up China's economy—and that their military disengagement would not leave a vacuum which he had any desire to fill, once, that is, Formosa had been returned to the bosom of China.

But in freeing themselves, the Americans also freed the Japanese. Hence the repeated warnings Chou gave his visitors, while at the same time trying to show the Japanese that there were other paths for them to follow. Chou En-lai told me very openly that because "France has shown that it's possible to conduct an independent policy toward the United States without losing their friendship," her voice "might be heard in Tokyo. Tell them—your influence can do nothing but good. You're a good example to Japan."

Chou En-lai did everything within his power to attack the Soviet Union. He used irony incessantly. "After half a century of socialism, they go begging for loans and advice to the Japanese and West Germans!" He accused them of having failed to prevent the President of the Federal Republic of Germany from being elected in West Berlin; Russia gave in on the question of the access routes to Berlin. If Chou reproached them for this, he did so by thinking of the reactions of East Germany. He was prepared to support the most hardline communists if that would draw them away from the Russians, whom he accused of being "soft" and "revisionist." So, where the interests of peace were concerned, his action against the "super-Powers" was not entirely without ambiguity.

Nothing takes precedence over the interests of China. For the moment at least, the interests of China do not seem to be a danger to peace. Like France, China makes her voice heard—often discordantly—in order to say out loud that peace means, first of all, letting the people find their own inner equilibrium.

Chou En-lai was Talleyrand in the role of Richelieu. He was a refined product of the *ancien régime* at the service of the new regime, a man who patiently wove the cloth of diplomacy while keeping all the threads in his own country. He was an enlightened man, patient and secretive, who, when called to play his national game in a world torn this way and that by ideologies, was always able to distinguish the ideologies from the interests they masked. He was a patriot dedicated to building the unity and strength of his country, who did so by charting a course between intrigues and hatreds, groups and factions, and with no support other than his own personal genius and the confidence of Mao Tse-tung.

During the successive, troubled waves of the Chinese revolution, Mao and Chou—an inseparable pair, although very different from each other—

always reappeared on the crest of the wave, in spite of frequently being hidden in the troughs between. The prophetic peasant and the cunning mandarin, the magician and the doer. In this system, whose description calls naturally on the vocabulary of religion, Mao, the Holy Spirit of the revolution, contented himself with acting—apart from a few lightning revelations—through the very Roman pontificate of Chou En-lai.

5

Poor Man's Medicine or a Major Medical Advance?

"A Great Victory for Mao Tse-tung Thought"

The recent achievements of medicine are one of the most surprising sights in People's China; in fact, there is no aspect of social life which tells us more about the Chinese way.

The day we arrived we had to wait for hours at the Shanghai air terminal because of a bad connection—storms were forecast over Peking and the pilot was taking no chances with a propeller-driven aircraft. Among the people who had come to see us off—in their blue trousers and white shirts—was a member of the revolutionary committee of the municipality of Shanghai. Standing beneath a humming ventilator fan, he answered all my questions.

"Is it true that a surgeon from your town grafts on arms and legs that have been completely torn off?"

"Of course. He's been doing operations like that for the past ten years or so. It's routine. But what's new is that the surgeons have given up classical anaesthesia for these operations and others like them and now use acupuncture instead."

These grafts, which French surgeons had told me had no equal in the West, were so commonplace here that they were not considered worth comment.

"Acupuncture as an anaesthetic," he went on, "has enabled medicine to make a breakthrough. After several years of experimenting, a Shanghai medical team has systematically replaced the Western method of anaesthesia with this one. It made great progress after the Cultural Revolution. In the

66

past few days, for example, we've been able, with acupuncture, to remove a cancer of the esophagus, to operate on a heart with a mitral stricture, and to take a meningeal tumor as big as a bowl of rice out of a brain. We remove lungs, the pancreas and thyroids, not to speak of ordinary operations on limbs and teeth. In Shanghai we've already done over five hundred operations of this kind. With acupuncture the paralyzed can be cured without surgery. A People's Army team has treated over sixteen hundred deaf-mutes since 1968 and ninety percent have been cured."

"How do you explain all these successes?"

"They are a victory for Mao Tse-tung thought."

I could not help glancing across at one of my companions who was taking part in the conversation. "They're mad, these Chinese!" he whispered.

The "Revolutionizing" of Medicine

Next day, in the aircraft—which had finally been able to take off—I was talking to a Chinese diplomat who had come to escort us. He confirmed, as if it were a fact: "It's a victory for Mao Tse-tung thought."

The following Sunday, we drove out of Peking early in the morning for the traditional walk along the Great Wall and a visit to the tombs of the Ming. Dr. Li Feng-chen, a member of the revolutionary committee of the town of Peking, rode in my car. As a doctor, what did he think of anaesthesia by acupuncture?

"It's a great victory for Mao Tse-tung thought," he said in all serious-ness.

Had acupuncture sprung from Mao Tse-tung thought fully armed like Athene from the brain of Zeus? We were going to be sitting next to each other for four hours and I wondered whether I would be able to get some clarifica-tion from him, for it was something I had great difficulty in understanding and believing.

"You'll get it straightaway," he assured me.

"I'm not a doctor."

"That's the point. A doctor would be prejudiced. Somebody who's not a doctor has an open mind. I've had a lot of difficulty in getting rid of the established ideas I'd acquired from my scientific education."

"*These things are visible to children and hidden from wise men,*" I muttered to myself, more and more puzzled.

"The breakthrough in our medicine would never have been possible had the Cultural Revolution not made Mao Tse-tung thought triumphant in all fields. Our great leader invited us to win victory over medical revisionism."

"How did revisionism reach medicine?"

"In medicine as everywhere else, there were two lines. The Liu Shao-chi line tended to reject traditional practices. It followed in the wake of Western medicine. It refused to experiment into the Chinese way. It limited itself to treating the sick from a materialistic and scientific standpoint. It limited medical treatment to town-dwellers, and then only to the privileged few. It wasn't concerned about the masses. It bowed to the medical establishment."

No doubt it was sufficient simply to reverse all this in order to define the line of Chairman Mao—reviving the Chinese medical heritage, increasing the range of experiments, remembering that the only element that counts is man, developing medical work in rural areas, destroying the medical caste system.

He continued: "The two lines were in bitter conflict for four years, until the revolutionary line triumphed. Medicine has been put in the service of the masses, and old practices and modern techniques have been brought together. The famous doctors, most of whom came from bourgeois and intellectual backgrounds, lacked political consciousness; they've been put in positions where they can't do any harm. After a period in the countryside, most of them acknowledged their errors—they lacked the proletarian ethic; they were reluctant to move away from the towns and to have recourse to traditional methods because what they sought above all was material advantage and fame. In the end they recognized the wisdom of Chairman Mao's directives."

"When and in what way did Chairman Mao come to formulate these directives?"

"He had laid down the principles in Yenan, and then he made his ideas on revolutionizing medicine more precise in an instruction of June 26, 1965. But there were many doctors who said among themselves that Mao wasn't a doctor and that only they could decide what was good for medicine. They had to hear the criticism of the masses before they began to take this instruction seriously."

The Treasure of Chinese Medicine

The black limousine glided with its horn blaring through a forest which looked like a chestnut plantation, and up an asphalt road which was full of hairpin bends. A warm drizzle had begun to fall.

Dr. Li Feng-chen leaned across to me and whispered: "I studied at the Peking Medical Institute and in the United States. Over a period of forty years I accumulated scientific equipment, wrote articles and sought only to increase my reputation. I was severely criticized. I began to realize that I had not bothered to follow the proletarian line."

A shadow passed over his face. It seemed better not to interrupt, and after a moment or two he went on: "Our Great Teacher showed us the light when he gave the order in 1958: *Rely on your own forces.* He applied this general line in particular to medical problems: *Chinese medicine is an inexhaustible source of treasure; one must try hard to retrieve this rich heritage, explore it, and carry it on to a higher level.*"

The *Nei-ching*, a treatise which goes back 2,200 years, contains very precise instructions for using acupuncture to treat migraines, toothaches, and pains in the throat, kidneys, joints and ears. Armed with the thought of Chairman Mao, Western-educated doctors began to study the Chinese tradition.

"What influence did the introduction of Western therapy have on Chinese medicine?"

"These two strains of medicine had remained rigidly separated. Western medicine was still unknown to the vast majority of the peasants; in the towns it had gradually forced Chinese tradition to retreat. No doctor was able to bring the two methods together. The two schools—Western and Chinese medical science—turned their backs on each other. The traditional chemists' shops sold powders, herbs, ginseng roots, and needles and figurines for acupuncture. The modern chemists' shops sold antibiotics, sulfamides, and special drugs. The traditional practitioners—half healers, half herbalists—hadn't the slightest notion of the biological sciences. Those who received their medical education at universities or abroad were totally ignorant of acupuncture and herbs."

Dr. Li Feng-chen looked as if he were about to fight an enemy who was quite close, or possibly even hiding inside him.

"The traitor Liu Shao-chi fought against the ancient practices, saying they were totally devoid of scientific character. The reactionaries of the Kuomintang had already let acupuncture fall into disuse. The renegade believed only in medicine that came from abroad. His followers in the medical profession brutally stopped the first attempts to use acupuncture as an anaesthetic in 1959."

The climb up the Great Wall interrupted our conversation. When we got back into the car, Dr. Li Feng-chen picked up where he had left off: "Today Chinese medicine has been rehabilitated. Acupuncture is taught at the University. The professors go up into the mountains with their students to find herbs. The healers of the countryside have learned the essentials of emergency medical care. The two medicines have now been fused in accordance with the invincible ideas of Chairman Mao: *Let the ancient serve the present, let the foreign serve the national; by developing that which has been accomplished, one creates something that is new.*"

We found this formula—which has any number of applications—on many hoardings: for example, over the entrance to the Sian archaeological museum, where it deals once and for all with the problem of the cultural heritage and artistic creation.

So instead of rejecting it, the Chinese integrated Western medicine with Chinese medicine; it neither dominated it nor replaced it. No longer are the graduates from the towns and the healers from the countryside members of two different races. This is one of the important achievements of Mao Tse-tung thought and the Cultural Revolution.

In Annex No. 2 of the Wuhan Institute of Medicine

An Ovarian Cyst Weighing Four Kilograms

The following morning we visited Wuhan Hospital, where we saw an operation for the removal of an ovarian cyst. Lying on the operating table was forty-one-year-old Madame Lei Ting-mei. She was showing signs of anxiety, and as she looked at us through the glass panel the tension was written all over her face. There were two acupuncturists, and they had each inserted two needles in her—in the calf and ankle of each leg. They were twirling the needles continuously. The surgeon, Lo Hsien-ying, was chatting with the patient, reasoning with her, and thereby, it seemed, having a soothing, psychotherapeutic effect on her. He then cut into her abdomen as if for a Caesarean section—and she did not flinch. Her anxiety had disappeared, and her face bore that air of calm resignation which has been a characteristic feature of the Chinese peasant for many thousands of years. The cut—which went from her stomach to her pubis—was opened up and held apart with forceps. And all the while the surgeon was carrying on a conversation with her. I asked our doctor guide, who was giving us a running commentary on the operation, why there was so little blood.

"He's applied herbs which have been known about for a long time but which have been used in surgery only recently. They have the effect of stanching the blood immediately."

He avoided further questions. All we shall ever know about these herbs is that they plug the blood vessels.

The surgeon removed an enormous oblong silvery lump from Mrs. Lei's abdomen. It was about a foot long and six inches thick, and it weighed more than eight pounds—heavier than a baby. At the precise moment that the surgeon cut the cyst away, the patient winced, but she soon became calm again. The cyst was laid in a bowl and shown to the patient. At first she was a bit frightened, but a moment or two later she was smiling broadly. Her head was raised so that she could eat. We wondered if this was intended to prove to us that anaesthetization is not accompanied by nausea, and that no disturbance is caused to the bodily functions. She made short work of some pineapple slices and mandarin oranges. The surgeon continued chatting with Madame Lei, going through his plans step by step. And then, with the speed of a professional dressmaker, he did the final stitching. All the while the acupuncturists were twirling the needles between their fingers.

An hour and half after the operation began, they pulled up Madame Lei's pajama trousers and she walked out with two nurses at her side—although not really using them for support. The surgeon whispered something to her, and she turned and gave us a friendly wave.

Boring into Bone and an Appetite for Pineapple

Meanwhile, another operation was underway. This time the patient was a forty-seven-year-old man, Chen Peng. Two acupuncturists were involved, each with two needles—in the left ankle, the left hand and the right arm. The same ceremonial and the same setting, but with two extra elements. X-ray photographs were taken of the patient's skull, and the surgeon, Lei Ling, spent a while with his head in Mao's *Little Red Book*, as if he were expecting to find there the technique for performing this difficult operation.

A gray sheet was placed on Mr. Chen's head, leaving exposed just half of his shaven skull. The surgeon took a scalpel and lifted a section of the patient's scalp, exposing the bone beneath. He then drilled a number of holes in the shape of a crown, and each time before he did so he tapped the skull with a mallet. He sawed from one hole to the next, until that piece of the patient's skull could be lifted like the lid of a box on its hinges.

Chen Peng showed not the slightest sign that anything was wrong, and calmly chatted with the surgeon. Meanwhile, forceps were poking about inside his brain, cutting and removing pieces here and there. There was a lot of scraping and mopping up, and finally the surgeon held up the tumor, which was the size of a walnut and covered with blood.

"Is he really not in any pain?" I asked the doctor who was with us.

"No, not at all. As you see, he's got a good appetite. He's speaking normally and playing with his toes."

It is said that the brain, although it is the center of the body's sensory system, is itself insensitive. But this is hardly the case when it comes to cutting the scalp, opening the skull with a mallet, and cutting into the meninges.

While the lobes of his ears were being squeezed, Chen Peng began to eat. The nurse was feeding him slices of pineapple. The doctor was at pains to point out that if only his hand had not been pierced by the acupuncturist, he would be feeding himself.

When we left, this operation had been going on for two hours and was still not quite over. The surgeon was adjusting the brain pan with his forceps before putting it back in place. He was getting ready to suture it as we were leaving. We were already getting behind our schedule, and we were never to know what became of Chen Peng. Even so, a number of us were shaking our heads in disbelief—although we had seen it with our own eyes.

Toward a Theory of Acupuncture?

I asked Madame Peng, a professor of biology at the Medical Institute of Wuhan University: "Is physiology able to account for acupuncture?"

"No," she said. "These phenomena are scientifically inexplicable. Nobody has ever been able to work out a theory. It's not known what the 'meridians' and 'cardinal points' are, or even if they exist. It can be shown how the brain gives orders to the limbs, but it can't be shown how the limbs can give orders to the brain to stop suffering."

"But do you believe in acupuncture? Would you use it yourself?"

She ran her hand over her hair. "Certainly! I've often had it, both I and members of my family. Just because a phenomenon can't be explained scientifically doesn't mean that it doesn't exist. If it's been proven by experiments which have been repeated many times, then this simply means that one day a scientific explanation will be found, but that at the moment theory is lagging behind practice. That's all there is to it. It's no reason for refusing to practice it, when it works."

Madame Peng accompanied me on a car tour of Wuhan and the surrounding area. She had with her several studies, some of which were in English, and these she gave me. She showed me that Chinese scientists were desperately trying to work out a theory of acupuncture, although they had not gotten very far with it yet.

"You did not rest satisfied after you had combined Western and Chinese medicine by taking the most positive features from each. How have you managed to go further with acupuncture in the past few years than in the three thousand years before that?"

"Through the work of the military doctors during the four years of the Cultural Revolution. They agreed to increase the number of experiments on themselves, to see how far you could go using needles for anaesthesia. They established that acupuncture prevented pain when a dressing was being changed; that if you inserted needles when a patient was in pain, the pain subsided immediately; and that if the needles were inserted beforehand, the patient wouldn't feel any pain at all."

"How can you tell that acupuncture is going to work?"

"When the needle goes into a cardinal point, the patient feels four things—a slight unpleasant pricking sensation, a heaviness, a tingling sensation, and local muscular discomfort. The acupuncturist must also feel the needle going in, as if it were being attracted by a magnet—the same feeling an angler has when he feels his hook being tugged by a fish. That means the effect of the vital energy, the Ch'i, has been obtained."

"Does the course of the meridian coincide with the nerve fiber?"

"Not quite. About half the cardinal points lie along the nerves. The other half don't, although they're in the immediate vicinity. There are some signs that the phenomenon of acupuncture is closely related to the nerves— *acupuncture doesn't work when the nerve near the point where the needle is inserted is itself deadened by local anaesthetic*, or paralyzed by hemiplegia or paraplegia. But there are also other indications that one can't reduce acupuncture to the functioning of the nervous system: when the illness is on the left-hand side of the body, the needle has to be introduced into the right-hand side—and vice versa. No doubt we'll have to look for a long time before we find a satisfactory theory. The nervous system and meridian theories don't offer a real explanation. As Mao says: *Man never really knows his own truth.*"

"What were the first operations to be undertaken with acupuncture?"

"Acupuncture gave instant relief in cases of acute tonsillitis. For the removal of the tonsils, pharmaceutical anaesthesia was replaced by acupuncture, and it was successful. It was equally successful with the extraction of teeth. But when it was a question of using it for large-scale surgery, then there were failures. The first few times it was used for the removal of lungs, the method didn't work. We recalled the words of Chairman Mao: *When one fails, one must draw one's lessons from this failure, one must correct one's ideas to make them correspond to the laws of the external world, and thus can one turn failure into success.*"

At that time people were content to leave the needles embedded in the cardinal points. The four sensations rapidly died away. However, when the needles were stimulated, the sensations persisted. This discovery was essential—it was sufficient to keep the four sensations going throughout the operation, either by turning the needles with the fingers or by making them vibrate with a weak electric current.

"These failures enabled us to understand how to improve our technique so that the patients were less nervous. Our research workers kept one another informed of the results of their observations. Since the Cultural Revolution our surgeons regularly visit their colleagues in other hospitals."

"Have methods developed through different experiments?"

"Certainly they have. In the beginning we used to introduce needles into a very large number of points—sometimes up to eighty for a single operation—but now the number has been reduced to at most three or four. For the operation on a cataract, two points are chosen from among several dozen which control pain in the eyes. For appendicitis operations only one point is now used, instead of the ten or so that were used before. Equally satisfactory results can be obtained from quite different points—for example, for the removal of a lung the needle can be put in a limb, the ear, the cheek or the nose and have the same effect. Finally, we've discovered that it's possible to replace deep penetration, accompanied by stimulation of the needles by hand, with a light insertion in the nerve fiber, accompanied by the passage of a weak electric current."

"So your method has evolved from inserting needles in a number of different points to using only a few; from seeking the best points to putting the needle anywhere; from deep insertion to vibration with electricity?"

"It's not a general rule, because the methods vary from team to team, and any one team will adapt its methods to the individual case. The essential thing is to apply the principle of Chairman Mao: *Practice, knowledge, again practice and again knowledge. This form repeats itself in endless cycles.*"

"Not the Sickness, but the Sick"

"If there are as many methods as there are teams and patients," I said, "it seems that you're not quite there yet."

"The number of needles, where they go, and the method of stimulating them are secondary. The essential thing is to produce the four sensations with sufficient intensity. Also, the relation between the patient and the doctor must be good. Chairman Mao teaches us: *Weapons are an important factor in war, but not the decisive factor; it is people, not things, that are decisive.* As it happened, we forgot this. And then acupuncture didn't work. Pain is subjective, and it's only alleviated when the patient takes part in the treatment with a clear and open mind. Otherwise, he winces in fear. If the four sensations aren't achieved, it's pointless to insert the needle deep into the patient or to twirl it for a long time."

"Even so, you can't do without 'things'! How could the acupuncturist work without needles?"

"Nowadays, for simple operations, some teams try to use just a pinch rather than a prick, or possibly pressure at the base of each thumb. In any case, problems aren't solved by a needle. According to Mao Tse-tung thought, *the material can transform itself into the moral, and the moral into the material, but it is always the moral which has decisive control.* In American hospitals, where the majority of our hospital doctors have been trained for the past fifty years and more, dozens of tests are done on the patient, as if he were a piece of biological machinery."

"Even so, this mechanistic conception of Western science has made great discoveries in therapy."

"The patient feels he's something other than the prisoner of a piece of machinery. As Chairman Mao says, *it's not a question of curing the illness by killing the patient, but of saving the patient from his illness.* Doctors often seek to evade their responsibilities by using chemical drugs to deal with illnesses which they isolate artificially from the patient. In this way they get out of trying to restore the patient's inner rhythm and equilibrium, which would be a much more difficult thing to do."

"What maintains this balance?"

"There are many things, but it is mainly the mind. Illness is imbalance. Health is maintained only by harmony between the two forces, the 'Yin' and the 'Yang'."

"Does the needle restore harmony?"

"Chairman Mao teaches that *the nature of a thing is determined mainly by the principal aspect of a contradiction, the aspect which has gained the dominant* *position*.* So in a society in which the proletariat and the bourgeoisie confront one another, when the bourgeoisie is dominant the whole society becomes bourgeois, and when the proletariat triumphs the reverse is the case. In the same way, there's a struggle between the stimulation caused by the insertion of the acupuncturist's needle—which stimulates the brain's ability to have control over the skin—and the sensation of pain—which weakens it. If the insertion of the needle is done under good conditions, it strengthens the brain's control function and reduces sensitivity to pain. If it is badly done, it's unable to raise the pain threshold and the brain in turn cannot master the pain."

"How does the stimulation caused by the needle overcome the surgical pain?"

"The insertion is more effective when it precedes the pain and occupies the whole range of sensitivity. The first excitation excludes the second. If the surgeon makes an incision before the needle goes in, the insertion is powerless to lessen the pain. But if the brain cells have received a good dose of stimulation through the acupuncture, the sense message of the surgical wound, although it's greater, isn't noticed. The ground has already been taken."

So a slight pain absorbs all one's attention and makes one insensitive to a greater pain. It is common practice in the West for a nurse to give a hearty slap to one cheek of a patient's bottom before she sticks a hypodermic syringe in it—the patient is taken by surprise and doesn't feel the injection he has been dreading. In a small way, the nurse is making use of the same phenomenon as the acupuncturist.

What seems to happen is that the needles send out sense messages which reach the central nervous system and attract its attention. The messages which are then emitted by the actual surgery run right into them and so fail to set in motion the sequence of events which normally leads to pain. This can be likened to the points on a railway line—a train comes along and, even if it is only a plate-layer's bogie, it releases the points and blocks the way for the express train that is coming up behind. This theory seems to be borne out by the fact that if a local anaesthetic is applied to a nerve next to the point where the needles are being inserted, the needles fail to desensitize the patient—the nerve no longer passes the sense messages given out by the jab of the needles and the way is open to pain.

"So, in other words," I said, "acupuncture is a kind of diversion? All it does is keep the cells which respond to pain occupied with something else?"

"A small sensation blots out a big one, if it comes before it. What's more, the small sensation—of acupuncture—must be created under good conditions. The patient must have a good understanding of what is being

---

*Mao Tse-tung, "On Contradiction," *Selected Works*, Vol. 1, p.333 (TRANSLATOR'S NOTE).

done to him. He must breathe from the abdomen as the surgeon tells him. And he must have the will to rise above any discomfort he may feel. If he doesn't do all these things, he'll be overcome by a feeling of oppression; his muscles will contract, he'll be seized by nervous tension, and the effect of the acupuncture will be nil."

"So a good relationship between the patient and the doctor is vital?"

"Yes. The patient must have confidence in the surgeon and his methods. And the surgeon must always be thinking of the state of mind of the patient, and must keep talking to him. Acupuncture is much more than just sticking a needle into a patient in accordance with some traditional practice. It's a desire to awaken a dormant force. If the acupuncturist is content just to give orders, he'll establish a relationship of authority, a father-son relationship rather than a relationship of equals. He will be putting himself above the patient, and this is paternalism. He should be his *equal*."

Madame Peng went on the offensive: "Western medicine takes over the personality of the patient. It's a palliative. Acupuncture, on the other hand, makes the patient participate to the full in his own cure."

"So, in the final analysis, one could do without the needle? Or even pressure on the thumb?"

"At the beginning of this century Freud decided to abandon the laying on of hands—used in hypnosis by Charcot—and proposed instead 'active collaboration,' in the shape of the basic rule of the free association of ideas . . ."

The car pulled up outside the hotel. Madame Peng looked me straight in the eye and said: "Mao Tse-tung thought has played a decisive role in the successes of acupuncture. Chairman Mao isn't a doctor, but he's given the doctors a sense of absolute devotion to the masses. He's also given the masses confidence in the doctors and in their will to heal. He has brought the two medicines together. There's now only one medicine."

And there's now only one China.

A Medicine for the Masses

"The progress of medicine and surgery is a direct consequence of the class struggle," we were told by the textile worker who made the speech welcoming us to the hospital in Wuhan. "Before the Cultural Revolution the cadres were in the best hospitals, while the workers had to wait at the gate, and often for a long time. The hospital staff, who specialized, as is the practice in bourgeois medicine, refused to take in patients whose cases didn't interest them. Hospital care was expensive. Some families had to sell their houses to pay for it. The Cultural Revolution gave birth to a mass health movement, which is in the process of creating a new medicine for all."

Serve the workers, peasants and soldiers. This instruction of Chairman Mao is inscribed above the door of the hospital in Wuhan.

Dedicating oneself to the masses presupposes that one goes for the simplest method. The successes of the new medicine have been in direct proportion to the simplicity of the methods used. The reduction of the number of points "enabled acupuncture to be popularized and was warmly welcomed by the masses." The best methods are those which everyone can practice. "The battle of our new surgery is won on the school bench."

"In order to prevent medicine from falling back into the bourgeois rut, it's vital that it remain under the control of the masses." Workers, peasants and soldiers are represented in the revolutionary committees of all the hospitals. "Before making an important decision on a question of surgery," the surgeon always "consults" the members of his team, the ward orderlies and sometimes, we were assured, even the cook.

Is a surgeon who has done years of study sincere when he takes the time and trouble to ask odd-job women for their opinions about a difficult case? Is he persuaded of the illuminating power of the masses? Or is he simply seeking to shield himself from his critics? Or perhaps he finds it more expedient to carry out orders willingly, because he would not be able to escape them in any case.

The Decentralization of Health Services

Center health work on the rural areas—this other slogan of Chairman Mao stretches along the walls of the lecture room of the Wuhan Medical Institute.

In 1965 the Chairman severely criticized the Ministry of Health, calling it the "Ministry for the health of the town-dwellers." "What is health protection? Mere idle chatter if it leaves aside the great majority of the peasants. The country areas have no doctors, no hospitals, and no medicines." In 1960, we were told, there were 48,474 qualified doctors—less than in France—and almost all of them were practicing in the urban areas. Also, in the towns there were 467,000 hospital beds, as opposed to some 150,000 in the country; the fifteen percent of the population who lived in the towns had seventy-five percent of the hospital beds.

Since 1965 there has been a movement—prompted by Mao—which has used persuasion and coercion to get some of the doctors and nurses out of the towns and into the countryside. Traveling teams from urban hospitals have been sent into the mountains.*

The progress which has been made with the driving force of the Cultural Revolution toward merging Chinese and Western medicine has enabled the new methods to become very quickly known in the army and in the country.

---

*The simplest teams are just three people—a doctor, a nurse and a soldier. Three is a good number for keeping a check on one another. *Numquam duo, semper tres*, as the Jesuits said.

Acupuncture, which is safe and economical, has played a fundamental role in the revolutionary transformation of the structure of the medical profession. Hundreds of thousands of "barefoot doctors" have undergone a rapid apprenticeship.

They have been trained by the method of the "five hundred": in *one hundred* days they learn to locate and use *one hundred* acupuncture points,* to prevent, diagnose and treat *one hundred* illnesses, to know and prescribe *one hundred* herbs and medicines, and to practice *one hundred* types of operations.

"Really? Which operations?"

"The simplest ones—for example, the removal of the tonsils, polypuses in the nose, lipomas, and abcesses; ligature of the *vas deferens*; abortion and scraping of the womb; simple childbirths as well as difficult ones in which forceps have to be used; setting fractures; plaster casts; the removal of bullets; strangulated hernias; sutures; and so on."

For more serious operations patients are sent to a hospital, where there are more qualified doctors.

"How are the barefoot doctors chosen?"

"They're peasants, workers, mothers, or soldiers who want to serve the people."

"They've no previous training, either specialized or general? How is it that they learn in three months to perform operations which aren't taught in the West until the student has done several years of medicine?"

"A distinction is made between common, everyday illnesses and conditions which a man or woman of good will can quickly learn to treat and more serious illnesses which require hospital treatment."

"It's well known that in Africa a large number of nurses do appendicitis operations. There's nothing of the witchdoctor about it; the problem is to make a correct diagnosis."

"It's better to do a simple operation, even if it's not justified, than for necessary operations never to be performed, for that leads to complications."

"So it's a bit like the West, where the use of antibiotics, although it's often excessive, has nonetheless eradicated numerous infectious complications."

"Yes, if you like. But the doctors and surgeons sent into the country haven't just seen to the training of barefoot doctors. They have themselves been 'reeducated' by the peasants, soldiers and workers. Their class consciousness has changed."

A very ramified health network has been set up—an infirmary in each brigade, a dispensary in each village, a small rural hospital in each people's

---

*Three or four are sufficient for one operation, but it is good to know many more, because the most effective points are not the same for all patients.

commune. "Now," we were told by the proud Chairman of the Revolutionary Committee of the Machiao People's Commune, who made us visit his medical center, "the population can survive illnesses and epidemics, even in the rural areas and in the mountains, and even in time of war, when there aren't any medicines. We've really changed our conception of the world, as our Great Leader requested. We have moved the center of gravity of the health service from the towns toward the countryside."

Bombard the Headquarters

"For thousands of years the exploiting classes have made medicine their private property," said the textile worker who was speaking in the name of the Wuhan hospital. A hierarchy had formed in the medical profession, parallel to the bureaucratic hierarchy which governed the country. At the top of the pyramid, "the doctors with the highest reputation earned a lot of money and got themselves a very bad name." The system lasted by and large until the Cultural Revolution. "The specialists arrogated to themselves a monopoly of knowledge and the exclusive right to grant and refuse diplomas and posts to their students." They had thus created for themselves life posts, which they kept "in their own selfish interest."

Medical education was still the same as before the Liberation; "copied from the West, it was based on long periods of theory"—eight years in the faculties of medicine—and it was aimed at producing "specialists," or rather "incompetents," while the prevention and healing of common illnesses were neglected. This made the shocking inequalities between the "elite," of which the doctors liked to form part, and the masses, whom they despised, even worse.

These specialists had all the bourgeois prejudices. "They had nothing but scorn for the traditional cures and pharmacopoeia"; they dismissed as incurable certain illnesses which the new, post-Cultural Revolution medicine has been perfectly able to cure. "Even the language they used" was meant for young people whose family background predisposed them to an "academic education" and "seeking comfort and privilege." They considered that what they knew constituted absolute truth, and that the works they had studied were infallible.

The Chinese faculty rejected those practices for which no theory had been worked out. After 1958 students were obliged to learn acupuncture, but the faculty was opposed to reducing the number of points. It instinctively rejected everything that was simple, because "this simplicity put its monopoly in question. We have refuted the theory according to which the more points are used the more effective the treatment."

In short, present achievements would never have been possible if the

hereditary power of the hospital specialists,* with their "scientific prejudices" and their "pretensions to know more than others," had not been shaken
by the will of the people.

The structure of the medical profession has been profoundly transformed by the *struggle-criticism-transformation* movement. "In the hospitals we
have applied Mao Tse-tung's instruction: *Bombard the headquarters*."

White-coated professors listened in silence as the textile worker gave us
the case for the prosecution in their presence.

The No. 6 General Hospital in Shanghai

Dr. Chen Tsung-wei, a tall man in his forties, shook my hand so hard I
thought he was going to break my fingers. Ironically, he turned out to be a
pioneer in the grafting of limbs. He is an athletic man with fine features, who
looks you straight in the eye. He also speaks good English. Besides being a
surgeon, he is also a member of the Revolutionary Committee of the
Municipality of Shanghai. He works at the town's No.6 Hospital, and that is
where, in 1963, he successfully reattached severed limbs for the first time
ever.

"They brought me a turner whose right hand had just been cut off by a
machine-tool. The stump, with the four fingers and half the palm, wasn't
even held on by a piece of skin. This kind of accident is common. In cases
before, we'd just sewn up the stump and, depending on how high it had been
cut, we'd fitted an artificial hand. I had never done a graft or read a report on
the subject, or even heard that it could be done. It was the workers who
convinced me to give it a try. The comrades who'd brought the man along
said: 'It's not easy to repair a broken watch, but the watchmaker manages.
Why don't you mend our comrade's hand, with the help of Mao Tse-tung
thought? Otherwise, he won't be able to work. He'll be lost to the construction of socialism. It'll be a defeat for the revolution.' The injured man and his
comrades felt so sure it would be successful that I consulted my team. To a
man, they said they'd give it a try. The operation lasted almost five hours.
Then, a day or two after it, a complication arose. Colleagues from other
hospitals came to my aid. In less than a year the injured man was back at his
machine."

This is a man of science. He reads the medical reviews regularly. He is
fully aware of Western knowledge in his field. Yet here he is telling—without
any evidence of astonishment on his part—of an event in which magic played
a crucial role. The workers who demanded that he perform this operation did

---

*One might say "mandarins," but this word, although of course borrowed from China, is
never used in this context by the Chinese.

not doubt his power, just as the Africans who brought a dying man to Doctor Albert Schweitzer had no doubt of his power when they said to him: "Great white sorcerer, you will heal him."

"Did you perform another operation soon afterwards?"

"Yes, very soon afterwards. Our entire team was received in Peking by the Prime Minister, Chou En-lai, and then by Chairman Mao, who invited us back three times after that. This gave us a lot of encouragement. We realized that we were on the right track and that we had to redouble our efforts in order to be sure of gaining new successes for the revolution. We tried other operations with increased ardor. Limbs severed at different points: the wrist, the forearm, the elbow, the arm, the instep, the ankle, the leg, the knee, the thigh. Clear, clean cuts from saws. Limbs that had been torn off or crushed and where the flesh was pulverized, so that several graftings were necessary. But it's suturing severed fingers that requires the most delicate work. We've had to take parts of nerves from legs and transplant them into fingers which have been cut off."

Standing next to him was the tiny figure of Liu Tse-fang, one of the first patients to have her fingers miraculously put back again. She was pretty, modest and had a lovely smile. She was his mascot.

"It was in 1966. I was nineteen. The operation lasted seventeen hours. During all this time the surgeon and his team had nothing to eat. They saved me, thanks to Chairman Mao and the Communist Party."

"How soon did you regain the use of your hand?"

"Four months later I was able to go back to work."

While she was talking to us, Dr. Chen Tsung-wei was watching her with a kind of respect, as if he had no say in what was from now on her story. I had to ask him a direct question to get him to say something.

"How did those four months go?"

"First, there was the healing, then the uniting of the two grafted parts, and then there was the rehabilitation."

He turned toward Liu Tse-fang as if to say: "She's the one who's interesting, not me." Or perhaps he thought she was perfectly able to say her piece herself.

"Now that my hand is better again, I'm working at the factory just as well as before. I can even play the accordion and knit. But more than anything else, I've worked to build socialism for the success of the revolution."

This time she seemed to have said as much as she could; she clearly had nothing to add. But Dr. Chen Tsung-wei came to her aid:

"This operation wasn't a complete success, though. The end phalanges of the four fingers haven't recovered all their faculties; they aren't very sensitive to extremes of temperature."

A light touch of self-criticism, but in fact this innocent remark does conceal a real problem—some operations of the same type have been discreetly attempted in France, and there have been serious disappointments concerning the recovery of feeling. A limb which has been grafted on but which has become insensitive is a handicap which patients find difficult to put up with.

"What is the average length of an operation?"

"There's no average; it can vary from two hours for a phalanx to twenty hours for four fingers. You never know in advance."

It depends on the nature of the accident and on the damage to the nerves. When a builder repairs an old house, he always makes allowances for difficulties that might crop up unexpectedly.

"When the operation lasts a long time, you don't hand it over to another team?"

"No. The same team must be in charge throughout. We keep ourselves from dropping by drinking tea or milk and by chanting quotations from Chairman Mao."

"How many failures have you had?"

"We've found since 1963 that twelve operations out of thirteen are successful. But it's in rehabilitation that success is less frequent. It quite often happens that a patient regains the use of only three of his four fingers, but this doesn't stop him leading a normal life."

"There's no rejection? Gangrene doesn't set in?"

"No, except where the severed section has had time to decompose. The operation must be done as soon as possible after the accident, within thirty-six hours at the outside. Also, the severed fragment must be kept under refrigeration."

(At this point one of my colleagues whispered: "If you lose a limb, don't forget to put it in the ice bucket.")

"Do you do grafts with limbs taken from dead people?"

"It's impossible. Rejection is immediate. At least, we haven't found a way of preventing it. It's only possible to graft from the same person."

"Do you practice on animals?"

"Yes, that's how we progressed after the first operation. Particularly with rabbits' ears."

"You've never tried a heart transplant?"

"No. I've studied many articles on the transplants you've done in the West, but we've decided to specialize in limb grafts. We're a nation of peasants and workers; we're still not quite used to mechanization and there are lots of accidents. Those who are injured must be gotten back to work, for the sake of production and even more for their own morale and the morale of other workers. But what's the point of prolonging a man's life by a few weeks when his heart has given out?"

With surgery as with everything else, China has made a political choice. There are two quite different societies facing each other across all these decisions. On the one hand, a comparatively simple technique which is available to the mass of workers. The exceptional cases and techniques are avoided; one is interested only in what can rapidly become of use to everyone everywhere. On the other hand, the rare privileged people who can be given a few more weeks of life at a cost of millions of dollars—although you never know whether this will make possible the development of a successful technique ten or twenty years from now. I remember Professor Christiaan Barnard's visit to France in 1967; he came swirling into my office like a *jeune premier,* followed by a horde of photographers and cameramen. The difference between the two societies is also striking in the way their medical achievements are made known. In the West, when the first operation was performed, the front pages were full of it. The patient lived only a few days, but great publicity was given to what was presented as a milestone in the history of mankind. In China, ten years passed and hundreds of grafts were performed before the news was made known abroad. Acupuncture operations remained a state secret until four hundred thousand of them had been done.

"Is your team still the only one performing grafts?"

"They're done in various parts of China, especially in Hunan. We've passed the results of our experiments on to all the hospitals in the main provincial centers, and they've passed them on to the hospitals in district centers, and then they in turn have passed them on to the dispensaries in the people's communes."

"Do you mean to say that dispensaries do this kind of operation?"

"No! But it's a good thing if communes which are very remote know exactly what the procedure is. It's essential that an injured man—no matter where he is—be sent to a hospital equipped to perform grafts within twenty-four hours."

Although No. 6 Hospital does all sorts of operations, it became famous for this specialty, and although several other hospitals also perform graft operations, Shanghai No. 6 is still the main one. We were told of disabled people being taken first to their provincial hospitals, but then being flown to Shanghai.

One would have thought Dr. Chen had nothing else to do but answer our questions. He was simple, serene and always smiling, a pure product of the revolution; his medical education had not begun until after the Liberation. He seemed to be widely respected—because of his professional talent? Because of his work as a member of the town's revolutionary committee? Perhaps also because of his human value; he gives one man back his leg, another his hand. He seemed completely surprised by the interest with which we asked him questions.

"Your surgeons," he said, shaking his head, "would do it just as well and probably better."*

Would do: was he implying "if, like me, they had the support of Mao Tse-tung thought and the affection of the masses"? He seemed to be sincere when he was explaining his vocation in terms of the revolution. Each operation enabled him to participate in the struggle in his country and in the world. When he restored life to a worker's hand, he was "increasing the production potential." When he grafted an arm on to a Vietnamese trainee who had had an accident, he was contributing to the "struggle of the peoples of Indochina against imperialism." Over the entrance to No. 6 Hospital there is the slogan: *Grasp the revolution, promote production*. It does not seem so absurd after a conversation with Dr. Chen.

Chinese Medicine: A Medicine for the Chinese

"Do you believe in the 'miracles' of Chinese medicine?"
"Yes."
"So do you think that people in the West are soon going to be able to benefit from it?"
"No."
"What? You contradict yourself. If they're serious, the miracles will be repeated in other countries. If not, it's a bluff."
"The Chinese aren't Westerners. The Westerners aren't Chinese."
"That's racism!"

Western Skepticism

No, in order for the new acupuncture methods to be accepted in the West, the medical profession would have to feel a pressing need for them, either spontaneously or in response to public pressure, and would have to consider them superior to the usual methods.

What one encounters is the very opposite. Chinese medicine was a subject of mirth even when Western medicine had made scarcely any advances at all. The oracular language Chinese doctors used to cover up their ignorance was a topic of great amusement for the European circles in Peking: "If you live to see the New Year, your forces will return with the spring and you can be expected to make a complete recovery," or "It is difficult to look at a patient's tongue when his elevated rank obliges you to keep your eyes fixed on the ground." Macartney's diary ridicules a medicine "of charms and

---

*Since then there have been several such operations in the West: an arm graft in Brussels, forearm grafts in Austria and France, a foot graft in Sweden, a thumb graft in California. In terms of technique the Western surgeons do just as well as their Chinese colleagues, but the social environment does not favor these kinds of feats.

mixtures." Even if it has been shown since that Chinese pharmacopoeia used homeopathy and some drugs like ephedrine several centuries before the Europeans, the idea is still current in the West that Chinese doctors are no better than Molière's.

How can one believe that sticking a needle into the calf affects the working of the liver? That acupuncture redresses and normalizes the course of some "vital energy" of which the biological sciences have never heard? That a needle in the lobe of the ear cures nervous depression? That a needle inserted in the thick of the thumb enables teeth to be taken out without the patient feeling any pain? None of this is common sense. Perhaps one could begin to take acupuncture seriously if, after the needle had been inserted, oscillographs were to detect the presence of electric currents, for which it would be possible to work out laws. So long as the Chinese themselves confess their ignorance of the real nature of the phenomenon, how can the Europeans be persuaded to overcome their mistrust?

Since we returned from China, our accounts of what we saw have met with good-natured skepticism. A certain doctor, writing in one of the big French evening papers, refused to believe in this "miracle anaesthesia." He suspected that some drops of "some anaesthetic" had been applied to "the mucous membrane in the nose of the woman with the polypuses"; that the woman with an ovarian cyst had been "given a rachianaesthetic" (that is, she had been "injected" with an anaesthetic syringe in her "rachis canal"); and that "before the operation the man with a tumor on the brain had been given good old Chinese opium."

Another doctor warned against the "pseudo health magicians," the "charlatans" who had recourse to "esoterism" instead of sticking to "the rigorous bases of an exact science." A third doctor asked whether there wasn't "some Indian hemp in the slices of pineapple swallowed by the patient. Everyone knows that for centuries the Chinese have studied the anaesthetic properties of Indian hemp."

Another doctor, the president of the main acupuncture society in France, said quite categorically that there had been subterfuge. "My position, which is that of many acupuncturists, is that *there is no such thing as anaesthesia by needles*. Preanaesthesia has always existed, in China as elsewhere. In Europe a surgeon will prepare his patient with morphine or other preparations which produce the maximum degree of relaxation. Or he'll administer curare to relax the muscles. You can get exactly the same effect with needles. But anaesthesia* by needles seems to me an error. I wasn't there in

---

*It seems preferable, when one is talking of acupuncture, to use "analgesia" rather than "anaesthesia." Although the pain is blocked, the feelings are not, and the patient continues to receive sense messages. "Hypo-algesia" would be even more accurate, since acupuncture does not suppress pain altogether, but merely reduces it to a tolerable level.

Wuhan, but the patients whose operations the French delegation witnessed were unfortunately not followed from their beds to the operating table. . . . I think the members of the French delegation who saw the operations have been deluded in their conclusions."

So two hypotheses have been put forward. Either chemical anaesthesia preceded the acupuncture—which would then be nothing more than a theatrical production which one could just as easily do without. Or acupuncture, which is useful for relaxing the muscles, is simply used as a preparation for real chemical anaesthesia, which is then administered secretly.

If the President of the Organization for the Study and Development of Acupuncture, who represents several hundred French acupuncturists, does not believe in analgesia by acupuncture, how can the fifty thousand doctors who are suspicious, not to say hostile, toward their acupuncturist colleagues—whom they feel lack the scientific rigor necessary for becoming qualified doctors—be expected to believe in it?

Systematic Doubt

Honesty compels me to say that not one member of our delegation was a doctor.* It is also true to say that we did not attend the preparations before the operations; so we cannot strictly say that at the pre-operation stage no recourse was made to the classic methods of anaesthesia.

To assume that there was a preliminary rachianaesthesia would be to doubt the intellectual integrity of the Chinese doctors: it seems to me that this hypothesis has to be ruled out.**

Can one possibly believe that China's leaders and doctors put on such a comedy to make the world believe they had discovered a new method of analgesia, while having recourse all the time to the traditional methods? The Chinese doctors we met, like the research workers and cadres, are men of sound judgment who are very strict with themselves. They seem to put forward only what they are sure of. A collective hoax on the part of men who studiously eschew self-satisfaction lacks a certain credibility.

---

*One of us, Marcel Béraud, a dental surgeon, did know something about anaesthesia. Since then a French doctor in Prince Norodom Sihanouk's entourage, Dr. Georges Pathé, has attended similar operations at the Shanghai Hospital No.6. French acupuncturists have too, and they have returned enthusiastic. Two Americans, Professor Grey Gimond of the Washington Bethesda Hospital and Professor Paul Dudley White, a cardiologist who was President Eisenhower's doctor, have also seen these operations. So have a Swiss medical mission (at the end of 1972) and a French one led by Professor Jean Bernard (in April 1973). It would be good if Chinese acupuncture teams were to apply their methods in the West.
**It was pointed out to us that light doses of a sedative (100 mg of luminal or 50 mg of dolosal) were given to relax patients, but these pre-operative treatments, which are common in the West, could not be confused with a real anaesthetic.

After man's first flight in space, Yury Gagarin's feat was called in question. The Chinese, like the Russians, are victims of their own taste for secrecy—where there's no mystery one suspects intrigue.

But for a long time, even in the West, acupuncture has been used with great success in treating functional disorders, allergies and psychosomatic illnesses. It has been used continually for pain. The Chinese have simply moved on a step from using it to cure natural pain to using it as a way of preventing pain that is provoked. And this spectacular extension of the use of acupuncture depends on a particular technical innovation—the needle is kept moving before and during the operation.

The great majority of Western doctors are certainly not prepared to take the step their Chinese colleagues took, prompted as they were by the Cultural Revolution. They will probably continue to view with skepticism both acupuncture and the equal doctor-patient relationship that exists in China.

The Incredulity of Western Patients

The Western doctor's skepticism might disappear if his patients pressed him enough. But how can they but share—most of them—his reservations? The Chinese insist on the moral factors—acupuncture is more likely to be successful the more confidence the patient has in the method and in the doctor. If he has a slight doubt about either, then he breathes with difficulty, his muscles contract, he sweats, and he becomes more and more sensitive to pain.

The proportion of failures is low, and no doubt this is because the Chinese people have become immunized against doubt over thousands and thousands of years. Since the time of the Tang emperors there have been figurines throughout China on which the points and meridians are marked and numbered. In many shop windows today—and not just in drugstore windows—you can see plastic mannequins of different sizes, from six to twenty inches high; their bodies are covered with finely drawn lines and numbers representing the meridians and points. There are dolls to suit all pockets.* Given away free with them are precise medical directions. You can also buy ears made of rubber, and they have twenty or so points marked on them, with all the various complaints that can be cured mentioned.**

The children adore these games—they play at nursing and curing one another's diseases. You even see them carrying around their necks a medical kit containing a case of needles, a bottle of alcohol and a tin of cotton wool.

---

*From 3 to 6 yuans (about 1 to 2 dollars).

**One kind of figurine is specially interesting from an educational point of view; it is a glass doll filled with water, and with holes pierced in it corresponding to the points. The holes are sealed with invisible adhesive tape. When the child inserts his needle in the correct spot, the water spurts out.

"We're practicing acupuncture so we can come to the aid of the masses and be of use in time of war," I was told in Nanking by a boy and a girl of about ten. And you could see the pride in their eyes.

A population conditioned in this way from nursery school on is all the more prepared to believe in the wonders of acupuncture. How can one expect the same from people in the West? The Chinese authorities must have had an inkling of this difficulty. The former Rockefeller Hospital in Peking* had started to use acupuncture on diplomats' wives during childbirth. A small boy from the European community was successfully treated by needles inserted behind his ear. But these operations were suddenly stopped, and no explanation was given; it was said that China did not want to take the responsibility for extending to Westerners therapy which was not their own.

"Do you think," I asked Dr. Chen, "that European doctors could use this method on European patients?"

"I doubt it," he replied. "In order to master the technique of anaesthetizing a patient with acupuncture, they would first have to do a lot of tests on themselves."

I fear he may be right. With the traditions of their therapy and the customs of their people to back them up, Chinese acupuncturists have been able to experiment—with some daring and at their own risk—on one another. They had the will to solve a national health problem quickly. They were fired by "the enthusiasm of the masses." What would motivate European doctors in their radically different context?

Anaesthetizing by acupuncture is undoubtedly the product of Mao Tse-tung thought, but it is also the result of necessity: the Chinese peasants did not have the benefits of medical science. In the West, Mao Tse-tung thought is not on the point of being adopted as an article of faith, and country doctors have been making the latest scientific achievements available to the rural population for a long time.**

Physiological and Ethnological Differences

Although various anatomical peculiarities distinguish the Chinese from the Caucasian and the Negro, we are not concerned with them here; but certain physiological differences can lead to different reactions both to pain and to acupuncture.

Poliomyelitis is known to be an illness of the rich; most underdeveloped countries are immune to it. A Westerner in the tropics is very likely to fall

---

*Since called the Anti-Imperialist Hospital, then renamed Hospital of the Capital after China decided to adjust its relations with the outside world, but known all along to the foreign community as the PUMC (Peking Union Medical College).

**But in the past few years, acupuncture has more and more become an acceptable method of treatment in the West.

victim to amoebic dysentery, although the natives rarely get it. The more comfortable man becomes, the lower his pain threshold. Central heating makes one feel the cold; material progress makes one hypersensitive. Our ancestors, who were used to washing with a jug of water and spending the winter in cold houses where the heat was concentrated around the fireplace, were more resistant to influenza than our generation, which has been softened by warm radiators and warm baths. Gradually, the mechanisms of self-defense get weaker; it is the hard life which strengthens them in order to protect us against illness and suffering.

No one—whether physiologist, psychiatrist, neurologist, or surgeon—knows exactly what pain is. What is more, no sociologist, anthropologist or ethnologist has ever been able to work out a law on the way pain varies according to social categories or racial characteristics. All one can do is observe that pain does differ according to temperament, race and standard of living. A tougher individual resists pain better than a more refined individual. Some people who are emotionally inclined to illness may tense up because of their pain, and then it becomes extremely severe. Others allow themselves to be calmed and even subjugated by a doctor who has gained their confidence; on these people pain has less of a hold. The collective psychology of a people very likely has a direct influence on these phenomena.

One of our traveling companions had to get treatment in Peking for tooth decay. While the dentist was using his drill, he was suffering so much that he asked for a local anaesthetic.

"You foreigners," the dentist said, "can't stand the slightest pain. A Chinese wouldn't feel a thing."

Another of our companions bruised his calf while leaping from a boat in Hangchow. For several days he complained of intense pain. They used acupuncture on him, but he felt no significant improvement.

"Do you think acupuncture would have eased the pain for one of your compatriots?" I asked the Chinese doctor who attended him.

"It wouldn't even have been necessary to use acupuncture," he replied, "for a Chinese in the same situation wouldn't have felt anything."

Larrey, the surgeon of the Grand Army, tells of making a grenadier swallow a glass of rum before amputating his leg. How can one distinguish the pain from the idea one has of it, the apprehension one experiences?

It does not seem unreasonable to me to suppose that the success rate in the West for using acupuncture as an analgesic would be inversely proportional to that in China: in other words, in the West there would be an overwhelming majority of failures and a small minority of successes.*

---

*The Swiss medical delegation asked that two of their members be given an analgesic by means of acupuncture. The Chinese doctors thought long and hard about it and finally agreed. It was a failure, and the Chinese doctors gave no explanation.

Ideological Preparation

No member of the medical team sitting around the conference table at the Wuhan Medical Institute made any reference to the preparation which went on before the needles were inserted. Several times we had to ask: "Do you prepare the patient in any way before he goes into the operating theatre? How long before? What do you do?" They would say he was "prepared psychologically" for "about half an hour." The doctor and the patient establish a dialogue "through studying the thought of Chairman Mao"; they "exchange views on the method to be adopted"; they create mutual confidence and an atmosphere of collaboration. For big operations this psychotherapy session is preceded by similar conversations over the previous two or three days.

"How do you cope with a patient who is not in sympathy with what you're doing?"

"At one time we used to treat the patient as an object; nowadays we try to persuade him."

"How do you relax the patient?"

"Politics are present in the operating theatre. We appeal to the patient to have the courage to overcome his fear of pain, to muster the will to live and get better, by convincing him that his duty is to fight for the revolution."

So it is the patient's pride as a citizen that is called on. He is shown that his personal destiny forms a part of a vast design; this must stir his vital energy.

"Do the sick ever refuse acupuncture?"

"It's very rare.* Almost all sick people in China are like those you've seen—they're lively, determined to get better to serve others, and full of enthusiasm for the thought of Mao Tse-tung."

The Second State

Here one is entering territory whose frontiers are difficult to trace. It's hard to deny that "inspiring confidence" in a sick person and inviting him to "participate" would help to calm him. But is this sufficient to ensure that the patient does not feel the pain of a major operation? They did not let us** into the mysteries of the preliminary conversation. What goes on? When we asked if they used hypnosis, the whole team protested. But had the question been properly understood? Had the translation that produced such categori-

---

*We did not manage to find out if these were counted among the ten percent admitted failures, or if those who did not cooperate during the preparatory psychological session were eliminated so the acupuncturist had to deal only with those who were well disposed toward his methods. I am inclined to accept the second interpretation.

**Or, so far, any other Westerner, it seems.

cal denials been accurate? Was this preliminary psychological treatment confined to suggestion? And didn't suggestion verge on hypnosis? Wasn't it possible to do hypnosis without knowing it?

In *La foi qui guérit*, the alienist Jean Martin Charcot, the father of the famous polar explorer, makes many clinical observations on suggestion and hypnosis. Isn't the state in which the Chinese patient chats to his doctor and eats stewed fruit, proving that he is fully conscious but feels no pain, close to Charcot's "second state"? It is certainly not real hypnosis, in which the patient enters a universe of which he will later have no memory. But is it not a modified consciousness, such as Mesmer created with electric currents and magnets? The phenomenon of "animal magnetism" brought to light by Mesmer has been caused since the beginning of time with various techniques.* But Mesmer did not have his roots in the Western tradition. Might acupuncture not just be a sophisticated adjunct to a phenomenon which is as old as mankind but which gradually disappears as the power of magic over man decreases?

The Chinese often give Westerners the impression that they live in the second state. The powers of suggestion exercised by collective thought know no limit when they are applied to a people whose receptivity is still intact and who have been duly conditioned.

Isn't the reference to Mao like the reference to the *hypnotist* which Freud made great use of in his essay *Group Psychology and the Analysis of the Ego?* Following Le Bon and Macdougall, he analyzed the suggestibility of crowds in terms of their identification with the chief, the ideal of the Ego, to whom each individual member assigns his mental energy.

Untransposable

"It has to be one of two things," one of France's top surgeons told me. "Either—and this is what I'd like to be the case—the feats you've witnessed are genuine, which means the Chinese are twenty or a hundred years ahead of us and so it's a matter of some urgency to get them to acquaint the rest of the world with their achievements. Or it's a bluff, and perhaps an unconscious bluff. In that case China is the victim of her own myths and one is bound to draw grim conclusions for the future of that country."

And what if there were a third hypothesis? What if the Chinese are neither ahead nor behind us? What if they are not even living in the same time span, in the same *age* as we are? What if they aren't even traveling along the same path as we are? What if they're making progress and making revolutions which are strictly their own?

Very special opportunities have opened up before Chinese medicine and

---

*Maybe Western medicine would have made progress in mastering these methods if the Académie de Médecine in Paris had not solemnly condemned them in 1840.

surgery. The Chinese have the good fortune to benefit from them; the chances of seeing Westerners benefiting from them in their turn seem remote. In order for their surprising successes to be achieved, many conditions had to come together, and in the West this stage is a long way off. Conditions like their age-old customs; traditional teachings in the school; popular belief in the power of tradition (even today, as we saw in Machiao, when two doctors work in a people's commune, one of them using Western methods and the other traditional methods, the queue is always for the latter); an 85 percent rural population which readily accepts such phenomena; an urgent need to set up a medical service recruiting from a population which assimilates more easily those techniques and procedures which have been laid down by custom; a Cultural Revolution which destroyed the mandarins of the medical profession; and a respect for Mao Tse-tung thought which brought doctors and patients closer together, within one single faith.

The Great Acupuncturist

Mao caused Chinese medicine to achieve an original synthesis between the old practices and modern methods in order to ensure control of the organic functions and to increase resistance to illness and pain. But what else did he do for China as a whole? Ensure control over the functioning of this vast society. Find the links and relations between the country's bodily organs. Reestablish an equilibrium which had been destroyed. Reduce the sufferings of his people by means of unexpected diversions. Reawaken its vital energy. To do all this for the most ancient and populous country in the world is no mean achievement.

Part II

Changing
the Individual

6

The Reshaping of Minds

The Revolution in Outlook

I asked a worker at the No. 2 Textile Works in Peking if he was satisfied with his pay. "Before the Cultural Revolution," he replied, "we were made to work for money. We were paid productivity bonuses. We were being corrupted and made bourgeois. We lacked political consciousness. Now we have come to understand that the workers must have no other aim but the revolution. No longer do we ask ourselves *How much are we working for?* but *Whom are we working for?*"

Everywhere we got the same answer. Some cadres went so far as to say: "It was the workers themselves who demanded the end of the bonus system. Before the Cultural Revolution their only aim in life was to live well and to provide a good life for their families. All they tried to do was get more, to make their lives more comfortable. It was an unhealthy motive and one which transformed them without their knowing it into bourgeois and revisionists. If it had gone on it would have put us all back in the past. But they recognized the danger. Serious study of Mao Tse-tung thought led them to discover that the real meaning of their work was to help the revolution. They denounced everything that diverted them from this aim."

"And what of those who didn't see it this way?"

"They cannot work. We must continue to reeducate them until they adopt the correct line again."

These are ritual statements, but it would be wrong to think of them as meaningless. This process of "reeducation" is not without difficulty or strain, for it is an attempt to change entirely the collective aims of life and the very mainsprings of all activity. Through and beyond the attitude to money, the object is to change man, his reactions, his values—in short, everything he has built up.

Hsu Ching-hsien, the brilliant leader of the Shanghai revolutionary committee and an influential Central Committee member, told me: "Even before the Cultural Revolution we in Shanghai maintained that the demands of production should not mean a reduction in political work. We felt there was a danger that the onward thrust of the revolution might be slowed down by material and egotistical considerations. It was necessary once again to launch the movement of revolutionizing society. Priorities had to be reversed. If we first set about changing men, we would then increase production much more quickly. Making the revolution means abolishing totally all that binds us to the ways of thinking and ways of life we have inherited from the past. So in this way the individual will be intellectually and morally regenerated. He will submit to the wishes of the collective. He will cast aside personal interest in favor of the exclusive interests of the revolution."

Hsu Ching-hsien, an elegant revolutionary with a finely featured face, was a man of thirty-six. In his light blue uniform with its stand-up collar, he had a striking silhouette. While he was telling me how to kill the old men within the new men (one felt he would really need to apply himself to kill the old man in himself), a hypothesis came into my mind. The "Great Leap Forward" was to have made China a great economic power. It ended in failure. In order to overcome it, or to cover it up, perhaps it had been necessary to assign other aims to the revolution. The basis of production was not firm and had to be changed. Since one couldn't increase consumption, one had to reduce the desire to consume. Since reality resisted this, it was necessary to see reality in a different way. The Cultural Revolution was in essence a revolution in outlook.

That is not to diminish its importance. Doesn't man exist almost entirely in the image he has of himself? For the Chinese this image is confused with the image they have of their supreme leader. In the last century Gustave Le Bon said that a passionate identification with the leader will enable the masses to achieve feats which go well beyond normal limits.

The Cultural Revolution was not just tactical, nor was it the result of cynical calculation; it was a strategy thought up by true revolutionaries in the wake of a serious setback. They had lost in spiritual power without gaining in material power. A spiritual hold had to be reestablished without delay—revolutionary ardor is an asset which runs out rapidly, and the Chinese communists recognized that if it was to last the revolution had to be both permanent and absolute.

At one time, China wanted to be rich; today she says she is proud to be underdeveloped. Anything which might detract from this feeling is officially discouraged: the Chinese should take on the pride of those who are poor and wish to remain so.

"Basically, what you want to do is change the character of a quarter of mankind. That's no mean undertaking."

"That's what we're doing. We are determined to get rid of the customs and culture which made China what she had become. We want to replace them with genuinely proletarian culture and customs. For as long as is necessary we'll brainwash those who don't understand.* We'll throw out those in authority who follow the capitalist path. We'll throw the workers, the peasants, the soldiers—and even the revolutionary intellectuals, although there aren't many of them—into the battle against bourgeois ideology, against the academic authorities, the reactionary cadres, and the whole educational, literary and artistic superstructure."

"Do you think China is already proletarian?"

"We're still a long way from it! What can be said, though, is that a proletarian China today seems nearer than it did before the Cultural Revolution. But there'll have to be even more Cultural Revolutions. The children inherit the mentality of their parents. Do you think the son of a landowner and the son of a Shanghai *comprador* become poor peasants or workers overnight, simply because their land or their money has been taken away from them? Not on your life. They keep the mentality of a landowner or a *comprador*. Even the bureaucrats gradually adopt the same mentality! *There's a class struggle being waged in people's heads*. Our duty is to help the proletarian in them triumph over the bourgeois."

Potential revisionism in the Chinese soul is destroyed. The dormant Khrushchev in each man and woman is killed.

A few days before, in Peking, Vice-Rector Chou Pei-yuan had told me: "Before the Cultural Revolution, teachers were preoccupied with getting chairs, and they were inculcating in their students the desire to get jobs. Now teachers and students have come to realize that they must disregard career and renounce personal ambition in order to become one with the broad masses of the people. Yes, we believe that man can be changed, even if he has to fight against himself. He can be changed if he cooperates, if he is convinced that the change will be for his own good and for the good of all."

Certainly, no more comprehensive attempt at "reeducation" has ever been systematically undertaken on so many million people with such determination—in the space of just one generation and under one and the same leadership. It is worth going to China just to see the way it is being done.

---

*He was the first and last Chinese leader to praise "brainwashing" in our presence (at least, that was the term the interpreters used).

The Techniques of Persuasion

We have seen how Mao Tse-tung thought is formed and articulated. Now let us see how it is propagated. On factory and farmyard walls, in the streets and railway stations, under pagodas and at the feet of bald mountains, vast red signs with gold lettering carry quotations from the thoughts of Mao Tse-tung and encouragement to the passerby to heed their injunctions: "To navigate at sea, one needs a good helmsman; to make the revolution, one needs Mao Tse-tung thought." At the Academy of Sciences: "Let Mao Tse-tung thought rule our research and our technology." On the trunks of plane trees; "Mao Tse-tung thought increases agricultural production." On the counter of the Chinese People's Bank: "Glory to Mao Tse-tung thought." At an aerodrome: "Mao Tse-tung thought guarantees us greater and greater successes." One of our delegation observed: "They should say it guarantees more and more rapid take-offs."

Cultural life is penetrated through and through with Mao Tse-tung thought. There is not a newspaper, a radio broadcast, a film or a ballet which does not quote some of the thoughts or actions of the Great Teacher. The source of all inspiration, the alpha and omega of letters, science and the arts is Mao Tse-tung thought.

Each day the papers are full of anecdotes quoted as an example for the nation. The international ping-pong champion owes his title to applying Mao Tse-tung thought. A revolutionary drain-cleaner says: "Thanks to Mao Tse-tung thought, I am now twice as efficient as I was." In the press, on the radio, through loudspeakers installed on street corners and village squares and from speakers on specially equipped trucks driving around the streets, the people are lulled, pestered and submerged by the omnipresent thought of Mao Tse-tung.

At four or five o'clock in the morning you are awakened with a start by the sound of amplified voices. You go to the window; children are in the hotel courtyard, reading into megaphones from the *Little Red Book*. You go downstairs, half-dressed, to tell these young propagandists to be quiet. They stop for a few moments, dumfounded by this incongruity. By the time you get upstairs again, they have resumed their chanting.

A measure of the ubiquity of Mao Tse-tung thought is the absence of any other. It is impossible to find a novel, a collection of poetry, an economic or sociological study, even a translation, in any bookshop; in the museums there are no books available about the pieces on exhibit. The works of Chairman Mao, in various editions and in all formats, complete and abridged, sit alone on the bookstands of railway stations and air terminals. The monopoly is broken—and then only rather timidly—by Marx, Engels, Lenin and Stalin, the seven plays of the revolutionary theatre, and some technical works.*

---

*This total dearth of books lasted almost six years, from May 1966 to February 1972. A certain number of titles reappeared for the Chinese New Year on February 15, 1972; they were either

"Mao Tse-tung thought study classes" have been introduced in all production units, public services, administrative offices, academic establishments, and nurseries. We saw them in people's communes and in factories. Either before or after work, a group forms a circle and discusses passages from the *Little Red Book*. In factories where the "three-eight" shift pattern operates, the study class is held an hour before each shift starts. The aim is to start with the *Little Red Book* and go on to study the Works themselves—in particular, the most difficult philosophical aspects whose "practical applications are a valuable aid" to the tractor driver, the pig-breeder, the machine operator, and the sculptor about to tackle a block of jade.

In an administrative office we visited in Peking the study class took place every day from eight until nine, and longer on Saturdays. We were told this was the usual period in offices.

The study period has the same ceremonial each time—the leader opens the *Little Red Book* to the page where the study session ended the day before, unless something topical or the wishes of the members of the group cause another passage to be chosen. He then reads aloud, half intoning, half reciting, and the whole group repeats each passage in chorus. He then talks about the passage, asks the group questions, and gets them to analyze and illustrate the text by finding contemporary examples. They are advised to continue their studies at home with their families. One of our delegation wondered if a couple's most intimate moments were ever interrupted by Mao study; as we shall see later, it is always a mistake to use irony where Mao Tse-tung thought is concerned.

In short, it was by means of the Cultural Revolution that the whole of China was transformed, in the words of Lin Piao, into "a great school of Mao Tse-tung thought."

In this enormous classroom care is taken not to "overexcite" a few brilliant pupils while the great mass of dunces slumber. Most certainly, the brilliant pupils are called on to become the pioneers of the revolution, but if they refuse they are expelled. The class is mainly for those who have difficulty in keeping up—that is, for the "broad peasant and working masses."

Mao Tse-tung thought demands a great deal, but it can bring its

---

reprints, like Kuo Mo-jo's essay *The Tercentenary of the 1644 Insurrection*; great traditional novels, like *The Dream of the Red Chamber*; old novels rewritten by their authors after the Cultural Revolution, like *Militiawomen from an Island* and *Mountains Enraged*; or—and these are the vast majority—translations, like Krupskaya's *Memories of Lenin*, Lissagaray's *The Commune of 1871*, Montesquieu's *de l'Esprit des Lois*, Lewis Morgan's *Ancient Society*, Thucydides' *History of the Peloponnesian War*, and Kant's *The Critique of Pure Reason*. This is only a beginning, but the bookshops are no longer temples consecrated primarily to the worship of Mao's works and secondarily to the works of the big four of Marxism. According to some witnesses, the crowd ignored the shelves reserved for the works of Mao and the founding fathers and made a beeline for the new titles. The list corresponds more or less to the list of his favorite books which Mao gave Edgar Snow in 1936.

rewards. Its teaching succeeds because it teaches success; it gives a sense of direction to daily life and enables man's humble lot to be transcended. The house is cleaner, the rice softer, the children more hard-working; Chinese communism knows how to bring these modest successes together and give them a wholly new dimension.

This helps us to understand how its hold on people can be so total without becoming intolerable. The teaching never stops. Each day, in addition to his rice or his bowl of noodles, the Chinese worker takes in a massive dose of ideology—at home, at work, and on his way from one to the other—and the dose comes in various forms—orally, in pictures, and in writing.

From Peking to Canton, from Sian to Shanghai, all Chinese, day after day, hear the same chants, repeat the same slogans, and react identically to identical *good things* and *evil things*.*

Thanks to Mao Tse-tung thought, the individual identifies with the group. He takes his point of reference and the behavior that stems from it from the same source. In evaluating both himself and others at group criticism and self-criticism sessions, the criterion is each individual's unquestioning acceptance of the established scale of values. Because of his devotion he is compelled to absorb the ideas of the Great Helmsman—his limitless confidence in his countrymen and his appeals for solidarity. This confidence is justified and this unity of purpose forged by the fact that all consciousnesses are imbued with the same ideas at one and the same time. But beyond these techniques, Mao Tse-tung thought draws its power of persuasion from an ideal of the collective ego which came before it. Chinese society wanted only to deify itself. It was also prepared to be obedient, to the point of reaching a degree of intolerance which to us sometimes seems barely tolerable.

Recitation

The newspapers, reviews, books, table talk, official speeches, technical reports and replies to questions are all the same—hardly anything is unexpected, and the identical clichés are heard time and time again.

Most of the local officials, teachers, workers and peasants we met spoke so quickly and so well that we had the impression that they were reciting their words. They never stopped to think, nor were they ever at a loss for words. When we asked them something point-blank, they replied without a moment's hesitation and, it seemed, without pausing to reflect.

In time we were able to see how this mechanism worked. The Chinese

---

*The success has been so great that the method has become more supple. The *Little Red Book* does not seem to Westerners in Peking to be as common as it was a few years ago, and possibly this is because it has become less necessary. Why "lay it on," since Mao Tse-tung thought has seized all minds?

are so voluble because their thinking is backed up by ready-made phrases, rather like the padding all eloquent people use here and there in their speech. And we were less surprised that those we spoke to had an answer for everything, once we ourselves had learned the replies by heart.

Everyone—from the workman to the farmer, from the salesgirl in the big store in Shanghai to the demonstrator at the Great Bridge over the Yangtse at Nanking—speaks like a book, or, rather, like one of those brochures with their predictable contents which are on display on the desks in hotel lobbies.

Collective Psychotherapy

Some cadres, going over the past few years, launched into self-criticism. A foreman in an electronics factory in Canton told me: "In 1966 I chose to follow the incorrect line of Liu Shao-chi, because I thought increased production was preferable to the rigorous maintenance of proletarian ideology. But during the Cultural Revolution the popular masses criticized me severely and made me realize that by acting out of self-interest I had become a revisionist. With the help of the works of Chairman Mao, I have now changed my view of the world."

At the Two Bridges rural brigade near Peking, a member of the Permanent Bureau of the Revolutionary Committee of the People's Commune, a man of forty-one, had told several of us much the same kind of thing about three weeks earlier: "I hadn't realized that when one works with profit as one's motive, one is traveling along the road toward the restoration of capitalism. Thanks to the fraternal aid of my comrades, who were unsparing in their criticism of me, and to further study of Mao Tse-tung thought, I have come to see just how false my ideology was and how my mind was being fed with bourgeois ideas. If I hadn't rectified the situation, I couldn't have worked as an official in a people's commune."

Similar results are achieved from group criticism and self-criticism undertaken during meetings which are held to extend the study of Mao Tse-tung thought. This famous technique is a universal and everyday phenomenon.

Nobody is exempt—the young boys from the hotel room service gather in the office and the staff on a train cluster on the platform at their destination to accuse one another, personally and collectively, of various misdemeanors. He who has not had his daily ration of self-criticism and criticism is in danger of backsliding.

All those among us who compared the China we saw with China before

1966 felt it was now a more relaxed country. The frantic tension of earlier years had passed. The hardened, depersonalized Chinese of the "Great Leap Forward" and the divided Chinese of the Cultural Revolution seemed to have become themselves again. Did they feel relief that they had gotten rid of the confrontation between Mao Tse-tung thought and "revisionism" which had lasted for so long? Had they found a certain spontaneity that had freed them of fear? Were they reassured that the country had regained its order and unity? Whatever the explanation, now that she had mastered the demons that were tormenting her, China seemed to be savoring her period of relaxation as a kind of renaissance.

Had Mao perhaps found the formula for a collective psychotherapy?

How long can this balance between constant supervision and spontaneity be maintained? This balance between joy and moral rigor? How long will the individual continue to regard his intimate relationship with the group as both a refuge and a source of satisfaction?

Although the prognosis is uncertain, the therapy is fiendishly consistent.

7

Education or Indoctrination?

First Years

Creches, nursery schools—from the moment a child first casts his eye on an object and begins to recognize forms, he is molded by politics. The first color he is made to appreciate is red. The first gestures he imitates are revolutionary—raising his clenched fist and stamping his heel on the ground. The first songs he attempts to sing are songs of war.

A baby has the words *Little Red Guard* on his bib. On the children's counters of the state shops the big dolls are peasant girls with rifles slung over their shoulders, soldiers in green with submachine guns and the *Quotations from Chairman Mao Tse-tung* bulging in their jacket pockets, or women miners with lamps on their helmets, Mao badges on their chests, and a slogan on their backs saying "May Chairman Mao Tse-tung live for ten thousand years!" Even more sophisticated are the animated plastic dolls shouting quotations from the Chairman into megaphones or the little girls who have the *Little Red Book* in one hand and a fly-whisk in the other and read Mao while killing flies.

At the nursery school of the Peking No. 2 Textile Works, about twenty children aged between two and four put on short plays for us. Hanging on the wall were large portraits of Mao, with drawings by the children on either side, representing such objects of national pride as a blast furnace, the launching of a satellite, and the mushroom cloud of an atomic bomb. Hanging out to dry across the room was a row of little red Turkish towels, each one bearing a child's initials and the words *Little soldier of the revolution*. The children came together to sing a military song. Then they split up again to mime, with their arms outstretched, the launching of the Chinese satellite. The smallest, the under-threes, wore trousers which were slit right up the small of the back. With their bottoms showing, they stamped their feet to celebrate the death of an enemy one of them had just killed with a miniature submachine gun. A little four-year-old girl sang a soprano number from the revolutionary ballet *The Red Detachment of Women*.

It was exactly the same at the nursery school in Meichiakou, the "Mountain Village of the Mei Family," in Chekiang Province—the same performances and the same themes. Little girls with their hair in pigtails and little boys carrying wooden guns acted a scene from the revolutionary ballet *The White-haired Girl*.

Physical education is so much more fun when it is turned into military exercises and the weights and dumbbells become rubber weapons. The children themselves seem to be made of rubber, for they are extremely malleable. They shout the slogans they have been taught with enormous enthusiasm and passion. China's small children are probably more certain of themselves and the things they are told than children anywhere else in the world.

A Village Primary School

Meichiakou has 1,344 inhabitants in 251 families. The school takes the children from seven to thirteen; it has five male and three female teachers and six classes.

I was told school is not compulsory. "How many children are there in the village?" "Two hundred and forty-two." "How many of them go to school?" "Two hundred and forty-two, of course." "Attendance is voluntary and yet everyone goes to school?" "It has happened that children refuse to go to school and prefer to play truant, but they don't do it for long." "Why not?" "Their comrades jeer at them. Their parents get at them. And their teachers put them to shame." In school, as everywhere else, it is a question of social pressure rather than formal obligation. The Chinese, children as well as grownups, do not have much time to be mischievous or idle.

Inscribed on the pediment of the school is an instruction from Chairman Mao: "You must concern yourselves with the affairs of the state and carry the Great Proletarian Cultural Revolution right through to the end." The subjects taught are in line with this; there is a political education course (which sticks as closely as possible to current Chinese developments), study of the works of Mao, Chinese literature (edifying stories drawn from the contemporary scene and socialist texts), manual training in production, singing (revolutionary songs), and sports (military). There is also drawing, but it is always imitative, never imaginative. Since the Cultural Revolution, flowers and animals have disappeared; what are drawn now are the Wuhan combine and the Nanking bridge. The older pupils do pictures of the local heroes of the liberation war and of "production."

Mei Ta-hsian, the teacher, explained to me that the number of hours devoted to Mao Tse-tung thought itself had just been reduced, since it had been integrated into all the other subjects. Children were taught to read, he said, with the *Little Red Book*, and it was also through the *Little Red Book* that politics and socialist culture were studied. Mathematics, physical education and drawing lessons also illustrate the maxims of the Chairman.

Unlike the esoterism of the mandarins, education is conceived as being for the children of the people—the people of this or that province or village. It is an integral part of the countryside in which the child grows up. When school is over, the teachers continue to set an example to their pupils by doing tough manual work.

"If the Cultural Revolution has given us one thing," Mei Ta-hsian concluded, "it has taught us to integrate our education better into the life of the brigade." It is the independent administration of the school by the village which allows and guarantees this integration—the brigade is self-sufficient and needs no support from the state in meeting the needs of its school. The school is the village's concern, and along with production it is the most important of its concerns.

A Barefoot Teacher

"How did the Cultural Revolution go as far as you were concerned?" I asked Mei Ta-hsian.

He pointed into the distance, no doubt toward Shanghai or Hangchow, and said: "The Cultural Revolution—it was in the towns that it really raged." Mei Ta-hsian was a quiet teacher in a village of quiet men.

He had been "born in the old society" in 1936. He had been brought up at first "in the ideas which were current among the privileged class of landowners and rich peasants." He had had to make great efforts to reach the level of a "socialist education." At sixteen, three years after the Liberation, his studies were finished and it was mainly "by practice" that he educated himself, by teaching in a number of different villages.

Now thirty-six, he had been teaching for thirteen years; he was married to a worker in the production brigade and they had three children. He said, with a smile: "We had to stop. Three is a lot, even too many, and one must set an example." His wife had earned 300 yuan the year before* and he had earned 396 yuan.**

---

*155 dollars.
**205 dollars.

So without hesitating he remembered to the nearest yuan what he had earned the year before. "How much will you get this year?" He did not know yet. It would depend on the harvest and on whether the revolutionary committee of the people's commune was satisfied with his work. As far as the brigade was concerned, once the deliveries of tea and rice had been made to the state, the workers—including the teachers—received their share of everybody's work in accordance with their zeal. There were no family allowances, no living allowances or other supplementaries; but, on the other hand, there were allowances in kind, and these included accommodation.

Mei Ya-hsian and his wife between them earned less than a factory worker in a town, but their needs were more modest. They bought everything they needed at the state shop, the only shop in the village, where prices were very low. All the peasants of his age looked the same; they all wore the same white shirts, plastic sandals and heavily creased trousers; they all had brush cuts and calloused hands.

He was a "barefoot teacher"; like the "barefoot doctors," his basic training had been very rudimentary and he had learned most of what he knew on the job. Like them, he responded promptly to needs which were not met at all before the Liberation.

One meets people like Mei Ta-hsian in every people's commune one visits, but they are often living alongside a different kind of person. The Cultural Revolution sent a number of teachers and young intellectuals out of the towns and into the countryside. They provided valuable reinforcements for the teaching units in the production brigades, but only reinforcements, for it was always fixed so that the barefoot teachers were in the majority.

The status of the secondary school teachers we met in the towns was scarcely any different; they too were paid by the municipalities and their accommodations were also provided free, either at the school itself or with a local family. But their monthly salary was double that of the barefoot teachers; it is more expensive to live in the towns than in the country. There is no distinction in salary or status between graduate teachers and self-taught teachers; only the nature and the quality of the service they give are taken into account.

The Young Red Guards

Education does not stop at the classroom door, but the methods are different outside school. It takes on the form of a giant game that lasts forever.

Not far from Sian, at the hot springs of Mount Li Shan, beside the white marble pools, pioneers were practicing their singing and chanting. Boys and girls aged between twelve and fifteen, wearing red scarves around their necks and carrying the *Little Red Book*, marched around the shrubs and through the ornamental pavilions to meet the challenge of the China of tomorrow with a grace that was reminiscent of the period of the Han and the Tang, who came to these springs and their lotuses to forget the worries of power.

How gentle and charming they have become, these tame adolescents whose elder brothers and sisters four years before had threatened the regime itself! These Boy Scouts of the revolution, having achieved the revolution in a somewhat haphazard way, were now content merely to sing about it.

In Canton the game seemed more serious and the Red Guards were unsmiling; although they were no longer on the rampage, they were still vigilant. They were mounting guard in the shops, two by two, boys and girls. Old men—probably intellectuals undergoing "reeducation"—were sweeping the streets under the watchful eye of these good students of Mao Tse-tung thought.

The children, who have been taught from a very young age to chant war cries, to dance extracts from new ballets, to read and write from the *Little Red Book*, to recite passages from it, and to march with clenched fists in the air, are spurred on by revolutionary competition; in each class one can spot those children who sing, dance and act revolutionary scenes the best. They are brought together into a troupe which goes to the towns or people's communes in the area, more to spread the word than to entertain people. School and the extensions of it are not intended to form interesting minds, but to create soldiers for the revolution.

In Nanking a troupe of "young Red Guards" put on a show which sent shivers down our spines. They mimed Vietnamese children at the front. They pointed their dummy submachine guns up to the sky, and the whistling and explosion of an American plane, which you saw as a shadow falling on a screen, made them dance with joy.

Then, dressed up as peasants and soldiers, they mimed the love that unites the people and the Red Army. A wind and string orchestra played *"The Young Red Guards Help in the Fields," "The Young Red Guards Learn to Grow Rice in the People's Commune," "The Red Guard from the Steppe Who Had Seen Chairman Mao," "The Red Sun Casts a Golden Glow over the Tachai Model Commune,"* and *"Mao Tse-tung Thought Illumines Tibet."* As a finale, sixteen young musicians and about as many singers performed "The Peoples of the World Will Triumph."

At midnight they accompanied us back to our hotel. Our heads were still spinning with the deafening sound of their drums and trumpets and the enthusiasm of these beardless soldiers and the passion of these girls. Their bright red-painted cheeks shone in the light from the lamps, as if the red of their armbands, ribbons and bouquets was not enough. "Our hearts are red," they shouted as they left us.

About seven o'clock in the morning, after a brief night's sleep, we passed a column of Red Guards in the street. Led by a girl carrying a portrait of Mao like the relic of a saint and a boy carrying the red flag on a bamboo staff lodged in his belt, they spread the word through loudspeakers. They were accompanied by gongs and cymbals. When we drew level with them, we recognized our friends of the evening before; we asked our drivers to slow down. Their faces lit up, and several of them waved at us. But they were on duty, and unrestrained enthusiasm would have been out of place. The day's tasks were before them—they had to go around the various districts distributing propaganda, seeing that the ideological level was kept high, rectifying errors. Where does it stop being a game, and where does the conditioning begin?

A Secondary School

In the Cuban Friendship People's Commune not far from Peking there were six secondary schools and twenty-three primary schools for a population of 38,000. We were welcomed in the school yard by hundreds of boys and girls between twelve and seventeen, all waving the *Little Red Book;* at a signal they all burst into applause.

Then the whistle was blown, and playtime was over. The pupils lined up and returned to their classes in orderly fashion. When our delegation entered a classroom, the children were putting their *Little Red Books* out on their desks. They used them frequently during the lesson, which consisted of a commentary on a *People's Daily* editorial.

Their curriculum was divided into three main areas: physical education, which was dominated by military gymnastics and the handling of weapons, moral education—which comprised communist ethics and Mao Tse-tung thought—and intellectual and practical education. Even in this last area, the only one which resembled anything taught in French schools, the influence of the revolution was still felt. Physics, chemistry and even mathematics were taught in conjunction with the school's workshops. The history that was taught was the history of the Chinese revolution; the geography was that of China. A little English and a little basic agriculture were also taught. As far as Chinese language and literature were concerned, only proletarian literature, the poems of Chairman Mao, works which praise the Great Helmsman, and the libretti of contemporary ballets were allowed. "Cultural" activities consisted of rhythmic recitals of poems, studies of songs from revolutionary operas and plays, and group writing of sketches about contemporary events.

Pupils and teachers take part together in work courses lasting a month and a half, and then they work in the fields for another month; most of the holidays are spent this way. The pupils attend school six hours a day, six days a week, for four years, at the end of which time they have learned the activities of everyday life.

Like all the other schools in the commune, the one we visited is under the ultimate direction of the revolutionary committee of the commune, and is administered on a day-to-day basis by its own revolutionary committee. Sitting side by side on these two committees are peasants, workers and soldiers, chosen for their revolutionary convictions to see that the education the school provides does not deviate from the line laid down by Chairman Mao.

National Education

"There's no doubt that it's in the village schools that the Cultural Revolution has had the most impact," Chou Chen-tung told me as we were climbing up a path in Meichiakou.

"I thought the countryside had been kept out of the Cultural Revolution."

"Not as far as education is concerned. The villages were not the scene of the same kind of disturbances as the towns, but they have been the first to benefit from the gains of the revolution. According to Chairman Mao's instruction,* the direction of the country schools has become the responsibility of the class of poor and medium-poor peasants."

Once again we were told that nothing had happened between 1949 and 1966. But in fact China made an enormous effort in these seventeen years to educate its youth and to create a uniform system of education. In the hundred years before the Liberation, foreign intervention had overturned the old imperial structures and thrown Chinese education into a state of anarchy; it had broken up as much as China itself had. It was impossible in practice to move from one kind of school to another; all one's schooling had to be in the same institution—with the Jesuits, the Scottish Presbyterians, or the Buddhists. There was no national education, since there was no nation.

The Kuomintang had tried to deal with this chaos in the period between 1927 and 1949. They had developed public education with some success, especially at the university level. But the many private establishments were still completely free to set their own timetables and curricula, to choose their own textbooks, and to use their own method of recruiting teachers and pupils.

---

*Applying Mao's directive of August 25, 1968, contained in an article by Yao Wen-yuan in that day's issue of *People's Daily*.

In the two years following the Liberation, the Communist Party completely unified the education system. The government schools were taken in hand by a Party cell, a political commissar and a school committee. The pupils and the teachers had to join a league of young communists and a trade union, respectively. In January 1951 the Ministry of Education called a meeting in Peking of all those who were running missions, schools financed by foreign funds, and private schools, and apparently "persuaded" them to accept the immediate transformation of their establishments into government schools. The system which was then created was a copy of the Soviet model. But here, as in other respects, the differences between the two countries led to a break, and the Cultural Revolution enabled China to take her own course. But clearly it is the achievements that have been made since 1949 that have brought the academic successes of present-day China.

Everywhere we were told that education is available to all children. But is this so in the remotest provinces—in Sinkiang, Mongolia and Tibet? We could not say, but it did seem to be true of the six provinces and eight large towns we visited.

We were also told that illiteracy was disappearing rapidly, not only because it was being dealt with at the source but also because evening classes enabled adults who had missed out on education to make up for lost time. We were told all the time: "Before the Liberation 85 percent of the population was illiterate. Now the situation is reversed, and 85 percent is able to read." What one used to see not long ago in the developed countries—grandmothers teaching their grandchildren to read—one now sees in reverse in China. The children, who are proud of having managed to grasp the basic Chinese ideograms, can be seen teaching them to their grandparents, and even sometimes to their parents. Of course, it is not a question of learning the 10,000 characters which are the prerogative of the scholar, but the 3,000 which are enough for reading the *Little Red Book* or the *People's Daily*, with which one starts. What would be the point of knowing the other ideograms, except to read useless and harmful books? Ignorance is on the retreat, and by the same token so is esoteric culture.

Although no statistics are published either on education or on other social or cultural matters, we were told that 120,000,000 children attend the country's primary schools and 30,000,000 go to the secondary schools.* The numbers have grown enormously under the communist regime. But universal education, which has been achieved by the creation of new teaching units in the most backward country areas, has been counterbalanced by a reduction in the period of study. Everyone goes to school, but for a shorter time than when only a few went.

---

*The man in charge of education on the Kwangtung Provincial Revolutionary Committee assured us that of the 50,000,000 inhabitants of his province, 7,000,000 were at primary schools and 2,200,000 were at secondary schools.

Education, the Birthplace of Society

A complete change in the nature of teaching has accompanied these successes. The urge to "revolutionize" primary and secondary education existed before the Cultural Revolution. Mao had always expressed his desire to give young people a simple education close to the soil, in which manual work and ideological training would be predominant, and which would be extended to all without discrimination. Experiments had been going on along these lines for a long time,* but the Cultural Revolution provided a magnificent opportunity to apply Mao's ideas on the "proletarianization" of education on a large scale. Hitherto they had not been able to alter the established routine any more than the winter sun had been able to filter through low clouds; then the storm cleared the sky. The schools—even the primary schools—were closed from June 1966 to February 1967. When they reopened, school textbooks had still not been revised, and so the only textbook that needed no revision—the *Little Red Book*—became the sole object of study.

In the new educational system, everything combines to turn the children into citizens of a revolutionary nation. The cult of heroic times remains vivid. As at the Kang-ta Institute in Yenan, the pupils absorb ideas while they are learning ideograms. It is no use teaching grammar or vocabulary with weak examples like "the tea is good," "my cup is small," "the cat has eaten the mouse." Those we spoke to ridiculed the old methods. The textbooks were full of "feudal and bourgeois rubbish," "flowers, birds and parks," and stories like the one about "Kung Jung, who left the best pears for his brothers." Now a child gets his political education and his cultural education simultaneously, with sentences like "To navigate through a storm, you need a good helmsman." Children and adults learn the alphabet and the catechism at the same time.

The revolution leaves little time for leisure. In China there is no association for "the defense of student youth" against adult oppression. A great deal is demanded of school children; it is not thought to be good for them to fall into lazy habits. A continual struggle against indolence is waged from the earliest years.

One of our delegation was worried about overworking the children. "Children don't tire as easily as grownups," Mei, the teacher, replied peremptorily. "It is good for them to have a lot of work to do. It's necessary for their growth."

More than that—in China you count on the children for the moral education of their parents, not just for teaching them to read. The regime

---

*These experiments had begun ten or even eighteen years before the August 25, 1968 directive, according to *People's Daily* (in a series of articles from October 18 to October 28, 1968).

sends the whole family to school through the children. They are given the task of fighting against an egotistical or retrograde mentality on the part of their family and friends.

Mei explained: "When the pupil goes home he tells his father and mother what I've taught him in class. He tries to make them share his socialist passion. He helps them get rid of egotism and revisionism, which they may still be suffering from."

So, the child has the responsibility of educating his family politically by holding a small family meeting every day. What could one do but believe those who told us that nothing matures children more than this task which the Party gives them of educating their parents?

The revolutionary loop is hooked: the "broad masses" push the teachers. The teachers push the children. The children push the adults. All go forward, prodded by one another. The school is the womb of the society of tomorrow; the society of today gives birth to its own future through the school.

A Military Training

"What do you want to do later?" I asked the young Red Guards in Nanking, after their display was over.

One of the five I asked wanted to become a worker; another wanted to be a peasant. The other three, two of whom were girls, said they wanted to join the Army—how better to make the revolution than by fighting for it?

In the school yard of the Two Bridges people's commune, boys and girls were marching past with rifles on their shoulders.

"Why does military preparation occupy such a big place in the life of the school?"

"We train the pupils in military exercises to give them a fighting spirit and a body that is tough and hardened to war," a teacher replied.

"Do you fear war, then?"

"Intellectual training is less important than civic and physical education. The pupil will become a good worker, a good peasant, or a good manager if he is first of all a good citizen. To be a good citizen, you must be a good soldier. To be a good soldier, you must be tough."

I asked the adolescents who danced with joy after they had "shot down" an American plane over Vietnam: "Would you be able to fire at a real plane?"

"Of course. We do target practice at school with real rifles twice a week. And on Sundays we go for practice with our parents."

It is the great family entertainment for the parents on their one day of rest a week. Everyone goes to the shooting range and waits his turn. All of them, from grandparents to children of four or five, are given guns and throw themselves down beside one another to take aim. When the target is hit, it topples over and reveals an ideogram; when all the targets have been hit, the ideograms form a slogan which says: "If the enemy sets foot on our soil we shall crush him." The marksman who misses his target suffers the shame of holding up the appearance of the complete slogan, so he either tries again quickly or makes way for a better shot.

Elsewhere boys make models of fighter planes and torpedo boats. Another game is a kind of military relay race. The school children run and pass to one another a sack stuffed with rags and bearing the word "dynamite." Each child must get around an obstacle course. Two stones mark the banks of a river, and the young revolutionary is supposed to jump across. A rope is stretched between two posts to represent a wall. If the child does not manage to jump across the "river" or trips over the "wall," the "dynamite" explodes and the mission has failed. He can make up for his blunder by falling on his arms to deaden the shock. One of his comrades then takes up the "explosive" and tries to run farther with it.

"Who are your enemies? China is not at war with anyone."

"The enemy is lurking in the shadows, waiting for the moment to attack us. . . ."

". . . We must train so we can destroy the revisionists and the imperialists if they dare to attack us."

"And what if they don't attack you?"

"Revisionism and imperialism are always on the lookout, and we must be ready to fight them at any moment."

"We are all little Red soldiers," a twelve-year-old girl told me, her eyes shining with conviction.

"Who are your greatest enemies, the imperialists or the revisionists?"

"They are both enemies of the people."

Apparently these young Red Guards prefer not to choose. Trembling with pent-up passion, they are prepared to play their part in a war: "If the enemies of the people invade China, our whole school will go to the front to exterminate the aggressor."

Where would this mysterious aggressor come from? From the East? There are some signs that indicate this—the little Red Guards keep up a sustained correspondence with their comrades in North Vietnam, Cambodia and Laos, "who are fighting with all their might against American imperialism." But there are other signs that the enemy is in the Northwest. Brochures printed in growing numbers stir up hatred of the Soviet Union.

At school children are taught to shout "Stick 'em up!" and "Don't move!" in Russian. They do not seem to know how to say it in English. In fact, the training is specialized. Young Chinese learn to shoot down American planes and to take Russian soldiers prisoner.

Classroom time is not enough; exercises are organized at night. The teachers go from house to house, waking up their pupils and taking them out by moonlight along mountain paths to round up and arrest a "counter-revolutionary," a "spy" or a "parachutist." The case has been quoted in the press of a school in Fukien province on the Hungchi peninsula whose pupils mounted guard day and night and patrolled the coast, taking part for real in the fight against the soldiers of the Kuomintang entrenched offshore on the island of Matsu.

Thanks to the Cultural Revolution and his ability to keep up the obsession with guerrilla warfare, Mao was able to re-create a climate comparable to that which he recalled with such nostalgia from the period before 1949. He remobilized his country in pursuit of an enemy who is continually being reinvented.

The school system has also inherited an iron discipline from the Yenan period. As in Kang-ta in 1936, the pupils are grouped into squads, platoons and companies; they learn how to handle weapons. And around five o'clock, when lessons are over, the pupils go home in columns of threes, marching with the perfect precision achieved by daily training. It is true that a visiting delegation never arrives unexpectedly, but even if the drill is brushed up even more for foreigners, the important thing is that the desire to put on this show is there. The visitors cannot think it is just a show, when, a quarter of an hour after they leave the school, they pass squads drilled to the same military precision marching down the road.

The same rigor reigns in the classroom. It is useless to look for examples of "non-directive teaching"; the pupils write to their masters' dictation in exercise books which are kept in excellent condition. They speak only when spoken to. Whenever you ask them a question, you have the feeling they are reciting; memory, which is given so little importance in the West, retains all its prestige in China. The truth, whether expressed by the master or the book, admits no imprecision. It is an order, a password, which must be learned correctly and repeated. It is rigorous and demanding, like a military handbook.

Thinking with the Hands

The secondary school at the Two Bridges people's commune houses workshops where teachers, workers and pupils work side by side.

In the first one, the electronics workshop, transistors and diode valves are made.* In the other one, they bend metal tubes under a blow-lamp to make tables, shelves, stepladders and chairs; most will be sold in shops but some of them will be used to furnish the classrooms next term.

"Before the Cultural Revolution," the official of the commune's revo-

---

*In other secondary schools in the suburbs of Peking they even make triode valves and printed circuits.

lutionary committee explained, "the pupils did not respect manual work. Now we have restored its honor. When they tear their trousers, they mend them themselves. If they break a seat, they repair it. They get used to being of service to one another. They cut one another's hair. In this way they are applying Chairman Mao's instruction: *Let us rely on our own forces.*"

In a carpenter's shop, the children make props for their school plays. A sheet-metal shop turns out sills for a car factory, which has sent a technician to the school to supervise the punching, filing, assembly and galvanizing.

All pupils spend one day a week in these workshops. But agriculture is not forgotten—half a day is spent in the kitchen garden, which provides vegetables for the school canteen.

In addition to this, at harvest time and at sowing time the boys and girls are sent into the fields to help with the work. They devote about one month every year to this.* All this naturally assumes that the students will call on the workers and peasants for help, and that they in turn will share the responsibility for educating the children with the professional teachers.** This entry of manual workers into the Chinese educational system is one of the main contributions of the Cultural Revolution.

In those people's communes where there are not enought craft teachers to ensure that schooling is complete, the "half study–half work system" has been introduced. For half the time the children get their practical education in the fields and workshops, where they are taught by the peasants and the workers themselves.

The teaching staff also benefits from other outside contributions. Officials of the People's Militia give courses in military theory and practice. The brigade's accountant teaches arithmetic. A "barefoot doctor" teaches the rudiments of acupuncture and pharmacopoeia.

In the primary school of the Meichiakou people's commune, "education for the class struggle" is dispensed by elderly "peasants," who come along to tell the children of the sufferings of former times. An old woman brings into the classroom the ladle she used to beg with in the "old society." The ladle is passed from hand to hand, as the children shake their heads in disbelief. An old man tells the history of his own family and of the whole village, with a fund of anecdotes. Happiness is relative; it exists by contrast with its opposite.

It is not only the teaching staff which has been revamped, but teaching methods too. Many lessons are given outside the classroom. In the "Dragon's Tea commune" the children learn to grow tea, get rid of insects, treat illnesses

---

*This is on top of a month's holiday in winter (in January) and a month's holiday in the summer (from the end of July to the end of August), although the latter is usually also spent in the fields.
**In the secondary school in the Cuban Friendship Commune, the factory workers and the peasants make up almost half the teaching staff.

and pick the leaves. In a rice commune near Shanghai the children are shown the various stages of rice-growing; mathematics lessons are taught in the fields—the pupils learn to measure the fields and to calculate the volume of a dungheap, the capacity of the granaries, and the harvest forecasts. In a fishing commune they are taught to fish, to make and repair boats and nets, to grow mussels and algae; engineering and accounting are also taught.

Commune officials and the part-time and professional teachers are full of praise for the new system. Before 1966 mathematics was taught, but the children were never told how to do the accounts for their production units; children who had learned chemistry never knew how to use ammonia. Now the children get on happily in jobs they once loathed, like repairing electricity faults, dismantling a switch and putting it together again, hammering metal on an anvil, binding textbooks. From the age of seven they practice to become complete producers as well as citizens. In this way China hopes to provide herself with a mass of qualified workers, of which there is still a most serious shortage, and to maintain a professional versatility which will solve all problems that crop up with great ease.

A Simplifying Revolution

One can find the origins of the new Chinese education system—or at least its broad principles—within Mao's personal experience: "I finally left primary school," Mao said, "when I was thirteen, and began to work long hours on the farm, helping the hired laborer, doing the full labor of a man during the day and at night keeping books for my father. Nevertheless, I succeeded in continuing my reading, devouring everything I could find. . . ."

Mao said one could leave school very early and continue to learn outside. Culture is both personal and social, something in which schooling does not play the essential role. Also, China needs producers, and lowering the age at which one leaves school expands the labor force. And finally, it is better to give a little education to all Chinese than a lot of education to a few Chinese.

We did not find a single leader or teacher who was worried about the way education had been held back when the Cultural Revolution closed the schools for a long time and completely changed the way they functioned. It was better, they felt, for pupils to lose a few years' schooling in order to get the education system onto a healthy footing. In the Third World education is like an army which consists entirely of generals and ordinary soldiers. The way to achieve development, rather than prestige, is to train warrant officers and corporals. Mao understood this very clearly.

In 1960 he was already advocating a reduction in primary and secondary schooling from twelve to nine years.* One of the famous Sixteen Points of August 8, 1966 concerns the shortening of the period of schooling. As a first step, each brigade must have its primary school, providing five years of education, and each commune must have its secondary school, providing a first period of two years, the second period to be introduced as and when possible.**

As Mei the teacher told me, "We reckoned that the education being given to children was much too ambitious. They were being made to take in large doses of literature, mathematics and history, of which they remembered practically nothing. Now we confine ourselves to teaching simple things, which we repeat over and over again until they really know them. And they remember best the things that are most concrete."

The mathematics, physics and chemistry textbooks have been replaced by photocopied coursebooks with lessons which take examples from everyday life and into which are slipped snippets of abstract knowledge, interspersed with songs and instructions on how to put on a play or how to draw a peasant at work in the fields. The cardinal rule is that education should involve what is economically useful. Any knowledge which is not practical is useless and harmful, for it tends to restore the class esoterism of the Confucian period.

Teaching must have its roots in the soil where the child lives. This is why the Classics are proscribed. They created a literary culture to which the worker, with his bare feet and calloused hands, had no access. They provided a game involving scholarly references which the children of the privileged classes played with ease and skill, while the children of the people tried desperately, but in vain, to join in. Here too, Mao drew a lesson from his own experience. In 1936 he told Edgar Snow how, resisting his father's pressure, he preferred practical books and stories to the great works of classical literature. "This annoyed my father, who wanted me to master the Classics, especially after he was defeated in a lawsuit due to an apt Classical quotation used by his adversary in the Chinese court. I used to cover up the window of my room late at night so that my father would not see the light. In this way I read a book called *Words of Warning (Shen Shih Wei-yen)*, which I liked very much. The authors, a number of old reformist scholars, thought that the weakness of China lay in her lack of Western appliances—railways, telephones, telegraphs and steamships—and wanted to have them introduced

---

*Before the Cultural Revolution primary schooling for the most part lasted six years—four years for the first period and two years for the second. Secondary schooling also lasted six years—two periods of three years each.

**The year 1972 saw the reappearance here and there, most notably in Peking itself, of the second period of secondary education. The period of schooling is thus only two or three years shorter than it was before the Cultural Revolution. But meanwhile seven-year education has become general throughout the country.

into the country. My father considered such books a waste of time. He wanted me to read something practical, like the Classics, which could help him in winning lawsuits."

Course without Obstacles

One of the most spectacular demands of the Cultural Revolution was for the abolition of "diplomas," "marks," "examinations" and "competition," which were termed the "vestiges of the old bureaucracy." We were surprised to hear these abhorred terms being used by people we spoke to, as if they had regained their prestige. Only primary school pupils with "diplomas" can go to the secondary schools; only secondary school pupils with "diplomas" can go on to universities. The pupils are given "marks" for their work throughout the year, and each term they have to take two "examinations." It is the end-of-term examinations, just before the summer and winter holidays, which are the most important; they last for four days in July and January. So have diplomas and examinations taken their place in the educational system once again?

The explanations we were given revealed some embarrassment. "Excesses were committed during the Cultural Revolution. Experience has shown that we must go back to a middle way, but don't think we've gone back purely and simply to the old system."

"But nonetheless you do evaluate the day's work?"

"Yes, but we've dropped marks in favor of signs which spur the pupils on to do better. On a bad piece of work the teachers write a quotation from Chairman Mao: *Be energetic and resolute. Strive to seize victory*. On a good piece of work, they draw a red flag at the top and write the slogan *Faithfulness to Chairman Mao*."

They seem to want to preserve the stimulus of emulation without falling into the excesses of competition. This is achieved in a curious way. The pupils are paired for their examinations and in their day-to-day school life. A mediocre pupil will be paired with a good one, whom he is exhorted "not only to catch up with, but to pass." They are judged together at the examination, in which they are allowed to help one another.

"One another? But surely it's only the stronger who can help the weaker."

"Oh, no," I was told. "You mustn't think that. You always have need of someone weaker than yourself."

Similar precautions are taken in sports. Teams meet on the football field and the volleyball court "not so that one beats the other, but so each can improve his performance through playing the other." At the end of the match, there is no announcement of which team has won. Each team knows perfectly well, but keeps the result to itself—the winners are discreet enough not to glory in their victory.

It is the same in school, where results are not announced. But if the examinations seem hardly any different from those in the West (we saw corrected and marked papers), they decide nothing in themselves. They aim to keep a check on what has been learned, not to judge the qualities and future of pupils. The virtues of the "soldier of the revolution" will count for much more in the end than the examinations.

Examinations have not been abolished, but their importance has been downgraded. They still serve as a means of keeping a check on knowledge and sustaining the pupils' energy. But like the knowledge they measure, examinations are designed to satisfy the needs of society, which implies the removal of any obstacle that prevents the group from remaining a group throughout its school career.

Diplomas, age limits, staying back a year, boarding and favoritism—there are so many routine obstacles in school that give sons and daughters of the bourgeoisie an advantage and put children from a culturally impoverished background at a disadvantage. One year just before the Cultural Revolution, twenty-eight of the thirty-three children who left Meichiakou primary school did not make it into secondary school. "All of them came from the class of poor and middle peasants. The five who made it were all children of rich or moderately rich peasants and cadres."

Now staying back a year has been abolished, and all children who complete their primary schooling are admitted to secondary schools. There has been an increase in the number of secondary schools—there is at least one for each commune—and the pupils do not have to board; those who live within six miles of their school walk or bicycle, and those who live farther away are brought in by brigade trucks. These measures, in addition to the radical simplification of the teaching, probably help to bring about "equal opportunity" and to simplify the social structure.

The Teaching Profession after the Cultural Revolution

The Cultural Revolution has affected "traditional" teachers more than any other social group. It has taken the responsibility of education away from them. China applies the principle better than other countries that school is made not for the teachers, but for those to be taught—and all the people are, have been or will be taught. The masters get their orders from peasants and workers. Gone is the superior status of the teaching profession; the authority to which the teachers are subordinated is determined by "the general consultation of the masses," who are better suited than any to "detecting the way the revolutionary wind blows."

The revolutionary committees to which the schools report seemed to us to be dominated by a type of man who was very different from the traditional teacher—the proletarian intellectual. Whether worker or peasant, he never beat about the bush—he spoke with the authority he drew from his ideological training. As they sat around this crude, self-confident figure, with his brush cut, his clean, sharp face and his lively eyes, the masters seemed humble by comparison. They looked at him before speaking, and were clearly under his orders. The first contact between the traditional teachers and these propagandists of Mao Tse-tung thought must have been pretty rough!

The combination of permanent staff and casuals has not been without its ups and downs. An official of a revolutionary committee told us that the best teachers, those whose experience was the most profitable and who interested the children most, were the amateurs. How could the professionals not feel bitter? The new education puts the professionals in a position of inferiority. In some schools the peasants are not content just to give lessons. They inspect the full-time teachers by sitting in on classes. In other schools it is the military who play the main role.

No attempt was made to hide from us the fact that the arrival in the schools en masse of these hastily anointed "teachers" had met with great opposition from the teaching profession. The traditional teachers had started by "bombarding the newcomers with jibes," calling them "illiterates" who only knew how to "look after cows," "tramps and beggars who knew only a few characters," "peasants who carried hatchets in their belts and knew how to run piggeries rather than schools." But in the end the jeering stopped; the established masters finally acknowledged their new colleagues' qualities "and often their superiority."

There is no difference in status or salary between the new teachers and the old ones. They are in the same category as agricultural workers and are paid according to the work points system.

Wherever there is a tendency to create an intellectual caste, it is ruthlessly smashed. "Our aim," we were told by a stern-looking propagandist of Mao Tse-tung thought, "is to use education to strengthen the dictatorship of the proletariat."

"Are the old teachers *a priori* suspect?"

"No, not all of them. Because they've been brought up and educated in the old society, many were not free to become proletarian revolutionaries. Today, with good will they can make amends for this."

If the good will is lacking, there is always the prospect of "reeducation." It is reasonable to suppose that good will has generally been forthcoming.

The Dialectic of the Master and the Pupil

Here too one can see traces of Mao Tse-tung's personal experience: "My Chinese teacher belonged to the stern-treatment school. He was harsh and severe, frequently beating his students. Because of this I ran away from the school when I was ten." Did Mao want to spare the children of tomorrow the suffering he endured as a child?

"Were you afraid of your teachers before the Cultural Revolution?" I asked the young Red Guards in Nanking.

One, a girl of thirteen, said: "Before, we never dared to criticize our teachers. Now we don't deny ourselves this right, and at the end of each lesson we criticize one another. But we do it in good heart because we're working for the revolution; we all have to learn something, we all have to teach something."

The Cultural Revolution has meant that children no longer see their teachers as sacred beings. Nowadays, the children, who are still pure, feel themselves worthy of purifying the adults. There is nothing that makes them prouder than to be called upon to "reeducate" their teachers. A communist of thirteen said: "The teachers used to prepare their lessons in an office, smoking cigarettes and drinking tea. Now we prepare them together. The teachers talk less, and we understand them better."

That is what we were told. Everywhere we went we saw respect for the teachers and order in the classroom. There is not necessarily any contradiction here; discipline can be agreed upon, obedience can be criticism. I would be prepared to bet, however, that in the minds of most children the dialectic was something less subtle. In other words, the teacher is no longer the dispenser of knowledge—and consequently of power.

The Romanization of the Orthography

"The Vietnamese did well to adopt the Roman alphabet such a long time ago," Chou En-lai told me. "At that time the number of people who knew the ideograms was infinitesimal. When new social strata came to be educated they were not troubled by the old alphabet and they made much more rapid progress. But we've waited far too long. We tried to Romanize the orthography in the fifties, but all who were taught it and upon whom we relied for the teaching of others were firmly attached to the ideograms. There were so many, and as we already had many things to change, we had to postpone this reform."

In the Yenan period, when the Red Army was looking for a more manageable vehicle for mass instruction, they worked out an alphabet of twenty-eight letters which was supposed to reproduce all the phonemes in Chinese; it was called *latin-hua*. It was tried out on school children in Paoan. The results were never made known. Again in the fifties it was trumpeted that the orthography was going to be Romanized in order to help with mass education. The reform failed before it really got going; as Chou En-lai explained, it came too late. But it was also because it came too soon; spoken Chinese had to be unified before it could be given a phonetic orthography. The ideograms were the only link among people who did not understand each other because their pronunciations were so different. To break this link would have been to Balkanize China. Universal education was assigned the task of spreading Peking Chinese.*

Kuo Mo-jo assured me that Romanization was now in sight. A uniform pronunciation was almost an established fact, and it would then be possible to move on to the alphabet stage. The old poet spoke of these prospects with a serene certainty, as if he felt his country was being borne along by history.

"Elitism" under Fire

The desire for "equal educational opportunity," which is the rallying call at teachers' congresses and political meetings in all Western countries (*Chancengleichheit* in Western Germany; *égalité des chances* in France), has been proclaimed throughout the Chinese revolution. In order to achieve it, it seems that Mao formed the maxim that "there will be equality of opportunity only if there is equality of standards; education must be leveled, since education must not be allowed to continue making society into a hierarchy."

Mandarins, mandarinate: the West borrowed these terms from China because she possessed—to the point of caricature—characteristics which the West recognized in itself to a lesser degree. Now the Chinese have done away with the one feature which had become symbolic of their country in the eyes of the rest of the world, and which doubtless remains in existence in every other country.

The Chinese have diagnosed in their own system all the drawbacks of the French system of education of which we have only recently become aware. And they have not flinched at taking the most radical of measures to remove them: the handicap suffered by children disadvantaged by birth or cultural background, the obsession with examinations, with competition, with the

---

*Pronunciation is still far from uniform, and the process has been going on since 1920. In addition, it is worth noting that the Japanese, who in many ways are so modern, have not forsaken ideograms.

Baccalauréat, the tendency toward abstraction in everything, the esoteric nature of culture, the sclerosed nature of teaching, the passivity of the pupils and the conservative corporate attitude of the teachers.

In the West the liberal system has tolerated the existing situation as well as the privileges of the establishment. In Eastern Europe, the communist system has shown itself incapable of preventing the reemergence of the "New Class," which Milovan Djilas has denounced and which is a class of leaders as closed and jealous of their privileges as any in the past. China is determined to destroy the hereditary establishment and to create men who are not heirs themselves and leave no heirs behind them. Will what has hitherto failed become possible in China?

The Cultural Revolution had the effect of making society more homogeneous. Schools came under the control of the producers; production units began to resemble schools. Workers or peasants rule at all levels; this removes any inferiority complexes that true proletarians might have, and makes those who are not true proletarians feel guilty about it. The technicians, engineers and cadres must now come from the ranks, like all those people whom the Cultural Revolution raised to leading posts. It is from the landless peasants and unskilled laborers that the brigades and workshops have come to expect innovations. The workers are constantly being encouraged to climb the ladder, but it is seen as a form of collective promotion rather than as a solitary climb. One of the most familiar pictures for the foreign visitor to China—either in reality or on propaganda hoardings—is of a group of workers huddled around their instructor in the shade of a mulberry tree, at the gates of a factory, on the edge of a field, or on the bridge of a cargo ship sailing up the Huang-po; they are listening intently, repeating what he says and taking part in a most moving and passionate session of self-improvement.

But for how long? In the long run, can this education, which is so simplified that it seems to be nothing more than professional training and political indoctrination, fulfill the hopes which the leaders have placed in it? Does its extension to the broadest strata of a backward peasant class make up for the lowering of its quality? Will the years that were lost because of the Cultural Revolution enable this rural country—which has been mobilized but at the cost of being turned upside down—to make a new "Great Leap Forward," only this time successfully? Will education, once it has been purged of "elitism" and placed under the control of the workers, peasants and soldiers who are already familiar with production work and ideological incantation, be able to fulfill its vocation of creating a new man, a worker who is morally, physically and intellectually fit to produce? We shall no doubt have to wait a long time before we are able to answer these questions, since China has staked so much in all these directions. Meanwhile, will China's children complain of having been deprived of their childhood? Or will they continue to be so sure of their cause—which will become that of successive generations—that "the triumph of the world revolution" will be assured?

When we left "Mountain Village of the Mei Family," the leading officials of the Revolutionary Committee, the peasants, the barefoot teachers, and the kindergarten mistress shook our hands warmly and applauded us when the cars moved off. The children sang in chorus: "We are the heirs of the revolutionary cause."

8

"Proletarianized" Universities

The Most Famous University

No foreigner had been in China's most famous university, the Peita in Peking, since the "Chinese May." It was at this university on May 25, 1966 that the first *ta-tzu-pao** was posted—the signal for the Cultural Revolution. Mao probably wrote it himself. Some days later, all lectures were stopped—definitively, for the Peita, when it tentatively opened its doors four years later in September 1970, had become a quite different university.

Mao chose this ancient and prestigious nursery of scholars and men of letters, the hybrid flower of Chinese civilization and Western knowledge, as the epicenter of the debate which was to shake China out of the torpor of *embourgeoisement*.

For months on end, two student groups confronted one another. One, guided from afar by the Great Helmsman, used inflammatory posters and violent demonstrations to denounce "feudal" teaching, the "revisionism" of the leading class and the *trahison des clercs* of those who had been cut off from the proletariat. The other group, which was being given behind-the-scenes encouragement by Liu Shao-chi, was trying to counterattack in the name of the order, the Party and the system that had been imposed on China since 1949. They exchanged not only arguments, but also blows and shots; in the scuffles at Peita many students and teachers were injured, some seriously.**

---

*Wall newspaper or big-character poster (TRANSLATOR'S NOTE).

**A female philosophy teacher, Nieh Yuan-tzu, a member of the Peking Revolutionary Committee, launched an attack on the President of the University when the call was given by Chen Po-ta, and she was seriously wounded on March 28, 1968 by bullets from the opposing faction.

125

The "Mao Tse-tung thought workers' teams" had to intervene to separate the two sides and give victory to the right camp.

The park bears no trace of these violent scenes. Bamboo trees and weeping willows screen the turned-up roofs of the pavilions; finely sculpted friezes run between the lacquered wood colonnades; pink lotuses and giant waterlilies float on the lakes. How could this luxurious paradise—which looks like the model for an old silk print—have been the scene of violent rioting? But there in the middle of the campus stands, rather incongruously, a gigantic plaster statue of Mao; on the pedestal a slogan in gold on a gules background says: "Brilliant University of Peking, Let Us Unite to Build the New University. . . . Dare to think, Dare to act, Dare to try." Those who welcomed us at the door of the horn-shaped porch, which was covered with old glazed tiles, had seen the struggle that had been waged in the name of the university. First, there was the Vice-President of the Peita University Revolutionary Committee, Chou Pei-yuan, a man in his sixties with aristocratic features, silvery-gray hair, gold-rimmed spectacles, a discreet hearing aid like the ones they make in Tientsin, long, delicate hands and an elegant smile. He spoke perfect English, for he had studied at the University of California and had taught at the University of Chicago. He spoke with great discretion of his past errors, of the agonized reappraisal provoked by the Red Guards and the wall newspapers, and of his conversion to the proletarian line. The repentant mandarin. An interpreter whispered to us that the President of the University Revolutionary Committee was a soldier, so it was thought we would "get along better with this man."

Standing beside Chou Pei-yuan was the leader of the Mao Tse-tung thought propaganda team, Tang Yung-yu, a young printing worker who had played an important role in the Cultural Revolution. With his comrades—workers from the various factories in Peking and peasants from the surrounding people's communes—he had occupied the university after the dramatic clashes of the spring of 1968 in order to "help the students to unite," to "eliminate the bad elements," and to "take leadership of the movement." He spoke incessantly and with great conviction. Chou Pei-yuan, who was old enough to be his grandfather, looked on deferentially, turning to him whenever we asked a question and patiently waiting for him to finish answering it. Around them stood other leaders of the propaganda team; professors of philosophy, history, Chinese and political science; students; and Red Guards, who stood out because of their armbands.

Before the Storm

This team did not ignore the university's past, but chose to depict it for our benefit in general, sarcastic terms. In the eighteenth century the park—

its lakes edged with hibiscus—was the home of a favorite of Chien-lung*;
Lord Macartney was a guest there. In the nineteenth century Yenching
University was established there, and this provided an "elite" education—in
English—for a handful of Chinese students. Its last rector, Leighton Stuart,
was also the last United States Ambassador in Peking. "Peita University is a
product of American cultural aggression," we were told. The same description is given of Peking's other university, the Tsinghua Polytechnic University, which was founded in 1911 with American compensation from the Boxer
War. Until 1949 Peita, like Tsinghua, educated "high officials and reactionary scholars, in the service of the Kuomintang clique."

Between 1949 and 1965 "the advent of the People's Republic hadn't
changed very much." The sons of China's great families were no longer being
educated on their own, but "about sixty percent of the students were still of
non-proletarian origin; they came from the *ancienne bourgeoisie*, from an
intellectual background, or from the new class of bureaucrats and high-
ranking cadres. Hardly more than a third came from the peasantry and the
working class, although these classes constituted nine-tenths of the population."

So, was the pre-Maoist social system still in existence—within this gem
of China's imperial past—after seventeen years of Maoism? Was a new class of
mandarins being formed, like the old one? "Rector Lu Ping, in collusion with
his friend the Mayor of Peking, Peng Chen, kept up the mandarin traditions;
with the support of the traitor Liu Shao-chi, the revisionist clique which had
usurped power in the university was sabotaging the orders of Chairman Mao.
It was adopting a method of teaching and syllabuses similar to those used in
Europe, the United States and the U.S.S.R.,"—Tang Yung-yu lumped them
all together. Of course, "bourgeois intellectuals dominated the Party Committee; there wasn't a worker or a peasant on it. . . . On the orders of the
traitor Liu Shao-chi and the revisionists in Moscow and of the Kuomintang,
the university's renegade clique relied for support on the enemies of the
proletariat. It spread perverse ideas. It prevented the serious study of Marx
and Mao. It encouraged students to become scholars, to achieve fame and to
take delight in the private possession of intellectual knowledge."

The inheritors of mandarin culture used the examinations and diplomas
as a way of keeping out or discouraging all those who had not benefited from
the same heritage. Had not a girl student of worker origin committed suicide
"because she only got a 3 in a test"?** The marking system was so important
that "it was harmful to the mental balance of the young." Cultural relations
with foreign countries had given added strength to this system. "The best

---

*The emperor who received the first English embassy in 1793.
**The marks go from 1 to 5.

students were sent abroad; they were immersed in capitalist or revisionist ideas and then when they returned they were entrusted with posts of power and responsibility." In short, the whole system "tended to discriminate against students of proletarian origin, to favor and confer privilege on the children of the bourgeoisie and to restore capitalism." Rector Lu Ping pretended he had forgotten that Mao had twice come to Peita between 1918 and 1920 to spread Marxism-Leninism, "sowing revolutionary thought and writing the most glorious page in the university's history."

Furthermore, the traitor Liu Shao-chi had concealed what should have been the two highlights in the history of the university since 1949—the gift of two calligraphies by Chairman Mao; in May 1950, "Let us unite to build a new China," and 1958, "Education must be in the service of proletarian politics and combined with political study." Nothing less than the Cultural Revolution was required for the revolutionary students to take cognizance of these precious gifts. But everything is costly in the long run; these acts of treason led the revolutionary students to demand nothing short of insurrection. The *ta-tzu-pao* put up in the university on May 25, 1966 and broadcast and published in the press on Chairman Mao's personal instruction on June 1 launched them into the attack; the mandarinal social structure, which had been protected and then reestablished over a period of seventeen years, came crashing down.

After the Storm

Fifty-one months without any teaching being done meant a total breakdown in the education of the intellectual elite. In 1971 higher education started up again here and there in an experimental way; it was the same in other areas of Chinese cultural life. Peita University took in a quarter of the students it was able to accommodate,* and it was one of the few university establishments which reopened.**

What other country would dare to cut out its higher education for four to six years? Nothing gives a better indication of the strength of revolutionary conviction than this deliberate sacrifice. If there is one point on which ideologists of both Left and Right—both developed and underdeveloped countries—agree, it is the fact that priority must be given to educating qualified engineers, technicians and doctors. Mao made a head-on attack on what he saw as a myth that could ruin the revolution: learning and

---

*In the academic year 1970–71, the first of the new era, 2,677 students—or "new students"—were taken, although Peita has the capacity to take ten or twelve thousand.
**About ten opened in Peking in 1971; about fifty remained closed.

scholarship cannot be a privileged, protected sector, a neutral zone. If the revolution is to be total—and it must be, or it will not survive long—it must forcefully assert its precedence over scholarship.

"Haven't you paid an enormously high price for your new methods?" I asked Chou Pei-yuan.

"No," he replied boldly. "The price is low for the transformation we've achieved. There was no way of avoiding it. We had to do everything in the opposite way. We wanted to educate proletarian intellectuals who would love the people, come from the people, and return to the people. We really had to turn the teaching methods upside down, since their aims were quite the reverse of what they had been. The aim we set before ourselves was to apply in all things Chairman Mao's instruction: *Higher education must produce workers with a socialist culture. It must educate men who prepare the people for revolution.*"

"I can understand that the revolution changes the content of literary and legal studies, but surely in the sciences and in technology the content must always be the same; how could the Cultural Revolution change trigonometry or science?"

"At first sight, the sciences and technology appear to be unchanged. But they're not seen in the same way; the approach is different. The new students no longer assimilate them in order to become scholars, to be placed above others like aristocrats, but in order to become builders of factories and organizers of production. They now know that they are all making their contribution to the development of the revolution in China."

"Isn't the main obstacle to these new developments the teachers?"

"Of course. It's mainly because of them that courses had to be stopped. They weren't ready for their roles as 'new teachers' for the 'new students.' They were in the habit of treating the students like recording machines. The break with the past has been difficult for them to make."

A third of the staff of the universities* have now been "reeducated" and are teaching and running laboratories; a third are being "reeducated" in the "May Seventh Schools" or are working in the fields; the other third have decided to work in the "social factory"—while keeping their links with the university, they go out and teach in production units.

"The teachers can teach again when they've shown they understand and accept the spirit of the Cultural Revolution—that's to say, when they've adopted the mass line. If it seems that they've not learned how to keep contact with the people, they're sent back for more reeducation and are replaced by men from the ranks. But above all, it is the students who teach the teachers, in accordance with Mao's principle: *The officers learn from the soldiers*. Thanks to the Cultural Revolution, we no longer have 'tape-recorder students.' All students are invited to put their spirit of invention into action and to educate

---

*In theory there are 2,133 of them, almost as many teachers as students.

one another morally, intellectually and physically in order to become better servants of socialism."

Rapid results are expected from these new methods and especially from this new attitude. Higher education has been shortened—a maximum of two or three years instead of the five or six before the Cultural Revolution. "Half the traditional curriculum is quite sufficient. One must get to the essentials and not waste time on subtleties which are forgotten immediately after the examination."

While the universities were closing their doors, the students were passing from the stage of being enthusiastic Red Guards to the possibly less exciting stage of "manual labor" and "reeducation among the masses" in the rural areas. Chairman Mao summed up the principles of the reform in 1968: "The universities must first of all be technical and scientific establishments providing a political education. The period of study will be reduced. The students will have to complete a stage of practical education at the grass-roots level first, and then they will return to it periodically."

This decisive intervention by Chairman Mao was transmitted through all the information media; the struggles between the various factions which had divided the student body ceased, as if by magic. *Roma locuta . . .*

Rigorous Selection

"We're still a very long way from making the university accessible to everyone," Vice-President Chou Pei-yuan told me.

"When do you anticipate that higher education will be available to everyone?"

"We don't anticipate it; we know perfectly well that this will be impossible for a long time to come. For decades only a very small proportion of young people will be able to go to the universities."

So the candidates have to be selected. But on what basis? Examinations? Competitions? This recruitment procedure led to the universities being condemned by Chairman Mao. Age? This would still favor those candidates from the most advantaged backgrounds.

Three conditions of admission were laid down:

1. The successful candidate must "possess a satisfactory ideology, have studied Mao Tse-tung thought in depth and have applied it in everyday life, know how to establish contact with the masses, and want to serve the proletariat";

2. He or she must "have acquired—after his or her secondary studies—an average of three years' practical experience* in a factory, in the

---

*"Five years is better, but in exceptional cases two is enough."

country, or in the army, and preferably in two of these three." Although as a general rule one has to have "completed first-degree education* and if possible second-degree education,"** workers, peasants and soldiers can be exempted from this: veterans are not required to meet any knowledge or age requirements.

3. Candidates must "have a solid constitution": *mens sana in corpore sano* is not a principle which is simply paid lip-service—it is in everyday use. Delicate constitutions have no place in higher education. In fact, from one end of China to the other, not once did we see a sickly or weak student; all the boys were strong and all the girls were healthy. The Spartans threw sickly children into a pit; the Chinese are content to keep them out of the universities.

A Maoist faith, practical experience in a job, and a well-built body— even these three together are not enough to ensure that one will be chosen. More than genuine selection criteria, these are conditions which it should not be difficult to satisfy. So how does the selection procedure—which to judge by the numbers *** must be either very thoughtful or very chancy—work in practice?

The explanations we were given boiled down to the following:

The young people who want to go on to a university announce their candidature in the production unit where they are working after they receive their secondary diplomas; during their time in the production unit their merit is judged by the way they work and behave toward their comrades.

At the end of the three years, "the popular masses" state their opinion of the candidate in the factory, rural brigade or military unit at meetings, where a clapometer is used.

The revolutionary committee of the unit, enlightened by the attitude of the masses, pronounces its decision on the candidates and decides whether or not to send them on to the university.

The revolutionary committee of the university makes the final decision. Does it perhaps bring in academic norms which the "broad masses" could have ignored? No, for it too is made up of representatives of the masses; workers, soldiers, peasants, and the representatives of the "new students"— themselves workers, soldiers or peasants—are in an overwhelming majority over the teachers.

At each stage it is the view of the masses which prevails.

I put my question in another way: "Do these three criteria all have equal status, or does one predominate over the other?" The head of the propaganda

---

*Six years, from age seven to age thirteen.
**Three or four years—from age thirteen to age sixteen or seventeen—depending on the school.
***One million students before the Cultural Revolution; barely a few tens of thousands six years after it began, against several tens of millions of young people with secondary diplomas.

team, sensing from my insistence that I was skeptical, replied promptly: "These criteria are right, since they are inspired by Mao Tse-tung thought."

One of his comrades, perhaps thinking that this arrogant *petitio principii* was not in itself consistent with Mao Tse-tung thought, added: "We're only at the beginning. We still lack concrete experience. The only thing we're sure of is that this new method seems better than the traditional method of competition. But we've still got a lot to do before we achieve our objective. We'd be pleased to hear your criticisms and suggestions."

While we were walking in the park, I continued the conversation in English with Chou Pei-yuan. His answers left no room for ambiguity. It seemed that almost all the boys and girls who finish their secondary education are in good health, and all of them are obliged to take a job. So, almost all of them meet the second and third requirements. The only condition which can be evaluated is the one concerning Maoist thought—the candidates must have unshakeable conviction. "Politics first,"* he said with a smile, as we walked around the lake.

The workers, peasants and soldiers, guided by the Party, choose from among their own ranks the best witnesses and best apostles of the new faith, so that they can go on to strengthen it still further and intensify their learning with it.

This system has naturally transformed recruitment. At Peita, where thirty percent of the students were proletarians before the Cultural Revolution, in the new era of real Maoist education a hundred percent** of the students are proletarians; the "new students" are, without exception, workers, peasants or soldiers and themselves the sons and daughters of workers, peasants or soldiers.

"What has become of the students who were in the middle of their studies in May 1966?"

"They were sent away in June 1966. A certain number of them remained to edit wall posters, lead enquiries, and take part in colloquia on the reform of education. Others, who became Red Guards, propagated the Cultural Revolution throughout China; but almost all of them were sent into the country or into the factories."

What are their chances of leaving these places? University places are costly. We were told that they were reserved for proletarian candidates who had not been infected for however short a time by passing through the mandarin university before 1966, but that in a few years' time "they'll have managed to raise their level of political consciousness sufficiently" and may be able "to be readmitted to the university." If Chou Pei-yuan is half opening

---

*In English in the original (TRANSLATOR'S NOTE).

**The Peking press indicates that eighty to ninety percent of the "new students" at Tsinghua University, the capital's other university, are of proletarian origin.

this door, it is more out of caution than conviction. In fact, all other routes to higher education have been firmly closed; only the proletarian route remains open. All criteria except revolutionary ardor have been brushed aside. This is the most crucial effect of the Cultural Revolution.

The Reversal

The Cultural Revolution has brought about the great transfusion. Intellectuals and bourgeois have been made willy-nilly into manual workers by being sent into the fields and factories, and from now on only those who are genuine manual workers will be allowed to become intellectuals. But still, all precautions are being taken to ensure that their proletarian stock protects them from the risk of contracting the intellectuals' illness, which is believing oneself superior to the proletariat. All of them, workers, peasants or soldiers, will reinvigorate themselves among the workers, peasants or soldiers at regular intervals: between secondary school and the university, during their time at the university, after they finish there, and regularly thereafter throughout their lives.

Certainly, even before the Cultural Revolution, periods spent in factories and on farms formed a part of the program, but like the homage of vice to virtue.* Students and teachers tried to get out of it by using all the strength of the mandarinal system. If they did not manage to escape it, it was a bad period which had to be endured in order to acquire a good image or at best a good conscience. Manual and intellectual work remained totally dissociated from each other, and only the latter contributed to education—through books and classes, which passed on "bourgeois" knowledge.

The system is now quite the reverse of this. The future doctor, government official, scientist or artist is not admitted to the university because he seems to be gifted in biology, the law, mathematics or painting; he is admitted because he is the son of a proletarian or a proletarian himself who—during his period of manual work among the proletariat—has shown himself to be a good agent of the proletarian revolution. His scale of values puts the interests of the revolution above knowledge, so that he can devote himself to his studies without losing his sense of direction.

"How were you appointed to your job?" I asked the air hostess who served us iced lemonade or hot tea throughout the journey from Sian to Wuhan.

"Because I was nominated for it," she replied, as she placed a napkin on my table.

---

*Reference to La Rochefoucauld's *"L'hypocrisie est l'hommage que le vice rend à la vertu"* (Translator's Note).

"But did you apply for the job? Did you want to be an air hostess? Did you dream of becoming one when you were a little girl?"

She burst out laughing: "No, never. But I wanted to serve the people. *A revolutionary*, Chairman Mao has said, *must serve the people where the people need him.*"

"So who decided that the people needed you on an aircraft rather than in a factory?"

"The revolutionary committee, on the recommendation of the broad masses enlightened by Mao Tse-tung thought."

She looked at me with her large, innocent eyes as if to say, "It's quite natural. How could it be otherwise?" One must assume, I am sure, that a planning department played its part in enlightening the judgment of the revolutionary committee.

"The broad masses—or the revolutionary committee of your unit—isn't there a risk that they may make a mistake, even if Mao Tse-tung thought is never wrong? Let's say you're prone to get airsick and the one thing you're not cut out for is being an air hostess?"

She laughed beautifully and said: "But that's impossible. A revolutionary doesn't have airsickness!"

Factories and Farms on the Campus

If its rules are not relaxed, Chinese society will undergo an unprecedented change. The barriers between intellectual work and manual work, between the leaders and the led, between the possessors and the dispossessed, will be broken down. Other revolutions have tried to break down these barriers, but they have always been built up again—most notably now in the Soviet Union. In China, will they disappear forever?

The Chinese revolutionaries are making sure that knowledge and learning will never confer privilege on anyone, over and above the grease of machinery and the mud of the paddy-fields. Selection for university in fact amounts to the manual workers choosing other manual workers who will continue with their manual work while they are at the university and return to it afterwards.

Once he has graduated, the student usually returns to the unit he came from originally. He rejoins it better equipped to serve the people, either in a managerial capacity or as a worker who is now able to bring to his job a more highly developed technique. He will always have to be lending a hand with the work; back again among the masses who chose him and who could remove him, he will not be under any temptation to adopt airs or postures of superiority.

We visited the farm and factory on the Peita campus, where teachers and students were taking turns doing the work. The stables and the workshops had been built in former pavilions by the teachers and their pupils. "Theory must be linked with practice." The university brings the village and the factory together within its own walls, which is the best way of putting an end to its isolation in society. So this is how Mao's instruction of July 22, 1966 on replacing the traditional universities by "establishments of applied higher education" is put into practice. All his instructions—to "reduce the period of study," to "educate technical personnel from the ranks of workers," to choose students according to "their experience," to make them "return to production"—are simply intended to persuade the masses to ensure that there is a link between the universities and industry, and this is something which liberal societies have generally discouraged.

The farm and the workshops we saw on this campus were reminiscent of the artificial village at the Petit Trianon, where Marie-Antoinette and her friends played at being shepherds and shepherdesses.

"How can people seriously believe they are in the fields or in a factory when they're obviously surrounded by university buildings?"

"Very easily," Chou Pei-yuan replied. "Even on campus you have to bend low to till the soil, the machines are coated with grease and your hands become calloused."

"Is this link you've established with industry and agriculture just an isolated case, or is it in fact something more general?"

"It's the general rule. Workshops, factories and farms are or will be associated with all the university establishments. They serve as practical guides for the education that is provided and as a guard against the temptation to escape into theory. All the universities that have started up again have a farm or a factory, and sometimes both; but only a few of them have been reopened, precisely because of the difficulties this raised."

In the whole of China before 1966 there were about twenty multi-disciplinary universities like Peita and Tsinghua and three to four hundred small institutions of higher education. No one can say how many there will be in the future, because the instruction Chairman Mao sent the Shanghai machine-tools factory on July 22, 1966 compelled the big factories to create their own institutions of higher education.

"One can easily understand the link between a university where science and technology are predominant and a factory; but where is the link between a university strong in literary and legal studies like Peita and a factory or a farm? Isn't there a risk that the teachers and students will regard these periods of work as an unavoidable nuisance or as a piece of folklore?"

With an expansive gesture, Chou Pei-yuan pointed out a red banner with gold lettering that was hanging on the wall; it said: "Literature must consider society as a whole as its factory." And he then developed this maxim of Chairman Mao: "When history students go into the factory or onto the farm, they ask the workers questions and make investigations so they can come to a better understanding of the exploitation of China before the Liberation."

Professor Su Chi showed us around the four biochemistry workshops of which he was director; they had been built by the students and teachers in a year and a half.

Now they make various anti-parasite powders, an anti-coagulant, insulin, antibiotics and a hemostat—all organic—here they do not seek to "synthesize" anything. Women sitting at small stained tables pour a red powder into large copper basins, stir it with a spoon, and strange deposits collect around the edge.

Revolutionary Utilitarianism

Professor Su Chi showed me a banner which was suspended over a copper cauldron in which a curdled, yellowish liquid was boiling. The banner read: "Education must train workers morally, physically and intellectually in the service of the dictatorship of the proletariat."

"Our university," he said, "must serve as a model for future multidisciplinary universities which will be directed mainly toward the arts, letters, law, economics and politics. The other university in Peking, Tsinghua, will serve as a model for scientific and technological universities. In the same way, the Tachai people's commune must serve as a model for agriculture, and industry must learn from Taching.

"All the poisonous disciplines have been removed from higher education."

"Poisonous—does that mean useless?"

"What's useless is harmful."

"So what are the 'useful' courses now?"

"The 'non-poisonous' courses go from Mao Tse-tung thought to 'revolutionary criticism' via a study of selected extracts from Marx, Engels, Lenin and Stalin, the history of the Chinese communist movement, the history of international communism, and Marxist-Leninist political economics. The students also learn to write."

This piece of information startled us. Would "red hearts" who were illiterate be admitted to the university? No. One has to remember that, like the mandarins of bygone days, today's students never stop learning to write. In their writing classes they use a brush dipped in India ink to paint their ideograms slowly and lovingly, with their heads bowed and their tongues lightly flicking across their lips—a beautiful piece of work.

"Wouldn't ballpoint pens do as well?"

"Absolutely not! Unless the downstrokes and upstrokes are formed very carefully, different ideograms can be confused."

Lessons in physical culture complete the curriculum. There are also special courses in Asiatic and Western languages, Russian, international relations, management, library science, econometrics, philosophy and literature.

There had been a lot of talk during the Cultural Revolution about stopping the teaching of the social sciences, which had the reputation of being harmful, or at least sensitive, subjects. At Peita University they have certainly been rehabilitated. No doubt the teachers had to show that they had undergone a long enough period of "reeducation."

These teaching programs have been gone through with a fine-toothed comb and they are now being taught using radically new methods. The old books have been abandoned; until new ones arrive, photocopied exercise books are used instead. There are no more examinations and there is no more competition; it is methods that are noted and checked above all, and this is done regularly and openly.

Everything possible is done to make education active. Students do not merely read and discuss a poem Mao wrote on war in 1928—a captain of the militia tells them about his campaign experiences. And if a student has to write on the subject "Power grows out of the barrel of a gun," he takes actual examples from the revolutionary history of Africa and Latin America.

The accounts are tempered by a touch of modesty: "At least this is how we try to apply Mao Tse-tung thought in education, but we haven't really mastered it yet. We make mistakes in our work. We've only been doing it for a year, and the universities were closed for over four years before that; we're at the experimental stage. We'd appreciate your criticisms. . . ."

"Isn't the greatest problem getting rid of the traditions of the past?"

"Yes, it is. Getting rid of them while at the same time maintaining them. The only way to overcome these contradictions is to return to the practical. And to do that, more 'three-way alliances' must be set up, so that the students do manual work side by side with the workers and the peasants. We try to experiment, produce and study the class struggle all at the same time. We learn from the experience of peasants, workers and soldiers by doing the same work as they, meanwhile studying our history. Each time, you see, it's a three-way alliance which enables the contradictions to be overcome."

In this way the mystery of the *practical factory*, which extends the university of literary and legal studies into life, is made clear. The scientific and technological university extends naturally into production factories, for which its workshops are a preparation, but it is in the "social factory," the building of the socialist society, that the student of Peita University will be welcomed. There he will be a new man, in "mastery of the work of the masses." Having become a source of socialist inspiration, his task is to prepare the masses for the great aims of the revolution.

"What becomes of the students when they've finished at the university?"

"It's very simple—they go back where they came from."

"Really? You mean, those who show a particular aptitude are not directed toward administration, agriculture, industry, teaching or whatever?"

I was asked to repeat the question; the notion of "aptitude" is as little understood as that of "gifts." The true revolutionary has an aptitude only to serve, and the needs of the unit to which he belongs come before the needs he may feel himself, if he feels any at all. His first duty is to his unit, which has sent him on for higher education more for the benefits it will get for itself than because of any merits it has recognized in him.

When we pressed them, they admitted that of course "some will change their posts and be drafted to do research or become teachers, *in accordance with the state's needs*." But almost all of them have the same destination—the place they came from.

This rule seemed essential to the disposition of manpower. It is a powerful motive for those who choose and for those who are chosen. It seals the union of theory and practice in the destiny of everyone.

These rigorous precautions no doubt explain the high esteem in which "literary" studies are held in China.

As a rule, in socialist countries scientists are treated with much more care and respect than literary men, who are held to be potential troublemakers. In China it is the men and women of the arts who run the show. Even on the farm and in the factory they play a vital role. They edit the critical articles in enterprise newspapers. They write the *ta-tzu-pao*. They take notes of the workers' ideas; they write reports and undertake investigations. They organize the Mao Tse-tung thought study periods. On holidays they organize groups to put on plays. They are the catalysts of the revolution.

It is clear that the universities of arts and letters are little more than Party cadre schools. When we asked if cadre schools proper still existed, they didn't understand. But why should they, since these new universities fulfill exactly the same function?

9

"Let Us Revolutionize Scientific and Technological Research"

Questions Which Have Remained Unanswered for a Long Time

What role does the Maoist regime plan for research? Did the Cultural Revolution attack research the same way it attacked the other areas of intellectual life, or did it pass by this highly prized area of activity with the idea that it should remain undisturbed at all costs? In the other communist countries research workers have the privilege of being aristocrats of scholarship. Yet the nature of the Cultural Revolution was to attack all privileges, to drown the aristocracies, and to return the intellectuals to the ranks. It would seem then that a fundamental incompatibility would exist between research and revolution.

I was asking myself these questions when I went to the Academy of Sciences in Peking. We asked questions about the situation in other sectors of Chinese society after the Cultural Revolution, but at least in these cases we had a fair idea of what the situation was before. The situation of research prior to 1966, however, is almost as badly documented as the situation after 1970. In the mass of publications on China, this chapter is missing.

Surprising Achievements

However, we know for certain that in various fields where advances can easily be measured, Chinese scientists have now overtaken the achievements of Western research. They have made some astonishing breakthroughs.

139

The atom bomb   China required much less time than any other nuclear power to get from the A bomb to the H bomb.*

Space   While Japan and the European Centre for the Construction and Launching of Spacecraft failed for several years in their attempts to put a satellite into orbit, China succeeded in launching two.**

Biochemistry   The Chinese have developed and administered on a large scale a post-conception pill which is taken once a month and is said to be a hundred percent effective; laboratories in the West are still trying to find the formula.

Surgery   As the reader will recall, Chinese doctors perform limb grafts—in which our surgeons are still at the experimental stage—as routine operations.

Oto-rhino-laryngology and anaesthesiology   Acupuncture is successfully applied, as we have seen, for operative and post-operative anaesthesia; it is also used to cure the deaf and dumb and to reanimate those who have been electrocuted. All this remains *terra incognita* for Western research.

So why are the Chinese, who are so discreet in all those areas where defensiveness or pride compels them to cover up their backwardness, even more secretive in an area where their initial successes should have given them great confidence? They are enormously humble: "You know, we're so far behind in science," I was told by Chou Ke-chen, Vice-President of the Academy of Sciences and a biochemist and meteorologist, who came out to greet us on the steps of the Academy of Sciences building. He was eighty-two and seemed to be stone deaf. Had acupuncture been unable to do anything for him? Is that why he had been chosen? Or was his deafness faked?

"But surely you didn't use an abacus for your thermonuclear missiles or for working out the trajectories of your satellites?"

We were sitting around a green-cloth-covered table on which there were pads of paper and pencils. On one wall was a portrait of Mao and on the opposite wall were portraits of Marx, Engels, Lenin and Stalin.

"You're right," Chou Ke-chen acknowledged. "China received a heritage from the *ancien régime,* but it was a very poor one. There was also some help from abroad, but very little. We have made some progress, but we must really be called backward." This remark seemed to echo Chou En-lai's.

The Secretary-General of the Academy came to his aid: "Our nuclear weapons are as yet only at an experimental stage. Our satellites are very small, and we've launched only two; there are thousands of others encircling the Earth. . . ." He punctuated his sentences with "dzhega, dzhega," the Chinese

---

*Two years and eight months separated China's first nuclear explosion from her first thermonuclear explosion; the United States took seven years and four months, the Soviet Union three years and eleven months, and France eight years and six months.

**Without suffering any failures, at least that the American detection system was able to monitor.

equivalents of "isn't it?" and "mmm?" which give the speaker time to find his words or formulate a thought. During the course of the conversation, our indiscreet questions precipitated a string of "dzhegas."

As elsewhere, we found ourselves piecing together the Chinese situation in the same way an archaeologist would reconstitute a Greek temple— starting with a metope or a triglyph hidden in the thick humus. We see things a little more clearly only after carefully comparing documents originating mainly in America with fleeting answers we got from Chinese scientists.*

Cross-checks** enabled us to come up with answers, but they are all conjecture. Answers will have to be checked against the facts as it becomes possible to establish them more firmly.

The Passage of the Hurricane

Were the scientists affected by the Cultural Revolution or were they bypassed? There is a definitive answer to this question. They were hit head-on. Research was thrown into the kind of confusion one can barely imagine—with a few exceptions, however, for work which was of interest to national defense.

Science as a whole could not have stayed on the sidelines. It was "one of the fields in which it was most necessary to change the customs, organization and state of mind." The new China did not want intellectuals who believed they were made of different stuff from other men. And "research, and especially fundamental research, offered a refuge for those intellectuals who refused to dirty their hands."

Already "this tendency was being revealed not only in higher education, but also in secondary education and even primary education—the teachers were obsessed with spotting pupils who were best suited to the scientific disciplines and were uninterested in the others." The few pupils who dis-

---

*In the conversations that follow, even more than in the other chapters, I have condensed many questions and answers, but without stating who is speaking.

**Of the following: a roundtable organized at our request at the Academy of Sciences; my various conversations with its President, Kuo Mo-jo; other roundtables at Peita University and at the Institute of Medical Research in Wuhan; visits to Nanking Observatory, the satellite-tracking center, and to the Canton Institute of Biology; individual conversations with university professors in Peking, Shanghai and Wuhan; the not very compromising but often instructive answers given by a biologist member of the directorate of the Academy of Sciences who accompanied us throughout our tour; the observations of several French and other Western scholars whose statements have not been published and who asked me not to quote them.

played special gifts for abstract thought were nurtured like hothouse plants. At the end of this long process, the scientists coopted those who most resembled themselves. This traditional university system "had not really evolved" in the seventeen years from 1949 to 1966. On the contrary, "the traitor Liu Shao-chi and his acolytes did everything to reinforce the disastrous effects" of this closed circuit.

Even the organization of research favored these tendencies. It was too centralized and in the last resort dependent only on the scientists themselves. The Academy of Sciences was the summit of a compact pyramid. Research was the fief of an elite which considered itself solely qualified to give itself orders. Being in theory under the Party and the Government, research was in practice free, since "the Party and administration cadres specializing in research lived in isolation with the scientists." Scientific research was also vertically integrated, whereas only horizontal integration would—by means of systematic decentralization—enable "research to spring from the bosom of the masses."

The organization which was so bitterly criticized was rather like that of Soviet research. The symbol and pivot of Soviet research is the scientists' city of Akademgorodok, near Novosibirsk—an oasis of privilege in the midst of sad Siberia, lacking communication with all Soviet reality outside the scientific and university community, although wide open to scholars from abroad.

I once had the chance to stay there—thanks to the hospitality of the mathematician Lavrentyev, who was its director. At that time the Cultural Revolution in China was at its height. "Those Chinese have gone mad," I was told by Soviet scholars who up to 1960 had spent several months a year in China. The symbiosis between the research being done in the two countries had gone very deep. "We don't get news from our colleagues any more. How they must be suffering in the face of all this foolishness!"

The Soviet scientists would have had plenty to fear if they had been in their Chinese colleagues' shoes. In their own retreat they have peace and freedom for their research comparable to that enjoyed by their colleagues at the Princeton Institute for Advanced Studies or at the Stanford Institute. "The Chinese research workers," I was told by a Soviet physicist, "had hopes of building a scientists' city in China just like ours. The poor devils! They didn't know what was in store for them. Their dream was shattered before it had even begun to be realized. They are dressed up in donkey's hats, jostled by louts and even forced to sweep the streets. It's appalling."

After the hurricane there was not a single Chinese scientist who did not realize that he had to give up any idea of locking himself up in an ivory tower. The research workers are reminded every day by the people that they belong to the people and that they depend on the people.

The Self-criticism of a Generation of Scientists

"Before the Cultural Revolution the scientists, who were followers of Liu Shao-chi, wanted to be served by an army of secretaries, technicians and laboratory assistants. They pushed all the menial laboratory tasks onto them. They behaved like satraps. They needed slaves. Now, they know that they have to rely on their own forces. They prepare their experiments themselves. They handle the broom. They form part of the broad popular masses."

The regime had brought the former exploiters to heel, but the scientists were tending to "become the new exploiters"; "the sons of the old exploiters were trying to find refuge in the world of research." A landowner exhorted his son to put science to bad use: "The peasants have taken our property. They have divided up my inheritance among themselves. It will not be yours to dispose of. But what they'll never be able to take away from you is what you've learned at the university." A well-educated government official was accused of having told his son: "Bury yourself in your books. This society is not going to do anything for us, because our family has a bad class origin. But if you study hard, you'll become a scholar and you'll have a brilliant future ahead of you."

These two fathers and sons had to submit themselves to self-criticism, the fathers for having given such advice and the sons for having taken it. The accumulation of cultural capital by the favored classes of former times became the accumulation of scientific capital and then monetary and social capital. In this way the continuity of the hierarchy was ensured. It is this continuity which the Cultural Revolution has broken. It raged across the country and with the likely result that there will be no more "inheritors of knowledge" just as there are no more "inheritors of fortunes." Coopting scholars has stopped being the modern counterpart of coopting owners of property.

"The caste of specialists had a tendency to escape into the abstract, protected by a jargon which was incomprehensible to all who were not members of the caste and which was capable of making the simplest things complicated. We have to cope with so many needs, there are so many gaps in our knowledge, and it's such a short time since we began to catch up, that we cannot afford the luxury of research which is purely speculative. We must fight against the temptation to do *science for science's sake*, because it's just another name for *science for the scientist!*"

"Do tell me," I said, "how applied research can progress without fundamental research."

"That's what a lot of scientists were asking before the Cultural Revolution. But they don't ask any more, because they've recognized their error. Why finance costly basic research, when the fundamental discoveries that are made are immediately published? Throughout the world it's a race to be first to make one's discovery known, since the one who announces it first is considered to have made the discovery. There are thousands of research workers in laboratories throughout the world all doing the same research at the same time. Why waste the people's money in the vain hope of seeing your name in the papers or, perhaps with luck, of getting the ridiculous Nobel Prize? What counts isn't fame—it's the usefulness, for the masses, of the applications that can be made of these discoveries. We must concentrate our forces on the practical use of research, instead of escaping into theory."*

Time and again we were told that before the Cultural Revolution the majority of research workers had come from the old exploiting classes. Even the others were scarcely any better; they entertained hopes of fame.

Nobody made these criticisms more vigorously than the President of the Academy of Sciences, Kuo Mo-jo, applying them to himself. He repeated his celebrated self-criticism to me: it is the self-criticism of a class, a society and a system. He no longer makes any distinction between the pre-1949 regime and the seventeen years that followed it. The year 1966 is an absolute beginning: the shattering and sudden awareness of the defects of the intellectual class, which had "clung to power and to its privileges as shellfish cling to rocks." "When I deciphered a stele which nobody had been able to decipher, I was happy because the newspapers reported it and because my colleagues envied me. Now I understand that I was mistaken and that you must work not in order to be in the limelight but for the good of the masses—for example, so that the people are more aware of their heritage."

I was worried by these remarks. Didn't this self-criticism which he served up to me with such an air of innocence amount to a criticism of me? He whispered it to me just as I sat down beside him, after replying to the toast he made in our honor.

That very morning we had seen his most recent achievement when we looked at the objects that had been discovered in the excavations of the Han tombs. The director of Chinese antiquities had confided in me that only Kuo Mo-jo had been able to decipher an inscription which went back several centuries beyond the tomb; but even he had not been able to discover all the secrets of this new Rosetta stone—he had put a black square around the word he had not deciphered. What mental agility in an octogenarian, and what proof of intellectual honesty! But what a gaffe I had just committed by publicly complimenting Kuo Mo-jo! I had forgotten that the object of my admiration should have been the "masses" in the midst of whom Kuo Mo-jo wanted—and was able—to be merely an anonymous worker. Kuo Mo-jo made me realize how much I was behaving like a mandarin by accusing him of having been one before the Cultural Revolution.

---

*Only Chou Ke-chen admitted that abandoning basic research could in the long run lead to an imbalance; since then it seems to have come back a little into favor.

Is he sincere? Does he really find compliments addressed to him personally out of place, because they allow people to think he might be susceptible to them? Deep down is he really flattered, and does he cover this up by constantly saying he is disinterested? Or is he afraid of "what will be said," and does he reckon on the interpreter publicizing his declarations of humility in the appropriate quarters? Or perhaps it is all these things, mysteriously mixed together? Isn't there one part of him which has resisted conversion, which continues to follow its own inclinations and to savor the pleasure of personal reward? *Video meliora proboque, deteriora sequor.* Perhaps behind his inscrutable face and his benevolent smile he lives in eternal conflict between the triumphs and reverses of his past.

Regeneration by Manual Labor

I picked up the conversation. "Aren't scientists excused from having to do manual work?"

"Oh, no," Kuo Mo-jo answered quietly. "Why should they be? Scientists are just like other men. They must obey the same rules as everyone else. In this way they learn to renounce the cult of the individual and endless intellectualizing. They realize the need to deal with the essential problems in order to resolve them as quickly as possible and as cheaply as possible."

"So, in practice all research workers must combine their own work with that of the workers and peasants?"

"Certainly. All the planning in research institutes and universities is arranged so that every now and again the scientific staff are taught the meaning of manual work. The scientists' work schedule provides for their frequent return to the masses."

"Isn't it very difficult to plan scientific work? Inspiration isn't turned on at will. And once an experiment has begun, you can't just leave it and go out and plant rice. You don't know how long it'll last."

"These objections apply to individual research, not to collective research. No one is indispensable. People can be rotated. The essential thing is that the team keep its continuity."

"But surely success in any taxing mental endeavor requires freedom from anxiety and distraction."

"Manual work doesn't hinder thinking. Quite the contrary. A rested brain makes discoveries more easily than an overworked one. The researcher who holds a broom or a spade in his hand is still thinking of his research; it's quite likely at moments such as these that he makes his discoveries."

"Hasn't this pursuit of the elite slowed down research?"

"It has both slowed down and accelerated it. In research, just as in education, production, diplomacy and indeed everything in China, the Cultural Revolution paralyzed us for four or five years. It delayed everything. But in order to stimulate everything. It gave our scientists a keen impetus. It spread the spirit of Yenan among them. They all felt themselves mobilized, body and soul, for research. They all realized within themselves the three-way alliance of the Kang-ta School*: a soldier fighting for his country, a student hungry for more knowledge, a proletarian devoted to the masses."

One can make fun of this mythological nostalgia, the historicism in this zeal to give present-day China the spirit of the 1930s, but one can also admire the absolute priority given to it as an aim.

"But you, for example—you don't have to do manual work."

Kuo Mo-jo laughed.

"Those like me who are way past retirement age are not made to do anything. But since Chinese science is short of researchers, we try somehow or other to remain active."

In the main university towns we saw that the old scientists lived comfortably and were spared from work in the factories and in the fields; only those who volunteered and those who had been subjected to the most bitter criticism did manual labor. But in order to avoid being cut off from the masses, they make regular visits to people's communes and factories. On the other hand, research scientists who are under sixty are compelled to do manual work. The historic decision of the Chinese Communist Party Central Committee, the Sixteen Points adopted on August 8, 1966, had been interpreted by many sinologists as a sign that the Cultural Revolution would spare the scientists and scholars.** But even if the *old scientists* were treated with the kind of care normally bestowed on fine porcelain, even if the military laboratories were able to continue operating in complete security, unlike the universities (all of which did not prevent the Chinese from welcoming the thermonuclear explosions as a victory for Mao Tse-tung thought), nonetheless the Cultural Revolution did not stop at the laboratory doors. It was the opposite of the situation in 1793—scientists were "needed" but they had to be fully committed to the cause.

Some Probes into the Depths of Chinese Science

Only by making a large number of observations and cross-checks can one form an idea of the level reached by Chinese science; here I am able to throw only a little light on what is still a fairly obscure area.

---

*The Yenan Anti-Japanese Military and Political Institute.
**The twelfth of the Sixteen Points said in effect that "the scientists whose attitudes were patriotic, who were also energetic workers and not against the Party or against socialism, and who maintained no illicit relations with any foreign country should be taken special care of."

For example, the two small nuclear explosions—equal to only about twenty kilotons of TNT—on November 18, 1971 and January 6, 1972 proved that the Chinese were in the process of miniaturizing an atomic "match" intended to serve as a detonator for the thermonuclear warheads on their rockets. The explosion of a nuclear missile at the end of a rocket's trajectory established beyond any argument that this missile has been miniaturized.

Hearing aids no bigger than a nut, which are made in a Tientsin factory and possibly elsewhere, prove that the Chinese have achieved a very satisfactory degree of electronic miniaturization.

More and more sophisticated Chinese-made computers are beginning to appear. Here too the Chinese have made exceptional progress. In October 1970 Tsinghua Polytechnic University in Peking looked like a temporary barracks; its departments of information science and precision engineering looked like the private workshop of a do-it-yourself enthusiast. The faith of the "new students" and the "new teachers" in the force of Mao Tse-tung thought made up for the rather charming lack of equipment. In the summer of 1971 Tsinghua was already looking more like an American campus, with extended premises and laboratories worthy of the name.

On December 25, 1971 Tsinghua University had just been given the most modern equipment. Students and professors, who a year before had had only one transistor computer, were making integrated-circuit computers on a production line. In the department of precision engineering they were designing and producing high-precision hydraulic milling machines which were computerized and silent.

Research in astronomy and radio astronomy, conducted in conjunction with the Chinese space program, is concentrated at the observatory of Nanking, which is perched on a peak six miles or so from the city, overlooking the great walls and shimmering lakes. We were shown a telephotometer whose objective lens, seventeen inches in diameter, was for satellite-tracking. We were told, though, that it was much less powerful than those used in the West, and that it was made entirely in China. There is always this alternation between humility and pride. "My glass is not a big one, but I do drink out of my own glass."

Late in 1971 a delegation of French experts were able to look over the "No. 1 Petrochemical Complex" in Peking; it consists of a petroleum refinery with an annual capacity of 2,500,000 tons of crude, and a synthetic rubber and plastics factory. A plant for the purification of waste is to be created by a unit producing motor oils. Nothing there really outclasses Western technology, but at the same time nothing is inferior to it. The most remarkable thing is that the complex was started in 1968, when the Cultural Revolution was breaking out; it seems hardly to have been affected by it.

"The Russians always pretended that there was no gasoline in China," I was told several times. "They wanted us to believe that we had to rely on their resources. Our geologists have now proved with acoustics that our reserves are practically inexhaustible. Right now our production is increasing so fast that it exceeds our needs."

Finally, we saw agronomists at work, determining which is friable soil, loess and sand; putting up screens, especially in northwest China, to combat wind erosion; and developing reforestation techniques.

There is no conflict between this evaluation and a report that China is a long way behind. Beyond the civilized humility, a little sincerity comes through in some of the things Chou Ke-chen told me: "I'm afraid to say where our mathematical science is with respect to yours. . . . You can't even imagine how far behind we are in high-energy physics. . . . If I told you how weak we are in cybernetics, compared to you or Japan, you wouldn't believe me. . . ."

No doubt these are some of the weakest aspects of Chinese research. The newest laboratories and the most modern factories, though, do not mean one can turn a blind eye to the vast number of workshops in which the machinery seems to keep going by some kind of miracle, as in a drawing by Dubout. So, although Chinese research scientists do reach and sometimes go beyond the level of Western research, the equipment used by the majority of the population is still extremely primitive; this is one of the paradoxes of China—some sectors which are very advanced internationally, side by side with wooden plows drawn by women.

How "Revolutionary" Research Is Organized

The failure of the "Great Leap Forward" of 1958–59, the sudden exodus of Soviet technicians in July 1960, and the three years of famine from 1959 to 1961 put an end to the implementation of new programs. The Cultural Revolution blew like a hurricane through the scientific community, which at the time was a real secret society. How was it that this series of disasters did not jeopardize the research programs—or did not jeopardize them more than it did? How was it that in some cases the disasters miraculously seemed to favor them?

The Academy of Sciences brought together the best brains in China, trained in some of the most famous foreign research centers. No doubt it was necessary for China to begin by concentrating the few research workers and all too costly scientific instruments and equipment in one area in order to achieve that "critical mass" short of which energy remains inert.

The Cultural Revolution broke this closed system and forced the research workers to enter "into close alliance with the people."

Now, we were told, each research unit works on local projects which are of immediate interest to the province, municipality or people's commune concerned. Or if a national project is involved, the unit cooperates closely with the local production units, so as to ensure a constant link between theory and practice. Now that it has been restructured from top to bottom, research has become as decentralized as it was once centralized. In this way scientific and technological investigations have, like any other discipline, broken free from the highly qualified elite who had monopolized them, and are now "fecundated by the spirit of the masses." This is perhaps one of the most profound and essential results of the Cultural Revolution, even though it is still one of the most hidden.

Instead of deciding everything, financing everything and controlling everything, as it did before, the Academy of Sciences now has just the rather modest role of giving stimulus and providing coordination.

"About sixty percent of the research institutes,"* we were told by the members of the Council of the Academy of Sciences,** "have purely and simply been put under the control of the provincial and local authorities; twenty percent are controlled jointly by the local authorities and ourselves; and only twenty percent have remained under our direct control. There is no longer the temptation to cut research off from practice. And no longer do we set up this screen between the research centers and the province which led the masses to take no interest in research."

"In view of the fact that some provinces are rich and others poor, aren't there differences in the amount of money put into research?"

"Yes, enormous differences."

"Isn't this inconvenient?"

"Possibly. But the advantage is that each province does its best, and tries to do better than the others. The masses are beginning to realize that their future depends on research, and they're putting their hopes more in new industrial and agricultural techniques than in the accumulation of capital, state aid or help from the other provinces. They don't want our country to lag behind others and to try to follow in their footsteps. Science has made great progress since it was placed under the control of the worker and peasant activists."

Echoes of Clemenceau's "War is too serious to be left to the military," but a Clemenceau who is a general. Science is too serious a matter to be left to the scientists; education is too serious to be left to the teachers; medicine too serious to be left to the doctors; art too serious to be left to the artists—it is the "Mao Tse-tung thought propaganda" groups which have revived it; national defense is too serious to be left to the army—it is the Party which controls the guns. And as for the Party, the masses must dismantle it now and again.

---

*It seems that before the Cultural Revolution China had about 110 research institutes (compared to ninety in the U.S.S.R.) and fifteen thousand research workers.
**Flanked by two others—the Academy of Medical Sciences (Western, of course) and the Academy of Chinese Medical Science.

"Does the Party," I asked, "give orders to the research workers, or does it give them complete freedom? Our experience in the West is that research workers are like wild ducks; if one were to domesticate them and clip their wings, they wouldn't be able to fly any more and would even lose their sense of direction. What, for example, do you think of the Soviet Communist Party's role in the Lysenko affair?"

"All scientific work is conducted under the direction of the Party," Chou Ke-chen said, "but that doesn't mean the Party says that $A + B = C$. The Party indicates the general direction and lays down the priorities. If need be, it intervenes to give the researchers ideological reeducation. But the scientific hypotheses remain the sole responsibility of the men of science. A Lysenko affair couldn't happen here now."

Did he mean it could have happened before the Cultural Revolution? At any rate, since the Cultural Revolution the relations between the Party and the research workers seem fairly clear.

The Party holds both ends of the chain in the name of the masses. First it commissions a piece of research, and afterwards it checks that the research worker has fulfilled his contract; as far as the intermediate links in the chain are concerned, the Party allows a certain amount of freedom.

One wonders if this way of doing things would eventually lead to anarchy. The Cultural Revolution seems only to be prolonged by this institutional chaos. The progress that has been made thanks to the interest in research throughout the country must be lessened by the drop in the quality of the research workers and of the research.

The answer to these questions is always the same. No doubt this great increase in research does involve useless investment and duplication of effort, but fruitful contacts are now established at the local level. Only a short time ago, everything had to be referred to the Academy of Sciences, and this slowed decision-making and stifled enthusiasm. Now, each factory and each people's commune supports the research which will help in solving its particular problems. If several different provinces end up doing the same work, competition develops between the rival teams. The research center which finds the best solution to a problem first is immediately cited as an example for the whole nation, and its solution is adopted.

This leads one to wonder if the balance China is trying to achieve—a balance between the centralization of broad policy lines and the decentralization of individual initiatives, between corporate discipline and autonomy of movement, between vigilant overall supervision and the flexibility of detailed implementation, between parallel experiments being conducted in a spirit of rivalry and the rapid publication of the results that have been obtained, between the *politicians* and the *scientists*—is not in fact likely to offer, in this field as well as in others, an elegant solution to the difficult problem of centralization and decentralization.

But as the Chinese say: "We're still feeling our way. We've made some progress, but we've still a lot to do."

Scientific Exchanges with Other Countries

The Cultural Revolution brutally severed cultural relations with the outside world. Chinese researchers and students who were abroad were recalled during the summer of 1966, and foreign students and teachers in China were asked to go home. All scientific exchanges were suspended for five years.

Chinese scientific publications were stopped; although they were resumed in 1971 for the benefit of Chinese readers, foreign scientists were unable to get hold of them. No scientific work has been published since 1966 by the Academy of Sciences, whose publications were prominently displayed in all bookshop windows before the Cultural Revolution.

Doesn't China's progress suggest that she was not left to her own scientific and technical resources?

It is a well-known fact that the Chinese nuclear program was able to count on the work of about a thousand atomic scientists, eighty percent of whom had been trained in Soviet research centers and twenty percent in American, British and French laboratories. Those trained in Soviet institutes had no choice. They crossed the border from Siberia in 1960, at the same time as the Soviet technicians were crossing it in the opposite direction. The others returned to China because of a desire to contribute to its development, because of a patriotism which had stronger pull than material comforts or political preferences, or possibly because of fear.

Now that their repatriation is complete, the sources of their knowledge might dry up. Or perhaps they are sure enough of themselves to have no further need of external aid.

One thing might indicate the opposite. Usually, the Chinese display a sovereign indifference to what happens abroad. Every man and woman in the country could echo the remark Emperor Chien-lung made to Lord Macartney in 1793: "What happens in your country doesn't interest me." But this was not so as far as the scientists were concerned. They asked one question after another.

Does this mean that Chinese scientists still form a little world apart from the rest of Chinese society? Or does it mean that because they are preoccupied with secrecy about the difficulties in their research programs, they are anxious for a resumption of exchanges—without, however, venturing to make proposals which properly speaking are the sole responsibility of the political authorities? But there is one hypothesis which must be considered—that the Chinese scientists know that no matter how praiseworthy their efforts and no matter how brilliant their results, their country cannot escape the law of modern societies whose progress is conditional upon the exchange of technology, ideas and men.

But a totalitarian regime does have one great advantage over a liberal country—it can receive without giving. Those we spoke to agreed when I observed that throughout the history of science discoveries had been made by looking over one's neighbor's wall, so it may be that the Chinese reserve the right to peer into their neighbor's back garden, without allowing him to look into theirs. China's embassies in the West, and even the "overseas Chinese," import tons of scientific literature, reviews and precision equipment into China.* Why should they deprive themselves, since the West is open to them? On the other hand, if the West did it to them, it would be nothing less than espionage.

Will Chinese scientists be able to follow, or even go beyond, the progress achieved by Western science merely by going through its publications? Educated outside China, will they be able to ensure their succession inside China? This is no mean task, although it is true that the regime has solved more serious difficulties. Concluding our discussions at the Academy of Sciences, Chou Ke-chen made this comment on the slowdown in China's progress after the withdrawal of the Soviet experts: "We must rely on our own efforts; necessity is the mother of invention, and we are spurred on by necessity."

Utilitarian and Utilized

A century and a half of decline has made one forget that for millenia China was in the forefront of world science and technology, that she continued to advance until the sixteenth century, and that she was only really outstripped at the beginning of the nineteenth century. Her genius was still directed more to invention than to discovery, and less to the pure sciences than to the applied sciences, like astronomy, meteorology, botany, medicine and pharmacy.

Because of the indifference of this self-satisfied society, no practical use was made of these discoveries. Printing from wood blocks was invented in China nine centuries before it was invented in Europe, and printing with movable type was invented in China four centuries before Gutenberg, but the first book actually to be distributed in China was the Bible. Promissory notes

---

*We met interpreters whose work consisted entirely of translating scientific articles from French and English.

on paper appeared in China five centuries before they appeared in Europe, but China waited for the pound and the dollar to come to corrupt her. When the Chinese invented gunpowder it was in order to make firecrackers; it was Western artillery which was to bring them to their knees. And it was Western navigators who brought the compass back to China; their ships were plying the seas, but there was not a Chinese vessel to be seen.

In short, the Chinese made discoveries but went back to sleep, regarding their inventions as useless toys. While they were asleep, the West copied them and made them into instruments of power.

Mao realized that science could no longer remain an amusement, or, in more modern terms, a prestige activity. China did not have a scientific spirit. A few scholars and fifteen thousand Chinese research workers were not sufficient to create Chinese science: it was the Chinese people, once they became fully involved in the adventure of learning, once they understood the power it could give them over their own development, who would—quite naturally—create a Chinese science.

It is important to realize that China has the time. She has no desire to go in for international competition; her society does not work on those terms. She intends to build her own future in her own time. By making higher education accessible to anyone, the Chinese have increased the number of people who may become scientists.

After one of our many discussions, one of our delegation could contain himself no longer. He confronted the President of the Revolutionary Committee of the Wuhan Medical Institute: "When a doctor is sweeping the yard or emptying chamber pots, how does his research get done? A scientist's time is so precious—why waste it by having him do work others can do? Aren't you putting the future of science in jeopardy by giving this priority to manual work, by this thing you have about proletarian education, by this futile squandering of brain power?"

The reply came with a smile: "The specialist who doesn't feel it beneath him to do the same job as the humblest of his colleagues is not only personally enriched by the experience but also establishes a relationship of equality with the members of the team. This is essential if he is to get the participation of everyone in the common task. Research can't make progress today if there's specialization between great scientists and doctors on the one hand and menial workers and ward orderlies on the other. It requires a collective desire to accomplish the common task."

Science should serve man, not be an end in itself. Its human finality is inseparable from the "social practice" of the scientists. The feeling seems to be that time wasted in this way is in fact well spent in human terms.

10

Communications

To Teach More than to Inform

When the Westerner, who is used to the rush of the "stop-press" news and "final editions," visits China he feels totally cut off from the rest of the world.

Once we left Peking, which is linked by teleprinter circuit with the outside world, we had the impression we were living outside time. We had newspaper headlines and radio news bulletins translated for us, but got practically no world news from any of them. We had to wait until we got to Hong Kong before we knew that Scott and Irwin had landed on the moon during our tour.

News in China is not printed because it is news but because it is useful. And it is not up to the reader or listener to judge what is useful—it is up to those who control the media.

If an item of news does not serve to educate the public, it is passed over in silence. When it heightens the revolutionary consciousness of the Chinese people it is made much of; the most auspicious moment and the best style of presentation are chosen.

The Chinese only reveal part of the game. The news which is most likely to interest the public is often not announced for some time. Mao's famous swim on July 16, 1966 was reported nine days later. Were they waiting for favorable circumstances in which to exploit it? Or had they not wanted to exploit it? Or did Mao give the go-ahead on July 25, after having refused it nine days earlier?

It was a year to the day before the world knew of an event which was the first signal of the Cultural Revolution—the dissolution on May 16, 1966 of a commission which had been charged with the task of reshaping education

154

from top to bottom; its proposals were judged to be incapable of making education truly popular. Another year passed, from the summer of 1971 to the summer of 1972, before people abroad, and then the Chinese themselves, learned of the disgrace and death of Lin Piao.

Any view which goes against the one which the authorities wish to publicize is censored, or presented under unfavorable circumstances so that it will be immediately rejected. No foreign papers can be found on the newsstands. With the exception of a few leaders, the Chinese are protected from any publication which is not official.

If the people are to continue working at the established rate, they cannot be allowed doubt and criticism which might weaken their enthusiasm. All news is passed through the filter of politics. "If we don't identify the revisionist tendencies in our ranks," we were told by a revolutionary leader in Chekiang province, "if we don't unmask the counterrevolutionaries who infiltrate us, the dictatorship of the proletariat will not become strong and firm. Politics must be at the command posts."

It is not a question of giving the Chinese news which, at best, they could not do anything about and at worst would disturb them. It is a question of explaining what contributes to the revolution in such a way as to "raise their level of revolutionary consciousness." *Explaining* is the key word.

The top leaders, the Party and the cadres in the production units all spend their time explaining; the citizens do one another the service of explanation. This continual process of explanation is a welcome contrast to thousands of years of ignorance.

"Explanation" is most often concerned with aspects of practical life which the general obscurantism of the past kept in the dark. This is what we must recognize, before letting our *liberalism* condemn without understanding. When we reproach the Chinese regime for releasing streams of propaganda, what we fail to remember is that this propaganda is most often directed at ways of dragging the people up from their state of underdevelopment. It is propaganda for spreading hygiene, for preventing or identifying epidemics, for helping in childbirth, for avoiding accidents, for learning to read, for going over from feudal customs to the new law of marriage. It is concrete propaganda, which speaks to the heart of the masses—about the abominations of the old system and the delights of the new, about the misfortunes brought by superstition and the joy of the grandfather whose grandson teaches him to read. In China one seeks not so much to inform as to educate.

The Educational Press

We wanted to visit a newspaper office, but this was the one request which was refused. As a consolation, we were shown ultramodern rotary printing presses at the Shanghai Permanent Exhibition of Industrial Achievements; these presses were able to print a six-color weekly using an offset process, but this riot of color seemed out of all proportion since the contents were so *deliberately* monochrome. It was this aspect which they did not want to show us. They considered our desire to see it preposterous; would we have had the nerve to ask to attend a meeting of a revolutionary committee, or a criticism–self-criticism session?

To judge by the end product, putting a newspaper together in China must be a rather dull process. One day's edition of the *People's Daily* is much the same as another's. Four million copies are printed, and the paper always carries the same kind of news—a Party editorial, the day-to-day details of a foreign delegation's visit, world news favorable to the Chinese, criticism of Formosa at the United Nations, indications of agricultural and industrial production (though without figures, as hardly any statistics have been given since the "Great Leap Forward"), sports, heroes of labor, the latest achievements of Chinese medicine, the full text of a top leader's speech, the progress of the agricultural cooperatives. There is nothing about what has happened in the world in the previous twenty-four hours—not a single news item. And there are no photographs, apart from posed pictures of official personalities.

The *People's Daily* has the same role as *Pravda* in the Soviet Union; it sets the tone for the rest of the press. The provincial papers, which do not come out every day, take up the same topics, adding some local news, usually about the progress achieved by a workers' team.

This last theme dominates the columns of the enterprise newspapers, which are pinned on notice boards in factories, institutes and offices.

In the golden age of the Tang dynasty, the Emperor Hsuan-tsung, a contemporary of Charles Martel, brought out the *State Monitor*, which echoed the wishes of the Emperor and the administrative hierarchy. It was the first printed gazette and was to continue to appear for the next twelve centuries. In this respect, too, China has revived her old traditions.

Watchwords and Slogans

We wondered whether circulation of the newspapers was too small, or their cost—moderate as it is—too high for people to buy them. Copies of *Jen-min Jih-pao*—the *People's Daily*—are posted on street corners. Passers-by crowd around to read them. The newspaper has become a poster. It blends into the ideological landscape—in China ideology is part of the landscape. The hoarding reigns supreme in the courtyards of universities and schools, in public gardens, along avenues, in ports and beside the road.

Most frequently it carries watchwords, and a good half of them seem to be the precepts of Mao Tse-tung. The others consist of slogans like "Liberate Formosa," "Crush Imperialism," "Save Food," and "Long Live the Five-Year Plan."

The Chinese language is a lively vehicle for the expression of strong ideas—each word has an astonishing impact, and the writing is decoration in itself.

Numbers are an incomparable mnemonic device. "Walking on *two* legs" means harmonizing agricultural and industrial progress. It also means using the most traditional methods and the most modern techniques at the same time.

The revolutionary committees are made up of a three-way alliance (peasants-workers-soldiers or workers-cadres-soldiers). "Forward beneath the *three* banners" was the favorite slogan between 1958 and 1960. This meant "follow the general line of the Party," "take part in the Great Leap Forward" and "help in the birth of the people's communes." The slogan survived the political developments. The red flag remains a trinity, and three banners flying from the towers mark the entrance to the Great Bridge of Nanking.

"The *four* plagues" were pursued—rats, mosquitoes, flies and sparrows.* The enemies of the people numbered *three* or *five*—these were the "three-antis" and "five-antis" campaigns. Against this the proletarian spirit is spread thanks to the "four withs" campaign (the cadres must *work–live–eat–act in concert with the masses*). The rural communes are engaged in the "five self-productions"—they must be self-sufficient in vegetables–oil–wood–meat–crockery. Agricultural development is to be guaranteed by the *eight* principles, peaceful coexistence by *five*.

Each time it is a question of a collective reflex triggered by a simple mathematical formula or poetic image. Once the reflex has been created, it has only to be sustained. One can then move on to the next formula, a rectification campaign, for example. It would be considered Rightist deviation for Party cadres to neglect doctrine for technical training and Leftist deviation to believe that ideology can replace professional competence. The balance is reestablished by a formula of synthesis: "Be Red and be expert."

When there is a change of tactics, some slogans disappear completely, and others appear and spread. The important thing is that the public feel that no views are being denied in the movement forward; the slogan of slogans is renewal in continuity.

Radio and Television

The radio broadcasts day and night, and there are sets in almost all homes. Most are enormous wooden boxes—what we used to call wireless sets. Transistor radios are just coming onto the market.

"The difference between radio and television is that television has the power of presenting a picture at the same time as sound; television has more

---

*The sparrows were rehabilitated after a number of autopsies revealed that they lived more off insects than off cereals. The fourth plague then became bugs.

advantages than any other means of propaganda." This remark by Ho Ta-chung, Director of the Radiophonic Research Institute, shows very clearly what store the regime sets by television.*

The first television station was opened in Peking in 1958 under a convention on assistance signed with the Soviet Union in 1956. Even today television is not widespread, because the prices of sets have been raised. Even though one can buy them in the electrical departments of the big shops, and there are a dozen or so manufacturers making them, they cost between three and seven months' salary for a factory worker and between five months' and a year's salary for a peasant. Thus, television is generally for collective use—in clubs in enterprises and people's communes and in the games rooms of barracks and schools.

A regular day's programs might be a Mao Tse-tung thought study course, a program for children, a talk on hygiene and health, a documentary on the latest advances in industry and agriculture, a report on students and teachers working on the land in a May Seventh School, and a revolutionary play on contemporary themes. On good days there may be a film about an episode in the Civil War or the resistance against the Japanese, or a foreign film like *The Battleship Potemkin* or *Lenin and the October Revolution.*

The national news is short and the items are usually several days late, either because of the time it takes for the film to be made by one station (of the inauguration of a dam or the reception of a foreign delegation) and distributed to the others, or because of the time it takes for the film's ideological content to be checked and approved. Foreign news tends to be a Chinese delegation's visit to Albania or North Korea or Africa, or a film on Vietnam.

What is most surprising for a Westerner is the number of repeats. "Dramatic pieces" like *The Red Detachment of Women* and *The White-haired Girl* are shown every week.

One of my companions asked incredulously: "Don't the viewers get tired of seeing the same program every week, when there's no other channel?"

"Not at all," was the astonished reply. "They are very happy."

In the club of the Peking cotton-weaving works groups of workers were glued to the screen, their mouths hanging open, fascinated by the program they were watching. We were told that the program was shown every week. After all, does the Western public tire of seeing the same old advertisements time after time? It seemed that these programs were the ones most viewers preferred.

The Loudspeakers

The most powerful of all the means of communication is still the loudspeaker. It can be heard droning away in village squares, in factories and

---

*It is estimated that in 1971 there were 200,000 television sets in China, one for every four thousand people; in France the figure was one for every four people.

workshops, and in the courtyards of apartment houses. It is to China what the transistor radio is to the West—but a transistor radio the listeners are not free to switch off. It wakes people up with the strains of the *Internationale*. It shrieks out at crossroads, but the policemen on point duty in their glass cabins interrupt its music, news or slogans to stop a pedestrian who has gone over the studs on the crossing or a bicyclist who has not moved over to let a car pass.

Plugged into the radio, the loudspeaker sweeps across the rice fields and sorghum fields where the villagers work. "Do you enjoy that?" I asked a peasant girl, pointing to the amplifier perched on a pylon. "Oh, yes!" she said. "That's how we can hear Chairman Mao's voice while we're working."

It was over the loudspeaker that we heard of the invitation to President Nixon; it was while we were visiting Peita University in Peking. "Attention, attention. In a moment there will be an important announcement. Attention." One of our companions heard the news at the same moment, beside the lake at the Summer Palace, while thousands of Chinese were celebrating the fifth anniversary of Chairman Mao's famous swim down the Yangtse on July 16, 1966. The swimmers were told the news in mid-stroke in the middle of the lake.

Loudspeakers installed at the ends of each wagon of every train dispense sound advice in stentorian tones. "Keep the corridors clear," "Give way to travelers who want to pass," "Get ready for the next station," "Carriage Number Seven is reserved for women with babies," "Don't push to get off the train."

A female announcer sits in a closed compartment, giving the orders into a microphone in a falsetto voice. She stops only to put on a record; the admonitions are interspersed with popular band music. The Chinese are not left in silence for a second; is there a fear that they will become bored or that they will think evil thoughts—or quite simply that they will think?

Mobilizing the Masses

Group Techniques

Making the message heard is not enough. In order to gain adherents to one's cause it is essential to reach the public in groups so that they will take in the message together, react to it as a group, discuss it and watch the effect it has on their colleagues. The impact of newspapers, slogans, radio, television and loudspeakers would be meager if they only reached individuals. This is why the daily meeting is an essential rite of the regime—it reinforces individual acceptance by social pressure. The latest issue of *Jen-min Jih-pao* is studied in groups, the latest orders are analyzed and considered along with the directives in the *Little Red Book*.

In exceptional cases, when it is a question of launching a new "campaign," the meeting can take several days. Then the "two-five" or the "three-eight" system is adopted. For two or three days one studies, discusses, and prepares the programs in theory, trying to foresee the difficulties that will have to be overcome and the new practices that will have to be adopted. There then follow five or eight days of work in which directives are put into practice. These are formed into concise formulas, which the loudspeakers then echo continuously and the banners hanging from the walls of places of work turn into an obsession. This process is continued for as long as is considered necessary.

This method is not confined to the masses. It is addressed just as much to the cadres. Since 1961 it has even been propagated among the intellectuals, under the heading "assemblies of immortals"—an allusion to the gathering of eight legendary sages. The intellectuals were invited by the Party to "absorb more of the brilliant thought of Mao Tse-tung" and to speak "completely freely so as to hasten the construction of socialism." Experience has shown that it is better not to leave the intellectuals on their own too much. Mixed meetings of "immortals" and "mortals" are safer.

Those responsible must bring all their good offices to bear in preparing the meetings. No room must be left for the unexpected: "Don't announce a meeting or recommend a directive if everything has not been thoroughly worked out. Be brief. The meetings mustn't be too long. All cases must be considered in detail." The meeting goes smoothly only if its conclusions are known by the organizers before it starts. On the other hand, the collective reaction is best produced spontaneously, when the participants are plunged into the meeting without having been able to prepare their defense. So the group replaces the individual. The demon of individualism is cast out; the deviations are rectified; the collective soul is shaped; a point of no return is reached. Who would dare go back on a promise made in a group? It is as binding as an oath.

The State of Permanent Mobilization

Westerners in Peking have not forgotten the mishap that befell a Mexican who was passing through the city a few years ago. He was staying at the Hotel of Peace (*Ho-ping Pin-kuan*) and had gone out for a walk on his own in the town. During his stay the current vogue slogan *Long Live Peace* (*Ho-ping Wan-tsui*) had become stuck in his mind. Not knowing how to find his way back to the hotel, he went to a rickshaw station. Instead of telling the driver the name of his hotel, he said the phrase which had been ringing in his ears ever since he arrived: *Long Live Peace*. The bicyclist repeated seriously:

Ho-ping Wan-tsui! The Mexican said it again, this time louder. The Chinese repeated it, raising his voice too so he should not appear to be less firm in his pacifist convictions than this foreigner. The Mexican then shouted back at the man as if he were deaf, stressing each syllable. The rickshaw drivers took it up in chorus: *Ho-ping Wan-tsui!* Pedestrians gathered round and joined in: *Long Live Peace!* It was building up into a mass demonstration, until a Chinese who spoke Spanish stepped in and saved the Mexican.

The Chinese always give the impression of being at the same time both calm and teetering on the brink of collective enthusiasm, smiling and yet on the point of bursting, reserved but available at the drop of a hat for a mass demonstration. The communications media used by the Party and the political themes it launches keep them in a state of permanent mobilization. What an unpredictable and disturbing power.

Spreading the Movement:
From the Snowball to the Avalanche

Technology is the servant of ideology. Over the radio—and every household has one; through the loudspeakers—which blare in every public place; on television—which is the main attraction in workers' clubs; and on the telephone—which is used only by sound Party men but which is available in every people's commune, the center can send its exhortations, orders and information to the most outlying districts in an instant.

The movement spreads more rapidly the more homogeneous the society, the more its barriers have been broken down, and the more it is perpetually urged to acquire a community consciousness. "Exchange your information" orders a slogan we saw in several factories. This advice is certainly essential. Everyone must be made to speak the same language and to share in the same projects. So the group protects the individual from his own temptations, and in this way one avoids imitating those egoists—mocked by Lao-tzu—who "never visit one another in their lives, although they hear one another's dogs barking and cocks crowing."

It is impossible to get away from this insidious invasion of your privacy. Did you forget to read the paper? You didn't quite catch what was said over the loudspeaker? But you're saved, because it will all be on the radio and television, on the hoardings, in the theatre, on the cinema and in paintings and sculpture. The orchestration is so powerful that it seems quite out of the question that an information campaign could fail.

In China the power of social pressure is such that each individual feels himself inevitably bound up with his fellows. Mao "provided a sense of direction," whether it be in ideology or technological innovation. The Prime Minister, Chou En-lai, "gave directives for the continuous mobilization of the masses." A resolution of the Central Committee puts such directives into practice. And then thousands and millions of cells set about spreading the principle handed down to them.

From Peking the watchword echoes through to the poorest village in the remotest province, losing none of its force on the way. It is like a snowball which grows into an avalanche and takes the whole population with it.

Whether it is a question of electrifying the rural areas, building blast furnaces in the villages or making underground bomb shelters, the method is the same.

In the liberal countries, where the law of the market place should in theory make the spreading of information easier, it often happens that hereditary distrust and social barriers present an obstacle to change. The Catholic nations of Europe have only very slowly adopted the technological transformations precipitated in the nations upon whom Protestantism left its mark by the Industrial Revolution. In India and Africa some remarkable advances, introduced by experimental rice- or coffee-growing centers, do not involve the population; the peasants of neighboring villages remain reticent or inert. It is many years—even decades sometimes—before new methods begin to be adopted on any wide scale. The cultural level of the workers does not enable them to be inspired spontaneously; the public powers are neither accustomed nor do they have the means to mobilize them rapidly.

In China, successful experiments—like the Tachai brigade, the Taching oilfields, and Tsinghua University—acquire a national significance over-night. By implementing the slogan "Economize on manpower thanks to the technological revolution," production at one factory in Shanghai was in-creased one hundred percent in a year, despite a thousand employees being detached for work in agricultural people's communes. The propaganda apparatus immediately guarantees experiments massive publicity through-out the country. The pioneers are presented as heroes; their unit becomes a shop window which the people are invited to admire. Emulation drives get underway in all the provinces, and they take the credit for the technological improvements which result; the exploits take on an epic significance.

So a totalitarian system, which in most communist countries leads in the end to bureaucratic paralysis, routine and atony, on the contrary seems here to give innovation and competition a role they probably do not have in liberal countries, where a monopoly on incentives for progress existed for so long. The Chinese people are united in a grand design because their leaders are able to appeal as much to the irrational as to the rational in them. The old society was blocked by the passivity of the masses, by the bureaucratic apparatus's alternating policies of interference and *laisser aller;* the new society is distinguished by a remarkable capacity for mobilization. If a concrete objective is presented simply, clearly and with perseverance, the society acquires confidence in its ability to attain it.

It is a form of auto-determination on the part of the masses. Their leaders put them under tension in order to make them achieve ends which they vaguely recognize are good for them.

Light Breeze and Gentle Drizzle

"There'd be no point," I was told by the Vice-President of the Revolutionary Committee of the Province of Hupeh, "in forcing the people to do what they don't want to do or what they see no sense in. Even if one put half the population in prison, nothing would be achieved. One must convince by repeating gently, and repeating again. That's how good principles get through in the end. We prefer the light breeze and the gentle drizzle to the hurricane and the thunderstorm."

This is the prevailing attitude in contemporary China. Most of the regime's leaders or their close relations—from Mao Tse-tung down suffered either at the hands of the Empire or the Kuomintang, or simply from the mandarin hierarchy. Certainly, they never retreated in the face of violence. But in ordinary times they choose persuasion over coercion. They try to make people submit voluntarily and gratefully to the new order which at first they totally rejected. Social constraint only occasionally appears in the form of savage coercion. Usually it takes the form of insistent but non-violent pressure, which the Chinese euphemistically call "fraternal aid"—and this the cadres and comrades dispense by making the individual aware of his social duty. They bring to their "fraternal aid" a curious mixture of respect for the other person, a desire to help him and a total lack of any doubt about the necessity and impending success of his conversion.

The human relationships on which contemporary Chinese society is based are very different from those associated with Stalin's Russia. After 1953, when the landowners were liquidated, the land was collectivized mainly through persuasion. The message was hammered home to the poor and medium-poor peasants that they would stand to gain more by joining a production brigade than by stubbornly remaining on their own. The privileged and their children were made to understand that they would have to live down their errors by working all the more enthusiastically for the revolution. Those responsible for the people's communes told us that collectivization had been carried out on an entirely voluntary basis.

"Voluntary? But if the voluntary decision had been not to go along with collectivization, would that have been allowed?"

"When the peasants understood the situation, they could not have any other opinion. If they were of the opposite view, it simply meant they had not yet understood."

Persuasion is total. The individual is assailed from all sides. No course is open to him but to agree. His only consolation is his enthusiasm.

With the leaders, how much of their tolerance is genuine, and how much is calculated? And with the led, how much is sincere assent and how much social hypocrisy?

It is difficult to say, but one must recognize the shrewdness of a government which is always ready to adjust its rhythm to the reactions of its citizens; to take "two steps forward and one step back"; to realize that it is always better to obtain a minimum of consent, in order to keep society's joints and muscles supple, than to force them to the point of contraction.

Liberating the Spirit of the Masses

Information Ascending—The Wall Newspapers

In Peking, Nanking and especially Shanghai, crowds collect regularly in front of hoardings, and those which attract the most people are the ones on which new wall newspapers have just been put up. These famous *ta-tzu-pao* played a vital role in the Cultural Revolution. Since then there have been fewer of them; they no longer cover the walls of China's towns as they did between 1966 and 1970, making them look like the Sorbonne in May and June of 1968. Even so, there are still hundreds of them—on hoardings, on walls, over factory gates, wrapped around trees, hanging under the arcades in the streets of Canton, along the banks of the Huang-po and along Shanghai's Nanking Road.

They come in various sizes; some are as small as a page of a school exercise book, others are large enough to cover an entire hoarding. They are stuck one on top of the other like enormous milfoils. Aggressive ideograms leap from them with their fists in the air, and they are often accompanied by drawings and caricatures. In a society which is strictly controlled, this is the free sector. The individual can intervene in public life by letting his imagination run riot. They are like giant loose-leaf complaint books.

Someone complains of poor service in a cycle shop: "I took my bike into this shop to have the chain mended. I was told to come back in a fortnight. I went to a shop in the next street, and they did the repair in five minutes. Which is the good revolutionary, and which the bad?"

This *ta-tzu-pao* was stuck up not near the good shop, but near the bad one.

"Why doesn't the shopkeeper tear it down?" we asked. "How can he tolerate being criticized in this way?"

"Those who want to tear down the *ta-tzu-pao* are reprimanded. The masses take their rights very seriously. Whoever put the poster up would get his comrades to come along while he put up another even more aggressive than the first. He would complain about the attitude of those in charge of the shop, who would be presumed guilty. So, it's in their interest to lay off and mend their ways."

Some of the *ta-tzu-pao* launch appeals. The local authorities are alerted to the poor state of a road which has been full of potholes for several months, or to the leaking plumbing in an apartment house. Others threaten invisible enemies: "Crush the chieftain of the revisionists." Most of them are specific, picturesque and striking.

The boards reserved for them are regularly covered with new papers. Even when the fever has abated, the worker sentiments are still forcefully reiterated through slogans, denunciations, sententious definitions, accusations, appeals: "Down with this!" "Up with that!" There is hardly a single one which does not end with exclamation marks or question marks.

What was the reason behind this strange practice?

"The *ta-tzu-pao* was the most effective weapon of the Cultural Revolution. It liberated the creativity of the masses."

In fact, it really does seem to be a new method of intervening democratically in the life of the city or the factory. Each helps the other by criticizing him—it is never a question of denigration, but of calling to order. These innumerable recriminatory placards may look as though they are presenting opposing views, but in fact they hold a single, united opinion. "Bad work," "false ideology," and "poisonous weeds" are denounced in the name of an identical proletarian view of life.

At the same time, these strange open-air protests bring the feelings of the common people to the very summit of the hierarchy. They guarantee that information and individual reactions get back to the leadership—what sociologists call feedback; and this is something which is very difficult to achieve in any society.

"The Masses Must Decide"

How is a balance achieved between the will of the government and that of the people? To what extent does the apex impose its will on the base, and the base on the apex? Aren't the procedures for giving the people the final say really just decoration to cover up what is in fact despotism? Or rather, is a genuine compromise being worked out every day between authority and democracy within the complex of social relations?

The natural state of any society is anarchy and idleness. In the words of Tristan Bernard, man is not made for work—his natural inclination is to do as little of it as he can. The Chinese leaders realized that of all the various methods different societies have invented for getting men to organize themselves and work, the least effective is to impose an authoritarian way on passive subjects. It leads to enormous waste because of inertia, indifference, malevolence and sabotage. They found that by far the most effective method was enthusiasm.

"The masses are the creators of history." "The revolutionary movement of the masses is naturally right." This is what the masses are seeing and hearing all day and every day. How could they fail to be persuaded? And if there are skeptics among them, either they are very quickly pointed out or they suppress their skepticism to avoid trouble. How does one distinguish between those who genuinely have faith and those who pretend, like Pascal's Christians who would kneel in church even though they were not believers?

The unbeliever who does not believe in the infallibility of the masses is warned about his deviation.

"The pseudorevolutionaries," Mao says, "love to behave like Lord Sheh, who was very fond of dragons but was frightened out of his wits when he saw one. They have been talking about socialism for years, but now that socialism has triumphed, they are frightened of it and recoil before it." The Cultural Revolution made it possible for this instinctive fear of the people—which overcame those who were supposed to be listening to them—to be denounced. The sacrificial knife immolates both the scapegoat and the doubt felt about popular power: "China's Khrushchev continually invoked the line of the masses, but when the masses really got moving he lost his head and poured out a stream of insults against them: he called them hordes of idlers."

A leader of the "Cuban Friendship" people's commune gave us his self-criticism the following way: "I'd let myself drift into directing in a bureaucratic and authoritarian manner. I was preoccupied with the views of agronomists and experts, and did not pay enough attention to the views of the workers. I had lost contact with the masses. Now I understand that even if it is necessary for engineers to be brought in, one must on no account overlook the participation of the masses."

How is this "participation of the masses" organized—other, that is, than by the ta-tzu-pao?

First of all, by the strategy of continual changes which Mao always followed.* He progressed through a series of small-scale experiments. His ideas on agrarian reform and peasant revolution he tried out first in Hunan, and then in Kiangsi and Shensi. He tried out his innovations on larger and larger scales, measuring the difficulties and testing the people's reactions. He got the masses to embark only on projects which they had already proved were realizable and desirable.

Another way to get the masses to participate, which has been used ever

---

*The only hitch in this strategy was the "Great Leap Forward."

since 1949 but which was reinforced by the Cultural Revolution, is to encourage invention. The Chinese worker and peasant are ingenious by nature. Back in 1793 Lord Macartney saw roller ramps made from logs moving boats over dry land and wheeled vehicles with sails being driven along by the wind. When you visit a people's commune or a factory, you are struck by the imagination of Chinese workers. No set ways are ever imposed from above; no attempt to try out something new is ever discouraged.

"If the worker isn't interested in his work," I was told by an official of the Peking No. 2 textile works, "he does bad work and what he makes often has to be scrapped. If he's really keen on his job, he tries to do it better than others. He increases his output and improves the quality of his work; he even invents new gadgets. The main question is not how many workers we have, or whether they've had enough training, but whether they're inspired with revolutionary ardor." Péguy must have had the same thing in mind when he told of the three stone-carvers; when asked what they were doing, the first replied: "I am breaking a stone"; the second said: "I am earning my living"; the third answered: "I am building a cathedral."

In order to encourage grass-roots participation, all achievements are amplified and widely publicized. It is not the Agriculture Ministry in Peking which dreams up and establishes modern methods; it is the Tachai production brigade which performs the feats and invents new techniques. The authorities content themselves with providing an enormous resonance box for such experiments. The "heroes of labor," the living proof of the zeal and competence of the grass roots, count for more than the directives from above. At best these would lead to "passive obedience" and at worst "passive resistance" and probably sullen inertia; the "heroes of labor" encourage emulation.

As Chou En-lai told me, "Chairman Mao Tse-tung is often away from Peking so he can keep in touch with what the masses are saying and thinking. He makes long tours in the towns and countryside." After a year spent conducting an investigation in Hunan in 1927, he was convinced that the peasants were ready to make the revolution. After a visit to the provinces in 1956, he was certain that the peasants were ready for the people's communes and that the cadres were too fearful of them. After disappearing in the summer of 1966, he returned convinced that the people would follow him if he eliminated Liu Shao-chi and the majority faction in the Party. A big decision taken at the top is not socialism, it is bureaucratism. Revolution is the will of the masses.

Who runs this game? The people who stir, or the man who interprets their stirrings? What does it matter? What counts is that the masses think they are being heard and the cadres remember to listen to them. In this way the dignity of the masses and the modesty of the cadres are ensured. The links of command and information in the Party and the organizations must be good conductors for transmitting the will of the leaders to the masses and the will of the masses to the leaders.

Cases of Volte-face

Respect for the masses—perhaps one need look no further for the reason why so many campaigns have come to an abrupt end and why there have been so many disconcerting changes of direction. Each time the Party has wanted to move faster than the masses, there have been failures; the Party has learned a lesson from this.

The "Great Leap Forward" sent the Chinese economy into a frenzied rhythm. The dissatisfaction of the masses put a sudden end to the utopian forecasts of 1958. The Chinese leaders quickly returned to a sense of proportion. In 1959 Chou En-lai started correcting the plan. In 1960 the Party was still priding itself on having limited the free market in the countryside. A few months later, it launched a campaign* which went in quite the opposite direction.

In 1966 and 1967 Chairman Mao gave his support to the theory of the "transmutation" of spiritual forces into material forces. In 1972 this theory was condemned.

Output bonuses were abolished by the Cultural Revolution as a symbol of revisionism; they reappeared in 1972. In schools and universities, manual work was presented as the essential part of education; in 1972 it gave way once again to general teaching.

The regime lurches forward, then retreats; and just when society has gotten used to the change, it goes on the attack again, corrects its errors, assimilates its victories, accelerates when it wants to, slows down to walking pace when it has to. This continual flux is a measure of the impulses of a people which dictates the possibilities of each and every moment. The submissiveness of the masses is far from being blind. Certainly the Chinese *leaders* fully deserve the name. They never apply the famous words: "I am their chief, so I follow them." But when they sense too energetic an opposition, they change direction.

If there is an element of democracy in the Chinese regime, it is in its capacity for self-correction. In his autobiography Mao told how he came to learn that only the masses could prevent their leaders from betraying them: "When Chao Heng-ti seized control, he betrayed all the ideas he had supported, and especially he violently suppressed all demands for democracy. We had organized a demonstration to celebrate the third anniversary of the October Revolution. It was suppressed by the police. Some of the demon-

---

*In the classic text of Li Fu-chun, *Raise High the Red Flag*, September 1960.

strators had attempted to raise the red flag at that meeting, but were prohibited from doing so by the police. They then pointed out that, according to Article 12 of the (then) Constitution, the people had the right to assemble, organize, and speak, but the police were not impressed. They replied that they were not there to be taught the Constitution, but to carry out the orders of the governor, Chao Heng-ti. From this time on I became more and more convinced that only mass political power, secured through mass action, could guarantee the realization of dynamic reforms."

Mao seems never to have lost this confidence in the masses. He asked of the Party and the organizations only that they serve as loyal intermediaries between the masses and the leader. The Cultural Revolution swept aside the mediation of the intellectuals, the Party and the bureaucracy, which had become somewhat dense, and reestablished a direct relationship between Mao and the people.

It is good transmission of directives which makes it possible to achieve a volte-face and at the same time to give the people the impression that the general line is being maintained.

The Westerner is often surprised to see the Chinese worshipping what they have burned, or burning what they worship. The "fraternal peoples of the Soviet Union" are suddenly rejected, in 1960, as "social revisionists." The Yugoslavs, who had hitherto been stigmatized as "social traitors," are promoted to the rank of "fraternal people," and so on.

Kao Kang, the "Stalin of Manchuria," Liu Shao-chi, "China's Khrushchev," and Lin Piao, "the ally of the reactionaries," are eliminated, although they had once been such beloved leaders. The Hundred Flowers campaign and the Cultural Revolution were launched and then suddenly stopped, without the regime apparently being affected or its capacity for advancement being diminished. There is talk of crushing the American jackals. The Chinese masses are ready to move off on a revolutionary crusade. Then it is decided to give a red-carpet welcome to the main representative of "bloody imperialism." The conversion is accomplished with ease.

In the days following the announcement—on July 16, 1971—of the forthcoming visit of President Nixon, we asked dozens of students, teachers, peasants and workers:

"For twenty years you've been saying in China that the number one enemy is the imperialist capitalism of the United States. Now, its leader is invited here. How do you explain this contradiction?"

The answers were similar: "Nixon is coming to China to try to find a way out of the impasse in which he's stuck. He has failed completely." "He can't get himself out of it in any other way." "He knows he's beaten." "He encounters so many difficulties in carrying out his policies that he's obliged to come and eat humble pie." A university professor told us: "In 1945 Chairman

Mao agreed to meet Chiang Kai-shek at Chungking and to drink a toast with him. Negotiation is sometimes a necessary phase in the victory of the revolution. It is a different way of carrying on the same battle."

Several people we spoke to quoted one of Mao's thoughts: "It is not because you receive your enemy that you adopt his line." We were told that this sentiment had been aired many times in the previous few months. We saw it on hoardings which had clearly been put up before it was announced that Nixon was to visit China. Slowly, the idea was absorbed by the masses. When the day came, they reacted perfectly.

In the weeks that followed, a campaign to explain these events was started. It developed the themes outlined by the Chinese we had asked point-blank on the spur of the moment. They were ready for us; the information they had been given supplied them with an answer to any question.

The Chinese masses have gotten so much into the habit of acting upon the most unexpected orders that no change of direction seems to surprise them. They know that there is a struggle going on which is never resolved once and for all. Politics has precedence over everything else. They do not feel their participation in the politics of their country is just a sham; they see it as a never-ending fight in which they are proud to be playing an essential role. At any rate, they act as if this were so.

11

The Tearing Down of Established Society

A May Seventh School

Some figures could be seen silhouetted against the light of the dazzling sky. A man pushing a wheelbarrow turned toward us, his face jovial. "What is he carrying?"

"It's human manure," Kuo Mo-jo said, leaning over my shoulder in the dark. I guessed that he was smiling.

"What does he do for a living?"

"He's a university professor. He's undergoing his reeducation."

This school—one of the two thousand "May Seventh Schools"—was about twenty-six miles outside Peking. Like the other farm-schools, or school-farms, the "Red East" school was started in accordance with Chairman Mao's directive of May 7, 1966.

"Isn't there a more reasonable way of employing a university professor than by making him carry barrowloads of excrement?"

"There's no more noble task. Civilization was born on the dungheap. It developed from the moment the nomads who were driving their herds across the steppe realized that by spreading their dung on the land they could make plants grow faster and thicker."

The university professor pushed his wheelbarrow down a furrow and then mixed its contents into the earth with his bare hands.

"There's no substitute for working with your hands. If you just tip out the dung and then cover the furrow with earth, it's much less effective as a fertilizer. You must make sure the earth and the dung are thoroughly mixed."

We were fascinated by this strange relationship between the intellectual and the dung. This cheerful smile of his—was it a façade, the forced smile of a wounded man making the best of it? Or the fixed smile of a captive who has fallen into the depths of despair and finds his situation comic in its absurdity? Or was it possibly delight at returning to an anal stage, and a complete absence of guilt because this return had been imposed? Or was it the beatific smile of the mystic who achieves bliss in extreme humiliation, saying with St. Paul: "We are made as the filth of the world."

In the end another member of the Standing Committee of the National People's Congress said to me: "I've done that work, too, during a stay in the country. . . . You get into the habit. It's tough for someone who's never done it, but in the end you pay no attention to it. In the meantime you win the esteem of the peasants, who have the advantage over us. They know that the first few moments are the hardest. They say: *He used to think he was superior, but now he's the same as us. He's not afraid of getting his hands dirty or putting up with bad smells.* That's how one becomes a good revolutionary."

Professors and students of Peita and Tsinghua Universities are fraternally united in this regenerative work. They are always coming and going between the cesspools and the cabbages. No doubt they began their studies or their profession by thinking in terms of a career, science and success. But here they are, confronted with themselves—returning to the state of their ancestors, peasants since the beginning of time; experiencing the pleasure of pain; seeking the esteem of the humble; answering the demands of the masses.

Around the farm are huts built by the pupils of the May Seventh School themselves. Inside them, beds are arranged as in a barracks; on the outside badly jointed parpens give the impression that it has been thrown together and is unfinished. Soldiers in green are in charge. The majority of those staying there are from the two universities in Peking, but there are also workers sent by their factories and peasants from the area; they had "lost contact with the masses," and here this contact is guaranteed. Everyone without exception wears the same blue gear and does the same work—apart from the fact that the peasants are in command and the intellectuals do the work.

There is a strict timetable: up at six-thirty to the sound of Mao's thoughts blaring over the megaphones. Communal toilet in a rather crude washroom at the end of each room—the men on one side, the women on the other. The living arrangements are strictly separate. Communal gymnastics, in trousers or shorts and vests. At seven-thirty a study session in Mao Tse-tung thought. At eight-thirty, breakfast. Work in the fields until twelve-thirty. Then lunch—boiled vegetables and rice. Half an hour's relaxation—ping-pong, volleyball, or a short walk. Then another session of work in the fields or workshops, or military training; when they finish at the May Seventh School the pupils must know their arms drill perfectly and must join the People's Liberation Army—"to defend the motherland from its enemies, no matter where they may come from." At four o'clock in the afternoon there are readings of Marxist or Maoist texts and group discussions while tea is served. Dinner at seven, and then reading the newspapers. At eight another study session or sometimes a show put on by the pupils. There are twelve hundred of them, and since the theatre, which is a kind of rural club where you can see the sky through the roof, holds only two or three hundred, they are packed in like sardines. The troupe—all amateurs—might give a performance of *The White-haired Girl*. Lights are out at ten-thirty.

"Is this kind of timetable appropriate to work on the land?"

"You can do more in four hours of enthusiastic work than in eight hours of passive work. In 1970 the 'Red East' School produced so many pounds of vegetables, so many quintals of rice, so many pigs and so many ducks.* In addition, working in squads of twenty gives great flexibility. While some are working in the pigsties, others are working in the ricefields or making megaphones in the workshop. But we've still got a lot to do, and everything's far from being perfect."

How delightful the mock humility of Chinese courtesy must seem after the real humiliation of tedious work! A professor of physics, an economics student and a member of the revolutionary committee of a district of Peking set off again, some with yokes or picks on their shoulders, some pushing wheelbarrows. They go off to plant fruit trees in alternate rows in earth which has already been treated with the precious dung. Although they are carrying different tools, they march forward in step and in close ranks.

"Why do intellectuals spend so many months doing work which peasants do much better, when China is short of intellectuals and the peasants are made redundant?"

The man next to me, who was a deputy and member of the Standing Committee of the National People's Congress, looked at me as if I had not understood anything: "That's a typical question from a Western intellectual." I had had this compliment before; most of our questions deserved it.

The deputy added, after a moment or two, perhaps fearing that he had upset me: "The pupils of the May Seventh School develop Red hearts. In the short term that's more important than productivity. We must get to the stage where the intellectuals are happy about no longer being intellectuals."

The May Seventh Letter

On May 7, 1966, three weeks before unleashing the Cultural Revolution, Mao sent a letter to Marshal Lin Piao in which he indicated that the army should become a "big school" in which the man of tomorrow would be

---

*We did not note the actual figures, but they were given in precise detail, contrasting as usual with the lack of data in the outside world on China's production.

formed. Cadres "who might submit to bourgeois temptation and fall back into revisionism" would come to "recycle" themselves under the authority of the army, which was to be transformed into a "big seminary." The "students," who would be of all ages, "would have to learn to work in factories, in the fields and in the army." In this giant forge the Chinese establishment was to retemper itself thanks to the study of Mao Tse-tung thought, production and its fraternal encounter with the proletariat.

The idea was not a new one; since the time of the Institute of the Peasant Movement in Canton, Mao had never ceased advocating free, compulsory and universal manual work. But in practical terms it was limited. It was the great upheaval of the Cultural Revolution which was to provide the opportunity to put these directives into practice on an unprecedented scale and to brush all the obstacles aside.

Possibly under the pretext of a return to the sources of the great Yenan period, some personalities whose positions were threatened sought to escape the shocks of the Cultural Revolution. Possibly the zeal of many intellectuals was linked with their desire to be forgotten. Nevertheless, the May Seventh directive has been put into practice everywhere—or so it seemed to us: in the revolutionary committees and the Party ranks, in the schools and universities, in the hospitals and the administration. Everywhere up to a third of the staff is away at any one time—either in a May Seventh School or in factories or in people's communes. When it was as widespread as this, the "recycling" could hardly be concealed; it was shaking China to its depths.

No doubt there were also economic reasons for this: the intellectuals are not the only ones who learn from the recycling; the peasantry, too, backward as it is, soaks up ways of thinking which are aimed at making the "Leap Forward"—which is still the unfulfilled dream of the Chinese leaders—easier to achieve. But the essence of the matter is elsewhere.

Mao's message to everyone, regardless of birth, qualifications or place in society, is the same: "You will be peasant and worker." This is the price the citizen pays for being "of the people," for sharing their troubles and worries, for living among them; it is the price the society pays for becoming socialist.

In the Wuhan Foundry

As we were walking single file beside the mills in the Wuhan foundry works—following behind a soldier in green who was chairman of the factory's revolutionary committee—workers gathered to see us. They seemed to have no particular job.

"They're the students," the soldier said. "They come here to forget what they've learned at the university and to plunge into working life."

"By doing nothing, don't they get in the way of the workers?"

"A little bit perhaps, but we're more concerned with ideology than with economics. The important thing is that they be trained and that they become true revolutionaries."

"Doesn't it get on the real workers' nerves to see idle students in their factory?"

"They're idle because they've just arrived. Soon they'll be starting work. The workers are proud that they're reeducating the students to make them into defenders of the revolutionary cause."

"Was the output of the students who came here earlier good?"

"Not always. Some fall ill and have to be sent back to the towns. Others have great difficulty doing as well as the workers. But the majority take the job to heart and reach a high standard; they leave full of enthusiasm."

In any event, this experience has made them discover the proletarian reality, and that is no mean achievement.

The Interlude of a "Top Leader" in Shanghai

At the ballet school in Shanghai we were told that artists also have to work in factories and on the land. I was astonished, and said so to Hsu Ching-hsien, member of the Chinese Communist Party Central Committee, who told us that "manual recycling" was the crux of political action.

"A dancer's legs and hands are so precious and so fragile," I said. "Isn't there a risk of injury?"

Hsu Ching-hsien leaped up; he drew himself up to his full height and gave me an ironic look. Determined to dispel this skepticism and intellectual complaisance, he said: "No one must be exempted from doing a period of work in a factory or on a farm. Manual work is good for everyone, even dancers. By doing it they learn to express the feelings of workers, peasants and soldiers. It is particularly important for us, the cadres; we—more than anyone—must mingle with the masses, to receive what they can teach us with humility. Mao said: *To teach others, you must first learn from them*. But it seems that at the Academy of Dance—in spite of what you say—it's a very long time since anyone went to the masses. I must look into that."

"In your view, how frequent should these periods spent working with the masses be?"

"Two or three months a year seems about right. Some stay longer, others not so long. Of my colleagues on the Shanghai Revolutionary Committee, the best is the Vice-President, beside me here. She spent three months in the country last year, and this year she's working in a textile factory for four months. I'm possibly the worst; I do barely one month. You know, you can always find excuses for not going. . . . And yet, when you're off sick, the work gets done just the same. So it all goes to show that no one is indispensable, and that one's reasons for not spending longer with the masses are bad ones."

He burst out laughing. His distortion of the proletarian line did not seem to worry him particularly, and his laughter infected the other members of the Revolutionary Committee.

When the outburst of communal gaiety had subsided a little, Hsu Ching-hsien continued in a slightly offhand manner: "All that should make it fairly clear to you that a Cultural Revolution is not enough."

During the meal that followed, I tried to make out whether this general uncontrollable laughter had concealed firm approval or a sarcastic view. A chat with Hsu Ching-hsien persuaded me once again that in China the laugh does not mean what it does in France.

"I'm off for the whole of next month," he told me, "to plant rice. But I know there's a difference between those who spend their whole lives planting rice and me. They know they've got nothing else to look forward to, whereas I know that for me it's only an intermediary."

I wanted to whisper "interlude" to the interpreter. But whether it is forced labor or recreation, this return to the soil has the same result. Can you imagine the Président du Conseil in Paris, the Lord Mayor of London or the Chairman of the Leningrad Soviet giving up his holiday to plunge into work with the proletariat?

"What's good during these periods is that there are no orders to be given; you receive your orders. And you appreciate the difference."

The Permanent Temptation of "Embourgeoisement"

Once again one finds that an essential characteristic of the Chinese revolution goes back to a reminiscence of Mao's youth. He told Edgar Snow how, when he was an assistant librarian, he had felt despised by intellectuals: "My office was so low that people avoided me. One of my tasks was to register the names of people who came to read newspapers, but to most of them I didn't exist as a human being. Among those who came to read I recognized the names of famous leaders of the renaissance movement, men like Fu Ssu-nien, Lo Chia-lung and others in whom I was intensely interested. I tried to begin conversations with them on political and cultural subjects, but they were very busy men. They had no time to listen to an assistant librarian speaking southern dialect."

Fifty years later it was possibly still the bitterness of the young provincial despised and cut by the mandarins, well established in their superiority, which appeared in the directives of the Great Helmsman.

Even a brief experience of the student life brought about changes in him which he witnessed dumfounded. He denounced his own *embourgeoisement*. "The soldiers had to carry water in from outside the city, but I, being a student, could not condescend to carrying, and bought it from the water-peddlers." Because he entered the cohort of intellectuals, he despised as much as he was despised. The mandarin prejudice in China is as deep-rooted as the prejudices of the nobility in France under the *ancien régime*: an intellectual would be cheapening himself if he condescended to do manual work.

Mao's confession was made public in a speech he delivered in Yenan on May 2, 1942: "I acquired at school the ways of a student; I then used to feel it undignified to do even a little manual labor. . . . I felt the intellectuals were the only clean people in the world, while in comparison workers and peasants were dirty. I did not mind wearing the clothes of other intellectuals, believing them clean, but I would not put on clothes belonging to a worker or a peasant, believing them dirty." That is what Mao said of himself. The difference between the intellectuals and the manual workers was confused in his mind—as in the minds of all his comrades—with the barrier between the refined and the vulgar, the agreeable and the disagreeable, the clean and the dirty. It is precisely this barrier which he wanted to tear down with the Cultural Revolution.

Putting the Intellectuals in Quarantine

"Liu Shao-chi and his clique supported a revisionist and bourgeois thesis which was inspired by the idea of the reconciliation of the classes." This was explained to me by the amiable leader of the Shanghai Revolutionary Committee. "In the same way, a few years ago, Yang Hsien-chen, the director of the Party School and a member of the Central Committee, reckoned there was no reason to pursue the class struggle in a socialist regime. This is a bourgeois trick to get people to believe there's no bourgeois spirit any more. The intellectuals still have three faults—they look for an easy life, they're egotistical, and they've no discipline. There's only one way of tackling these faults and that's by crushing the intellectuals, by putting them in quarantine and making them live among the workers and peasants. Well before the Cultural Revolution the *three likes and the three withs** gave us this aim; since then all we've done is to make this system more general."

In fact it was in Shanghai that the movement to reform the intellectuals

---

*Eating, living and working like (and with) the workers and peasants.

was most vigorously pursued, probably because there were more intellectuals there than anywhere else. The intellectuals had to give up their "comforts" and their "arrogance," and to blend into a work community in order "to gain inspiration from the genius of the humble."

Toward the end of the Cultural Revolution, Mao told a Western visitor, in a private conversation: "The intellectuals had no contact with the masses. The case of a Tsinghua professor is typical. Now he goes to the factory, but very often he's unable to answer the workers' and students' questions. The texts he used were decades old. A teacher can talk and talk, but he can't solve actual problems. Once he's rubbed shoulders with the masses, it's better."

Hsu Ching-hsien told me: "The intellectuals are pushed by an uncontrollable force into believing they are a superior breed. This pretension is ridiculous, but when they've been reeducated by the workers, peasants and soldiers they become more reasonable. You can make something of them."

"How do you define an intellectual? At what point does someone become an intellectual?"

"The intellectuals are people with secondary school diplomas."

"Junior or senior?"

"Junior is enough."

It is as if one called all French children with school certificates "intellectuals." When all Chinese have reached this level (and education is spreading so fast that this could be by the end of the present century), will they avoid the faults of the intellectuals?

The Pulverization of the Classes

When the Westerner hears the terms "bourgeois" and "privileged" being used all the time in China, he does not really grasp what they refer to. He feels he is in the most equal society on earth. All Chinese—young and old, men and women, city-dwellers and those who live in the country—dress alike. There is only one vast homogeneous class. One type of man—the worker with calloused hands. So how can there still be a class struggle?

It is precisely because Maoism is vigilant in denouncing any attempt to cease "being a people" that China seems to be the most "people-like" country in the world. The obsession with the struggle against the bourgeoisie is the reason for the disappearance of the bourgeois class.

The activists of the Left quickly found in China, as they did in all other countries, that the "bourgeois spirit" was not being tracked down and stamped out with sufficient vigor. The young people of Hunan published some very strange documents in the heat of the Cultural Revolution, and although they had certainly not read Milovan Djilas's book on *The New Class*, they were frantically denouncing the "new aristocracy" and the "new bourgeoisie," the "restoration of capitalism," the "dominance of the bureaucracy" under the influence of which they said the Party, the army and the nation's cadres had fallen. They founded the *Cheng wu lien* movement to denounce "the antagonism between the new bureaucratic bourgeoisie and the people's masses."

"The former holders of power exercise their bourgeois dictatorship under the leadership of Chou En-lai"—just as before the Liberation. They "dupe the masses who are still hypnotized by social-reactionary practices." No one has dared to cut out "the evil at its roots by suppressing the reactionaries and the bureaucrats who are in the service of reactionary tendencies." Only "a few isolated culprits have been ousted." Some officials have been dismissed, but "these are stratagems for keeping the old system." In 1968 Mao abandoned his pursuit of the revolution and became "the prisoner of the bourgeois"; he "gave himself up" to those who were working to "stamp out the revolution."

What a pathetic confession there is in these declarations! Before in their turn being denounced by the masses, the leaders of the *Cheng wu lien* tried to lead them into an assault on an impregnable hierarchy. Their iconoclastic passions were in the same vein as those of Mao himself. He too saw society becoming stratified before his eyes, a hierarchy being re-formed, classes being reborn and his egalitarian ideal being reduced to nothing. He did not succumb before this law of nature; he called on the young to smash everything. Can one blame them if they got furious when they encountered resistance?

Mao stubbornly pursued an aim which the Soviet-type communists long ago gave up trying to achieve—the establishment of a completely egalitarian society. Everything that singles the individual out is bad; everything that blends him into the mass is good. Stripes were abolished in the army. Maybe this is also the reason why no attempt is made to achieve great feats in the field of housing—the more the Chinese crowd together in rooms which have been transformed into dormitories, the more the collectivist society becomes established. Education, dancing, games—a uniform rhythm of life and information create a common way of thinking and living.

Chinese society is a society of continual mixing. The principle is the same as in purification plants, where powerful agitators shred up various substances and artificially introduce the aerobia which abound in mountain streams. The thousands of different groups and castes which made up the former Chinese society are reduced to shreds and rubbed against one another, air bubbles are passed through, and they are purified and regenerated by this mutual contact.

The Citizens Are Interchangeable

Kuo Mo-jo leaned across and whispered: "Men must be like the waves of the sea, so that you can't distinguish one from another and so that they're always taking one another's place."

The great dream of the one-dimensional man—to do away with classes and castes, you have to abolish all specialization. "We abandon the principle," Kuo Mo-jo went on, "that *I teach and you cultivate your field. We each do our own thing*. We say the opposite: *the peasant teaches, the teacher cultivates the field. We're all prepared to take one another's place*." This is why the big universities have small factories, the large factories have small universities, the villages have workshops, and the combines have farms. To bring the intellectual closer to the manual worker and the worker closer to the peasant, but more than that to create a single race of men—all of them being workers and peasants, manual laborers and intellectuals. The "three-way alliances" which are so often invoked do not always have the same meaning. Sometimes it is the "soldiers-cadres-revolutionary masses"; at other times it is the "peasants-workers-soldiers." Sometimes it is the "intellectuals-workers-peasants," sometimes it is the "teachers-students-proletarians," and sometimes it is the "three-way alliance of the ages" invented by Chou En-lai—old, young, middle-aged." But whatever it means at any one time, the formula represents an act of faith in the virtues of "mixing"—bringing different groups together revives the structures and injects new blood.

Each person is careful to achieve within himself a harmonious "three-way alliance." The interpreter I had, Chou Chen-tung, is a young career diplomat—in so far as one can speak of a career in a system which rejects the very principle, since everyone must be prepared at any moment to be mobilized for whatever task the revolution assigns him. Chou Chen-tung, though, is an example of the "three-way alliance" between the intellectuals, the soldiers and the proletarians; at one and the same time, he went through the university, served in the army and underwent "reeducation" in the country. He has the precision of speech of the intellectual, as well as the gestures and fine sense of nuance. He has the punctuality of the soldier, and also the sense of authority and respect for authority. And if he does not have the appearance of a proletarian, he does have the ideology. When he translates, the most simplistic pieces of propaganda become convincing, and are made even more attractive by his sweet smile as he beams from behind his thin glasses. At this level of refinement, the "three-way alliance" in practice attains the perfection of the *Spiritual Exercises* of Saint Ignatius Loyola.

Mao's "directive of May 7, 1966" stressed the idea put forward in the early writings of Marx—and one which disappeared in his later works—of interchangeability as the only way of preventing the permanent establishment of a leading elite, that is, of an established power. Anyone, whether a worker, a soldier, a peasant or an intellectual, must be capable of doing anything. "We other propagandists of Mao Tse-tung thought," we were told by someone we met at Peita University, "we're ready to fight on all fronts—the revolution, production, and if necessary war. Pick in hand, we can go back to the soil. Pen in hand, we can denounce the bourgeoisie. Microphone in hand, we can inform the masses. Gun in hand, we can defend socialism."

Fifteen Girls in the Fields and Peanuts

Of the many stories we were told, we thought the most important was the one about the fifteen girls and the little piles of peanuts; this is a story borne out by official documents.

During the Cultural Revolution hundreds of thousands of young people left the towns voluntarily to go into the country; not just to get the fresh air for a few weeks or months but with a view to settling down there for the rest of their lives. This is what fifteen young schoolgirls from Talien did: they left the town to regenerate themselves by doing manual work.

Going to the people to be the people . . . "In May 1966, when the mountains were covered with flowers, drums were beating and gongs sounding in a little village perched on a hill. . . ." This idyllic scene serves as a setting for acquiring revolutionary consciousness. "Grandmother Lin, who had suffered much in the past and had a deep hatred for the old society, got up earlier than usual and prepared a meal for the young girls in memory of past sufferings." It consisted of bran pancakes and soup made from wild plants with a piquant flavor. "Grandma Lin put the pancakes on the table. She started talking about the old days, how she had to beg for her food and how the landowners took pleasure in setting their wild dogs on her. . . . The young girls cried with her and ate their bran pancakes and bitter herb soup."

The first benefit of this peasant life is to make the young girls understand the deep significance of Mao Tse-tung thought and the need to avoid revisionism: "Grandma Lin was seized with violent rage and asked the young girls—'That great rogue China's Khrushchev says *there are advantages in exploiting the people*; he wants us to return to the past and start suffering again. Can we allow that to happen?'

" 'Never!' cried all those who were present. Cries of 'Down with China's Khrushchev!' and 'Long live Chairman Mao! Long live, long live Chairman Mao!' rang out along the valley."

One incident must have opened the eyes of the fifteen girls more than any theory lesson. This took place in a barn, where the members of the commune were sorting peanuts. Suddenly a woman, an "unhealthy element," cried out: "Let us put our peanuts in little piles so that the bonuses can be given out according to the number we've gathered. That's how we'll create competition." When the young girls heard that, they immediately understood that this was no small affair—it was a question of the class struggle. That night they went around to the peasants' houses to study alongside them the teaching of Chairman Mao: "Politics commands; that's the heart of everything." They criticized and rejected the revisionist theories of China's Khrushchev, according to which "production commands" and "material stimuli" are to be used, private gardens and the free market are to be extended.

Late in the night the young girls and the poor and middle-income peasants ran to the barn. When they saw the little piles of peanuts on the ground they thought that they were not "piles of peanuts" but "piles of egotism." They took wooden shovels and put all the little piles together in one big collective pile.

Next day the young girls made a bright red flag on which they wrote: "Struggle against yourself, decry revisionism!" With the flag held high, they marched to the barn. They planted the flag before those who were sorting the peanuts conscientiously, speedily and tidily for the revolutionary cause. That was how the young schoolgirls "spent two years of struggle in intimate contact with the invincible thought of Mao Tse-tung."

Overjoyed at the discovery they had made and at the resistance they had successfully mounted against the traitor who had come insidiously among them in the form of a "woman who was an unhealthy element," they decided to make their home in the mountain village. Today they are presented as an example to all school children in China.

The *Hsia-fang:* Punishment or Privilege?

Nothing demonstrates the ambiguity of "reeducation" better than the equivocal status of the periods of manual work. They may mean enviable promotion in the scale of revolutionary values or dreaded deportation to corrective labor camps. It is either the one or the other, depending on the case.

"Those who haven't recognized their errors," we were told twenty times, "do manual work until they've understood, until they're back on the right line." From the deposed President of the Republic, Liu Shao-chi, to the most junior member of the Party, from Rector Lu Ping to the most modest barefoot teacher, manual work seems to be seen both as a punishment and a salvation.

"Doing manual work" means "being thrown into the dustbin of history" for top personalities, but merely "being reeducated" for small fry.

The delegation poses with Prime Minister Chou En-lai and President Kuo Mo-jo.

One of Alain Peyrefitte's conversations with Prime Minister Chou En-lai.

The leaders of the Wuhan Provincial Revolutionary Committee.

A portrait and slogans welcome the passengers at the Sian air terminal.

The cave in Yenan, the end point of the Long March, where Mao lived like a peasant.

The interior of one of the four caves at Yenan where Mao lived for eleven years; it is now a destination of pilgrimages.

Peasants threshing corn in the province of Shensi.

A rural commune in Hopeh: men, women and children are all working.

A young worker outside a steelworks in a suburb of Wuhan.

A woman takes her grandchildren for a walk near the Summer Palace outside of Peking.

An open-air revolutionary show at a people's commune.

Traditional junks and foreign and Chinese cargo boats in the port of Shanghai.

New bicycles, wrist-watches, sandals and plastic belts: a rising standard of living.

The Shanghai Ballet School: art must play its part in the revolution.

At the Wuhan iron and steel complex a worker puts in six days a week, has no annual vacation, and gets 60 yuans ($31.00) a month.

Crude equipment in a foundry.

The poet, archaeologist and historian Kuo Mo-jo; at eighty he is a national monument.

Prince Sihanouk says of Mao Tse-tung: "We are brothers."

A French class at Peking University. The students are workers, soldiers and peasants. *"Un révolutionnaire ose reconnaître ses fautes et les corrige rapidement."*

A lesson in Mao Tse-tung thought: a critical reading of the *People's Daily* in a people's commune.

Sunday in a Shanghai park.

Removing an ovarian cyst under anaesthetization by acupuncture.

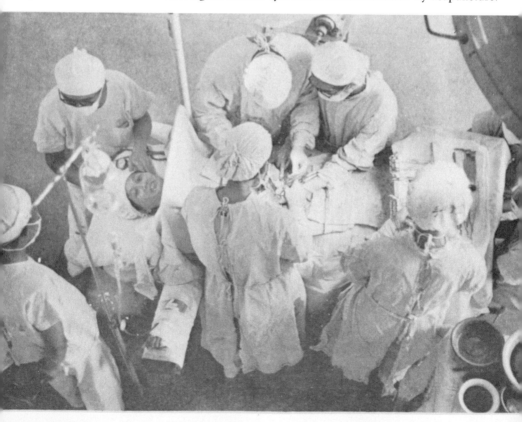

The Forbidden City; in the background, the Palace of the People and the Museum of the Revolution.

Young people looking through the windows into the forbidden rooms of the Imperial Palace.

Above: Handwritten wall newspapers.

Above left: Lovers in a Shanghai park.

Just over the border in Hong Kong, an old beggar woman—a sight that is no longer seen in People's China.

You ask where one of the leaders eliminated in the early stages of the Cultural Revolution has gone. Or one of those who played a key role in the first phase of the Cultural Revolution but who was crushed by the very machine he had helped set in motion. The answer is mechanical: "He is where he should be," and then: "He's doing manual work (*hsia-fang*)." How long will his "reeducation" last? No one knows. "It'll all depend on his attitude to his work."

Not everyone shows an exemplary attitude. Various witnesses told us that during the Cultural Revolution the intellectuals, students and cadres working in the people's communes took advantage of the first period of troubles to scatter like a flight of sparrows.

In Talien the fifteen girls who had been cited as an example to us had to confront groups of young people who, while claiming to be Red Guards, were trying to avoid the *hsia-fang*. All the signs are that a good number of students and school children thought like these bad Red Guards and not like the pure young girls.

It is not easy to shake people out of their habits. The ancient Chinese custom of binding feet was not intended as a torture but as a way of making women unsuitable for any work and even for standing upright. High society Chinese used to have fingernails several inches long—not for aesthetic reasons but to show that they did nothing with their hands. Before 1949 Chinese students always firmly refused to keep themselves by doing small jobs. In the same way, when the Cultural Revolution was in full spate the Red Guards seized on the marvelous pretext of "surveillance over the administration" to get back into the towns.

The army's intervention was needed to hunt down the Red Guards and "stray intellectuals" who had left their posts. It required all the power of the propaganda apparatus to get the countermovement underway.

But candidates were also being turned down without explanation. Many students, convinced by the propaganda, or realizing that all doors would stay closed to them until they had done their stint, or simply wanting a change of scenery, made repeated and unsuccessful applications—they were not wanted.

We heard a number of views like this one from a schoolgirl: "I was absolutely determined to show that whether I was bourgeois or not, the very hardest work didn't frighten me, so I asked to be employed on any job in the far-off Sinkiang desert, as a 'pioneer,' or in the Lanchow oil wells as a 'shock worker.' I knew these jobs required considerable physical effort and I really wanted to prove what a determined communist I was." These regions are China's Siberia—to work there is an honor. "Most of my classmates who were taken on for this work had failed their exams." Yet her friends were taken as pioneers, and she was not. So the "class origins" of a young bourgeois girl can—in spite of her diplomas—be a handicap which bars the way to *hsia-*

fang, whereas these very same origins compel others to go to do *hsia-fang* as a matter of priority.

No doubt "reeducation" through work must remain somewhere between punishment and privilege so that these aims can be achieved. If it were only a punishment it would turn the Chinese countryside into one enormous labor camp. If it were only a privilege there would be a risk that recruitment would soon dry up. At some point vaguely and mysteriously situated between these two extremes "reeducation" through work provokes both terror and enthusiasm by turns.

The Feats of Quiet "Reeducation"

The most astonishing thing about the Chinese methods of "reeducation" is that they seem to take place with a minimum of drama. "It's better to indoctrinate than to compel," I was told by many people, among them Chiang Kuei, leader of the Nanking Provincial Revolutionary Committee, a strapping man who looked as if he had been around. He went on, amid bursts of laughter: "Almost always things go very well. The cadres or intellectuals who need to be reeducated recognize the benefits of reeducation after some time, and they ask for more of it. It's only then that they can be sent back where they came from."

There are so many cadres who reproach themselves for having remained isolated from the masses, so many students who come to realize that they must transform their view of the world, so many teachers who confess to having remained bourgeois, but how many of them are sincere in claiming that they have undergone a genuine spiritual change of heart? How many of them are secretly champing at the bit, hypocritically proclaiming their conversion only to shorten their ordeals? It is very difficult to give an answer. On the other hand, it does seem that although the slightest unorthodox thoughts are mercilessly tracked down, they are pursued with a minimum of physical violence. Although four-fifths of the members of the Academy of Sciences have been sent into the provinces, none seem to have been killed or put in prison.

On a poster over the entrance to the Wuhan iron and steel complex there is a directive from Chairman Mao, dated September 11, 1968. It says: "Many of the students educated in the old-style schools are capable of integrating with the masses; they are welcomed by the workers, peasants and soldiers." In fact, it must often happen that workers, peasants and soldiers welcome outcast intellectuals with kindness. A few words of friendship inspired by pity can change the course of a soul and give courage to the despairing. "Those who are irremediable are very few," Chiang Kuei assured me, "those

who stubbornly continue along the capitalist road and don't want to understand. But we leave a way out even for these people; we're quite happy to
submit them to corrective treatment for as long as it takes." Most will recover
one day: those who are shaken up enough to adopt the mass religion without
reservations or who are clever enough to pretend—in other words, those who
play the game. On the other hand, those who refuse "reeducation" will
continue to suffer it. Such is the irony of the *hsia-fang*.

Periodic Brainwashing

"Again and again," Hsu Ching-hsien, the young leader of the Shanghai
Revolutionary Committee, told me, "you must wash your brain. If you forget
to do it from time to time, the capitalist spirit will soon return. This
brainwashing is painful; you feel the pain of it for a long time. That's
precisely why you must do it. If you didn't suffer from it, it would mean it
had become useless."

He went on, with the smile of a Buddha on his lips: "Ten or a hundred
brainwashings are needed in the life of a man. Ten or a hundred Cultural
Revolutions are needed in the life of China, if she is to remain Red for a
thousand or ten thousand years. The dictatorship of the proletariat can only
be established by rooting out all bourgeois influences. If one were to forget
the class struggle, even for a moment, this would be enough for a counterrevolution within each individual Chinese and throughout the country. The
Communist Party would become a revisionist party, that's to say a fascist
party. One would see the whole of China change color; it's almost done so
before. Red doesn't last well; it fades."

"Do you think," I asked, "that the differences between technicians and
peasants, between manual work and intellectual work, and between town
and country will gradually disappear? And aren't differences of origin among
the young beginning to reappear?"

Hsu Ching-hsien rubbed his elegant hands together: "Of course. As
long as a boy or girl hasn't been steeped in the revolutionary struggle, there's
a risk of succumbing to the temptation of the easy life, of restoring
capitalism. This temptation must be destroyed all the time."

The danger threatens young and old alike; it is human nature, and it is
always trying to come through.

"If we try to inculcate in the young a Marxism-Leninism of the past, the
revolution will stop. We won't make them the heirs of the revolutionary cause
by teaching dogmas, but by tempering their proletarian spirits. No one is
born Red. The young who were too small to have taken an active part in the
Cultural Revolution must all make a revolution themselves."

Apathetic and Activist

"Are the cadres and intellectuals who are sent to be 'reeducated' really animated by revolutionary zeal, or do they seek to do as little as possible?" I put this question to Hsu Ching-hsien. I did not ask it because we had noticed—either in the country or on building sites—many of those malingerers one sees in the Soviet Union, Poland and elsewhere. To tell the truth, most of the workers we had seen had been busy—not very quick perhaps, but steady. Would the apathy which seems to be everywhere in state systems also be present in the May Seventh Schools and other corrective work-places?

"Alas," Hsu Ching-hsien replied, "there are many bad elements who slip through and bring with them a taste for comfort and laziness. Some time ago, the pupils of a drama school who had been sent into the country to do agricultural service set themselves up for a comfortable holiday in a large house. They had a wonderful time there. But after they were there three months it was noticed that they had not cut any sugar cane. They had pretended to when there was an inspection, and then after the inspection they had rested again. There are cases like this from time to time. We've still got a lot to do to inspire the masses with revolutionary energy. Fortunately, although there are a few black sheep, there are many, many white sheep."

"Do the young people demand a return to the austere Yenan principles?"

"The great majority of young people today want to be—at one and the same time—workers, intellectuals and soldiers. They're aware that politics must take precedence over technology, but without making it disappear. They want to return to the purity of former times. They want to prepare for a people's war, even if this war is only to be fought on the production front."

According to what Hsu Ching-hsien says, it is the mystics who once again have the upper hand in this country. But for how long? The words of this charming revolutionary are still in our heads: "Ten or a hundred Cultural Revolutions are needed in the life of China. . . . Ten or a hundred brainwashings are needed in the life of a man."

12

"New Thoughts" or a Conservative Revolutionary Art

A Permanent Exhibition of Pop Art

The *ta-tzu-pao* are more than simply a powerful means of communication. Often, after they have finished their day's work, peasants, workers and young people spend the whole night drawing, writing and painting—which of course in China is all one operation, since writing involves drawing and painting. They do not produce their characters and illustrations in a slap-happy way—they try to find the most satisfactory way of adapting their inspiration to aesthetic requirements. They are well aware that of the thousands of *ta-tzu-pao* on display it is the most vividly painted which catch the eye—caricatures of bureaucrats and revisionists, shining portraits of Mao, pictures of partisans leaping out from the jungle and peasants perched on their tractors. The Cultural Revolution has really created a mass art.

One member of our delegation protested that posters in which the drawing was so stereotyped and the execution so crude could not possibly be considered art, especially since all the country's great artists had been "deported" either to the May Seventh Schools or to rectification camps. It would have been very surprising if the vast leveling process which had affected everything else in China had not also had its effect in this field. The fashionable painter had disappeared along with the industrial "boss" and the top scientist, the medical and university "mandarins." The only individuality which can be celebrated is that of the Great Teacher himself; only the masses are considered to have creative talent.

So the man in the street is invited to become a painter himself. China has sent her artists into the fields—but all the people have become artists. In France, house painters could scarcely call themselves "painters"; the *real* painter is an artist, a "Monsieur," even if he is a bohemian. The house painter is an artisan, a workman. In China it is difficult to distinguish between the artist, the artisan and the skilled worker. All over the People's Republic, peasants are decorating their houses, municipal employees are perched on ladders coloring enormous hoardings depicting a soldier bent under the weight of a sack of corn or a worker carrying a machine gun, children are decorating their classroom walls with watercolors, and workers are decorating their factory walls.

These spontaneous artists are seldom creative; they get along mainly by imitating, like art school students who set their easels up in front of the *Mona Lisa*. Inspiration does not change: a creative person, Bergson said, "has only ever expressed one thing," constructing his own universe to live in forever more. And in China inspiration is collective; it is not the individual who is creative, since all he does is passively reflect the accepted models. It is the whole Chinese people. They have covered the country with pictures of Mao and ideograms cut out of gold paper. You find them from one end of China to the other, but you find them only in China.

Tapestry-making in Hangchow

We spent a morning visiting the silk and tapestry factory in Hangchow. In a room with windows looking over a lake surrounded by willows, men and women were bent over their drawing boards, sketching the outlines of landscapes and portraits from postcards—the house in Shaoshan where Mao was born; the first revolutionary post Mao set up on the Chingkang heights; Mao speaking at the Institute of the Peasant Movement in Canton; a portrait of Chou En-lai*; portraits of Marx, Engels, Lenin, Stalin, and the leaders of fraternal nations like Prince Norodom Sihanouk and Enver Hoxha; and scenes from revolutionary ballets. In all, there are about twenty different subjects, all specially selected and reproduced in various sizes and materials, in black and white as well as in color.

Once the sketches have been drawn—in sizes which have been decided on by the factory revolutionary committee—the artist's work is taken over by electronic machinery. With five hundred automatic machines and six hundred thousand punched cards, the tapestries can be turned out several thousand times more quickly than by hand: an invention—we were assured—of the factory workers themselves.

---

*And, in the summer of 1971, of Lin Piao.

"Really? Weren't they helped by engineers? Weren't they influenced by techniques used abroad?"

"No, no. It was the broad masses who invented and developed this process."

Everything comes from the broad masses—and returns to them—the choice of subjects (those preferred by the masses), the sketches done by artists who are condemned to remain anonymous, and the ultramodern manufacturing process.

As in most Chinese enterprises, the nine hundred production workers are divided into three teams because of the level of demand; orders flood in all the time from every province. Every House of the People, every club and even the most modest family dwelling asks for a picture of Mao wearing his bathrobe after the famous swim down the Yangtse, Mao playing ping-pong, or Mao on the tribune of the Gate of Heavenly Peace, his hand raised in salute as thousands of Red Guards march past.

"However much we increase the rate of production," the leader of the revolutionary committee explained, "we can never manage to meet the demand. Before the Cultural Revolution, this factory was concerned mainly with turning out tapestries of emperors sitting under their canopies, courtiers in sedan chairs, court dancers and mandarins. The people are no longer interested in these castoffs of the old society. What they want are scenes from contemporary life, and they demand color, not just black and white."

From the loom, then, come the wart on Mao's chin, the drop of water on his toe, the tip of Stalin's moustache, Lenin's goatee, and Chou En-lai's dazzling, mischievous eyes—all in twelve colors, faultless and utterly predictable, turned out with the speed of a machine gun.

Artisans of Art or Artisan Art

Austere, high buildings, put up recently, we were told, but already beginning to look shabby, with the roughcast flaking off—this was the Peking artisans' studio. Tung Ching-yang, Vice-President of its Revolutionary Committee, told us its history. Before the Liberation the artisans had worked on their own account, but the competition that developed between them put them at the mercy of the foreigners who were exploiting China. Then beginning in 1949 collectivization gradually came in, and the first thing that happened was that individual work was coordinated. Then, in 1952 cooperatives were set up, and in 1958 three cooperatives merged to form this studio, with its eight hundred workers.

"So, it was progressive 'étatisation'?" We were asked to repeat the question; it did not seem to mean anything to him. After all, the state had nothing to do with it—it was "initiative from below" that had "demanded this regrouping."

In Peking there is now not a single artisan working alone. Other workshops specialize, but this one incorporates everything—painting on silk, painting on glass, lacquer work, cloisonné enamels, ceramics, and sculpture in ivory, jade, carnelian and coral.

We were told that "collectivization meant that important progress could be made." Techniques were modernized. As recently as 1965, cloisonné enamels were being made over charcoal, but now electric ovens are used. Electric machines are used for cutting hard stones instead of the old pedal machines. There are mechanical lathes for polishing sculptures. The blue of the Song ceramics—the "color of the sky after rain"—used to fetch the highest prices in the West, because it was not being made any more. The secret had been lost for five centuries, but it was reinvented thanks to Mao Tse-tung thought: "Rediscover what is best in tradition."

Like any move toward efficiency, industrial progress meant splitting up the production process among various specialists—apart, that is, from the prototype. No longer does one man conceive a work, plan it and produce it himself. The unique artist has faded away. The individual artisan has disappeared. The masses have become artisans. The piece of ivory passes from hand to hand. One man draws people. The next man does the trees. Each—we were told—requires a quite different technique. One man carves a landscape on a piece of hard wood, while another lingers over the contours of a face. A worker cuts semiprecious stones on a mill covered with diamond powder. One of his comrades agglomerates the ivory powder. Others are working with pliers and glue brushes to fix the cloisons of copper. Still others are polishing the eight hundred round cloisonnés the studio turns out every day. One person is printing delicate motifs on the insides of miniature bottles whose necks are so narrow that only the thinnest brushes can be used. Another applies a layer of lacquer—always the same—on the copper of the vases. As we watched all this, we asked ourselves: Is this art, when workers repeat the same deft maneuver for eight hours at a time, and then at the end of their shift another team takes over from them, and then another—twenty-four hours a day? Are they art—these objects turned out by their thousands, all identical? Yet there was great dexterity in the precision of these movements, tirelessly repeated, and these romantic landscapes and epic characters did bring a kind of dream world into many homes.

Traditional and Revolutionary Subjects

There are some artists who see the work through from beginning to end, from conception to the finishing process. They are the ones who create the models for endless series. Their subjects fall into two categories.

Either they imitate traditional art, or—as is most often the case—their subjects are contemporary. If they are traditional, they may be balls of ivory carved to look like lace, in which the sculptor manages to carve—through holes he has made in the outer shell—thirty-two other balls, embedded one within the other and each turning freely. This takes two years. There are also big paintings, lacquered screens inlaid with hard stones. And there are pictures of birds sitting in palm trees, flowers around a lake, and upturned roofs from the period of Confucius.

In the case of contemporary subjects, a block of ivory might be carved in the form of the heroine in the *Red Detachment of Women*, dancing a *jeté-battu* beneath the palm trees of Hainan island and holding her submachine gun above her head. The Great Bridge of Nanking might also be a subject—in hard stones of the appropriate color and with red flags made out of coral on top. Or perhaps a "chain bridge" to commemorate one of the glorious moments of the Long March.* Or a Treasure Pagoda on its topaz sugar loaf high above the steep hills of a pink quartz Yenan. We watched an ivory sculptor at work on a game of ping-pong; one player had slit eyes, the other was a "long nose"**—his jaws hanging open as if he were chewing gum.

Who says what the subjects are to be? "Nobody. The workers decide themselves," we were told. But when precious materials are involved—like a block of jade or gold leaf—is the job given to the worker who asks for it? "No, of course not. The workers with the least experience start with ordinary materials like wood and soft stones. The Revolutionary Committee keeps the expensive materials for the most highly skilled workers." And these craftsmen do not seem to worry about the extra value they are adding to these materials. One old sculptor had spent six weeks working on a beautiful piece of coral, and he was reckoning that the job would take him not less than a year. His work will be exported through Hong Kong and will be sold for thirty thousand yuans.*** A rapid calculation shows that the price of this sculpture is the equivalent of twenty-five years' wages for the sculptor. But has it ever occurred to him to make the same calculation himself?

Innovation and Conservation in the Proletarian Aesthetic

These partisans in their peaked caps holding high the red flag, and these episodes from the revolution fashioned in inlaid rosewood—are they representative of the true proletarian aesthetic? Chinese art has been given a revolutionary content; has it found revolutionary forms? Evidently not, and our little group was rather disappointed about it. We were told that the

---

*The famous crossing of the Tatu River (TRANSLATOR'S NOTE).
**Chinese nickname for white men.
***About 15,500 dollars.

essential thing was that "contemporary subjects" had been introduced on a massive scale. What is more, they said with some humility, "The reforms are far from complete; proletarian aesthetics have still not fully mastered Mao Tse-tung thought." To a Westerner's eyes, Maoist realism is every bit as inflated and pretentious as the Stalinist-style plastic arts, and probably more so. But do we in the West apply the appropriate criteria?

In art, as in every other field, the regime has broken with tradition. Instead of orders coming from the Court, the mandarins or the rich "Westerners," they now come from the revolutionary committees, the proletariat and the fraternal countries. The taste of the workers, peasants and soldiers has replaced that of the elite. And it is hardly surprising that there is a great difference between them.

Cloisonné vases, jade Buddhas, agate mandarins and amethyst palankeens were smashed by the Red Guards in 1966 and 1967—in the name of the proletarian line. These remnants of the imperial past were distracting the people from the revolution. The same techniques are in use today. Wrinkled old jade and ivory sculptors now produce work based on contemporary themes. White-haired goldsmiths and lacquerers turn out partisans and Red Guards. The Cultural Revolution is being sculpted. The Chinese imagination is thus peopled with stock characters.

"Basically," said Chou Chen-tung with a delicate smile, "bourgeois aesthetics and proletarian aesthetics have opposite aims. You in the capitalist world treasure objets d'art which are rare, and you despise those which are seen everywhere. Here, though, we reject forms which are different from the accepted models, and so the accepted forms are everywhere." Forms which are endlessly repeated and seen day in, day out by hundreds of millions of men and women.

These objets d'art are the only decoration which is officially permitted. Whenever we were received by high officials, it was always in the same surroundings—the same wicker armchairs with the same loose gray covers, the same teapots, the same spitoons, the same ashtrays on the same little tables. The spirit of Yenan still drives China's leaders; from the troglodyte houses in the Garden of Jujube Trees to the drawing rooms of the Palace of the People they have kept the same simple lifestyle, the same supreme contempt for elegance in the general surroundings of their daily lives. At first this absence of style came as a shock, but in the end one comes to wonder whether this might not in itself be a kind of style.

Revolutionary Music

The orchestra pit at the Shanghai Opera. The instruments are like those we have in the West, except for some Chinese gongs and violins. An ordinary orchestra pit in an ordinary opera house. In fact, if the conductor and the members of the orchestra were not dressed in gray uniforms with stand-up collars, you would think you were in Paris, London or New York. The music seems only superficially Chinese; apart from occasional ear-splitting crashes on the cymbals and some flute tunes which seem rather highpitched to the French ear, the overture and accompaniment to the ballet, *The White-haired Girl,* could have been European.

Otherwise, it seems to be a potpourri of Tchaikovsky, Lalo and Johann Strauss. Tunes keep coming back, and you find yourself wanting to whistle something from *The Queen of Spades, The Bartered Bride* or *The Firebird.* If you close your eyes, you are back before the war listening to an orchestra playing a medley of mazurkas and skaters' waltzes at a bandstand at Divonne-les-Bains or Bourbon-Lancy.* You wonder if the composer has been plagiarizing. The audience listens to these arrangements in silence, enjoying them all the more because they hear them so often.

For the music of these revolutionary operas is interchangeable—*The White-haired Girl, Taking Tiger Mountain by Strategy, Shachiapang* and *The Red Detachment of Women.* It is not long before one has heard the whole repertoire. The only instrumental work is a piano concerto called *The Yellow River.* You listen to the music in the concert hall or the opera house, and then you hear it again on records; on the radio—where the works are broadcast in full as well as played in snatches as signature tunes; over the loudspeakers; and from the lips of children who hum the tunes as they walk through public gardens. The whole of China is haunted by these tunes. In fact, they have become a kind of common language. A few tunes ringing in the heads of eight hundred million people as though they came from an invisible barrel organ.

"Who is the composer?" we ask.

"There isn't a composer. This music has been composed by the masses, armed with the invincible thought of Chairman Mao."

Hanging above the orchestra pit of the Wuhan Opera is a sheet of calico bearing a calligraphy by Mao Tse-tung which says: "With that which is foreign, make something national." If the broad masses have begun to compose works based on Western themes, it is because Mao urged them to do so. He made a decision which assumed some importance in the Cultural Revolution—on his orders, the opera *The Red Lantern* was transcribed for the piano and not for a Chinese instrument. It is hard to believe the Peking newspapers when they say the Chinese were spontaneously full of enthusiasm for the piano. The papers presented Mao's decision in the form of a real detective novel of the class struggle. "Counterrevolutionary revisionists" had succeeded in burying the joyous news of Mao's decision in silence for two and a half years. "But the counterrevolutionary revisionists did not admit defeat easily. They said the piano had to be smashed to pieces. They wanted to dissuade their comrades from using this instrument for revolutionary ends."

---
*Spa towns (TRANSLATOR'S NOTE).

Naturally, "insults and sabotage on the part of the piano's enemies could not . . . shake them."

Faced with an art form which enshrines revolutionary works in European music, a traveler determined to be enthusiastic about it said that "Chinese music brings together in a very happy combination the Chinese secular basis and the melodic scale of the West. This makes for extremely attractive music of great emotional power." Another visitor, somewhat more reticent, agreed with one member of our delegation: "It's not Chinese. It's half Viennese, half Russian. It's utterly conservative. The *Yellow River* concerto is so evocative of the play of the water that you'd think you were standing under a shower at the municipal baths. Is that revolutionary music? At best, it's 'neo–I don't know what' music."

But hasn't music which is on everybody's lips and which engages the latent energies of a people achieved its revolutionary aims?

How the Wuhan Acrobats Knock the Big Stick out of Their Hands

We were very anxious to see an acrobatic display. Trapeze artists, conjurors, clowns and foot-jugglers are traditionally the pride of China. Their displays, which had no political content between 1949 and 1966, were suspended during the Cultural Revolution, because they were expected to be more than just exhibitions of tumbling and cycling. The acrobatic shows had just been resumed. So were they now able to perform without being revolutionary—while everywhere else art for art's sake was in disgrace—or did their performances now serve socialism?

Wuhan is an odd town, where there was quite a bit of violence at the time of the Cultural Revolution. It is also the town Mao chose when he decided to astound the world by diving into the Yangtse. Traditionally, the acts were announced by actresses, and in such loud voices that they deafened the audience. In one of the numbers—called "lotus"—plates were spun on the end of long flexible sticks. How do little revolving cups and waving flowers glorify the "great victory of the socialist revolution?" How do the "chair games"—in which chairs are balanced one upon another—and the "feet games"—in which young girls lie on their backs and roll barrels with their feet—glorify "the Great Leap Forward on the different fronts of socialist construction"? Or are "revolutionary realism and romanticism"—which the program speaks of—coming together?*

---

*"Socialist realism" must "depict the everyday life of a people building socialism"; "revolutionary romanticism" acts as a corrective when reality is not so rosy—it "rectifies the artist's tendencies toward pessimism."

Certainly, the man in the street was up there on the stage, but the women were more coquettish and the men more agile than in real life. The peasants were represented celebrating the rice harvest, but the balancing acts were so stunning—seen in this operetta setting—that one easily forgot any ideological content they may have had. What could these feats and skills be demonstrating? How did they illustrate Mao's instruction: "The basic task of socialist literature and art is to try to represent the heroic image of the workers, peasants and soldiers. It is only with such models that our arguments will appear convincing, that we will be able to hold our positions firmly, that we shall be capable of *knocking the big stick out of the reactionaries' hands"?*

However, these appetizers were soon followed by the main courses. The conjuror came on—as a poor peddler who turns his pocket handkerchief into a Barbary duck in order to meet the needs of the masses. Then a bicycle pyramid was built up into an attack on the heavens. They were Vietcong bicyclists, armed with submachine guns, defending their land against American planes. The bullets whistled past, and some of them punctured the tires on which the pyramid rested. An American plane fell out of the sky—to cheers from the bicyclists and the audience. And so the classic trick cycling act ended up with an explosion of hatred by a group defying gravity with its impassioned movement.

After the Vietcong partisans came the Chinese military. Up near the roof pilots flew from ejector seat to ejector seat. Sailors pirouetted around a red flag.

And then there was the star act—an acrobatic navigator trying in vain to reach a lighthouse which he has to repair on a cliff. Although he makes the most daring leaps—which are so skillful they deserve to be successful—each time he falls back onto his boat, which is being tossed about in a storm. Finally he has an inspiration. He gets his *Little Red Book* from his pocket, and with one final, perilous leap, he makes it. It is like Astérix swallowing the magic potion.*

For the finale, the whole troupe came together, with rifles and submachine guns ready, *Little Red Books* held to their chests, singing a military song, and bringing to an end a show which has by sheer force earned the poster descriptions "revolutionary" and "anti-imperialist."

The auditorium of the Wuhan Opera, which was packed with young people, was electrified from the very first act. The audience hummed with delight at the feats of the acrobats, held its breath when they faced danger, gave support to their exploits, burst out laughing when the bicycle tires were punctured, and exploded into wild cheering. But the audience seemed to us

---

*A popular French cartoon character, Astérix the Gaul, who fights the occupying Romans with the aid of a magic potion which gives him superhuman strength (TRANSLATOR'S NOTE).

to be quiet and rather reserved when there were political allusions. The revolutionary argument seemed more of a concession than a conviction.

The Purge

A quick look at what was on in Shanghai revealed that this town of more than ten million inhabitants had been offering the same five plays and films *for the past three years*. And what is more, attendance is considered a political act, and therefore an obligation. A number of films from before the Cultural Revolution are banned. There is now no individual creativity or seeking after fame. In the whole of China when we were there there were only seven plays, ballets and operas, and all of them under the direction of Comrade Chiang Ching, Chairman Mao's wife.* The people have "reeducated the cadres entrusted with literary and artistic work and reorganized the ranks of writers and artists." The other shows are only variations on this repertoire. The inspiration is the same, whether the performance is by a folk troupe like the one from Yenan, troupes of "young Red Guards" as in Nanking, or troupes of acrobats from Wuhan.

The public had been used to variety. In 1962 over 50,000 different plays were being performed—they were either based on the classics or produced spontaneously after the Liberation. The Peking, Shanghai and Canton Operas devoted themselves primarily to traditional works. So over 200,000 actors and singers were doing their best to preserve and enrich the nation's theatrical and operatic heritage. In the cinema, there was great variety— films from China, the Soviet Union, Czechoslovakia, Yugoslavia and even the West, among them the Hollywood version of *David Copperfield*.

This intensive cultural life has been slowly stifled since 1964. The "Festival of Peking Opera on Contemporary Themes"** selected thirty-five plays. Then an artistic revolutionary movement got underway that became a prelude to the Cultural Revolution. The traditional repertoire was to be replaced by modern revolutionary plays. The Peking Festival—in which Madame Mao's influence was predominant—was hailed by the press as a "victory of the socialist Chinese Revolution."

The thirty-five plays of 1964—from the 50,000 listed in 1962—were later reduced to seven. Out of the vast repertoire which had been built up during the twenty years traveling companies spent entertaining the troops and during the first fifteen years of the Communist regime, hardly anything remained that was genuinely considered to conform to the victorious line. Even the seven plays that became models were purified still further in the crucible of the Cultural Revolution.

---

*Later to be accused by the regime of Hua Kuo-feng of having plotted against her husband.
**Held from June 5 to July 31, 1964.

As Lin Yang-yang, the ballet master of the Shanghai Opera, told us, "Our first attempts to bring onto the stage subjects taken from contemporary life ended in failure. Our artists slavishly copied the socialist realism imported from the Soviet Union. The masses instinctively felt that this model did not correspond to our line; it had been imposed on our writers and playwrights by bureaucrats who got their jobs on the orders of Moscow. This arrangement was wrong. We gave our dramatic art greater depth by linking it up with the oldest traditions of Chinese opera. Then the public realized that we had found the true way, the Chinese way."

What Lin Yang-yang did not tell us was that in the rigorous screening of the vast repertoire played up to 1964 it was not only the plays on contemporary themes—in which it was not felt that ancient China was reflected—that were cast aside, but also the many more plays which national and local traditions had handed down—and in which the spirit of present-day China was not expressed.

But Lin Yang-yang's answer leads one to suspect another reason. In order to get the Chinese to respond enthusiastically to works you want them to like, you have to put an end to the ruinous competition of traditional and foreign shows which attract more people. After this draconian process of selection, the public was no longer free to reject the seven plays that were retained, since they became the nation's only ones.

Destroying Harmful Germs

Maybe there is more to it. A foreign film, a traditional opera or a contemporary play which was not strictly in accordance with "the line" would introduce harmful thoughts and would risk destroying in a few hours the achievements of several years of proletarian development.

In the autumn of 1959 Marshal Peng Teh-huai was dismissed and replaced by Lin Piao for having bluntly criticized Mao Tse-tung at a Party plenum for errors during the "Great Leap Forward." A short time afterwards a play by Wu Han called *Hai Jui Insults the Emperor* was put on in Peking; in the form of an allegory borrowed from Chinese history, it told of the disgrace of an upright—but too outspoken—mandarin. The play enjoyed a great success, and Wu Han published a follow-up in 1961 under the title *Hai Jui Dismissed from Office*.

There is nothing as fragile as an authoritarian regime when it gives free rein to heresies. The army had to be brought in to put an end to Wu Han's "insurrection." The "Army Cultural Commission on Art and Literature" took as its first target this work of Wu Han, who had dared to use an allegory to attack Chairman Mao. The military soon settled their accounts with this offensive on the part of bourgeois ideology—of which these pamphleteering plays were only the precursor, the "refuge of anti-proletarian views."

Even those works which were the most revolutionary in their inspiration were screened—works like *Taking Tiger Mountain by Strategy* were scrutinized by a commission chaired by Madame Mao, and all concessions to the "revisionist line" were denounced scene by scene and line by line.

"Burning All Books" or "Fahrenheit 451"

These principles resulted in a general sterilization of literature. "In pre-Liberation China letters were a purely artificial activity," we were told. "Inspiration was for only a minute section of the population. The slate had to be wiped clean, and that's what we did."

One of the first acts of the Cultural Revolution was to close the bookshops. Hsi-tan arcade in Peking—where many of them were—became a dead alley; closed shutters were covered with slogans like "Let's put an end to the trade in reactionary trash!" "All books to the rats!" and quotations from the Chairman such as "Literature must serve the masses. It must be created for them and be used by them."

So the Cultural Revolution began a process of elimination. Not a single literary work was printed for five years. Those reopened bookshops we visited carried only speeches and writings of Mao and technical books. The official documents of the Great Proletarian Cultural Revolution and the library of Peita University contain references to poems, plays, articles and even novels written by peasants, workers and soldiers, but it does not seem to be very easy to get hold of them.

Everyone knows Truffaut's classic film *Fahrenheit 451*, in which Julie Christie, because the authorities are burning all books, learns her favorite book by heart. China at times reminds you of the same strange world. But in this respect (as in many others) Mao's policy is in keeping with Chinese tradition. The powerful Chin Shih Huang-ti, who built the Great Wall of China, issued a decree banning all books, especially Confucian texts. His successor, although concerned that the people should have enough to eat, maintained that books merely complicated life. "I conquered the Empire on horseback," he said. "What good are classical texts to me?" The Chin decree was not repealed until the reign of the Emperor Wen. Scholars then set about the difficult task of trying to locate old texts; some were discovered in walls and tombs, and others had been memorized by several generations.

Even in the libraries, readers can only get hold of certain carefully chosen foreign authors, like Balzac, Dickens and Zola—"witnesses of the decomposition of bourgeois society." They can get Gorky and Mayakovsky, but neither Pasternak ("a renegade") nor Solzhenitsyn (a "traitor who accepted the Nobel Prize just like Sholokhov").

Toward the Resumption of Artistic and Literary Activity

Will China's literary and artistic production—which has been interrupted since 1966—be resumed?

We were told that this earth could not last forever; the authorities were anxious to "get the creation of socialist art and literature going again." Efforts had to be made to "train and educate workers, peasants and soldiers." But it would still be necessary to "take account of political quality in selecting the creators."

In spite of these assurances, no writer has appeared on the scene, or at any rate none to whose work the public has access. Almost all of the writers who were publishing before 1966 belonged to the generation of the Leftist intellectuals who blossomed after the Movement of May 4, 1919 and threw in their lot with the party in 1949. Only Kuo Mo-jo has officially survived.

It is certainly clear that the Cultural Revolution has not kept its promises as far as the arts are concerned, and that the "masses" have not succeeded in creating the masterpieces that were expected of them.* It would seem essential to return to the pre-1966 policy which allowed those with talent to express it, and which allowed *individuals*—with names and a reputation—to write, compose and paint. It will no doubt be a long time before writers and artists who have been so brutally treated are prepared to come out into the open again. The backlog in the economy has quickly been made up by increasing production, but how can the lost years in the arts be made up?

---

*In the arts as in politics, a volte-face is not impossible. American artists, playing classical as well as modern music, have been acclaimed in China. A few years ago jazz and Beethoven were being censured as "bourgeois music," so what does this sudden turnabout mean? And why should the Chinese now have access to the arts from other countries, but not to their own arts, which have a tradition going back centuries?

13

The Exemplary Characters of
the Repertoire

Terrifying or Admirable Monotony

As we have seen, only seven "model revolutionary works of the theatre" remained in the sieve of the Cultural Revolution. Not eight, but seven— which were destined to be a unique system of reference. The two biggest dance troupes, at the Peking and Shanghai Operas, present them as revolutionary ballets. Color films have been made of them, and these are shown in all the cinemas and every day on television. Local companies put them on as plays. The music from them is on long-playing records, and boxes are sold in all the big shops for next to nothing. But you cannot buy anything else. Sketches are taken from them for school children and Red Guards.

In fact, there were probably no more than seven *chansons de geste* in France between the tenth and thirteenth centuries. And for five centuries the Greeks had nothing but the *Iliad* and the *Odyssey;* children learned to read from them, and they were recited in public. In Italy, too, popular culture was based on just a few operas.

The Chinese imagination is peopled with only a few characters—and they are all peasants, workers and soldiers. Chinese of all ages, both sexes and any status share the same aesthetic experiences, learn the same lines and are lulled by the same rhythms. These refined and expurgated works offer the people the quintessence of what they should love and hate, the perfect models which they should imitate. Hundreds of millions of minds follow the same handful of adventures in the service of identical revolutionary aims. These works—which are known by heart and are sung and danced in factory creches and in the most remote people's communes—offer the Chinese, who until recently led very separate lives, an extraordinary means of communication. Grandmother Li, the young Hsi-erh, and the heroic railway pointsman Li Yu-ho are now part of the cultural heritage of all Chinese from Tibet to Manchuria, from Mongolia to Hainan.

The transformation of the traditional theatre was the starting point for the Cultural Revolution, and it has become its culmination. This limited repertoire molds a collective outlook.

We saw three of these seven works—*The White-haired Girl, The Red Detachment of Women* and *The Red Lantern*.

The White-haired Girl

The Shanghai Opera—the second most beautiful hall in all China, after the Banqueting Hall of the Palace of the People in Peking—is packed with workers. They are all wearing white shirts and blue trousers, and it is difficult to tell the men from the women.* The *White-haired Girl* was composed in 1945 and is *the* work; it was first produced in Shensi on the boards of a company which was entertaining the troops there. It quickly became famous. It was exported, then transformed into a "revolutionary ballet on contemporary themes"; it survived the Cultural Revolution with the stamp of Madame Mao, and then became something of a craze, with people flocking to see it in order to weep at the misfortunes of the gentle heroine and to rejoice at her rescue.

The action is set in a village in the province of Hopeh during the resistance war against Japan. The beautiful Hsi-erh, the daughter of a poor peasant Yang, and her fiancé Ta-chun, a peasant from the village, are preparing for the New Year festivities; Hsi-erh intends to present her father with some humble gifts. Huang, a landlord, sadistic despot and collaborator with the Japanese, comes to abduct the young girl. He finds her alone. But then her father Yang comes back. The landlord kills him before his daughter's eyes. He abducts her and keeps her as a servant and slave. He treats her cruelly. Hsi-erh manages to escape into the mountains and to elude her pursuer; she lives a solitary existence.

Her hair turns white. Her fleeting appearances provoke a superstitious fear among the mountain people. They place food on an altar at the foot of a grotto, as if she were a goddess. All she lives for is vengeance. "As season succeeds season, my hatred grows fiercer; the howling of the wolf, the roaring of the tiger are nothing to be feared. I hope, yes, I hope, I hope that the red sun will appear in the East!"

---

*A theatre ticket costs from 4.5 to 6 *mao* (about 25 to 30 cents). A cinema ticket is from 1 to 2 *mao* (5 to 10 cents). (The *mao*, incidentally, has nothing to do with the Chairman's name.) The tickets are usually not on open sale; they are distributed in collectives.

In the end the village is liberated. A detachment of the Red Army arrives, beating the drum to "punish the despots and the traitors." The villagers put out the flags and pursue the fugitives. Huang, the landowner, is calmly executed on stage without any kind of trial after a brief "people's judgment." The crowd gasps with pleasure when the revolver is fired and the petty tyrant falls to the ground. Hsi-erh recognizes the head of the Red Army detachment. Yes, you have guessed—it is her fiancé, Ta-chun. The White-haired Girl sings a hymn to the sun: "The sun is risen! Thousands of years of suffering and hardship now see the sun rise! The sun is Mao Tse-tung! The sun is the Communist Party!" But Ta-chun reminds her that the revolution cannot just be concerned with personal vengeance: "The proletariat can liberate itself finally only by emancipating man." Everyone swears to pursue the revolution to the end—until the old injustices are abolished forever.

It is easy to see the ancient Chinese myths behind this contemporary story—the "white goddess" worshipped by the peasants; the persecuted woman who prefers to flee and go mad rather than submit to oppression*; the sun myth applied in turn to a pagan divinity, to Buddha and to Mao Tse-tung.

At the end of the show—as at the end of all shows—the company comes back on stage to sing *The East Is Red*; they stand there joyfully waving their *Little Red Book*s. The audience is on its feet applauding. Then the company joins in, in the communist tradition, showing the audience how much they appreciated their attentiveness, and making an offering of mutual homage to the work that has brought those on both sides of the footlights into communion.

It is a beautiful show that is never boring. Of course, the music is completely European in inspiration—with the exception of some popular tunes, a Chinese violin solo and a few gong beats; the choreography is uninventive—except for acrobatic leaps in the battle scenes, *jêtés battus* by soldiers brandishing submachine guns, and folk dancing by the villagers. All this leaves the Western aesthete with a sense of frustration. But the consummate skill, the gracefulness and the long legs of the star Mao Hui-fang and her comrades** ensure the success of the show. It is the precision of the performance, its speed, the colors, the beauty of composition and the meaning of the collective movements that attract the audiences.

With its technique copied from *Swan Lake* and its realistic decor (which even reproduced the effects of the sunset and lightning streaking across the

---

*Chou En-lai came across such a woman, who would let no one come near her, and who lived in a cave like a wild animal; her whole family had died of famine, leaving her a demented orphan. The villagers brought her food at night; she would come out to get it and then run back to her lair. No one dreamt of seizing hold of her.
**The role of Hsi-erh is so tiring that there are three other dancers who take over the part in turn.

clouds), it could be called a "monument of conservatism," and indeed it was so described by one of the group. Yet, although there is much that is conventional and stereotyped, it still projects the dramatic intensity of a myth which exalts the great principles of the revolution.

The Red Detachment of Women

The Red Detachment of Women is very much like *The White-haired Girl*. Written in 1964 and adapted in 1970 to incorporate the principles of the Cultural Revolution, this six-act ballet is put on by the Peking Opera Troupe and has the same star as its twin ballet put on by the Shanghai Opera Troupe.

The beautiful Wu Ching-hua is, like Hsi-erh, a poor young peasant girl who is cruelly mistreated by her master, a wicked landowner, and then saved thanks to communist partisans. She then joins the ranks of the women's section of the Red Army. These women wear khaki shorts and shirts, and apart from their hearts, the only red they sport is an armband bearing the words "Red Army." The Party representative in the detachment, Hong Chang-ching, an intrepid communist, dies at the stake without saying a word. The martyr's blood brings forth its harvest of partisans. Wu Ching-hua, whose revolutionary consciousness is born out of resentment against her master, redoubles her hatred for her oppressors. She finds herself at the head of a vanguard of the proletariat bent on dying for the cause of the revolution.

Tang Hai-kuang, the oldest of those who went to the performance with us, took it upon himself to tell me what was happening, and to comment on it. The action took place on the island of Hainan, where he came from himself. Normally a man of few words, Tang was unstoppable; he told me how he had fought in the resistance on Hainan, and how the play was based on fact. He became quite emotional when he told of the extortions of the landowner.

Of course, the master is executed in the last scene, and the humble peasants end up as victorious warriors.

The Red Lantern

The Red Lantern is rather different; it is not a "ballet," but a "model Peking opera."

It is a winter night in a town in Northern China occupied by the Japanese. The communist railway pointsman, Li Yu-ho, is on the station platform waiting for a liaison man. When the agent leaps from the moving train, he is fired upon by a Japanese patrol. With the help of his comrade, Wang Lien-chu, who is also a member of the Communist Party, Li Yu-ho manages to shield the wounded man from his pursuers and put him up at his house. After exchanging passwords and holding up the red lantern, Li receives the precious secret code which he is to deliver to the partisans.

The Japanese know about the important code, and are looking for the liaison man. They get hold of Wang Lien-chu, Li Yu-ho's comrade, and torture him; they get him to talk and to join up as a mercenary police officer. Because of the cowardly traitor Wang, the net tightens around Li. But before he is arrested, Li lets his mother and seventeen-year-old daughter Tieh-mai in on the secret. His daughter cries out:

> Now my aims are high and my way is clear.
> Blood must pay for our blood,
> Our children take on the cause of our martyrs.
> Here I raise the red lantern, let its light shine far.
> Oh, father!
> My father is as steadfast as the pine,
> A communist who fears nothing under the sun.
> Following in your footsteps I shall never waver.
> The red lantern we hold high, and it shines
> On my father fighting those wild beasts.
> Generation after generation we shall fight on,
> Never leaving the field until all the wolves are killed.

Li Yu-ho resists torture, and, covered in blood, sings of his unconquerable hope for the success of the revolution:

> Once the storm is past flowers will bloom,
> New China will shine like the morning sun,
> Red flags will fly all over the country.

He and his mother are then shot by a Japanese execution squad. As they fall, they cry out: "Long Live Chairman Mao!" The Japanese release the young Tieh-mei, with the intention of following her in order to get hold of the secret code. Tieh-mei, who is grief-stricken but galvanized into action by the deaths of her father and grandmother, raises the red lantern and cries:

> Oh, grandmother, oh, father, I know what you died for. I shall carry on the task you left unfinished and be the successor to the red lantern. Nothing can stop me from delivering the code to the Cypress Mountains and avenging your bloody murder.

She manages to escape with the code, and reaches the partisans in the Cypress Mountains. They ambush the enemy and wipe him out. They celebrate their victory, holding their weapons above their heads. Tieh-mei holds up the red lantern. The stage is flooded with light.

A quotation from Chairman Mao draws the lesson from the opera: "Thousands and thousands of courageous men and women have given their lives for the people. Let us raise high their flag. Let us advance along the path marked out for us by their blood!"

A Collective Art for Personal Use

Why is it that a theme which in Europe has been the subject of so many films and novels is expressed in China solely through the medium of revived opera? It is because this medium corresponds more closely to tradition and speaks more clearly to the masses. As long ago as the thirteenth century, the struggle against the Mongols was the subject of epic plays, with solos, acrobatics, group tableaux, flags waving, duets between a popular hero and a foreign oppressor, scenes just like the one in which pointsman Li Yu-ho defiantly stands up to the Japanese captain. In this respect, the revolution is identifying itself with the deepest traditions of the country. It sets against a background of the *Internationale* the eternal struggle of the patriots, the horror of the invader, the denunciation of collaborators, and the bravery of the young who bear the burden of the sacrifices.

The four other model works* have also become the subjects of a vast iconography: posters outside cinemas, portraits of the heroes and pictures of scenes in shop windows and on hoardings, sculptures in studios. A brief analysis of the themes of these works throws light on the private inner world of the Chinese.

*Taking Tiger Mountain by Strategy*** tells an authentic tale of the Red Army in the winter of 1946. A commando has been given the task of cleaning up a region which is infested with bandits. Yang Tzu-jung, the platoon leader, is able to combine cunning trickery with absolute devotion to the Party. By a stratagem, he manages to steal into Tiger Mountain and right up to the bandits' nest. Thus he leads his men to victory.

*On the Docks**** is the only one of the seven works that is not set in a military context. The opera is about a dockers' brigade in the port of Shanghai. The sacks of corn and rice which they handle are a link between socialist China and the fraternal countries of Asia, Latin America and Africa; the "world struggle" against imperialism depends on them. Clear the decks: sabotage has been discovered and it could bring about a catastrophe. Then, a solo by a student docker, the young Hsiao Han, who, having fallen prey to the "bourgeois temptation to make a career," tells of the ideological states of mind which led him to be partly responsible for the sabotage. "Helped by his comrades and the Party officials," he ends up acknowledging his errors and swearing to dedicate his life to the "line" of Chairman Mao. He realizes that the perfection which is demanded of every Chinese is vital for the success of the world revolution.

---

*We did not see them, but they are not hard to imagine from the color pictures, records and libretti we were able to bring out with us.

**Written in 1958 and revised in 1963 under the direction of Chiang Ching, it was recast in 1969 by the Shanghai ballet school under the impulse of the Cultural Revolution.

***Written in 1963 in Shanghai, revised under the direction of Chiang Ching in 1969.

*Shachiapang** is set in a small village south of the Yang-tzu Chiang and in the middle of the marshland which gives the opera its name. Wounded soldiers from the People's Liberation Army have sought refuge there. Hunted by the Japanese and their collaborators, they are saved because in this village they are "like fish in water." Thanks to the determination of their Political Instructor, Kuo Chien-kuang, a model revolutionary fighter; to a trick on the part of the Party liaison man; to an old aunt who resists torture; and to the complicity of anonymous villagers, the wounded succeed in rejoining the Red Army, which liberates the village.

Raid on the White Tiger Regiment takes place in a Korean village in 1953, after the breakdown of the Panmunjom talks. In order to smash an "American-puppet" offensive, a reconnaissance squad called "Dagger" has to penetrate deep into the enemy lines and wipe out the "White Tiger" regiment's command post, which is generally considered impregnable. The leader of the "Dagger" squad, Yang Wei-tsai, who inspires his men with his daring and coolness, sets off into the night and risks his life to fulfill his mission. In the finale, the Chinese volunteers and the Korean soldiers celebrate the "great victory of Chairman Mao's military thought," and then go off on another mission.

So, a new genre has been created, and it is difficult to define—ballet? opera? opera-ballet? The two pieces which are called ballets, *The White-haired Girl* and *The Red Detachment of Women*, have parts which are sung. The other five, which are called Peking operas, have sections which are danced. In the same piece there are dances, songs and symphonic music. Techniques borrowed from Western choreography and sets and music which are quite European are mixed with traditional features of Chinese opera—gigantic leaps, mock sword fights, and the unfurling of flags. New wine in old bottles.

The amazing thing for the Chinese audience is to see on the stage an adventure which they have just lived through in real life, and to see that it also fits into the great fresco of their eternal history. It is both folklore and Liberation. Dream and reality come together. This art can be profoundly moving for those for whom it is created.

Out in the streets of Shanghai one evening, we saw the tower in which the English had installed a replica of Big Ben. It was almost ten o'clock, and just before it began striking came the chimes of *The East Is Red*. Outside the cinemas there were huge crowds, the only queues we saw in China. They were waiting to see the film versions of *Taking Tiger Mountain by Strategy* and *The Red Detachment of Women*. They were going to see the last performance; it would end after midnight, which is very late for people who normally go to bed early and get up early. Could there have been a single person in the queue

---

*Written in 1964 under the direction of Chiang Ching and revised—also under her direction—in 1970.

who had not already seen the original on the stage several times? What were they expecting of the film? We noticed in the theatre that the audience reacted much more favorably to the acrobatic dances than to the songs of anguish or triumph, and much more favorably to the cleverness of the production—the way it presented snow falling or the sun rising—than to the fervent declarations of loyalty to Chairman Mao. But the Chinese make a good audience. It is certainly not a single aspect of a work which appeals to them; it is the work as a whole—the dramatic intensity of it, the catchy rhythms, the magic of the colors and the different scenes, the words and the music. A total spectacle, to which film adds its own special magic.

In the Wings

Our cars came to a halt in a park on the outskirts of Shanghai. It was alive with cicadas. Although it was not yet eight o'clock, it was hot. The famous Academy of Dance—which performed *The White-haired Girl* on stage and on film—was waiting for us, with *Little Red Books* in their hands, all ready to go. On the top floor of a modern building (which was already looking old), dancers, conductors and musicians were practicing. Near me was the director, or rather the leader of the Academy's Revolutionary Committee; he was a military man, wearing green denims and a cap pulled down over his ears. But he had no insignia to indicate his rank. He might have been an ordinary soldier, a captain or even a general. His fine features and aristocratic profile were those of a mandarin's son. But how was one to know? Ballet students, with their hair pulled back with elastic bands, served tea. The corps de ballet was demonstrating some basic exercises. The boys were in blue tights, black shoes and white sweatshirts with sleeves. The girls wore yellow tights, pink shoes and red sweatshirts. The pas-de-deux, *entrechats* and *pas de bourrée* might have been from *The Nutcracker* or *Giselle;* all they had added were some leaps and bounces which soared to an almost incredible height. A gentle breeze blew through the windows, which were open all the way down both sides of the room; carried on the breeze was the chirping of the cicadas.

We might have just stood there naively admiring the beautiful way they carried their heads, their lively faces, fine hands and sinewy legs, but then someone opened our eyes to what was really going on.

The *jeune premier*, who had the face of the hero in a popular novel, started the discussion with a public confession: "I was born into a family of poor peasants. At the Academy of Dance I received a bourgeois education which left a deep mark. It was not until the Cultural Revolution that our school adopted the proletarian way and I understood that the tatters of the past had to be thrown onto the rubbish heap. In the end the ballet turned its back on the ignominy of revisionist aesthetics. Now—it expresses only the revolution, the horror of the old times, the heroism of the partisans. It has taken as its aim the political education of the masses. All the students at the Academy of Dance now understand that they have to become the ambassadors of the headquarters of the proletariat."

We asked the name of this *jeune premier*, who had recited his profession of faith without faltering and in such a strong voice. The question was avoided. "Here, there are no stars. He's just one of the artists. What counts is the troupe."

"But how are we to identify him?" one of our journalists asked.

"Just say: the actor who plays the part of the hero Ta-chun, leader of the Red Army detachment."

The ballet master was the next to speak. He was a charming little man with a slightly effeminate face, but eyes which were burning with revolutionary faith. He agreed to give his name. He was Ling Yang-yang. He explained the method he uses to express revolutionary feelings with traditional choreography. "The classical language of the ballet liked to represent a utopian hope by a series of graceful leaps, like a bird flying into the wind. We have transformed this figure into a movement of revolt."

As he spoke, he made gestures with his index finger. His eyes sparkled.

"Leaps in Western ballet often indicate illusion and irresoluteness, as in *Giselle* when the wilis float hesitantly into the forest. In China, the leap— with arms raised and fists tightly clenched—expresses the force of the revolution." Lin Yang-yang demonstrated, by raising his arm, clenching his fist, and putting his spinning leaps to the service of revolutionary ideology.

"The solo—which ends in a virtuoso pirouette—was a piece of bravura, noble in style. It was intended solely to direct the audience's favor toward the leading dancer. The Chinese solo—which is identical to the Western solo apart from the mask-like expression and the final pose of the crack shot— expresses the people's fury with the landowner."

So the same movement which expresses the affected feelings of bourgeois society symbolizes—for the Chinese—class struggle.

"We've taken the pas-de-deux and transformed it into a movement representing anger with the landowners. Likewise, your classical duet represents love. Romeo turns around Juliet. Woman is the willing prey of man. It's a reactionary idea. For us, the woman can be in the center and the man can turn around her on condition that this represents not love but hatred, on condition that the woman is a poor peasant and the man is the landowner trying to seize her."

Lin Yang-yang did a few steps as a demonstration. "Point work—the favorite way of parading one's love. Raise a fist above the head and Juliet's ecstasy is transformed into the desire for vengeance."

All the ideas and feelings have their conventional forms. But love itself has changed its meaning. "It's no longer the egotistical search for pleasure by two people. It's two people's determination to make the revolution for everybody." The landowner's hand placed on the dancer's waist "is the humiliation which breaks out in the struggle between the classes." The duet between the peasant man bringing home a sack of flour and the young peasant woman who is there to welcome him "is the friendship of work, the people helping one another." Bourgeois love has been replaced by the hope of two people for a better future for the proletariat.

So these are a few figures of Chinese classical art: the walk of despair on the knees; dancing around and around to express disarray; a series of leaps to symbolize the struggle; sudden dashes, with gun in hand, to represent the will to vanquish.

I asked Lin Yang-yang how the dancers were recruited.

Out of tens of thousands of candidates, only 155 were selected—65 boys and 90 girls. Two criteria are used above all: their proletarian zeal, and their physical suppleness and dancing technique. For the leading dancers physical appearance "is also a consideration." But a good revolutionary outlook and instruction by the poor peasants in cooperative manual work play an essential role. To express revolutionary themes, you have to be on the right line yourself.

Hsu Ching-hsien, the leader of the Shanghai Revolutionary Committee, did not go along with this optimistic statement. He told us he regretted that the Academy of Dance had not been back to the factory or the countryside to do manual work for a long time.

The conductor of the orchestra, who is also a composer, defended himself vigorously against the criticism that his music lacked originality.

"Is your music really avant-garde?" we asked.

"If what I am told is right, for you in the West avant-garde art consists of jigging about in a group, stark naked, to discordant music which sounds as if a cat were walking up and down a piano keyboard. For us, the arts revolution must take place at the roots, not in the form. Music is original if it expresses new feelings by means of a classical technique."

Thirty young female dancers in costume then burst onto the floor. They were supposed to be members of the People's Militia. They were pointing guns and raising their pistols and curved sabres—in a ballet which was full of pirouettes and somersaults. Then they formed a "chain bridge." This recalled the famous episode in the Long March, and was a group composition rather like Rude's "Marseillaise."* Its colors were blue and red, and it had a great feeling of movement, with rifles and yataghans. It was raised with such force

---

*François Rude (1784–1855), the French sculptor whose best-known work is the bas-relief group "Le Départ"—also called "La Marseillaise"—at the foot of the Arc de Triomphe in Paris (TRANSLATOR'S NOTE).

and faith that Chiang Ching was surely right when she said: "It is inconceiva-
ble that, in our socialist country led by the Communist Party, the dominant
position on the stage is not occupied by the workers, peasants and soldiers,
who are the real creators of history and the true masters of our country. We
should create literature and art which protect our socialist economic base."

It was quite clear from the demonstrations of the Shanghai Academy of
Dance that Madame Mao's injunction had been largely fulfilled. China has
found her own solution to the main problem that confronts artists today—be
they in the "free" world or the socialist world—that is, how to create a new
aesthetic which is truer, more authentically expressed, and closer to real life.

The Ultimate Goal of Revolutionary Art: Proletarian Pride

Printed in the program of one of the performances was a letter Mao sent
to the Yenan Peking Opera Theatre in 1944. It said: "History is made by the
people, yet the old opera (and all the old literature and art, which are divorced
from the people) presents the people as though they were dirt, and the stage is
dominated by lords and ladies and their pampered sons and daughters. Now
you have reversed this reversal of history and restored historical truth, and
thus a new life is opening up for the old opera. That is why this merits
congratulations."

The regime keeps the workers hard at it, in fact harder at it than ever.
But it is careful to give them in exchange the reward of dignity. Not only
their dignity as Chinese, as members of a nation which has regained its
power, but also their dignity as proletarians, as members of a class which has
won its power. Why didn't the theatre ever present peasant heroes? Because
before the Liberation the workers were considered to be no worthier of
figuring in a work of art than the beasts of burden they resembled. Now they
have mounted the stage. They have become heroes. There are in fact no other
heroes but them.

At the Academy of Dance, the *jeune premier* "who plays the part of the
revolutionary hero Ta-chun"—although still insisting on his anonymity—
told us this very personal story: "The first time I danced the star role in *Swan
Lake*, I invited my mother to come and see me. It was the first time she had
been to the theatre. She was a poor peasant. She'd had hardly any education.
After the performance I asked her if she'd liked it. She started to cry. She had
not felt at all involved in what she'd seen; she hadn't even realized what it was
about. The characters weren't real for her. The story meant nothing to her.
She felt despised by all who were taking part in the performance."

Frédéric Mistral, the Provençal poet, vowed to write only in Provençal
after he had proudly recited one of his French poems to his mother, and she
had burst into tears because she could not understand it. The star dancer in
Shanghai swore to reform himself when he saw how his mother had reacted to
Swan Lake.

"I asked my mother what she thought I should do. She advised me to return to the village and work in the fields. I understood that I had to wage the revolutionary struggle by resisting Liu Shao-chi, who maintained that the ballet cannot reflect contemporary life. With the help of the masses, I understood much better Chairman Mao's instructions: 'Make foreign things serve China,' 'Keep what is good in the literary and artistic heritage,' 'Serve the people.' I took part in the Academy's production of *The White-haired Girl*. And this achievement—in April 1964—proved that the Peking Opera, a reputedly impregnable citadel, could be stormed and revolutionized. Since I've been dancing in contemporary revolutionary ballets, my mother is proud of her son; she grasps the meaning of the themes, which correspond to her own experience of life. She is happy to see that her class, the class of poor peasants, holds a place of honor, by providing the heroes, while the landowning class provides the traitors."

Proletarian Communion

In front of the Sian archaeological museum, there is a hoarding which bears ideograms in Chairman Mao's own handwriting. They say: "Whom to serve? That's the basic problem." Since the Cultural Revolution, spiritual life is tolerated only in so far as it is within the reach of the masses.

The sculptures and stained glass windows of the cathedrals illustrated themes from the Bible so that the people could understand. Works of art created in accordance with Chinese tradition can on their own assume the magical, incantatory power which moves people to the point where they understand. Folk performances were always popular. One of the great Chinese classical writers, Pai Chu-yi, a poet and top civil servant who was a contemporary of Charlemagne, tried his work on washerwomen. If they did not understand it, he would go back to his desk and try again. He wanted his poems to be appreciated as much in the village as at Court. Molière, who tried his plays out on his cook, was of the same view. It is at times of decadence that art parts company with the common people.

The aesthetes who create works for other aesthetes consider, either consciously or unconsciously, that the common people are unworthy of them. In China, the audience no longer feels despised by the artist—maybe because the artist had to endure the scorn of the people during the Cultural Revolution. Each evening a common work is created on the stage; the mutual applause of actors and audience at the end of the performance underlines the reciprocal nature of the created work.

The communion between the troupe and the audience is only the reflection of the communion staged by each of the seven model plays. The characters themselves are not isolated beings. They are part of the people by virtue of their social origin, their living conditions, the affection they have for them and receive from them. The revolution is not the concern of a few courageous experts. Those who are at the battle-front need the help of the masses. Li Yu-ho, the pointsman in *The Red Lantern*, sings with his mother and his daughter, Tieh-mei:

> People say that family love outweighs all else,
> But class love is greater yet, I know.

The Proletarian Hero

The visual impact, the music, the feelings and aspirations these works arouse encourage each Chinese to emulate the characters on the stage. The Cultural Revolution was rigorously selective in choosing these prototypes of the new China. They are the incarnation of all the virtues necessary to overcome the obstacles and difficulties which stand in the way of the revolution: "Bravery and daring, speed and persistence, a spirit of sacrifice and fearlessness." To guarantee the future of socialist China, the people must be willing to outdo themselves.

These exemplary communists all belong to the three-way alliance of workers-peasants-soldiers. On the stage they represent the vast majority of the population, who had never previously figured in the theatre, except as object of derision. They share a code of living: fervent devotion to the Great Teacher and everything he stands for, faith in the invincibility of the Party, courage in the face of challenge—remembering all the time the "Open, sesame" of the *Little Red Book:* "Be resolute, fear no sacrifice and surmount every difficulty to win victory." Revolutionary faith which rouses the humblest workers "to the point where they astound their executioners with the intrepid serenity" with which they meet torture and death. A cunning which makes up for an unequal struggle with imagination—all blows struck against the enemies of the people are good, all dodges and tricks that lull them into a false sense of security are allowed.

Above all, it is patriotic passion which rouses the audience. The revolutionary who confronts his adversaries does not yield to the temptation to keep quiet and humble himself in the hope of saving his skin. He insults them with the passion of warriors in the *Iliad*, in fact with all the more passion if he realizes that his situation is hopeless. Before dying, he will have the supreme satisfaction of knowing he has told his enemies what he thinks of them. Consider, for example, the pointsman in *The Red Lantern*, who sings:

> The Japanese militarists are wolves
> Hiding their savagery behind a smile.
> You kill our people and invade our land . . .

In fact, there are only ever two choices—sacrifice or dishonor. The Chinese theatre is so conceived that wavering is no longer permissible.

Class Hatred

What is it that enables Hsi-erh to overcome the terror of being alone in the mountains? What is it that prevents Wu Ching-hua, the little slave girl in *The Red Detachment of Women*, from despair until she rejoins the Liberation Army? What is it that acts as a support to Yang Wei-tsai in *Raid on the White Tiger Regiment* when he is told that his old aunt, a Korean peasant, has been assassinated by American imperialists? Each time it is the passion for revenge.

> The anger of the celestial warriors rises to the skies!
> *Class hatred* wells up in their hearts;
> May our comrades turn their grief into a force!
> Blood debts are only paid with blood.

The people become united behind a common hatred of oppression, domestic or foreign, and their rage is turned into action. The Party, guided by Mao Tse-tung thought, harnesses this violence and channels it into revolutionary energy. Injustices which have been suffered demand justice. Heroes who are jeered at regain their dignity only by punishing those who caused their indignity.

The Anti-Models of the Repertoire

There are anti-models as well as positive models competing to form the judgment of the masses. The didactic underlies the whole of the Chinese revolutionary theatre. Vice is stigmatized and virtue praised. Two character types are offered for loathing—people from the past, a past which can always return, and people who have slipped through into the present.

There are the old oppressors; they are made to appear so odious that as soon as they appear the audience roars its hatred. The landlords in *The White-haired Girl* and *The Red Detachment of Women* are interchangeable; they wear straw hats and European suits, have gold watch chains in their vest pockets, and lean on imperial canes. They are greedy and bloodthirsty. The dowagers with their tiny feet—in the same ballets—treat the young slave girl even worse because they themselves are incapable of doing anything apart from beating people with their canes.

There is also a more contemporary character—the communist who has lost his way, such as the student who falls victim to revisionism in *On the Docks*. Insufficiently armed with Mao Tse-tung thought, he is seized by the bourgeois temptation of egotistical schemes, but he is regenerated by self-criticism and by being pardoned by the Party. So, too, the militant Wang in

The Red Lantern, who weakens under torture and gives his comrade away to the Japanese is paid for his crime with a promotion to police officer in the Japanese brigade.

Before the revolution there was no individual good or evil. Error was pardonable, since the whole of society was in error. Since Mao has given an answer to all questions, error has become unpardonable. Either one follows the line or one deviates from it. The ideal is very clearly laid down, and if one transgresses, it is entirely one's own fault. Even betrayal under torture is a crime.

Key Themes

The Party, the Army and Death are the three key themes of the repertory.

All the heroes, without exception, belong to the Chinese Communist Party. Seeing them, the masses are better able to understand how much they owe the Party. In order to win victory for the revolution, the Party members accepted such discipline, encountered so many dangers and bore so much suffering that it is impossible that all this could have been in vain.

Some characters are seasoned militants—men like Hong Chang-ching, the Party representative in *The Red Detachment of Women,* who is seen singing the *Internationale* as he is dying at the stake. Or the political instructor, Kuo Chien-kuang, the "model revolutionary fighter" who inspires the wounded in the village of *Shachiapang*. Or the pointsman, Li Yu-ho, in *The Red Lantern,* who is fearless under torture. None of these men are weak when put to the test.

Others are young recruits, like Hsi-erh in *The White-haired Girl*—the wild girl, white as a ghost, who is hunted in the mountains; like Wu Ching-hua in the *Red Detachment of Women*—the peasant girl from Hainan island who flees from her master and joins the detachment; or like little Tieh-mei in *The Red Lantern*. These adolescents all have the ardor of the new convert. Like their elders, they are fired by their faith in the invincibility of the Party and the infallibility of Chairman Mao. As Li Yu-ho sings in *The Red Lantern:* "Brought up by the Party to be a man of steel, I fight the foe and never give ground."

The fervor of these militants is contagious. Their example transforms those who witness it. They put the teachings of the Chairman into practice. If one does not deviate, one is triumphant over plots and traps. But step a little too much to the right or left and one is defeated. The revolutionary theatre—like educational establishments, like the army, and like the Party—is a "school of Mao Tse-tung thought," the most alluring and the most surreptitious influence on the innermost recesses of souls.

The army is there in fine outline behind any revolutionary action. Six of the seven model plays are essentially military. In the seventh, *On the Docks,* the army appears at the first threat of sabotage. There are many variants on the same theme; submachine guns, soldiers, standards, children blowing trumpets, villagers with guns in their hands—all become an obsession. The Chinese have been humiliated by the superiority of those who invade them for too long not to seek some kind of compensation in a triumphant militarism.

Death is always on the horizon. Every Chinese knows by heart the Mao saying which is recited in the primary schools: "All men must die, but death can vary in its significance. . . . To die for the people is grander than Mount Tai . . ."* There are deaths which have no meaning—those which do not advance the cause of the revolution. There are deaths which have a supreme meaning—those of heroes who are killed in action in the class struggle. This is the choice every Chinese communist must one day be capable of making: martyrdom over betrayal.

Death never strikes at random. It metes out justice by eliminating the traitors and oppressors. It is exemplary, and covers heroes with a halo of glory in a final act of apotheosis. The heroes bring history to life on the stage, and it is a history for which they have lived and died. The people relive it with them, as their own history.

One might say that the principal character in the Chinese revolutionary theatre is war. The war of resistance against Japan, as in *The White-haired Girl, Shachiapang* and *The Red Lantern;* the war against "American imperialism," as in *Raid on the White Tiger Regiment;* the war of liberation against "the reactionary forces of the Kuomintang," as in *The Red Detachment of Women.* But since all these wars are over, this militarism might seem outdated.

But it is not, according to the Chinese. The fight against imperialism can always start up again. Fraternal solidarity with all the people of the world is an ideal which must always be pursued. The hydra of capitalism is continually being reborn. Revisionism is as much of a threat today as feudalism was in days gone by. The heroic episodes from wars of the past must be used to re-create a climate which is essential in order to maintain revolutionary dynamism. The spirit of devotion, sacrifice and faith—the spirit of Yenan—is always necessary for the progress of the revolution. The repertory is only one of the methods of reviving and communicating it—probably the best one.

---

*"Serve the People," September 8, 1944, *Selected Works*, Vol. 3, p. 227.

Part III

The Successes

of the

Chinese Way

14

The Multitude Controlled

The Challenge of Sheer Size

China at first sight seems like a monster with a thousand heads. You are dazed by the vast numbers of people—a multitude of children with gay, laughing faces, bicyclists going around in tens and twelves, and groups of people who gather to stare at you in curious silence.

Shanghai, which is served by Air France, has more people than any other town in Asia: ten million. When we got there, the weather was so bad that we had to stay the night before going on to Peking. Although it was dusk, the streets were lined with people as we drove into town. We wondered whether the crowd had been called out on our behalf. But our stopover was unplanned and unexpected.

Cheers rang out from the crowds, and it was with great difficulty that the cars got through. People were spilling over into the road, and more were coming up side streets. There were hundreds of thousands of children, youths, grownups and old women in black—but the majority by far were young people.

Soon we realized what had happened. A few minutes before we arrived, an announcement had come over the loudspeakers that the North Korean Prime Minister and several of his ministers had come. This government delegation from a fraternal country was on a state visit and had had a warm welcome in Peking. They were being accompanied by Chou En-lai. The people thought we were the North Koreans. If the crowd had moved just one step forward, our convoy of cars would have sunk without trace. It would have been like a river bursting its banks.

Constantly Overpopulated

We have seen that "the masses" keeps cropping up in the language of communists. And in China the word takes on its fullest meaning. Nowhere in Europe—not even in the most populous areas—does the density of population strike the traveler so forcefully as it does in China.

On warm nights people crowd into the streets and sleep on camp beds, thousands of them packed close together, their rows stretching for several miles. The next morning, the beds disappear as if by magic. In just a few minutes they are replaced by men and women of all ages in shirts and shorts doing their exercises, and then by swarms of bicycles.

The first few days one is so surprised by all this that one wonders whether they have been forced into it by exceptional circumstances. Are all these peasants in the countryside gathering for a harvest festival? Are these townfolk going out into the streets for some revolutionary anniversary? Experience shows that these guesses are naïve. Macartney wrote that "this immense population likes to live outdoors and in large numbers." China has been overcrowded constantly and for centuries past.

The Immensity of China

China is not only densely populated, it is also gigantic. You become obsessed by the distances—endless rivers whose lower courses are like the arms of great seas and mountain ranges which are the highest in the world. The sheer size of the country increases the problems caused by overpopulation. China is eighteen times larger than France, and the population is sixteen times as great.

Sixteen times? Or fourteen, or eighteen. Demography is not the least of China's mysteries. No one was able to give us exact figures. Those we were given varied by 200 million.

"Censuses" have been published since the sixteenth century. In 1661 the population was 104 million; in 1756 it was 192 million; in 1792 333 million. Macartney had no illusions. "One can hardly assume that the Europeans are able to verify whether the population of this vast empire, which is bigger and has more people than any other in the world, is or is not a third of a thousand millions."

One hundred and eighty years later we are hardly any further forward. The first census really worthy of the name was in 1953, and it gave the population as 582 million. In addition, a survey of thirty million people produced a figure for the birth rate of 37 per thousand. The survey gave a mortality rate of seventeen per thousand, hence a population growth rate of two percent, one of the highest in the world. After that, it increased, and then dropped appreciably. American demographers reckon that the population of China must be increasing by at least fifteen or twenty million a year. So, if it was about 530 million in 1949, it would have grown to over 800 million in 1968, and to between 850 and 880 million in 1972; if the growth rate continues at this level, there will be 1,000 million Chinese by 1980.

The figures which crop up in the speeches of Chinese leaders are so much rhetoric. The authorities do not seem keen on providing serious information, if there is any. Prince Sihanouk told me he reckoned the population was between 800 and 850 million. Chou En-lai was present when he said this, and did not contradict him. In public the Prime Minister speaks of 700 million, and this seems to be the official line. American researchers, analyzing all available information, have come up with figures ranging from 750 to 900 million.*

The authorities do not often refer with any degree of precision to the population of the country as a whole, but they are less shy in talking about towns and provinces. Everywhere we asked, we were told that the population of the six provinces we visited had increased since 1949 by between fifty and sixty percent. But this is not final proof of anything. After all, immensity is immeasurable.

Anxiety and Pride over Numbers

In a Western country such imprecision would be alarming. It is probably even more alarming in a country which claims to have a totally planned economy. How can you draw up a serious plan if you do not know within twenty-five percent how many people live in your country? This kind of ignorance is hard to understand in a system where a close check is kept on everyone, where urban districts and rural "brigades" are strictly delineated, and where information is rapidly centralized.

Is this kind of uncertainty a sign of indifference or anxiety? It could be said that the Chinese hide themselves from problems that frighten them. Until quite recently infanticide was common among China's poor peasants. Admittedly, Marx always wanted to hold Malthus up to ridicule.

It is possible that the Chinese are overwhelmed by their own numbers—that it is a kind of nightmare for them, and yet at the same time they feel it is cause for pride and faith in their future. Until they bring good fortune, their numbers are a curse. The average population density in arable areas is more than 650 per square mile; in the south of the country it is 2,000. For centuries this country has had a population which is beyond its means. It boils down to a single problem—how to keep overpopulation down so that

---

*But an atlas published in Peking in 1972 gives a figure for 1970 of 697,260,000. What happened to the other 50 or 200 million Chinese? "Died in labor camps," American experts coldly reply, but this of course is sheer conjecture and can be neither proved nor disproved.

the country can survive economic crises and get on the road to prosperity. It did not seem to us that China was completely free of this problem, but she is much less its prisoner than she was.

The Challenge of Anarchy

When you visit Peking you are still shown the tree—to the east of "Coal Hill"—where the last Ming emperor hanged himself, abandoned by all but his faithful eunuch, while a Manchu emperor was preparing to take his place. As a punishment for having allowed the last truly Chinese emperor to end his life, the tree was put in chains.

The history of China is filled with dramatic incident—emperors overthrown by vassals whose help they had called for, feudal lords rising up against the central power, peasants fighting the feudal lords. There is probably no other country in which the tradition of anarchy is so strong. The Chinese people—encumbered by their numbers—have never shown an aptitude for self-government. They never experienced the long steady progress we see in European history—the gradual birth of a collective conscience which came to flower in free cities and towns, merchant and craft corporations, liberal professions ruled by their Orders, pluralist political parties, and trade union movements. Conspirators joined secret societies. Conflicts were settled with the sword. Whenever a new dynasty came to power it was because the one before had shown itself incapable of stemming the rising flood of rebellion. Strong men answered the people's call to turn the chaos to order. The strong men grew weak and anarchy returned. As Genghis Khan said, when he launched his hordes on their conquest of China, "Our descendants will dress in gold, eat rich and sweet food, and press the prettiest women to their bosoms, but they will forget that they owe it all to us." The prophecy came true, and the process was repeated many times over. Up till now Mao's companions have avoided this fate. They seem to have decided to take measures specifically designed to avoid it, such as imposing on themselves a monastic style of life.

Between 1839 and 1949 anarchy was endemic. There was continual insecurity, except in the European territories. There was fighting in the provinces, but it was so general that no one knew where the front was. Whenever one went out into the country, one would hear the crackle of gunfire. Even the Japanese—in that part of China which they controlled—held only the large towns and the railways. When one side seized land back from the enemy, they would wipe out the population which had welcomed him. In fact, when Chiang Kai-shek recaptured Kiangsi from the revolutionary army, he shot several hundred thousand peasants.

Rebellions and reprisals threw whole populations onto the roads and reduced them to vagabonds. An official count in the 1920s of the number of displaced persons in only half of China's eighteen provinces was as high as 56 million. No doubt part of this floating population could have gotten jobs in industry—which was growing at the time—but many became bandits and some became mercenaries in the armies of the "warlords."*

All travelers were advised to take an escort with them. Teilhard de Chardin was accompanied by about ten soldiers when he went on his palaeontological expeditions. Brigands did not attack travelers if they thought they stood to lose more than they would gain. A country of plundering. Beggars fleeced by thieves. Thieves fleeced by bandits. One big racket from top to bottom.

Break-up

According to Voltaire, only small states are governed democratically; the bigger ones are doomed to anarchy or despotism or both. Walter Lippmann also wrote of the "ungovernability of the great empires." Can the methods which have been proven effective for small units be extended to large units? In many universities—Berkeley, California, for example—we have seen relations between staff and students get worse as classes get bigger, even though the staff-student ratio has been maintained. How can one apply to China a system which works well in Hong Kong, Singapore and Formosa? Although the people are the same, there is a difference not only of degree but also of kind.

The traveler is overwhelmed by the diversity of China. What unity can there be between crowded towns on rivers, ricefields which look like patchwork quilts, steep mountains, and immense desolate plateaus where humanity is at the mercy of the great winds? What unity can there be between the tall, thin Chinese of the North and the short, stocky Chinese of the South? Or between the alien populations—the Tibetans, the Turcomans, the Lolos, the Mongols and the Han people, who are themselves so diverse? Between provinces which do not speak the same language and where, so the proverb says, you only have to go ten *li*** and the people do not understand one another?

If there was some excuse for the Westerners involving themselves in the affairs of China, it was that the Chinese seemed incapable of administering themselves and the country was bound to break up. When the Empire fell, the "warlords" carved the provinces up among themselves, and the conflicts between them plunged the country into the kind of ruin and decadence not seen in Europe since the time of the Hundred Years War and the Grandes Compagnies which ravaged France.

---

*Army chiefs who behaved like potentates, first allies and then adversaries of one another.
**The *li* is about a third of a mile.

This break-up of China reached its height under the Japanese occupation. The territory which remained under Chinese administration was split into three parts, each governed by one of the "heirs" of the "Father of the Chinese Revolution"—Yenan by Mao Tse-tung, Chungking by Chiang Kai-shek, and Nanking by Wang Ching-wei, in collaboration with the Japanese. These three men, who had fought under the same banner, had become diehard enemies. This was China.

Victory of the Multitude over the Multitude

"Have you been carrying out a population policy?" I asked Chou En-lai.

"In the beginning we may not have given this problem the attention it deserved," he replied. "But today we're reaping the benefits of what we have done. Our population growth rate is now down to under two percent."

The reader may not be aware that the population policy of the Chinese People's Republic has had many twists and turns. I think they can be summarized in the following way.

Encouragement to Have Children

In the first few years of the regime, the authorities were making a massive effort to reduce the mortality rate. Since they did not bother with birth control, they in fact encouraged population growth. Orthodox communism claims that overpopulation is a strictly capitalist phenomenon which results not from there being too many men but from society being badly organized. Limitation of population seemed contrary to their doctrine. Indeed, Mao said many times that the greatest asset of the Chinese was their number.

Doctrine was given support by circumstances. To start with, China had enormous problems of underproduction, and needed to concentrate all her energy on finding better ways to use and extend land for cultivation.

In addition, the regime wanted to eradicate barbarous practices. Up to 1949 it was not uncommon for newborn children—especially girls—to be drowned, left abandoned on the side of the road, thrown to the pigs, or sold. Infanticide was banned for the first time under the marriage law of May 1, 1950. The law said: "Parents have the duty to bring up their children. They must neither maltreat them nor abandon them. It is strictly forbidden to drown or commit other similar crimes against newborn children." In order to stop these traditional crimes, one has to get at the motives and convince people that a large number of children is a good thing. In a climate of Malthusianism, it might have been possible to replace traditional methods by others which were less cruel, but which did not have the advantage of simplicity and effectiveness.

Meanwhile, the results of the 1953 census seem to have led Peking to realize the difficulties that were likely to arise if the population continued to increase at the same rate—or if the rate itself increased, which was in fact what was happening, since mortality was dropping fast.

The Chinese leaders yielded to the evidence: they had to choose between population growth and economic growth. In order to take off economically, it was necessary to lighten the load and lighten it quickly, since children are merely consumers for a long time before they become producers.

Campaign for Limiting Families

A family planning campaign got under way in 1954, and was in full swing two years later. In September 1956 Chou En-lai told the Eighth Congress: "We are in favor of a suitable regulation of reproduction!" In February 1957, in his big speech launching the "Hundred Flowers" campaign, Mao gave China the order: "Birth Control."

But this campaign—although it is still going—has had a series of strange setbacks. It was completely suspended from 1958 to 1961. During the period of the "Great Leap Forward" the authorities stressed the incomparable benefits to the country of its large population of young people. In the expected "prodigious economic development," China was not going to have too many workers, but too few. The failure of the "Great Leap Forward" in 1959, the bad harvests followed by famine between 1959 and 1961, and the departure of the Soviet technicians in 1960 made the leadership very aware of the terrible difficulties they were heading for. The order to limit families was renewed in 1961, and with even greater urgency. Contraceptives were distributed free, sterilization encouraged, and abortion made easier. There was also a movement—which continues—to encourage later marriage: at thirty for men and twenty-five for women. There was a spectacular press campaign. *Women of China* encouraged its readers to get their husbands to have vasectomies. *Youth of China* showed Chou En-lai expressing his admiration for a young woman of thirty-two who had been married twelve years without having a child.

But it's only human nature . . .

We asked dozens of young women workers and peasants about the family planning measures, and from their replies we gathered that they had met with solid resistance in the towns and calm, passive resistance from the rural brigades.

In an authoritarian regime one must not always take campaign slogans literally. The people are not so quickly persuaded; human nature is not manipulated easily.

We noticed that most of the people in the street were young. It was the same in all the towns we visited. The vast majority of them must have been born in 1967 or 1968. Of course, it is possible that there are more little children in the streets because the older ones have other things to do. But it has been stated quite categorically that the Cultural Revolution led to a tidal wave of sexual freedom. There was the closing of the secondary schools and the colleges, the Red Guards marching on the big centers, and the freedom given to young people of both sexes—all this increased the opportunities for the practice of sexual freedom in 1966 and 1967. Not that the unbridling of one or two million Red Guards—among a mass of eight hundred million— could of itself have had any measurable effect on the population. But it is not impossible that a psychological climate prevailed which encouraged a new crop of births. The Chinese press breathed not a word of it. We heard only discreet references to this period of collective, uninhibited liberation.

But habits die hard. Mao Tse-tung acknowledged philosophically in December 1970 that contraceptive methods had not brought much of a change to the country's population curve—families still did their utmost to secure the male line. "In the countryside a woman still wanted to have boy children. If the first and second were girls, she would make another try. If the third one came and was still a girl, the mother would try again. Pretty soon, there would be nine of them, the mother was already forty-five or so, and she would finally decide to leave it at that." However powerful the means of persuasion at one's disposal, one cannot quickly change the thinking of a whole people.

Slow Progress in Limiting Families

The campaign for late marriage and a maximum of two children resumed more intensively than ever in 1968. "Two children are quite enough; large families are a hangover from the past, like bound feet and child marriage." Many times we heard young women repeating this. Did they really believe it? They certainly seemed to.

Since 1970 the official campaign has developed, bringing in a variety of coercive measures.

In a number of towns we were told that a couple who were expecting a third child ran the risk of being separated by being assigned to enterprises several hundred miles away, of having their children and accommodations taken away from them, or of being forced to live in separate male and female dormitories. But we were not able to find out if these were just vague threats, or if in fact they were carried out.

Chou En-lai's discreet but firm remarks led me to think that after the old doctrine, which had not been really thought out, had been implemented and thrown into reverse time after time, now at last a clear plan had been drawn up and should begin to bear fruit—at least in the villages. There was new and more extensive propaganda on restricting the birth rate, contraceptive methods were widely available, and people were encouraged to adopt a monastically severe moral code.

We were able to confirm that the contraceptive propaganda was accompanied by practical measures of all kinds; that effective contraceptives—the pill, the pessary and the coil—were available free of charge to couples through the dispensaries in the rural communes, factories and towns; that teams went around to all the most distant hamlets, giving information to the peasants; and that abortions using acupuncture were done on a large scale—in fact, in the dispensaries of the Machiao rural commune, "this is going on all year round."

Three Conclusions

Three conclusions can be drawn from our observations and investigations. They are as follows:

1. The delay with which the birth control campaign was launched, and then the stops and starts it underwent, have in practice canceled out its achievements for twenty years. The birth rate seems to have stabilized between 1953 and 1972 at around thirty-five to forty per thousand, while the mortality rate dropped to fifteen per thousand. The natural growth rate, then, must have climbed some years to over twenty-five per thousand and by 1970 to have dropped to not much under twenty per thousand. In other words, the annual population growth must have gone from about ten million in 1949 (twenty per thousand in a population of 500 million) to nearly twenty million in some years in the 1960s (twenty-five per thousand in a population of 800 million).

2. However, a number of developments since 1968 seem to have stopped at least any increase in the rate of growth, if not the actual growth in the population. These developments include the elevation in the cultural level of the masses, the anti-illiteracy campaign, the increased number of family advice missions and centers, the ease with which people can obtain contraceptives, free abortion, and the harsh measures taken to discourage early marriages and large families. In the years to come, these measures could have the effect of actually reducing the rate at which China's population is increasing; if Chou En-lai is to be believed, this is already beginning. From the experience of Japan and other countries which have adopted measures to control population growth, though, it seems that there is a period of at least a dozen years before any results become evident. There is a good chance that

between 1980 and 1985 China will have a population of over 1,000 million, and it is not impossible that by the year 2000 this figure will have risen to 1,500 million.

3. Although the measures taken to limit the population have not yet borne fruit, the country is beginning to master the insoluble problems which have beset it for centuries as a result of its overpopulation. Its resources seem to be developing more quickly than its population is growing.* China is getting richer, not poorer. In spite of the hesitant conduct of population policy, Marx seems to have been right, and Malthus wrong.

Ants and Cicadas

Who is the mysterious pointsman who controls the lives of China's multitudes like trains going in and out of a marshaling yard? Everywhere there are men and women coming and going, in a hurry but not an excessive hurry. Some are so bent over that their chests are horizontal; they drag behind them carts loaded with sand or cement. Some carry piles of bricks balanced on their heads. Others push cartloads of dung. Trucks go past, packed with men and women standing in the back singing songs, intoxicated by the rushing wind. Armies of workers build workers' dwellings, factories and dykes along rivers. There are cohorts of bicycles, whole companies of bicycle-rickshaws, and large numbers of tricycles pulling enormous loads of hay, crates, wood, vegetables and coal. Morning and evening, you come across tiny children piled six at a time into little boxes hitched to the back of a pedal-rickshaw, being taken to or collected from nursery school.

Whenever you go out of the towns, you see hundreds and even thousands of men, women and children digging, hoeing, plowing, carrying things, sowing and planting; others are working compost and human manure with their bare hands before spreading it on their vegetables. All their movements are so well drilled that the casual observer might think it was a show put on specially for him—like an enormous amusement park with real-life characters.

It is all reminiscent of a painting by Hieronymus Bosch. Teams of men pulling barges up rivers, plunging down into the bowels of a mine, rowing their sampans when there is not enough wind, sailing along canals, and stooping in ricefields beneath a sweltering sun.

In Sian, Shanghai, Peking and Canton activity was still going on at building sites at eleven o'clock at night. Under powerful arc-lights, hundreds of workers were harnessed to little carts loaded with materials, climbing up scaffolding, and working away with trowels and hammers.

---

*It is difficult to be more positive. The population-cereals ratio was about the same in 1972 as it was between 1950 and 1960—about 140 pounds per person per year. The press is insisting more than ever on the production of cereals—which "commands everything." Imports, though, still take up a significant proportion of China's weak currency reserves.

Why do the ants need the cicadas? Is it the attraction of opposites, or the need for contrast? Have the Chinese, who are a living symbol of hard work, concluded a pact with the symbol of laziness? Day and night, in the towns as well as in the country, you can hear cicadas singing. Why have the Chinese allowed these useless insects to live, when they have gotten rid of dogs and flies and once were even in pursuit of cats and birds? Maybe deep down they have a need for this noisy reminder of a civilization and leisure which is not theirs.

What is the principle behind the movements of these inhabitants of the hive? What is it that makes them tick? Are they fleeing from the poverty, misery and hunger of the past? Are they racing toward a promised land, a paradise which they have already glimpsed and which will one day be within their grasp? A China without poverty, without suffering and without hunger. A China which has achieved harmony.

An Ungovernable Country Governed

Even though harmony has not yet been achieved, there is at least peace. Mao's victory in 1949 gave China a peace she had not known since the beginning of the nineteenth century. This benefit seems to have come on its own, having nothing to do with ideology or political and economic organization, yet it is so massive and so new that it had immediate repercussions on the prosperity of the Chinese people.

After the storms of the Cultural Revolution, order now reigns everywhere. From Peking's great avenues to the mud roads of the People's communes, and from the platforms of the big stations to the most far-flung provinces, one single authority lays down the law. And since 1949 this authority and this law have been challenged only by the intellectuals, during the "Hundred Flowers" campaign, and by the young, in 1966 and 1967—and on both occasions Mao had encouraged them to do so.

The regime had to survive many tests, many years of civil and foreign wars, bad harvests and natural disasters in order to give this subcontinent the means with which to feed, clothe, house, educate and contain its teeming population. The regime managed to get over all these dangers and keep a terribly vulnerable subsistence economy intact. The regime gave life to a country which was not viable before. It was seriously believed that the Chiang Kai-shek regime, which in twenty-two years had not solved a single one of the tragic problems that beset China, would take over from the communist regime.* The United Nations continued to entertain this belief even twenty-two years after the establishment of the People's Republic.

All parts of China which had lost the habit of being administered are affected. Their populations are controlled and disciplined for the collective

---

*Other than the problem of territorial sovereignty.

cause. Their essential needs are satisfied. China counts only on "her own forces" in overcoming her difficulties. Her public services function. She is no longer overburdened by her own size. She faces up to her own destiny. In short, this country which had long been the one country which was considered ungovernable is now being governed.

15

The Feudal System Eradicated

The Forbidden City

"The Forbidden City" is the name given to the vast palaces where twenty emperors of the Ming and Manchu dynasties kept their power and wealth from the fifteenth century on. It is hard not to view it as a symbol of the "China City," access to which was forbidden to the mass of Chinese by a clever system of political and social hierarchies to which only the emperor held the key.

The Court of Peking—a medium for all the ambitions, vices, virtues and intrigues that inevitably accompany absolute power—is still intact. The visitor can see its familiar gold columns, incrusted thrones, ebony screens, state beds, jade ornamental ponds, summerhouses and gardens. Our guides brought to life the characters who had long since left this golden prison—the all-powerful emperor whose precarious life was threatened by the dagger and the cup of poison, and the courtiers, concubines and eunuchs who satisfied the whims of this demi-god. Although much blackened, the picture they painted was none the less instructive.

In the Hall of the Union, which holds the twenty-five seals of the Empire, they have carefully preserved a screen with the two ideograms *wu wei*, ("Abstain from action"), which give us the golden rule of a paradoxical political art. A society which was rigid and whose continuing existence was guaranteed by the status quo. A world aswarm with people. An unchanging system—closed in on itself and condemned to drag on until the excesses of its own degradation brought about its downfall. An image, too, of Chinese

231

society, whose feudal, divisioned organization—with its continual tendency to reproduce inherited patterns—condemned the Chinese people to a static existence to which they could see no end.

The Classes

Although it was not split up into as many castes as Indian society and although there was in theory a certain fluidity in it, Chinese society was strictly divided into four classes—the scholars, who formed the leading class and from among whom the nine grades of civil servant were recruited; the peasants; the artisans; and the merchants. Then there were those who were *déclassé*—the beggars (who in fact formed powerful corporations), the actors and the prostitutes. And, finally, the "outclassed"—the eunuchs, whose castration assured them of a job at Court and who were therefore influential and rich; because they were separated from other people and from one another, they were never removed from the source of power.

In his own analysis of Chinese society, Mao added to this traditional and functional classification. He subdivided the class which was by far the most numerous according to wealth into agricultural workers, poor peasants, medium-poor peasants, medium-rich peasants and landlords.

As society became modernized, new social strata made their appearance: the business bourgeoisie, the non-mandarin intelligentsia, the workers. But up to 1949, the divisions remained more or less intact; the new, young classes were simply added on to the old classes, and the two lived side by side.

The Celestial Bureaucracy

Mencius justified this system in the fourth century B.C. "Some people do brain work, and some do manual work. Those who work with their brains govern; those who work with their hands are governed. Those who work with their hands feed those who work with their brains."

China is one of the very few countries in which—before the modern period—the possession of power was justified by the possession of knowledge. The justification was largely hypocritical, since in the majority of cases it was being fairly wealthy that enabled one to get the education necessary to gain access to power. Of course, education cannot simply be bought; one also needs hard work and talent. The Chinese ruling class naturally developed a certain pride in thus "purifying" their power. Their greatness and their misfortune both sprang from this. They certainly did not despise riches but, on the other hand, they never held them in excessive respect. The merchants occupied the lowest rung on their ladder of moral classification, because their wealth was redeemed neither by knowledge nor by anything they made. The mandarins were perfectly capable of trading or prevarication—these were just personal failings. Doing business would have been a social failing.

China was richer and more technically advanced than Europe in the time of Marco Polo, and she could certainly have had an industrial revolution centuries before Europe, had it not been for this repulsion on the part of the scholar-civil servants toward the market economy and bourgeois freedoms. She rejected this revolution a second time when the merchants of the West brought it to her in the nineteenth century.

This second rejection condemned the ruling class to social revolution; Chinese society would probably not have broken up in the twentieth century, in conditions which made violence inevitable, if the scholars had accepted the rules of the market economy, as the Japanese ruling class did with success and less ideology. But perhaps their resistance has finally borne fruit; what they rejected has been finally rejected by China as foreign graft. The last class has not become the first; the ideologues still govern China, and with relentless rigor.

The faults of the mandarins were numerous. Although the Confucian ideal required that they be "gentlemen" (*chun-tzu*), solely concerned with the public good and with justice, they shared one characteristic with the "common men" (*hsiao-jen*)—they were guided by self-interest. And self-interest very often became class interest; most of the civil servants were themselves landowners, and when the emperor asked them to take away landowners' monopoly of agricultural profits, they displayed a certain lack of zeal. They were inclined to break the very laws which they were responsible for implementing; as bureaucrat-landowners, they clung to their lands like shellfish to rocks. It was their job to collect taxes, and so they held the middle-income and poor peasants at their mercy. From the fifteenth century to the end of the Kuomintang, they behaved like local tyrants.

Clan and Custom

Neither the power of the emperor nor that of the scholars would have lasted long if the entire social and moral organization of the Chinese had not treated authority and tradition as sacred.

Society was simply a collection of "clans" in which all the family cells were subject to the absolute authority of the rich uncle. This was especially so with marriage, which was always arranged by the parents. Mao himself was married at fourteen to a young woman of twenty; he ran away and never saw her again.

Everyday life is permeated through and through with ritual, taboos and superstitious practices. The peasants use up their feeble resources in costly ceremonies in which force of custom is often stronger than religious belief; "He who prepares a marriage feast forgoes buying an ox."

Geomancy forbade the digging of a well to the east of a village, even if it was the only place where there was water. For centuries, the people destroyed China's forests in order to get fuel with which to cook their rice. They were afraid that if they dug for coal, which was in the ground in large quantities, they would awaken the Great Dragon. The question was how to escape from superstition when it was compounded by social pressure.

The Social Scourges

The chasm that separated the ruling class from the ignorant and superstitious masses encouraged corruption.

Under the Empire, people who held a tiny shred of power built up fortunes. The eunuchs systematically exploited all who had dealings with the Palace. Bribery and corruption were rife from top to bottom of the bureaucratic pyramid.

Under the Kuomintang, American money went to making the civil servants richer, while famine was spreading throughout the country—our last glimpse of China as a country in which the great wealth of the few meant more misery and a greater decline in the fortunes of the vast majority. And this became a terrible scandal—the begging, the filth, the prostitution and the drug-peddling and drug-taking. There is no shortage of documents on the social scourges which assailed China before 1949.

There was even trading in children and young girls. In the tin mines of Yunnan you can still meet workers who were sold in their youth like slaves. Selling a child to an artisan, an industrialist, a procurer, or a landowner was often a way of saving it from death and of buying vital weeks of survival for those left behind—it was a milder form of infanticide.

Changing Equilibrium

So this society which had been taught by Confucius that the first virtue was benevolence and respect for others had reached the criminal point where its citizens were renouncing one another.

The Chinese were not blind to these contradictions, but all they saw were abuses. There were plenty of reformers, both emperors and ministers, but when their virtuous authority had cut off enough heads to end the most flagrant abuses, their own deaths sooner or later relieved the tension, and equilibrium was reestablished one notch lower down.

No one—neither the emperors nor the leaders of the young republic— came near the essential elements which governed this equilibrium: the worship of the past, the privilege of knowledge protected by its intrinsic complexity, and the law of the landowners.

If Chinese communism has a chance of making something that lasts, it is because it has been able to establish the basic elements and principles of another equilibrium.

The Peasant Condition

In the heart of peasant China, in the mountain village of the Mei family, the old grandmother Shun explained the revolution to us.

She told us how bad life was in the old days, and it was as if she still could not quite bring herself to believe they were past. Four-fifths of the land belonged to only four families, and the other fifth was shared by a hundred families. For the privileged few, new houses, patios and finely carved furniture, for everyone else, hard work and destitution. As she proudly showed us the three rooms in her half of the house and her few pieces of whitewood furniture, she said again, in case we had not understood the first time: "We didn't have enough clothes; we had no furniture except for two mats, and they had to do for the whole family; we never went to school; and often we went several days without eating."

She was talking of the past in the way the old often do when they want to scare the children, and of course the social and agrarian situation in China has generally been more complex than that of this village in Chekiang Province. But putting questions of exaggeration and oversimplification aside, the truth as the Chinese see it is that before it was everything for the few and nothing for the rest, whereas now it is something for all.

This achievement came about through the collectivization of the land. Chinese communism did not feel forced to the same degree as Soviet communism to make the agrarian revolution *against* the peasants. Stalin went back on nearly a hundred years of individualism in Russian agriculture, and so there were strikes and sabotage on a large scale, as well as repression and famine which cost eight million lives.

Blood was shed in China not because of stubborn opposition on the part of the masses, but in order to consolidate victory; it was sacrificial blood, like that of the landowner in *The White-haired Girl*.

A country whose rural and urban population densities are close to one

another demands that work be collectively organized. The Chinese have
always known it. The revolution merely meant that the responsibility for
organization became collective instead of being undertaken by the landowners, who would then get all the profit.

The equality came about in power, not distribution. It contributed to
the reinforcement, not the dissolution, of the community; it was protection
against the return of "feudalism." A revolution within Chinese reality.

Now at last the peasant condition has been transformed. The misery
might be as terrible, but it seems lighter. If one taxes the fruits of labor, it is
not to extend and decorate one's own house—which stands in full view of
envious eyes—it is for the brigade. The Chinese peasants toil as much or
possibly more than before, but they do not have the feeling that they are
kowtowing before the profiteers. Their fatigue is just as real, but it is no
longer humiliating. They bear it better because they have escaped from their
servility.

This factor cannot be measured. But suffice it to say that it alone is
enough to change people's lives.

Egalitarian Poverty

It is not only in the country areas that the Chinese have moved from the
contrast between degrading poverty and offensive luxury to a uniform
tolerable poverty. The highest salary we came across was that of a surgeon—
280 yuans a month. An unskilled laborer gets 35 yuans, so the ratio is eight
to one. The leaders themselves set an example of modest living.

It is sometimes said in irony that those in China who were living in
wretched conditions continued to do so and that those who were not joined
them, so the progress has not been great. But the irony falls flat, because the
benefits that have been obtained are twofold.

First, poverty before 1949 was synonymous with filth, epidemic and
famine; nowadays poverty is above the bare subsistence level. It is always
decent. Quantitatively the difference is not enormous, but qualitatively the
threshold has been crossed.

And just as important for the equilibrium of society—the riches of
yesteryear have disappeared. The privileges that gave the Chinese the consciousness to form a nation have ended. Some of the former landowners,
bourgeois businessmen and factory bosses have kept some of their wealth, but
what can they do with it? The night life has gone. You cannot buy cars; they
are reserved for the collectives. Anyone who went out to restaurants or the
theatre every night, or who spent large sums in shops selling jade or fans,
would quickly be identified as someone who wore the silk clothes of the old

mandarins. No one dares to display how comfortably off he is in so Spartan a climate. China prefers money-hoarders to pleasure-seekers. She has reduced her rich to the austerity levels of the great misers.

It is certainly not true that hundreds of millions of indigent paupers have gained access to opulence and good living, but it is true that they are no longer hungry and that they no longer have before their eyes the privileges of the rich. The regime has won the gratitude of the masses for this gigantic leveling process.

Aristotle claimed, "Rebellions are always born of the desire for equality." Mao realized that true revolution demanded equality of desires or at the very least equality of the means of satisfying them.

Energy Mobilized

Mao also realized that the revolution would only last if it took place first of all in people's minds. It did not consist of distributing weapons, food and land, but of giving the peasants the desire to fight, the taste for working intelligently, and the will to conquer their own land.

This is perhaps where the Chinese leaders have best shown their understanding of the human soul. In order for the Chinese to consider the revolution as their own affair, they had to make it themselves. In order for them to cultivate the land with the pleasure of acquisition, they had to seize neighboring properties. The revolution did not emerge spontaneously out of peasant misery. It was inspired in the peasants by the Party, but the Party had the skill to convince them that they had wanted it all the time. It is as if Mao made use of the exhortation addressed to Moses: "Take strength and courage to *conquer* the land which God *gives* thee."

Bad Cards Mao Made into Trumps

Mao often said: "China will only cease being a poor and weak country when she ceases being a feudal country and becomes a country controlled by the people."

The Maoist regime knew how to extract from the misfortunes which were destroying China the psychological resources which were necessary to free her of them. China's past provided Mao with the materials that enabled him to build the future.

One might argue that in any case things would not have continued to get worse for very long. Even a dictatorship of the Right or a liberal democracy might have been of as much benefit to China from the point of view of technological progress as communism. Feudal practices would by themselves have fallen into disuse. It was not necessary to establish communism in order to ensure China's take-off.

But any attempt at writing Chinese history must take into account two basic facts:

On the one hand, it was all the more difficult to get the Chinese people out of their feudal conditions because they constituted such an enormous, inert mass. Mao succeeded in moving them. He made what was a weakness into a strength. His revolution was essentially religious and national.

On the other hand, with a dictatorship of the Right or a liberal democracy, China would very likely have been colonized—by a few great powers whose economic and political domination would no doubt have developed her resources, though it would also have drained them.

Values had to be turned upside down before the Chinese peasants roused themselves from their apathy. Contrary to the theories of all Marxists—Mensheviks and Bolsheviks, Bukharinites and Leninists, Trotskyites and Stalinists—Mao proved that the peasants were qualified to make the revolution.

He gave them a political aim toward which they could strive and directions on how to get there. He organized them, motivated them, guided them and set them in motion. He proved to them—with small, progressive experiments—that the hope he was holding before them was not false, that his program was as realizable as it was stirring. By distributing weapons to them, Mao was arming them more than anything else with the conviction that a fundamental transformation of their condition was becoming a possibility. The task of the Red Army—which lived among them—was as much to convert them and train them as it was to fight the enemy. In short, it is faith which has changed everything.

The End of the Feudal Era

Officially China emerged from the feudal era in 1911. Sun Yat-sen imagined that its effects would be overcome in the space of three years; in practice, a good half-century was required before the peasant masses freed themselves from the exploitation which had kept them in misery.

However cruel were the social plagues which assailed the Chinese people, they did not prevent them from living. They were even in a way part of their biological balance. A thousand-year order had introduced its degrading customs into the collective economy. Everyone somehow or other put up with it.

Even after the Liberation, the peasants were still paralyzed with fear in the face of their fallen idols.

In his novel, *The Sun Shines over the San-Kan*, Ting Lang depicts farmers who do not have the courage to arrest the tyrant who used to oppress them. A look from him, which only a short while before filled them with terror, still makes them lower their eyes. The weight of tradition is too great for them. They still secretly bring him the rent. They only manage to rid themselves of their fear in an upsurge of sadistic violence. Communism planned the break and sealed the revolution in blood. Hence the fierceness of so many "people's tribunals" toward "corrupt civil servants," "landlords who abuse their power" and "local tyrants." A leader of the Hupeh Provincial Revolutionary Committee told me with terrifying calmness: "It was often necessary to condemn their old lord to death in order to deal with the peasants' faint-heartedness. As long as he was still alive, they feared that he'd regain his power."

Feudalism is a social structure, but much more it is an attitude of mind. Has it been completely eliminated?

As a professor at Peking University told us: "The Great Proletarian Cultural Revolution had as its aim to wipe out feudalism and bureaucratism. Bureaucratism is reappearing all the time like a dragon's head. Even feudalism is hard to get rid of." Mao was able to arouse the will to fight in the peasants of Hunan and Shensi, and it was necessary to keep this spirit alive all the time in order to remove the vestiges of the old regime.

The Domination of the Social Scourges

Along with many other observers, we were able to verify that the social defects and ills that followed on feudalism and were its symptoms have in fact disappeared.

With illiteracy, a whole medieval way of thinking has been swept away, driven out by the philosophical, social and moral code encapsulated in the *Little Red Book*. Minds once dominated by fear, supported by resignation, open to all manner of superstitious beliefs, which created and were also the victims of a thousand phantasms, are now filled both with the certainty that they can achieve a very great deal and the awareness that they owe everything to *themselves*. To use Toynbee's classifications, the Chinese, who were once "Zealots" quick to turn to the dim and confused past for explanations of the present and codes of behavior, have become "Herodians," who build their own present with the help of their own idea of their future. Of course, the transformation will be complete only when the generation brought up with this new attitude becomes adult. In any case, the young laugh at the "foolish" old beliefs.

Prostitution has completely disappeared. As a leader of the Shanghai Revolutionary Committee told us, "It was the easiest thing in the world to get rid of pimps and procurers in 1949, but it took a long time to reeducate the women, to teach them to live by working and to find jobs for them to do. Some had to undergo a long process of reeducation. Some slipped back into their old ways, but not many."

The communist regime also succeeded in getting the addicts off opium. One is not told a great deal about this, but a Shanghai doctor did reveal a little. "With some inveterate smokers," he said, "it took several years to get them off it. To start with, they were isolated from other people. Many couldn't stand being deprived of their opium, and had to be given painful treatment in hospitals. Usually we had to give them the drug, and then gradually reduce the dosage. But now this particular scourge has been wiped out, and we're not prepared to see it return."

Robbery and corruption also seem to have been eliminated, at least as social phenomena. Not, of course, that Mao Tse-tung thought has been able to "reeducate" pickpockets, bandits, blackmailers, shady civil servants and gangsters; but what one can say quite definitely is that nowhere does the principle "Crime doesn't pay" apply better than in this land of eight hundred million puritans. How *could* it pay? In a society which is as egalitarian and "open" as China, any fortune someone might acquire is instantly suspect and can easily be pinpointed. Even the petty thief would be taking enormous risks, out of all proportion to any likely gain.

The Chinese naturally feel this improvement in the moral climate of their society very deeply. A mystique of unselfishness has been inculcated in each and every one of them. They do not seek to acquire money. They seem in fact to be afraid of it. When you are in a shop or taking a taxi or rickshaw and you offer a fistful of money without knowing exactly how much there is, they refuse to take it as if it were something evil. They reckon up how much you owe, pause for a moment, and then with great embarrassment they take a small note and a coin from your hand. They seem afraid that they will burn their hands with it.

I asked a technician at the Wuhan Iron and Steel Works: "Which quality do the Chinese respect most in their leaders?"

Without a moment's hesitation, he said: "Their honesty." And then, after a pause, he added: "It was corruption that brought down the Kuomintang."

From Destroying the Past to Rediscovering It

Whatever their opinion of the regime's merits, observers who knew China before the Liberation are all agreed on one point: China has become almost like another planet. She has gone through not so much an evolution as a mutation. They recognize almost nothing of the China they knew when they lived there.

"Before the Liberation . . . ," the old woman at the Tea Commune kept saying. She was still marveling at the progress that had been made. But by going on about it, she was also recognizing the need to "kill," again and again, the very recent past which she still feared might return.

In the Forbidden City or the Summer Palace, it is still systematically being "killed"—Tzu-hsi and her lovers, Kuang-hsu and his favorites, and the naval funds squandered on marble boats for the lake. In the library of Peking University the visitor is shown the empty shelves which used to hold the valuable manuscripts and ancient books which Chiang Kai-shek carried off to Formosa. All the time they are killing what is feudal, reactionary and capitalist in each and every Chinese.

The not so young who go on about how bad things were in the past do it because they fear the youth will forget. The horrors of yesteryear are constantly being recalled, and this serves as a measure of the progress that has been achieved. What are today's low salaries, uncomfortable housing and harsh regime compared with these terrifying memories?

But condemnation is selective. Mao knew how to gain support from the past when necessary. After all, the greatness of past centuries is the surest springboard for national ambition. Agrarian collectivism is descended from a thousand-year-old tradition of peasant mutual aid. The ideograms used at the court of the scholar-emperors of the seventh century are still in use today—to express Mao Tse-tung thought. On red and gold hoardings on every street corner you can see Mao's instruction: "Make the past serve the present."

In 1938 Mao Tse-tung explained himself at somewhat greater length when he said: "The history of our great people over several millenia exhibits national peculiarities and innumerable treasures. As regards all this we are mere schoolboys. Contemporary China has grown out of the China of the past. We should sum up our history from Confucius to Sun Yat-sen and we must constitute ourselves the heirs of all that is precious in this past."*

There is acupuncture; the restoration of archaeological treasures; the sick who smile as they get up from the operating table fit and well, thanks to an ancient practice which has been revived and tirelessly improved; the young Pioneers who come miles every Sunday to march along the sacred way, between the stone animals, to the tombs of the Ming emperors—where once no mortal was allowed to set foot. What is it that they come to seek in this secret plain, hemmed in by hills and heavy with the scent of oleanders? Perhaps the memory of another Long March—that of the Han people four thousand years ago.

Compared with these forty centuries, what is a quarter of a century of

---

*Mao Tse-tung, "The Role of the Chinese Communist Party in the National War," report to the sixth plenary session of the Sixth Central Committee of the Party, October 1938, *Selected Works* Vol. 2, p. 209. A translation is also to be found in Stuart Schram, *The Political Thought of Mao Tse-tung*, Pelican Books 1969, p. 172. (TRANSLATOR'S NOTE).

communism? But what achievements there have been—and we should not be afraid to say so. There is no precedent for such a radical metamorphosis of such a large number of people in such a short space of time. Mao's great feat was to have given the Chinese the feeling that while abolishing the past in so many fields they were at the same time remaining faithful to the best of their heritage. If one thinks of this four-thousand-year period of Chinese history occupying just one day, communist rule represents the last nine minutes, but in this brief space of time more has been done to transform this people and their land than in the whole of the rest of Chinese history.

16

The Restoration of the
Middle Kingdom

The Navel of the World

The ancestor of the Chinese is at rest at Choukoutien, about thirty-five miles from Peking. He lived in China 375,000 years ago and, as far as palaeontologists know, he is the oldest man in the world. At any rate, the Chinese do not doubt it for a moment. In his glass case, "Peking Man," or *Sinanthropus pekinensis*, is the first link in the longest chain; the first man of the "first civilization on earth"; the father of the "noblest people," "the most numerous people," "the most fully human people on earth."

Every day some two thousand visitors come by bus from Peking. Workers, peasants, school children and soldiers come to see for themselves, by pressing their noses against the glass, how the many thousand years of Chinese history merge into the history of the human species, and to see how the eight hundred million people who are trying to build the most revolutionary nation on earth are also the product of the most ancient civilization on earth.

At Paipo, a neolithic site in Shensi Province about thirteen miles from Sian, there is a "museum of the earth." It lends itself just as much to educating archaeologists as to edifying the public. A huge wooden hangar has been erected over the excavations to preserve and protect them. As we moved along the catwalk, among the remains of igloo-shaped huts, grain silos, graves, drains and dry-earth ramparts, a young palaeontologist with her hair in pigtails was explaining that Chinese man had been ahead of all the other races at all periods in history. She pointed out that the silos were outside the huts and that there was one silo for a number of huts. "Grain," she said, "was

243

common to several families. The social regimen was communism. The Chinese were communist five thousand years before Karl Marx."

The temptation to be sinocentric is a strong one, especially when you see the purity of the pottery and the polished stone tools, which are several thousand years older than similar tools discovered in the West, if not than those found in Egypt and Mesopotamia.

China Alone

Whatever you do, whether you go for a Sunday walk along its restored section about sixty-five miles north of Peking or lean over through the portholes on the section between Peking and Sian, the Great Wall takes your breath away. It is a crenellated, winding wall that stretches for about two thousand miles, clinging to steep slopes, plunging into valleys and clambering up to the mountain tops. Millions of men worked to build it, and hundreds of them died of exhaustion doing so. Our guide told us that their bodies were thrown into the mortar and became part of the wall itself. You can still find their bones among the stones. Under the old regime you had to be prepared for anything. Human blood has always been the best cement. Intended as protection against the raiding nomads from the steppe, the Great Wall was a double line of defense inside the belt of deserts and high mountains that encircled China.

China has always considered herself "the only civilization under the heavens." At the edge of Eurasia, she constituted a massive block, isolated from the rest of the continent by this double barrier and from the rest of the world by an ocean. Born in isolation, China's civilization was one of tilling the soil, not of barter. The world was China. The first Jesuit missionaries wrote that "one must realize that the Chinese, supposing as they do that the Earth is square, claim that China is the greater part of it. So to describe their empire, they use the word *t'ien-hia*, 'Under-the-Heavens.' So, with this admirable system of geography, they were able to confine the rest of humanity to the four corners of their square." Impenetrable and inaccessible, China remained until the last century just about as ignorant of the Western world as Europe was of America before Columbus. She was and no doubt still is—deep down in the minds of the Chinese people—"the Middle Kingdom." She occupies the center of the emergent world. The universe revolves around her. The other people are thrust out onto the periphery.

Shielded by this wall of stones and men, why should the Chinese feel the need to know anything else but China? Mao Tse-tung had never been outside China when he went to Moscow before the Liberation; he never went to a neighboring country, not even Vietnam or Japan; and he spoke no foreign languages. Chou En-lai was an exception; along with Chen Yi, he was one of the few Chinese leaders to have been to the West. The Chinese are capable of the most humble submission to anyone who symbolizes and reinforces the national bond, and they have a deep-seated collective pride; they are not really curious about anything which is not Chinese.

The Suzerain Empire amid Its Vassals

China has always established herself by opposing others. The Chinese people used to reject foreigners as inferior. Up until the fifteenth century Chinese civilization was acknowledged as superior by all Western sailors and merchants. From the sixteenth century, though, when Western civilization had caught up, the two worlds remained impenetrable and incomprehensible to each other. The European was like a strange animal for the "heavenly" Chinese, and vice versa. Each was ignorant of the other. Each was the other's barbarian.

At the beginning of the eighteenth century, Father du Halde wrote: "Everything that comes from abroad—whether letters, gifts or envoys—passes as a mark of submission."

When Lord Macartney led the first British embassy to China, the Son of Heaven demanded that he acknowledge his supremacy by kowtowing—making nine genuflections, each time touching his forehead to the ground. Lord Macartney's reply was that he knelt before no one but his own king. After months of bargaining, the emperor ended up by agreeing to see the ambassador unofficially at his hunting residence. He replied to George III's missive with the following "imperial mandate": "O King, compelled by the humble desire to participate in our civilization, you have sent a mission. Your ambassador has paid homage to my Court. The terms in which your memorandum is couched reveal a respectful humility which is worthy of the highest praise.

"As for your demand that one of your subjects be accredited to my Heavenly Court, this is contrary to all the customs of my dynasty and is quite out of the question.

"Governing the whole world as I do, I have only one aim in view—to uphold perfect government and to fulfill the duties of the State. Foreign overtures do not interest me. I have ordered your envoys, your bearers of tribute, to go in peace. It becomes you, O King, to respect my feelings and to show greater fidelity and loyalty in the future in order to guarantee peace and prosperity to your country by perpetual submission to our throne."

Right up to the eve of the First World War, the emperors, shut away in their Forbidden City, did not really understand that China's importance in the world was relatively limited and that the ships from Europe represented a danger to her.

The last sovereign, Empress Tzu-hsi, kept the formula "Governing the whole world . . ." in her decrees. Even in the twentieth century, imperial edicts spoke of the duties of the French and English as if their sovereigns were subjects of the Middle Kingdom.

On the night of August 22, 1967—when the Cultural Revolution was at its height—the Peking offices of the British chargé d'affaires were surrounded by a hostile crowd and set on fire. The chargé d'affaires himself was roughly handled and spat upon, and the people shouted phrases at him that he did not understand. When protests were lodged with the Ministry of Foreign Affairs, a Chinese diplomat replied: "The chargé d'affaires only had to lower his head. That's what the crowd was demanding. If he'd done it, the tension would have been reduced straightaway."

A Hundred Years of Humiliation: Sharing the Melon

It was under the reign of the Mongol emperors that a Franciscan, Jean de Montcorvin, a contemporary of Marco Polo, set up the first missions in China. At first the Chinese were tolerant of a religion that they did not take very seriously. Then the Ming emperors learned that the missionaries kept their links with Rome and became more suspicious. Saint François-Xavier tried in vain to land in China, before dying on an island off Canton. But for all that, the Society of Jesus was not discouraged. At the end of the sixteenth century the Jesuits adopted the Chinese language, Chinese customs, Chinese dress and Chinese names. But they were unable to obtain authority from Rome to alter the rites to bring them into accord with local traditions. They felt this freedom would be necessary if they were to succeed in converting the emperor—and such a conversion would undoubtedly have meant the conversion of the entire Heavenly Empire, just as the conversion of Constantine led to the conversion of the Roman Empire.

Whether they liked it or not, the Western missionaries showed intransigence. They no longer accepted any compromise between their dogma and Chinese traditions. They tried to propagate Christianity by spreading its benefits. But success was limited; only a tiny minority were baptized, and their compatriots referred to them contemptuously as "Rice Christians"—because during the frequent famines the missionaries handed out rice to their parishioners. The converted stood out from their half-starved neighbors by their healthy appearance.

This situation irritated the Chinese more and more as time passed. Throughout the nineteenth century there were many incidents which did a lot to poison relations between China and the Western Powers and to compromise the spread of Christianity. Whenever there was a demonstration against the missions or a missionary was murdered, European governments felt obliged to intervene with force or threat of force to protect those whom they considered to be under their jurisdiction. In the end Peking was forced to sign an agreement recognizing the missionaries' right to carry on their evangelism as they wished.

Nothing was more calculated to make Christianity appear as a foreign body, and even as a foreign agent. The converted appeared disloyal to their own country. Was it possible to tolerate their recognizing a Western sovereign who would impose his views through a clergy which was answerable only to him, in his distant capital, either Rome or London?

The China of yesterday never made a clear distinction between the spiritual and the temporal, and present-day China does it no better. And in the nineteenth century the West was of hardly any help to her in doing so.

So the missionaries, quite unaware and in all good conscience, did a great deal to awaken Chinese nationalism. Probably no other influence contributed as much to setting China against foreigners as their efforts to convert her to a religion which had been unable to integrate itself into the country, stubbornly sticking to bread and wine rather than the rice and tea which the Jesuits would have preferred. The massacre of the Boxers* bore bloody witness to this.

Drugs, Spearhead of Western Civilization

Just as they felt no need to absorb the spiritual values of the Christian West, so the Chinese felt no need to buy European food. In this respect, too, they reckoned they were self-sufficient.

China fascinated Europeans, who were attracted by her unheard-of riches and the prospect of unlimited profit. But nothing that the foreign merchants had to offer in exchange interested the Chinese—nothing, that is, except opium. Although it had been used for a long time, its use was very limited. Foreigners started to import it clandestinely through Canton, by buying the complicity of the local civil servants. As Macartney wrote, "Great quantities of this heady drug are brought into the country, in spite of all the

---

*The Boxers, whose name comes from the Chinese *I Ho Ch'uan*, or "righteous, harmonious fists," was an antiforeign movement that developed in China in 1898. As a result of the Opium Wars, the weakened Ching Regime had been forced to grant sizeable territories within the borders of China to foreign governments. Encouraged by the dowager empress Tzu-hsi, the Boxers were soon attacking foreign territorial leaseholds in Chihli, Shansi and Shantung provinces. By June of 1900, approximately 140,000 Boxers were occupying Peking and besieging the foreign embassies there. A force of British, French, Russian, German, Japanese and American troops, fighting its way through from Tientsin, finally lifted the siege in August. The outcome was an agreement in which China was forced to pay an indemnity of $333 million, greatly increasing her national debt, and to permit foreign troops to be stationed on her soil, in return for which the Western powers would refrain from partitioning the country (EDITOR'S NOTE).

precautions the Government takes to stop it. The customs officers gladly allow themselves to be bribed. And then after they have got the money in their pockets for letting the contraband opium through, they often become the first purchasers. Most of the ships that come from Bengal bring opium, but Turkish opium—which comes in British ships—is preferred and costs almost twice as much. The Governor of Canton is putting the Cantonese on their guard against the effects of opium: 'The barbarians are drawing enormous profits from the Middle Kingdom with the help of a substance which is vile and disgusting. But what is so utterly odious and deplorable is that our compatriots are surrendering blindly to a treacherous and destructive vice, to the point where their folly leads to death, and that the many cases of this happening do not open their eyes to the dangers involved.' In spite of this statement," Macartney concluded, "the Governor of Canton takes his regular dose of opium every day."

In the estuary of the Canton River, we were shown the remains of Fort Bogue, which the English fleet attacked and destroyed in 1839 in the name of free trade, so that the European merchants could get the authority to sell this honorable merchandise. Thus began the first war with the West. China lost it, but there were others to come.

These same warships forced China to open her gates at one and the same time to Western missionaries and Western opium. The Treaty of Nanking, which served as a model for the other "unequal treaties," bound the "heavenly" authorities to recognize as legal both the traffic in narcotics, which had been prohibited since the eighteenth century, and the missionaries' right of establishment, which had hitherto been contested—two very different ways of violating China.

China Dismembered

China was militarily and technically inferior, and in this struggle she was decisively beaten. Bit by bit she lost her borderlands and traditionally dependent territories.* She was reduced to the eighteen *han*** provinces, which the Westerners divided into spheres of influence—Kwangsi to the French, the Yang-tzu Basin and the Canton River to the British, Shantung to the Germans, Inner Mongolia and Manchuria to the Russians and the Japanese. The "five ports" open to the West in 1842 had by the beginning of the twentieth century grown to over a hundred.

On the coast and up the valley of the Yang-tzu, the concessions put the keys to China in the hands of the Powers.

They removed numerous maritime and river ports, like Tientsin,

---

*Cochin-China in 1867, the territories of the Amur and Turkestan in 1871, Korea in 1885, Annam, Tonkin and Cambodia between 1885 and 1887, Burma in 1886, Formosa and Manchuria in 1895, Tibet in 1904, and Mongolia in 1921.
**Those inhabited by people of genuinely Chinese ethnic origin.

Shanghai, Canton and Hankow, from the jurisdiction of the Chinese authorities. And all industry—even the public services, such as transport, water, gas and later electricity—was in the hands of foreign companies. The foreigners administered justice in disputes between Chinese and foreigners. In Shanghai one can still pass in turn through each of the four towns into which the city was divided—the international concession directed by the English and the American consuls; the French concession under the sole direction of the French Consul-General; the Japanese concession; and finally the Chinese town itself, reduced to a number of densely populated districts.

The Chinese still speak with a sense of shame of the "semi-colonial" state into which their country had fallen, but Sun Yat-sen condemned the euphemism. He said: "We use this expression 'semi-colony' for our own consolation. But in reality, given the economic oppression of the Powers, China is not just a semi-colony—she is suffering worse conditions than any other real colony. . . . China is the colony of every country with which she has signed a treaty. We are not just the slaves of one country. We are the slaves of all countries."

In order to understand how the Maoist regime was able to take root in China, one must understand how deeply the Chinese, a proud people, suffered after the most tragic collapse in their history. In the course of a single reign, that of Tzu-hsi, the "rebel barbarians" became the "foreign Powers" and even the "dominant Powers."

In 1908 China was at their mercy. With "unequal treaties" and revolts, Western reprisals and Chinese revenge, and then more "unequal treaties," the foreign Powers treated the Heavenly Empire like a melon from which—in the words of the bitter Chinese expression—"they cut themselves juicy slices."

From the Opium War right up to 1949, American, English and French currencies were in free circulation, and this use of foreign money led to continual inflation.

A plutocracy got rich on speculation and the exploitation of China's human and material resources. As Teilhard de Chardin wrote: "The invader is a leech whose only function so far seems to be to suck the country dry."

Before 1949 China seems to have been a series of towns transformed into Towers of Babel, a gigantic slum with one tiny district of offensive prosperity; money flooding everywhere without the Chinese getting more than a few small coins for selling their souls. This at any rate is the vivid memory of the Chinese today.

The Impact of a More Efficient Civilization

The shock encounter with the West was humiliating, and although the impact was to some extent absorbed by the sheer immensity of China, it nonetheless rent the fabric of traditional Chinese civilization. The China of

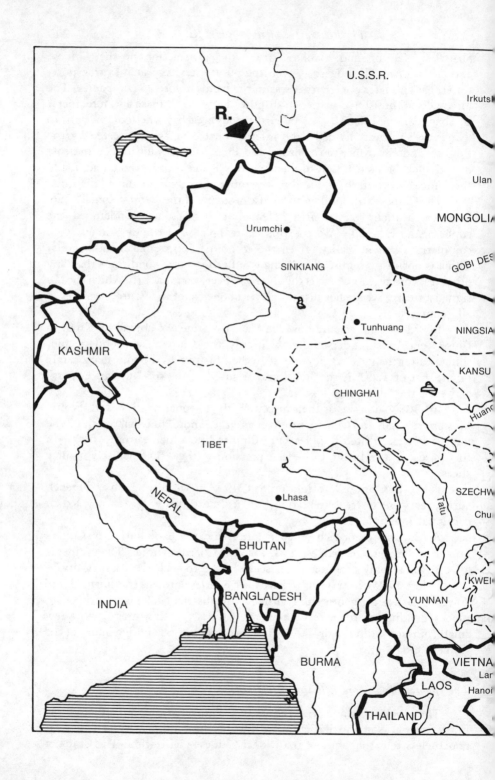

The Middle Kingdom Dismembered

the old clans, the landed bureaucrats and the ignorant masses collapsed in the twilight years of the venerated idols. The war against the foreigners, the civil war, and the renewed outbreak of famine precipitated the ruin of the traditional economy by throwing millions of the sons and daughters of ruined peasants onto the already overflowing labor market. The deciding factor in causing the revolution was economic bankruptcy—in particular, rural bankruptcy. Things really had reached the point where "everything was excluded except the extremes." The traditional combination of feudal oppression, landowners' abuse of their position, a remote and impersonal bureaucracy, and Western imperialism suddenly produced an explosive mixture, and the resultant blast was unavoidable.

China had been cut off from her origins and forced to acknowledge her military, economic and social inferiority. She thus hesitated between two possible courses of action—falling back on her own resources or integrating with industrial civilization, something that had hitherto been prevented by the established order.

China split in two on the issue. The urban, coastal and industrial communities opted for industrialization and foreign domination; the agrarian communities and those which valued China's past rejected change and the foreigners who brought it.

Because she had not been able over the centuries to acclimatize herself to the world progressively by opening up her frontiers and having regular relations with other countries, China was suddenly plunged, by this foreign domination, into a brutal "deculturizing" process.

The shrewdest of China's scholars realized that the country was falling into a relationship of dependence simply because she had scorned an interest in others for such a long time. Liang Chi-chao wrote: "The countries of Europe compare their systems and are continually spurring one another on. In this way the talents of their peoples get richer by emulation. China proudly considers herself great and powerful, and declares that no one is her equal."

The majority of cultivated Chinese feel their duty is to challenge and question the thousand-year-old dogma of the superiority of their civilization.

At first China's eclipse was put down to nothing but Western military power. It was thought that in order to protect the only true civilization one had only to borrow this power. As Feng Kuei-fen wrote in 1861, "What we must learn from the barbarians is just this one thing: good strong boats and cannons that hit their target. . . . We must adopt the barbarian's own tactics of force in order to keep him in check."

Another scholar, Hsueh Fu-cheng, also accepted the idea that China had to borrow technology. "Let us acquire the Westerners' knowledge of machinery and mathematics, with the intention of protecting the Way of our sages. . . ." The reformers' rule became: "Learn the barbarians' superior technology in order to keep them in check."

The final military defeats of the Empire and then its fall opened the eyes of the Chinese elite. It was not enough just to leave Chinese civilization unchanged and cover it with a veneer of foreign technology. A number of people began to draw the alarming conclusion that the Middle Kingdom could not content itself with choosing just some of the external attributes of Western civilization; it had either to accept them all or to allow itself to be dominated by Western civilization.

Only with Sun Yat-sen, and especially Mao Tse-tung, was China able to escape this dilemma and discover a third way, the Chinese way.

It was no good just copying one aspect of Western civilization, and it was dangerous to imitate it in its entirety and in a servile manner. China had to rethink her whole economic, political and moral philosophy.

Today the choice is clear. China has decided to imitate some of the great Powers' achievements as rapidly as possible—the nuclear and thermonuclear bombs, nuclear submarines and intercontinental missiles. But as for the rest, she is too proud to stoop to imitation.

The Primacy of Independence

Building the Nation

"Classical China," Kuo Mo-jo told me, "did not really feel herself to be what one could call a nation. Rather, she thought of herself as a civilization with a message for all men and as a fatherland."

Of course, in order to survive as a nation, China had to accept that there were other nations in the world. Moreover, being closely integrated in the patriarchal system, the Chinese were too loosely bound to the central power to have much feeling of common destiny. In Sun Yat-sen's words, "We are like scattered sand. We have no real national unity." It was a question of achieving national unity by regrouping the clans. "Why does China want to make the revolution? We have no cohesion and no resistance, and this is why we have been invaded by foreign imperialism and oppressed."

The Maoist revolution was more than anything else the building of a nation. It consisted of replacing the integration of the clan into Chinese civilization with the adherence of individuals to the Chinese nation.

"Nationalism" is the most important of Sun Yat-sen's "Three Principles"; the other two, "democracy" and "socialism," derive from it. The principle, *min-tsu*, refers at one and the same time to the people, the nation, the race, and the independence both of the Manchu emperors and of the Western invaders. What Sun Yat-sen defined, Mao achieved—thanks (and he was the first to acknowledge it) to the Japanese and American militarists, unwittingly his best agents.

The Sian Incident: A United Front for National Liberation

Maoism's strength is that it managed to symbolize the passion for national independence, and the Kuomintang's failure to do so was its greatest mistake.

In December 1936 Generalissimo Chiang Kai-shek was inspecting the anti-communist front in the North. Soon after he arrived there, he was taken prisoner by his second-in-command, Marshal Chang Hsueh-liang, whom he had come to exhort to be more active in fighting the communists of Shensi. Chang rightly criticized him for being concerned only with fighting Mao's troops and not bothering with the Japanese, who had conquered Manchuria and were encroaching farther on China's sovereignty. This conflict contained the essential choice which lay before China—to give priority to national unity against the foreigner and abandon the pursuit of the communists, or to give priority to the struggle against the communists and leave the way open to the foreigner.

Chiang was freed after being held prisoner for thirteen days. As our guides explained, "Chou En-lai arrived in Sian to convince the army commanders in the Northeast to release their prisoner. The Chinese Communist Party thereby enabled a united front to be formed against the Japanese aggressor. Chiang Kai-shek wanted to step up the struggle against the communists. The opposite in fact happened. He was freed—through the mediation of Chou En-lai—on condition that he promised to make war on the Japanese, to reorganize his government, to eliminate the pro-Japanese elements and not to attack the communists."

Whatever the precise tenor of the Sian talks, the fact is that Chiang Kai-shek, the man who had been mercilessly massacring communists for ten years, established a "united front" with them, accepted Chou En-lai as Mao's permanent representative, and resolved to be firm with the Japanese. This firmness of course led six months later to war.

The Sian affair lies at the heart of the Chinese revolution. Chiang Kai-shek was undeniably fired by a fierce nationalism; he detested the Japanese, but spontaneously he gave priority to the struggle against communism, not to the struggle against the foreigner.

Having given priority to the class struggle from 1923 to 1936, Mao's genius inspired him to reverse this during the war of resistance against Japan.

Mao stated this national priority in the most categorical manner in "On

New Democracy." This basic text dates from January 1940, but it was so unorthodox that it was not published in the Soviet Union until after Stalin's death. It completely broke with the theses of the Comintern and proposed that the leadership of the Revolution should be entrusted to "four revolutionary classes"—the poor peasants, the workers, the petit bourgeois and the "national capitalists." In short, the bourgeoisie, the intelligentsia, the mandarins and the "compradors" had to choose between the last two classes if they were to rally to the regime, which indeed they did in large numbers in 1949. These four classes, under the direction of the Communist Party, had to lead a revolutionary mission whose first objective was anti-imperialism—Japanese and then American. The second objective was anti-feudalism—aimed against the warlords and the landowners, who were allies of the Japanese. Even today the Chinese flag symbolizes this theory: one big star, which is the Party, directs four smaller stars—the four classes—which are put on the same footing.

The Patriotism of the Proletariat

Marx believed that the proletariat of all countries would unite spontaneously in an anti-capitalist International. In 1914 Jaurès and Lenin reckoned that this ineluctable union would be enough to prevent the First World War. And in 1917 Lenin thought it would be sufficient to establish peace. They all forgot one thing—that the proletariat has the most uncompromising sense of patriotism.

The Chinese Communist Party took direction of a vigorous struggle against the Japanese invader. It harnessed the patriotism of the rural masses. In 1931 it declared war on Japan, which had just annexed Manchuria. It was a purely theoretical gesture since the communist bases were a long way from the Japanese troops, but nonetheless it had great significance.

On the other side, the Kuomintang, who did not dare to breathe a warlike spirit into the peasantry for fear of upsetting the bourgeoisie upon whom they relied for support, found themselves thrust onto the defensive.

The Japanese had given Mao's troops their historic chance, by enabling them to embody national passion. Their conquerors, the Americans, completed the job by supporting Chiang Kai-shek, and thereby finishing him off. The process which was to begin all over again in the Vietnam War was underway.

Because the Kuomintang did not dare to go all the way in stirring up national feeling, the communists were able to rally—in Mao's words—"the national bourgeoisie, the intellectuals and all non-reactionary forces into a united common front to resist the Japanese."

Chinese China

Control over people living on the outskirts of the Empire had escaped into the hands of the colonial powers.

Now these alien populations—which history brought into the China of the Han—once again form an integral part of the Chinese nation. The Manchus, the Mongols of Inner Mongolia, the Muslims of Sinkiang, and the Tibetans are all bound once again to the central power, in accordance with a federative principle which hardly gives the national minorities any chance of expressing their differences. Several nationalities, but one fatherland. The Constitution of the People's Republic declares: "The People's Republic of China is a united multinational state." Of course, "all nationalities enjoy the freedom to use and develop their language and script, to keep or to reform their customs and habits," but "any action aimed at undermining the unity of the nationalities is forbidden."

China has ceased to lay claim to Korea, the Indochina peninsula, Burma and the Himalayan states, although not long ago they were her vassals. But, using a new form of words to express a long-lasting state of affairs, she arranged to have at her disposal the firm friendship of "sister nations"— North Korea, North Vietnam, Sihanouk's Cambodia and Souphanouphong's Laos.

In short, the Middle Kingdom restored its natural frontiers, indissolubly linking with the Han population the majority of the national minorities, which once constituted an unstable colonial zone of "tributary" nations, and forming with the others a protective ring of "sister nations."

Independence regained. There is no doubt that it makes the Chinese people very proud and gives them a calm confidence in the future. Each peasant, each worker and each soldier has assimilated the theories of the "paper tiger" and the "fish in water."

People do not talk about the "nuclear strike capability," but they certainly think about it. Ever since October 1964, when China exploded her first atomic bomb, the people have greeted every new stage in the development of a nuclear weapons system with wild enthusiasm. They feel themselves not only masters in their own house, but also well on the way to being invincible, something they have never been before, even with the Great Wall.

I was told that many peasant women who still pray to ancestors and spirits believe that the ancient emperors continue to keep a watch over China. And no doubt Empress Tzu-hsi is jumping with joy to see her ambition realized and the Middle Kingdom free from foreign occupation, capable of going its own way and saying what the emperor said to the King of England's first ambassador: "What happens in your country is of no interest to me." This time China says it with impunity.

17

The Conquest of Poverty

One Calamity after Another

China before 1949 was a medieval country. She had a population which was continually stricken by natural disasters—floods and drought; invasions of locusts, rats, mosquitoes and flies; and both endemic and epidemic diseases, including bubonic plague and cholera. There was complete ignorance of the real causes of these phenomena and a total lack of hygiene. Also, the Chinese were breeding like rabbits, although there was mass slaughter on an equally grand scale. There were magical practices and puerile superstitions. There was also illiteracy, which barred the majority of the population from the more elevated mental activities and, with the exception of a tiny educated minority, reduced the conveying of information to a simple word-of-mouth procedure. China's three great religions—Buddhism, Taoism and Confucianism—reached the people in a very irrational form. There was an underlying restlessness which would culminate without warning in uncontrollable rumors, great panic, fear and mass hysteria.

The Poorest Country in the World

How was this immense population, mostly illiterate, to assimilate the bare minimum of culture and rationalism without which it would not be able to conquer all its affliction, misfortune and backwardness? From being the fabulously rich country to which Christopher Columbus had tried to find a route, China by the nineteenth century had become one of the poorest in the world, and she certainly remained so until the middle of the twentieth century. A report from the League of Nations in 1939 gave the average income per head as twenty-nine U.S. dollars; this compared with thirty-four for the Indies, 282 for France and 554 for the United States. A United Nations report of 1949 still placed China behind Pakistan, India and Indonesia. In 1949 the average Chinese was eating twenty percent of the calories consumed by his European counterpart; his average life expectancy was twenty-five, compared with sixty-four in the United States. "In the country, where organization has broken down," Teilhard de Chardin observed, "it means unspeakable misery. And on top of all this, there's the cold. If there were a recorder of human suffering all over the face of the world, what would we not have to read at this very moment!"

Changing the Course of the Yellow River

Nature gave this misery cataclysmic dimensions. When you fly low over the Yangtse or the Huang-ho, the Yellow River, you can see how they can bring either abundance or terror and destruction, depending on whether they can be brought under control. In normal times, they carve a course for themselves between alluvial deposits. After a few torrential rains, they inundate thousands of acres of arable land. After a period of drought, they are reduced to a trickle; the soil turns to yellow dust and the harvests dry up.

The chronicles of ancient China praised the foresight of the emperors who had the rivers dredged instead of raising the dykes. But the ancient precept was rarely respected. The bed of the Yellow River has risen over the years and in many places is several feet higher than the plain; you can see the sails of the junks floating past above the ricefields. Of course, the ricefields themselves are vulnerable to a break in the dyke or a flood.

The Huang-ho has changed its course and its mouth twenty-six times. Both Marco Polo and Lord Macartney reported that in the view of the Chinese themselves the country had suffered more from the Yellow River bursting its banks than from war, famine or plague. Emperor Kuang-hsi made a hole in the levee in order to drown a rebel army; in so doing, he caused a flood in which a million people perished. . . .

Vicious Circles

Poverty has always followed a vicious circle. Soil is friable because trees do not have time to grow: destitute peasants are forced to eat the leaves and bark and then to sacrifice the rest to make huts and light fires. Loess is swept down by mountain torrents because it is not held in place by trees. Crops are laid to waste alternately by flood and drought. By blocking the flow of rivers, silt is continually raising their levels and forming natural dams which make the water burst its banks. And then on the very eve of a promising harvest, the locusts come—and in only a few short minutes their mandibles will have pulverized one field after another of rye or wheat.

These terrifying images have not been painted in retrospect by communist propaganda in order to stress the merits of the present regime. All the travelers' tales agree.

Once again, what Macartney said about the risks to the rice harvest is devastatingly accurate: "When the plant is green, drought makes it wilt. As it becomes ripe, the floods come and do it just as much damage. The birds and the locusts—whose numbers are so great that a European cannot imagine them—swoop down on them in preference to any other seed."

Over the next hundred and fifty years things simply got worse. Before 1949—in fact, before 1937, since the war with Japan was just one more disruptive factor of many—everyone felt powerless in face of this tangled series of cataclysms. The documents are there for reference. There is a whole library of them, from Marco Polo's *Divisament dou Monde*,* dictated in a Genoese prison ten years before Joinville** wrote his *Histoire de Saint Louis*, to the United Nations enquiries after the Second World War. For example, there is the report by Dr. Stampar, the public health expert sent to the Nanking government in 1933 by the League of Nations. His conclusions make one shudder. He maintains that there is *no* solution in sight. "If all the rich nations of the world pooled their efforts, they would not manage to pull China out of her stagnation."

Famine

China before 1949 presented the traveler with the same kind of sight which he still sees today in places like Benares—a vast number of beggars with amputated limbs; children covered in sores; scraggy, underfed black pigs and dogs; most people wearing rags and tatters, but a few in brocaded finery. When the elements got angry, famine swept everything away. The peasants were ruined already, and when there were droughts or floods they had nothing at all in reserve. So there was nothing that could prevent famine, which was often complicated by typhus or plague and so terrible that men

---

The Travels (TRANSLATOR'S NOTE).
**Jean de Joinville (1224–1317), counselor to Louis IX who wrote his biography; written between 1305 and 1309, it tells of the Crusade of 1284 (TRANSLATOR'S NOTE).

became cannibals. Travelers were inevitably struck by images of hungry people: "skeletons staggering around on bones which were once legs and stretching out their hands which are now bones toward the rice which is their only hope of salvation"; a man who "sways there in the scorching sun, his testicles dangling from him like withered olive seeds—the last grim jest to remind you that this was once a man."

In each of the affected provinces, deaths were measured in hundreds of thousands. In Suiyuan, on the border of Mongolia, the administration admitted to three million deaths, but foreign experts sent there by the International Aid Commission for Famine in China gave a figure of six million.

There was no need to travel to distant provinces—famine could be seen just as easily in the big towns.

As one witness reported, "Winter after winter in Shanghai, when I left the house to go to work there would be three or four corpses on the pavements—they were Chinese who had died of famine or cold during the night. What I found most shocking was that when I showed alarm and distress the Chinese passers-by who had gathered around began to laugh. Was this an absence of nerves? Indifference to human life? Or was it the age-old practice of hiding one's emotions out of prudence or manners? I really don't know."

Powerless Parrying

Not knowing how to treat the malady, the only thing to do was laugh it off. Or run away from it; or put up with it and make the best of it; or somehow ward it off. Running away from it meant massive, panic migrations, often involving hundreds of thousands of men. Many others attempted to accommodate themselves to it; before Chinese cooking became the rich man's luxury, it was the poor man's stand-by (and no doubt that is why it is now so highly prized)—its subtleties were born of the need to make anything that was edible actually pleasant, and to give some flavor to a very ordinary, basic dish. Warding it off involved superstition and magic, which were practiced just as much by the people as by the emperors. The latter chose names which they thought would bring down heavenly blessings on their empire—names like Chia Ching (Great Happiness) and Hsien Feng (Universal Abundance); one crafty minister even went so far as to change the name of the *Unfaithful River* (so called because it frequently left its bed) to *Immutable River* in the hope that it would show itself worthy of its new name.

It was all very well laughing off China's problems, resigning oneself to them, or trying to ward them off, but in the end there was bound to be a revolt that would come and sweep away these emperors and ministers. Sun Yat-sen put the problem in a simple and dramatic way when he said: "The question of hunger is the most important question in people's lives. . . . The ancients used to say: Eating is the people's heaven. . . . When everyone throughout China has enough to eat, and at a reasonable price, then we shall be able to say that the problem of the people's life has been solved." A modest ambition and at the same time a titanic challenge. Sun Yat-sen was unable to fulfill his ambition and fell; Mao took up the challenge.

Or rather—and this is the heart of the revolution—Mao made the people take it up for themselves. He saw the ambivalence of this misery, the fact that it was an atrocious thing to be subjected to but at the same time a motivational force of incomparable power. "Our poverty and our destitution are bad things on the surface, but in reality they are good things. Poverty provides the impulse for change, action and revolution. On a blank page everything is possible. You can write and draw what is newest and most beautiful." Mao's revolution was truly that of a Chinese, of a man who suffered hunger himself. He told how he never had either meat or eggs until he left home, although his father had passed from being a "medium-poor" peasant to being a "middle" and finally a "rich" peasant. He retained a vivid memory of the Hunan riots, when starving peasants were executed for begging their landlords for food.

There is not a single Chinese over the age of thirty who cannot remember a year when there was famine; there is not one who did not have the feeling that his life changed completely when this menace was removed from his everyday life, "as if he crossed the bridge leading to heaven." It is not surprising that Mao was able to demand so much from his people.

Eating Their Fill

Anyone who would dispute that in the past quarter of a century there has been a vast improvement in the lot of China's peasants, workers, youth and old people is neither honest nor sincere; his opinions are worthless.

Certainly we could not say that in China all is for the best in the best of all possible worlds; but what we can say is that we saw people who were well fed and apparently free from poverty, even if they lived modestly by the standards of our consumer society. They were well dressed, although their clothes were somewhat uniform (usually blue cotton trousers and white shirts for both men and women), and the children and young people were healthy and strong. Whereas before 1949 observers reported that children were often covered with infected sores, nowadays as soon as a pimple appears on their skin, out comes the mercurochrome.

It is not just the big towns and industrial areas that present this picture of health and harmony—it exists even in backward Shensi, one of the provinces where observers noted a famine in the autumn of 1960. No attempt was made to hide from us the fact that that year had indeed been a hard one. Food shortages were a definite possibility and rationing was strict, but when we spoke of famine, they simply laughed at us. They assured us that there had not been a real famine—with people eating roots and eventually one another—since the Liberation. Famine or food shortages—let us not quibble over words. What does seem certain is that after three years of great hardship from 1959 to 1961, the problem of hunger has not reappeared.

The country around Yenan, which is poor and mainly worked by hand, also has its share of cultivators, trucks and tractors. Not long before, tractors had been seen only on cinema screens. Many peasants own bicycles with nickel-plated rims, double frames, strengthened forks and luggage-racks strong enough to carry a man or a quintal sack of corn. You do not see any very fat Chinese, although pagoda statues and Meissen buddhas might have led you to expect them; you do not see any very thin Chinese now either.

Travelers who knew China under the old regime insist that the people are now taller. After many centuries of deprivation, the Chinese often used to look like stunted children. Nowadays, although they are still smaller than Europeans, the Chinese—especially in the south of the country—seem well built. Every morning you see thousands of young people doing gymnastic exercises on the pavements and swimming in the lakes around Peking and Wuhan; they give an impression of strength and health.

But rationing *is* still in force. Everyone must get his food from the shop assigned to him, and he is limited to a certain quantity of rice and a certain quantity of tea; he cannot go beyond this limit. We were told, though, that this is more a question of rationalizing than rationing. There are so many Chinese and the ancestral fears are still so very much alive that it would take only the smallest panic for the shops to be ransacked and for the weaker customers to be driven—from one day to the next—to begging for their living. Needs are not defined *a priori*; a figure is set and any purchase in excess of it would constitute stockpiling, or, in other words, hoarding. Each person is allowed thirty pounds of wheat, flour or rice a month, half a pound of oil a month, and six yards of cotton fabric a year. The threshold is certainly not very high, but it is said to be above subsistence level, so that the majority of Chinese—reassured by the very strictness and severity of these regulations, whose sense has been carefully explained to them over a long period—are not buying all they are entitled to. In this way consumption can be kept a little below production.

Furthermore, there remains a vast free sector. At any time of the day anyone can eat in a restaurant, where prices are cheap, buy ice cream on the street corner, or—in Peking—go to the Jenmin or Tien-chiao market. The crowd presses around the stalls, handing over small sums of money for fried fish, lacquered duck, roast pork, tripe, rice balls and soy sauce. The children make a mess of themselves with candy and chocolate ice cream, while musicians scratch away at violins and entertainers tell tales to a delighted crowd.

The River Tamed

Mao got rid of hunger, which had been the spectre haunting Chinese life for centuries. He also tamed the Yellow River, a feat whose symbolic importance overshadowed all other benefits.

For three thousand years attempts had been made to master this river which is at once China's provider and destroyer; Mao showed the Chinese that it was within their reach. Between 1957 and the end of the century, forty-six dams and canals will have been constructed; there will be navigable stretches of 1,200 miles from Outer Mongolia to Shantung. In the end a vast plain half the size of France will be protected and regularly irrigated.

In the golden book of the Sanmen Dam it has been written: "If the Government of the People's Republic did nothing else and disappeared tomorrow, the Chinese nation would remember with gratitude for a thousand years that it mastered the Yellow River."

The control of the river must symbolize for many Chinese the possibility of control over their destiny.

The victory over hunger and the domestication of the Yellow River are genuine achievements, and in later chapters I shall be describing how they were accomplished. But mainly it is the incessant hard work of the Chinese people which has brought such benefits to all.

Conquering the Spirit of Poverty

It is both rare and very moving to see an entire people living by the hope which they place in the future, a hope which is all the stronger because it stems from a confidence in themselves. Behind all the indoctrination and ideology, what each Chinese we met was really saying was: "I am building a new China."

In ancient China the expressions most often heard were *pu yao chin*— "that's how it is, it's of no importance"—and *mei yu fa tzu*—"one must accept." "My father had decided: I could but obey." "My stepmother takes me

for her servant." "The landowner demands his due." "The locusts are coming." *Mei yu fa tzu*.

Mei yu fa tzu and *pu yao chin* are infra-dig expressions. They made it
possible to live with poverty, by accepting it. Nowadays the emphasis is on
action and collective responsibility. The rest will follow—to conquer poverty
one must stop accepting it.

18

An Agriculture That Feeds
the People

A traveler about to land at Shanghai has an unforgettable view—fields with furrows straight as a die, divided into plots as far as the eye can see, glistening in the sun in a mosaic of color and reflected light. Every inch of soil seems to be utilized; hanging gardens cling to hillsides, valleys are cultivated, the fields come to within a few inches of houses, railway lines and factories. It is like an enormous jigsaw puzzle which the Chinese put together, take apart and put together again every season. The fields are enclosed within a geometric grid of innumerable irrigation channels. The houses look minute, grouped together in hamlets with their little clumps of trees. On a battlefield hundreds of thousands of square miles in area, the Chinese have taken on a gigantic struggle with nature—with mountains, torrents and rivers, as well as with soil erosion and drought.

Centuries of infinite patience and hard work have finally turned the soil into a landscape with meandering waterways edged with dykes, a tapestry of green, roads and canals. Few lands give such a vivid impression of agriculture as a fine art. And the success masks the effort that has been put into it.

Away from the alluvial soil of the Yangtse and the Huang-ho, there is none of that very fertile soil found in Europe and America which requires hardly any work. In fact, the soil is friable and easily exhausted if an attempt is made to increase the yield—as happened at the time of the "Great Leap Forward."

The Primacy of Agriculture

China's great wealth lies with her people; her history is the history of her peasants.

Every year the emperor himself used to open the farming season by marking out three sacred furrows. This ritual acknowledged the vital role of those who fed the Empire, of the peasants who came immediately after the scholar–civil servants in the social hierarchy. By raising them one more notch, the revolution was recognizing their importance in China.

China is hundreds of millions of men and women cultivating their land to feed themselves. China's economy still has the wonderful simplicity of primitive times. The criterion of success is also simple: that these people should eat their fill.

In this respect—as we have already seen—the success of Chinese communism is incontestable, and in fact it is hardly ever in dispute. The figures prove it: in 1965 China imported 400 million dollars' worth of cereals, whereas today the level of imports is very much lower—and lower still in proportion to foreign trade. And one can see proof of the success of Chinese communism: there are no half-starved faces, no swollen stomachs; everyone looks healthy. It may seem rather ordinary to get enough to eat, but for the Chinese people it is a novelty. It is difficult to estimate the impact on their lives of this hitherto unknown sense of security.

This landscape is the work of centuries, and this success which took many years to achieve was in no way accompanied throughout by good fortune and happiness. The entire paradox of China is evident in the contrast between a very old landscape, which suggests that revolutions are just passing tremors within the immutable, and the peasants, who are fully aware that they are living in new times, because they are at peace with one another, confident of the morrow, and masters of their land as they have never been before.

One comes to realize how very little it required for these peasants to inherit their land—merely the overthrow of the existing order, merely a revolution.

The Impossible Agrarian Reform

The basic issue in China has always been agrarian. Since the beginning of time, ninety percent of the population has been peasants, more often than not working on land which they did not own. The land has always been the near monopoly of a minority of families, and the mass of peasants have been forced to put up with the hard conditions of tenant farming, which were almost always aggravated by the debts incurred in time of famine.

It was always famine which thwarted efforts to bring ownership and work together. China did not experience the slow progress made by the peasantry in the West, the gradual and continual erosion of feudalism. Periods of egalitarianism constantly alternated with lapses into a desperate struggle for existence. The mechanism was always the same: a jacquerie of desperate men would be led by an energetic or cunning pretender in a revolt to overthrow the dynasty and dispossess the great landowners who made up the court; then the land would be distributed among the peasants; but very quickly a famine would come along and force them to sell it back for a pittance, perhaps for a sack of rice or millet.

Shih Huang-ti in the third century B.C., Wang Mang in the first century, and Prime Minister Wang An-shih in the eleventh century all tried and in their various ways failed: As a chronicler wrote of the first of these attempts, "The strongest, greediest and most base of men numbered their fields in thousands, while the weakest were left with a patch of land too small to stick a needle in."

Each successive dynasty filled the Danaids' jars—the Song, the Mongol Yuan, the Ming, and the Manchu Ching confiscated large holdings and gave them to the peasants, thereby improving their lot for the time being. But making the peasants richer did not mean the consolidation of land ownership, and the continuance of private property always brings about— with the help of famine—the reestablishment of the *latifundia*.

In order to put an end to this endless fluctuation, it was necessary to pass from reform to revolution, from breaking up and distributing land to the complete abolition of private property. But why should a regime which relied on the support of the mandarin elite and which had received the mandate of preserving society have decided on these extreme measures?

Because they were not able to solve the agrarian question, the majority of the imperial dynasties collapsed under the impact of peasant revolts. The last dynasty, the Manchus, was no exception; the *first* internal shock it suffered—with the Taiping rebellion—foreshadowed the end. In the valley of the Yangtse between 1850 and 1864, the Taiping established a communal system of administration, with a "law on the land" which was very close to the agrarian solutions of the communist regime; in fact, as a young man Mao was passionately interested in the history of the Taiping movement.

The Manchu dynasty stamped out this uprising, but was it going to draw the appropriate lesson from the experience? A decree of Empress Tzu-hsi suggested it might: "I perceive how calamities from within and aggression from without have come upon us in relentless succession. . . . But today definite progress has been made toward necessary reforms."

But the Court recoiled in the face of its own boldness, and kept going back on its decisions. It sent students to Europe, and then recalled them. It commanded a powerful navy, and then assigned its finances to building a marble pavilion beside the lake of the Summer Palace. The land it dared not touch.

Everyone was dissatisfied and frustrated, both the advocates and the opponents of change. One thing at least was agreed—that the mandate of heaven had been withdrawn from the Manchu dynasty. Sun Yat-sen invested himself with it.

The Powerlessness of Sun Yat-sen and the Kuomintang

Outside Nanking stands a high hill dedicated to the memory of Sun Yat-sen; it has been very attractively planted with larches and spruces, and laid with lawns. Visitors from abroad are invited to climb several hundred steps to the mausoleum, the work of the French sculptor Landowski, where they are encouraged to stand in respectful silence before the reclining white marble effigy of the first great man of the Republic.

On Peking's Tien An Men Square hang portraits of Marx, Engels, Lenin, Stalin—and Dr. Sun Yat-sen. Sun's widow, Sung Ching-ling, is Vice-President of the People's Republic of China. And in November 1966, the centenary of the "Father of the Chinese Revolution"—as he is known on both sides of the Formosa Strait—was celebrated in Peking with great ceremony. Isn't it strange that the People's Republic of China takes such care to stress its descent from the founder of the Kuomintang? In Formosa, in fact, Sun is the object of a cult comparable to the Mao Tse-tung cult in mainland China.

This piety in a minor mode is indicative of ambiguity. The Maoist regime takes the Sun Yat-sen legacy and at the same time transforms it; Mao claimed to have taken over what was best in the Chinese heritages in order to fulfill the promise it entailed rather than repudiate it.

As regards the land, the promise was a simple one: "Nine out of ten peasants own no land. Farmers must cultivate the land for themselves. Now, agricultural produce is for the most part taken by the landowners. If we cannot solve this very serious question, it will be impossible to ensure that the people live."

Sun Yat-sen's influence remains as strong as ever because he made a broad outline for the future. His teaching suggests a synthesis between Chinese tradition and adaptation to modern civilization. His influence was such that nothing could happen later without reference to him.

Sun Yat-sen sacrificed the landowners without hesitation to the small farmers: "The power of the big landowners will be swept from the continent of China. Profit from the land will be raised and only the peasants farming themselves will get land from the state. In this way the people will devote themselves more and more to agriculture and no land will be left abandoned." But at the same time he refused to change the distribution of wealth: "In China today, where industry is not yet developed, there is no place for the Marxist class struggle and the dictatorship of the proletariat. There can be no question of distribution where there is nothing to distribute."

As a child Mao often spent nights reading the clandestine writings of Sun Yat-sen. In 1911—after the Wuhan rising—he enrolled in the republican forces, and assisted in the trampling and defeat of Sun Yat-sen. He must often have reflected later on this mixture of aggressiveness and faint-heartedness. What he learned was that only aggressiveness paid.

Why did the Kuomintang—which could have sought the support of the peasants—neglect to do so? Because it was essentially the party of the towns. Its policies failed to consider the rural heartlands of China, and this was where it lost out.

The Kuomintang established two Chinas. It gained the support of the industrial and trading cities along the coast and tried to bring China into the Western world. It abandoned backward, antiquated China with its primitive country areas to the landowners and former warlords, who raised taxes and put down any seditious movements.

Agrarian reform was talked about but never undertaken. In 1930 the Kuomintang declared that the land rent would be limited to 37.5 percent of the harvest—instead of at least fifty percent, which was often being demanded. But this was never implemented. An agrarian reform was announced again in the Kuomintang program of 1945, but it was never even started. The poverty of the peasant masses was intensified by exorbitant rents, accumulated debts, uncertain harvests, old-fashioned agricultural methods and the passivity they had inherited from their forefathers.

The Kuomintang, then, dealt only with the privileged sections of society, and thereby was condemned—as they were—for continuing a policy which allowed half the country to remain impervious to progress.

Between 1921 and 1931 the Chinese Communist Party followed a parallel course. Its aim was to take root among the workers in the industrial towns and defeat the enemy on his own ground.

The crushing of workers' revolts in Shanghai and Canton enabled Mao to impose his seemingly outlandish idea of bypassing nascent industrial China and getting the peasant masses on the move.

Luckily for him, a third party was interested in the industrial fringe of China—Japan was to take possession of it from 1937 to 1945. When the Kuomintang troops were swept back from their coastal and urban base into the interior by the advancing Japanese troops, they found themselves hurled into surroundings in which they were very out of place. As they became less and less capable of governing the rural areas, all the Kuomintang could do was to cling to a superficial power; in its dying years, the Kuomintang remained a prisoner of its own modernist origins. Their political action was addressed to an urban China, and the form of combat they chose was that of an industrial nation. Their chances against an industrialized nation like the Japanese were nil, and they were soon ousted.

From that moment on Mao was able to marshal the peasants simultaneously against the landlords, who supported the Kuomintang, and the Japanese invaders. Rarely in China's history has there been such a favorable coincidence of circumstances—popular feeling against exploiters and national feeling against an invader. The Kuomintang had promised a lot in thirty years, but they had done nothing to bring to the rural areas the radical reforms that were so sorely needed by the vast peasant proletariat of a poor and backward country. The failure of the Kuomintang and the success of the communist jacquerie formed the basis of what is essentially original about the Chinese model.

"Rely on Your Own Forces": With the Production Brigades

Machiao, in Kiangsu Province, is one of the 80,000 people's communes specializing in rice-growing. In actual fact, these communes are more like big cantons. The basic cell is the production brigade, which corresponds to the traditional village. The production brigade owns the land, although it is a moot point whether "owns" really means anything when the owner cannot rent or sell the land; nonetheless, whenever we spoke to people we met about the state being the owner of the land, we always got a quick and strong reaction: "It's not the state, and it's not the people's commune. We own it—the production brigade."

The symbols are stronger than the reality. . . .

Each brigade has its revolutionary committee—just like the people's commune, the municipality and the province—and deals only with the revolutionary committee of its commune, which determines each brigade's production targets and, when the harvest shows a surplus, demands permission to keep the surplus in order to undertake certain investments. This power only covers investments of medium importance—for example, putting up new buildings or modernizing minor equipment. Surpluses used up in this way must not exceed ten to thirteen percent of production: profits—which are still allowed—remain under strict control.

Bigger investments for projects like soil improvement, irrigation works and reforestation involve state aid in the form of subsidies or technical advice.

The state also intervenes when communes cannot guarantee their own consumption requirements, and provides them with the cereals they need.

Each commune is autonomous. The principle is, as always: "Rely on your own forces." But the amount of freedom left to the individual brigades seems to vary quite a bit from commune to commune. In Machiao it seemed extremely limited, whereas in Mei Chia Wu, a tea commune near Hangchow, the brigade's revolutionary committee seemed able to lay down the production plan, decide on the distribution of wages, direct small investments and organize agricultural and political training.

Ever-present Practices of the Past

We were under no illusions that all communes are as progressive as the ones we visited; they indicate one possible future for the agriculture of this developing country, but they are not representative by any means of the reality of China's rural life.

For every dyke erected by the Dragon's Well brigade, countless rivers remain untamed both throughout the vast twenty-eight million acres under cultivation and throughout the virgin lands abandoned to flood and drought.

As for mechanization, it is still very limited, in spite of the principles that were laid down by Mao Tse-tung and the plans that have been clearly expressed by Chou En-lai. Even Machiao, which is a model commune, has only twenty-eight tractors for 20,000 workers.

Over hundreds and hundreds of square miles, the only machine to be seen is the train; it crosses land which has only ever seen and known animal power. And, of course, the cheapest, most skilled and toughest of the animals is still man. One sees carts being drawn by mules and donkeys which look half-starved, but the horse is little used. One sees few cows and oxen, especially in the North. Everywhere, it is man who carries things and pulls carts; sometimes he is even harnessed to a plow. In fact, some parts of the country, like Hopeh, hardly use animals at all.

The Chinese are still not very good at fertilizing their land. In Japan—where the degree of mechanization is much higher—ten times more fertilizer is used per acre. The substitute methods are picturesque rather than effective: the odd little squares of canvas one sees hanging under the hindquarters of mules and horses to catch precious manure. And, as we have seen, man has replaced the animals in this respect as well. In fact, China has not yet been able to acquire the chemical industry which her agriculture so very urgently needs and which is the only way she can achieve prosperity.

Productivity is also very low. Twenty or thirty men produce as much as one man on a modern American farm. If China's productivity were on a par with that of the United States, twenty million farmers would be enough to achieve today's level of production.

What is more, agriculture is still suffering from the aftereffects of the events of the past decade—the years 1960–61, with the withdrawal of Soviet experts and various natural climactic disasters, and the Cultural Revolution, with all the new difficulties it created.

The importance of agriculture is symbolic. The peasants often use the roads to dry their hay; even on the main road from Shanghai's international airport into town it stretches two-thirds of the way across. It is not a rejection of what is modern, but why should modernity be encouraged? China is by and large an old-fashioned country, but one without complexes. The peasants have priority by virtue simply of being peasants.

Something else that impressed itself on our memories was the sight—as we left Sian, in Shensi Province—of the road filled with hundreds and hundreds of carts. All pulled by men and women, some of them were weighed down with sand, coal, cement sleepers or carefully stacked bricks; others with hay, rice, watermelons or aubergines. The whole of the surrounding countryside had been mobilized to serve Sian. The seemingly total absence of any mechanical means of transport was compensated for by this great mass of people moving slowly toward the town like a vast human conveyor belt.

Work seems to have become second nature to everyone: They do not do periods of intensive work separated by hours of rest or days off; they just have short breaks now and again on the spot. They eat whenever they can, and they sleep in the rough or near their machines. The breaks are intended mainly to provide time in which to plan the next task and to obtain advice from the study of Mao Tse-tung thought. Millions of peasants and their children live this way, as though their common aim were to make the land work for them after thousands of years of famine and degradation.

Eaux et Forêts

Eaux et forêts—the name of the French rural administration springs to mind when I think of the immense tasks the Chinese peasant has to undertake in order to gain control of his environment. Systematically and patiently—at the brigade level or on a regional basis—China is rebuilding her forests, which have been progressively destroyed over many centuries, and regulating, damming, conserving and utilizing her great quantities of water.

An impressive attempt has been made at reforestation. Thousands of millions of trees have been planted in towns and in the country, along roads and on windswept plateaus.

Along the dead-straight road leading to Peking, the trees provide the traveler with a cool shade which is most welcome. Pines, poplars and willows spring up among dwarf acacias. They are all less than twenty years old. To see trees that are older than the regime itself, one has to go to places like the Summer Palace, the Forbidden City and the lakes of Hangchow.

In the ten years after the Liberation, over five thousand experts were trained and sent all over China. More than 125 million acres—an area about the size of France—have now been replanted.

The emperors put a Great Wall around China to keep out the Huns from the West; with the weather just as with politics, danger lies to the West. China is now protected against the west wind by a new Great Wall of forests, sometimes over six hundred miles long.

In the construction of the canal from the Yangtse to the sea, the martial arts were used for peaceful purposes. The same men who learned to build earthworks during the war with Japan, digging tunnels to link one village with another, opened this 120-mile waterway, which drains a huge region and protects it from flooding.

The harnessing of water is a real battle. When fifteen communes in Lin Hsien district decided to dig the "hero" canal in 1958, it was not clear whether it was to be a mark of respect to the heroes who had fought in the Liberation or to the communes themselves. In any event, this local undertaking assumed proportions that fully justified the pride shown in it. The whole job lasted ten years; 35,000 people worked on the main canal and, overall, as many as 100,000 people worked together. Except at harvest times, almost half the population of the district worked on it.

In the end, after 19,000,000 work days, three-quarters of the entire district was irrigated by a network of canals stretching over six hundred miles. Fourteen hydroelectric power stations were producing about 4,000 kilowatts, and by 1975 this figure was due to have reached 15,000 kilowatts. So half the district's 485 brigades have electricity. The district is also self-sufficient in cereals, and even sends large quantities to other parts of the country.

The rivers have been dammed and dyked. Torrents that have been tamed now produce electricity as well as irrigate fields that were previously impossible to cultivate. The peasants know what all these works mean for them: "Without this dyke," they say, "without this irrigation canal, we would have died of hunger in a year like this."

Agriculture Takes Off

The "Great Leap Forward" fixed a figure of 500,000,000 tons of cereal as the target for Chinese agriculture. It is still far off. Chou En-lai presented the record harvest of 1970 as a great success, and it was only 240,000,000 tons.

In fact, it was probably twenty percent above the figure for 1965 and fifty percent above the figure for 1952, but in this period the population grew by about the same amount.

In 1971 the harvest was reckoned to be 250,000,000 tons—about ten million above the previous year—but there were some 15,000,000 more mouths to feed. The 1972 harvest, according to Chou En-lai, was four percent below that of 1971, so it was back at about 240,000,000 tons.

Thus China's agriculture—which seems to progress in fits and starts and to vary greatly from one year to the next—is still lagging behind the growth in population. It seems neither to be losing nor to be gaining much ground.

Enormous efforts have been made—especially if one thinks in human terms—to deal with the main cause of agricultural disasters, the terrible pattern of the country's waters. Every possible advantage has been taken of this period of peace, and no doubt these two factors together explain how production has advanced to the point where the needs of the population have up to now been met.

As for hydraulics, the hardest and what seems the most "profitable" part of the job has been done. Now, it is in the battle for production that the war will be won or lost. And of course, China has realized—albeit rather late in the day—that the key factor in this field is chemistry. The soil is often naturally poor; it has been exhausted by thousands of years of exploitation and possibly thrown out of balance by the intensive "hothouse" development undertaken during the "Great Leap Forward." Only fertilizers can enrich soil like this. The "green revolution" which is beginning to produce such astonishing results in India has not yet been undertaken in China.

There has been a great increase in the production of chemical fertilizers—from 6,000,000 tons in 1965 to 16,800,000 tons in 1971. The target figure for 1975 was 35,000,000 tons.

There have been important cereal surpluses, and these have enabled stocks to be built up which probably amount to 50,000,000 tons. "In time of war," I was told, "it would be impossible to destroy all our reserves."

These are more than mere figures. They are proof that something really fundamental is now on the move in China, so that in the end there will be an agrarian reform which will not break down in time of famine.

Of course, the population is also increasing, but it is not improbable that from now on growth in agricultural production will exceed population growth. Perhaps Malthus's curves, which seemed at one time all too evident in China, will be reversed.

One can easily understand the reasons for the tight "hold" the Chinese communists now intend to keep on the population. They must give themselves time to increase production and productivity in order to feed their vast population and to make more and more of the workers available for work in industry. Before the Chinese economy can take off, it needs a solid runway.

19

Industry Has Two Meanings

Ping-pong Balls

Relations between China and the United States were resumed—in the eyes of
the world—across a ping-pong table. And one of our last visits was to a
factory near Canton where ping-pong balls were made. When we arrived, we
were wondering whether they held a privileged place in China's system of
symbols, for Kuo Mo-jo had said to us in Peking: "We have made the world
revolve around a ping-pong ball." Here, though, we shall look at ping-pong
in terms not of a new style of diplomacy but of a certain style of industrialization.

Our hosts took great delight in telling us their factory's history, or, more
accurately, their adventure. In the beginning was Mao. The Chairman had
said: "Sport must be developed to strengthen the physical constitution." A
few Cantonese workers discovered a specific application for this general idea:
ping-pong balls must be made. "Relying on their own forces," about a
hundred of them set up shop some twenty miles out of town. All they had was
a cauldron which they heated over a domestic hearth; they had no machinery
and hardly any idea how to set about the job in hand. "During the day we put
up tents under the lychee tree* and in the evening we started building
houses. But we encountered serious difficulties, because we didn't understand the technique for manufacturing ping-pong balls." They bought

---

*Lychee, or litchi, is a small, pulpy and juicy Chinese fruit; the inside is rather like a peeled
grape.

materials from the ironmonger with which they made waffle-like molds in which the balls took shape.

The authorities were wary and had given them only a very tiny subsidy. In fact, their misgivings were borne out by the first results. The balls were far too light and burst like bubbles when they were struck by a bat. But these pioneers were not discouraged.

This was 1960. Now the factory produces 1,600,000 ping-pong balls a month, and they told us proudly that the best of them are used in championships. But it was by no means all plain sailing. Liu Shao-chi had a hand in it.

"Those who supported the renegade's line seized on our difficulties and they advocated imitating foreign technology as the only method. Luckily, this line was criticized, fought and in the end swept aside. The creative spirit of the masses has enabled original solutions to be invented which—by developing mechanization—have increased and improved production."

As a matter of fact, the methods used do retain the authentic local flavor of resourcefulness. Celluloid sheets are steam-distended and pressed into hemispheres; these are then stuck together. To test their roundness, the workers simply roll the balls down an incline, at the foot of which are small cups. The best-quality balls roll straight down toward the center cup—these are the ones that are used for competition matches. "Deviationist" balls—the ones that are badly balanced and hence veer to left or right—are for general, everyday use.

For a moment we wondered why we were being shown these rather amusing operations. Could the manufacture of ping-pong balls really be taken seriously? In fact, a new shop in the factory was turning out silicon parts for use in transistors—very delicate work done in a vacuum to keep the dust out. Ping-pong balls and electronics in the same factory—and produced by the same men. They made the decision themselves to embark on this new venture, simply because of a campaign which said that this kind of production would be useful. The workers moved from cauldrons to precision engineering. That is the key to the system; it is an anti-system system. Ten years after the ping-pong ball decision, another of the same kind—the workers' initiative; lengthy discussions to decide how to respond to a directive from the Chairman or, in the second case, to a campaign; a decision is suggested but not planned; there is no concern about whether it is economically rational; no bother about the technical aspects; and each team is absolutely confident of its own ability.

The second stage is in fact even more astounding than the first. We were told that it was the subject of some disagreement among the workers. The factory could have developed its production, or extended it to cover other sports equipment or other uses of celluloid. Quite apart from the unanimous condemnation of the "economism" of the renegade Liu Shao-chi, the decision to go into silicon production was almost a provocation in itself.

Industry—Industrious

This anti-system has its own methods: the factory is also a "production brigade"—not a production *unit*, a pawn on the economic chessboard, but an element in the social structure. Production is an aim, but the social group which pursues that aim is not a means to that end; it is its very foundation, its vital living cell.

But economic considerations do enter into it. Although productivity leaves plenty of room for progress, investment is next to a minimum and made as safe as possible.

Production got off the ground with hardly any state aid; the aid increased as the workers proved their success. If this Canton factory is to be taken as an example, the state has found an effective way of spreading industrialization at minimum cost.

The state brings out individual initiative, but the workers create the investment by their own work. They are able to feel that the enterprise is their achievement and their property. In this way a network has grown up of small and medium-sized enterprises which were set up with a minimum of initial funding. This system ensures a connection between the needs of planned production and the initiatives encouraged in the masses. We sensed that the Chinese were just as proud of their small factories—which are still very much like craft workshops in the way they operate—as of their most important industrial combines.

Although no one brought up the topic, the dates spoke for themselves: the enterprise was born at the time of the "Great Leap Forward" and its second stage was launched during the Cultural Revolution. In many respects these two movements had the same inspiration behind them; the Cultural Revolution made good the failures and disappointments of the "Great Leap Forward." Liu Shao-chi complacently denounced the "Great Leap"—and was eliminated by the Cultural Revolution. Like the "Great Leap," the Cultural Revolution advocated the industrialization of China from the bottom up. Liu not only "stifled" the masses' vigorous efforts in industry, but also ordered the closure of tens of thousands of medium-sized and small enterprises which had been set up, accusing them of not being sufficiently profitable and of being incapable of ensuring rapid development.

For many different reasons, what is needed is industry which is close to the people—in other words, close to the peasant. Where there is no commercial organization, the only way to adapt production to consumption is to bring them together physically. Where there are no adequate means of communication, an industry which is dispersed about the country is essential, for it cuts down the need for transport.

It is also practically invulnerable, and one should not underestimate the advantage this has in the eyes of the Chinese. Chairman Mao once defined the aims of industrial development in these terms: "to make the revolution and to promote production; to improve our work; to prepare ourselves actively for a war." The men who lead China have all made one war in which victory depended on being able to organize a number of provinces in the interior and to live off them.

Only by decentralizing industry can its symbiosis with agriculture be guaranteed, and without this symbiosis there can be neither social equilibrium nor economic development. Chinese society aims at making the worker versatile; the man who was a laborer yesterday may be a farmer today, and a weaver or a mechanic tomorrow. Once industrial production takes root in the rural areas, three parts of this aim will have been achieved. As for development, it depends on the cooperative interaction of industry and agriculture—industrial power depends on an improvement in agricultural productivity freeing labor from the land, and agriculture will only become more productive if industry gives its support in the form of chemical fertilizers, electricity, machinery, equipment, trucks and bicycles.

When it comes down to it, dispersed industrialization furthers the principle of the "primacy of the political": the factories do not acquire so many cadres and technical men that their sheer size becomes an obstacle to revolutionary management. The workers are in on everything that is going on, and the pursuit of better productivity and technical innovation cannot become the private concern of experts and specialists. "Make the revolution and promote production"; one can't exist without the other—the revolution encourages the creativity of the workers and thereby promptly enables production to make its long-awaited "Great Leap Forward."

Blast Furnaces and the Farmyard

The Peking No. 2 textile works and an electrical engineering factory in Shanghai each employ about two thousand workers. The rice commune's cement barge factory employs several dozen. In Canton the sports factory has a work force of 280, and the one in Nanking employs 150. In Hangchow—the silk capital—we visited a factory which employed 1,700 workers, and there were twenty other factories like it in the town; even in this ancient industrial center, concentration is avoided.

Wuhan, though, was different. Sixty thousand workers, four blast furnaces, and an annual output of more than three million tons of iron and steel products. If the term "heavy industry" means anything, it means the Wuhan iron and steel works.

The blast furnaces seemed to have been the center of an ideological war of which Mao was the eternal winner. The first one,* built with Soviet aid in 1958, produces between 1,500 and 1,700 tons of steel a day. The Chinese built the fourth one on their own; it was producing 3,000 tons a day, and we were told it would soon be producing 4,000 to 5,000 tons. And the method of construction is as important as the achievement itself: they managed to complete it in four months, and the whole region was involved.

Even so, a visit to Wuhan leaves one with quite a different impression from a visit to, say, one of the big steel complexes in France. It is not a splendid, well-oiled, smooth-running technical machine. We were shown electronic machines which can weigh loads in motion, laminates being moved by magnet cranes, and the automated feeding process for the blast furnaces. But what struck us as we walked through the combine was the anarchic jumble of workshops, depots, workers' houses, single quarters, maize fields and kitchen gardens. No separation here between life and work. Black pigs rummage about in the slag. Ducks and children wander about between the buildings.

This combine is an autonomous world all its own. Two or three thousand people earn their living there or live there. The combine has twenty schools, as well as People's Liberation Army units, a hospital, stadiums, a center for "ideological reeducation," cooperatives, and fields under cultivation. The whole complex carries out the directive Chairman Mao gave when he inaugurated the first blast furnace in 1958: "A great enterprise like the Wuhan iron and steel works can be gradually transformed into a combine which will make the widest variety of iron and steel products for mechanical, chemical and construction engineering; it will also devote part of its activities to agriculture, education and military training." This instruction is religiously written up on a hoarding at the works in letters of gold.

All things considered, blast furnaces are built here in the same way ping-pong balls are made in Canton—without too much concern for economic rationale. The location of the works seems rather odd,** since Wuhan is a long way from the iron- and coal-mining areas. The figure for total production which we were given is about the same as was given in 1964—so in spite of two new blast furnaces, output does not seem to have increased.

---

*The first of the four currently in production. Hanyang, one of the three towns which make up Wuhan, has been a big steel-making center since well before the war.
**On the other hand, the combine is near a big river, so everything is transported very cheaply. The Wuhan iron and steel industry was very active under the British in the 1920s and 1930s.

But what seems to concern the responsible officials much more than this is the ideological level of the workers: how the work of 60,000 men is to be "revolutionized."

Industry—Industrial

In short, does China have genuine industry? One is tempted to say that she doesn't, especially since the word has no meaning for the Chinese, or at any rate it has a threatening connotation. Industry has an autonomous existence and exists as an end in itself only in the minds of engineers and technocrats. Liu Shao-chi no doubt did not commit all the crimes of which he has been found guilty, but he was a useful scapegoat. He represented the values that Maoism was trying to wipe out. By accusing him it was possible to get the masses to accept an opposite hierarchy of values, which subordinated the myth of industrial production to other, stronger myths.

Of course, this subordination cannot but have consequences for production itself. However much we are assured that the revolutionary spirit increases productive capacity tenfold and however many times we are given proof of it, the fear persists that very often ideological tension is a distraction from work and inhibits creativity.

One must bear these reservations in mind in interpreting the great slogan of industrialization: "Walking on two legs." Sometimes it means that China's economy rests on agriculture and industry, and that one cannot be sacrificed to the other. At other times, it means that China's industrial effort is divided between rural light industry, which is widely dispersed, and urban heavy industry, which is highly concentrated. But even in this second case, the dialectical opposition of these two branches of industry does not give grounds for assuming that heavy industry is likely to be a hotbed of economism. Because the desire to develop the small and medium-sized enterprises is very largely political in intent, one must not conclude that therefore the industrial concentrations will be safe from the "primacy of the political."

A Nationalist Industry

China's politics are basically national. Chinese are modest out of politeness and a sense of decency, but they are not very good at hiding their immense confidence in themselves. It is useless to compare one's achievements with those of others; it is enough simply to assert them.

The Permanent Exhibition of Industrial Achievements in Shanghai is a display of nationalism. Here is the glory of China's massive effort to solve problems of advanced technology "by her own means." Specialized dictionaries have been used extensively in order to make sure that the quality of the success comes through in English and French: machine to align a camshaft, planer for bevel gears, coordinated single-column reaming machine, monocrystal silicon oven, electric welding drill, multi-purpose command system for industrial electronic computers.

No sector of industry is omitted. Freighters and pedal-generators for villages without electricity, 32-ton trucks and teleprinters, buttonhole machines and scientific measuring apparatus—not to mention petit-point portraits of Chairman Mao. Everything meets the same high standards. Maybe there are no jet aircraft, but we were assured that the Chinese were perfectly capable of producing them. When we asked specific questions, it became clear from their answers that the finest of these machines were not yet in serial production; it was the future that was on show. For the present the Chinese generally have to have recourse to foreign industry.

Nationalism and ingenuity work hand in hand to ensure that these borrowings are incorporated into the Chinese way. A foreign machine is very often bought just in order to be studied, taken apart, rethought and put together again in order to meet the users' own needs and ideas. Why respect the habits of the capitalists? We were given the example of the workers at the Shihchiachuang thermal power station.

"The output of the generators must not exceed the limit fixed by the manufacturer": for many years this had been the rule for generating equipment, a "taboo" area of the energy industry according to certain bourgeois technical "authorities." Refusing to blindly put their trust in these foreign dogmas, and especially in an area labeled "forbidden," the workers "courageously transformed this foreign equipment and raised its productive capacity by fifty percent."

Results

In short, how powerful is China industrially? Firm figures simply are not available. Those we have are only approximate: 21,000,000 tons of steel, 300,000,000 tons of coal, 26,000,000 tons of petroleum and 125,000 million kilowatts of electricity. All these figures indicate that important progress has been made.*

---

*But it is difficult to be precise. For example, Chinese figures for 1957 and 1958 put coal production at 300,000,000 tons. If, however, we take the more realistic figure of 130,000,000 tons as a basis, the annual growth in production is well below the twenty percent increase estimated by some enthusiastic observers.

In 1971 Chou En-lai told Edgar Snow that in the previous year industrial production had reached 90,000 million dollars; according to *People's Daily*, the figure for 1971 was ten percent higher.

The communist regime set out with the very poor industrial legacy left by the "old society." It took care not to build a prestige industry rapidly, pouring all available capital into it and setting it apart from the peasant China, which would then be condemned to rot and waste away. Instead, money was put into long-term development and slow industrialization, transforming the enormous human potential of the rural areas. "Industrialization is a prolonged war," a guerrilla war waged in all corners of the land.

Industrialization modifies the peasant mentality; it supports agriculture and increases its productivity, and, in return, the means are created for investment. The fact that there is a very low level of productivity—which is perhaps more noticeable in the big industrial concentrations than in the smaller local enterprises—is not because of incompetence or lack of goodwill on the part of the workers; it is because of the shortage of equipment. Industry is ready to make great advances, but does not itself hold the keys to its progress; the future of industry rests on the balance between agricultural productivity and population growth.

20

Between Subsistence Economy
and Exchange Economy

People were bicycling over the Great Bridge at Nanking, and this contrast seemed to sum up the problem of China's transportation system. Chinese transportation also "walks on two legs," but the two legs are not of the same length.

The West stole their inventions from the Chinese, and now the Chinese are doing the same in reverse. In China, the bicycle is omnipresent and has many uses. Rusty old bicycles and gleaming new ones carry and pull everyone and everything. For a long time to come the bicycle will be the only mode of transport available to the "broad masses."

The bicycle's success is no doubt due to the fact that it is a kind of mechanical illusion, a bogus machine. It is driven by muscular energy, and in China man has always been the most widely used beast of burden, so the bicycle makes his task easier without in any way breaking his monopoly. It is a masterpiece of ambiguity; it carries its driver.* It could hardly be more appropriate to the Chinese way, since it is driven by man's "own forces" and does not depend on any external source of energy.

While the bicycle remains the most widespread means of transport in China—because it is the most economical—the Great Bridge of Nanking

---

*Bicycles are, however, rather expensive, in view of the low level of wages; an ordinary one can cost 150 yuans, or about 68 dollars, which represents five months' wages for the laborer or one month's for a manager.

stands as a token of her leaders' determination to equip her with a modern communications network.

China only *seems* to be a vast country; in fact, the Yangtse cuts her in half from east to west. A broad and powerful river, the Yangtse allows small cargo boats to get the four hundred miles up to Wuhan, which lies at the very heart of the country. It made a great impression on Marco Polo: "This river runs for such a distance and through so many regions and there are so many cities on its banks that truth to tell, in the amount of shipping it carries and the total volume and value of its traffic, it exceeds all the rivers of the Christians put together and their seas into the bargain."

Seven centuries later, going down the Huang-po is just as impressive. Sitting comfortably on the deck of the Friendship Boat, we took a twenty-mile trip and discovered another China, one that contrasted strangely with the picture we all had of ricefields and peasants bent over their furrows. Both banks were packed with metallurgical factories, blast furnaces, petrochemical plants, thermal power stations, naval dry docks, and the quays were lined with wharves, goods and cranes. Everywhere, workers, dockers, sailors and truck drivers battled their way between enormous crates and packing cases, horns blowing and engines backfiring.

For centuries, China had all the advantages of this splendid natural waterway between west and east without the inconveniences; the Yangtse was not an obstacle to north-south communications, for ferries do not involve any cargo transfer when cargo is carried on a man's back. It was after the coming of the railways and the roads that the Yangtse really cut China in two; it hindered the establishment of any rapid connection between north and south, at least to the east of Wuhan, where the first bridge was.*

When it was opened in 1968, the Great Bridge at Nanking transformed the situation.

Old-fashioned Transport

"With no railway and no good roads, this is the real essence of China . . . ," Teilhard de Chardin wrote in April 1924. This was a traditional state of affairs, and the revolution did not change it all that much.

Naturally, there are few private cars; a handful of ancient Soviet models are used for important people. On Tien An Men Square in Peking—which is about three or four times the size of the Place de la Concorde in Paris—there were only a few buses and trucks to be seen; they stood out sharply amidst the swarms of cyclists, blowing their horns all the time to clear a way.

---

*Apart from the Nanking Bridge, there are only two bridges over the Yangtse, and both were built in the 1950s by the communists with Soviet aid; they are at Wuhan and Chungking.

In the suburbs of Peking, we came across the convoys that supply the capital. There are not many trucks; merchandise is carried day and night in heavy carts drawn by animals, in cycle-rickshaws, and in sacks, cases and hampers on handcarts.

Public transport is spotty and always overcrowded. There are very few trains and they are extremely slow, doing an average of thirty miles per hour on the Peking-Shanghai run. Air travel—so necessary in countries like China which are so vast—is still an exceptional luxury. Shanghai has a population of ten million, and in three hours at the city's airport we did not hear a single aircraft take off or land.

Some Development of the Railways

There is a basic hindrance to the growth of road transport: the low level of production of gasoline and diesel oil. There are only three to four hundred thousand trucks on China's roads. Priority has been given to the railways, and progress has certainly been made. One can get from Peking to Urumchi in Chinese Turkestan—a distance of 2,300 miles—in four days.*

In 1949 the rail network covered 18,000 miles. In a little over twenty years the communists have increased this by half. There are now double tracks on the Peking-Wuhan line, and soon there will be on the Peking-Shanghai line.

Electrification has also begun, along with the installation of a system of electric signals and centralized controls. Various types of cars are being built, including double-deckers. But production of locomotives seems to have run into serious difficulties.

Removing the Problem

It is not impossible that the inadequacy of the infrastructure will soon present an obstacle to economic development. We did not get the impression that the Chinese leaders were inclined to give priority to this very important sector. From the way things are going, it seems that in these difficult areas they have found numerous reasons for pushing in the direction of widely spread industrialization, of the autarky of each province—and even of each district.

On January 1, 1972 *People's Daily* rejoiced over the fact that the good

---

*Urumchi is the town's Turkish name; in Chinese it is Wu-lu-mu-chi.

harvests had finally enabled the provinces of the North to satisfy their own needs—for the first time for centuries. So Chairman Mao's instruction had been carried out: "Change the situation which requires cereals to be transported from South to North." This is what makes the Great Bridge at Nanking something of a paradox.

Small-scale iron and steel production, cement manufacture, the processing of agricultural products, and repair and maintenance centers can all exist side by side in the same place. They can all be done locally. So can prospecting and exploiting raw materials and sources of energy. In this way one avoids the cost of transportation and also the problem of transportation, which is then limited to the production of bicycles.

Foreign Trade, a Means for Autarky

Each part is autarkic and the whole, too, is an autarky. There is nothing new in this; China has always been a solipsistic society, believing there to be no civilization beyond her borders. Macartney—the "Ambassador bringing tribute from England"—was unable to discuss questions of trade; he arrived in the middle of celebrations of the emperor's birthday and was received only for the gifts he bore.

Even today it is clear that communist China goes in for trade with other countries only through necessity. Foreign trade is just one way of reaching autarky. China is not opening up as a market of consumers; she is seeking to complete her own system of production. She needs certain raw materials, certain semi-finished products and certain advanced equipment—and these the international market can offer on terms which are advantageous to her.

What will happen when China has filled in the gaps and is in a position to stand on her own feet? Will she withdraw from the international market, in accordance with her traditions and philosophy? Or will she be caught up in the wheels of foreign trade?

Since the end of the Cultural Revolution, imports and exports have returned to their 1966 levels, which are way below those of 1958. In 1970 imports rose to 2,000 million dollars and exports to 2,200 million, which is about the same as the level of foreign trade in Norway and Austria. China's main imports are manufactured goods (although she does not import more than she exports, and she imports no consumer goods, except Swiss watches), chemical products, food products and raw materials.

She exports manufactured goods, raw materials and food, and so the structure of her trade is similar to that of an industrialized country.

A careful balance is preserved, and in this respect Hong Kong plays a vital role. China buys nothing from Hong Kong, but sells the colony its daily food requirements. The net profit in 1970 was 470,000,000 dollars, and this enables China to cover her trade deficit with Japan and Europe.

Since the spectacular drop in trade with the U.S.S.R., China's main trading partners have been Japan and Hong Kong, then—a long way behind with over 200,000,000 dollars' worth—comes the German Federal Republic, and then—with between 150,000,000 and 200,000,000 dollars' worth—come Singapore, Canada (wheat), Britain, France and Australia.

21

Take-off

"China is a relatively backward country." This is official doctrine.

In conversation the adverb changes, as modesty surrenders to precision: "China is setting out from a very backward base," Chou En-lai told me. "She'll need at least a hundred years before she catches up with the industrially developed countries."

My feeling is that as China progresses, there will be many surprises in store for us. There have been some already: who expected her to explode a nuclear device? Launch an artificial earth satellite? For ten years the Chinese leaders kept their economic achievements a secret. Then in 1971 Chou En-lai gave Edgar Snow the two small figures we considered in an earlier chapter: 90,000 million dollars' worth of industrial production and 30,000 million dollars' worth of agricultural production. Western experts' calculations of China's wealth were turned upside down. If the figures are true—and because Chou En-lai spoke so rarely, they are credible—China's economic strength is twice as great as the experts had thought. With the necessary adjustments for China's economic structure, a figure of about 125 billion dollars is obtained for the 1971 Gross National Product—this is between the GNP of West Germany and that of France.* This gives a per capita income of 145 dollars—equal to that of Japan in 1913 and Taiwan in 1962 (but without the American aid and with all the limitations of size and "relying on one's own resources").

---

*See the Appendix.

Chou En-lai may have predicted it would be a hundred years before China catches up with the advanced countries of the world because China does not like these comparisons. In fact, of course, they have very little scientific value; the units of evaluation are inappropriate from the start. And the Chinese absolutely reject their ideological value.

Those who rely on their own resources want to be judged according to their own criteria. To be a party to the statistics game is to sacrifice oneself to the myths of industrial societies which rival one another in their growth rates, Gross National Product, per capita income, rate of investment, and so on. If one rejects the "economism" of the "imperialists" and the "revisionists" one cannot logically interpret the Chinese situation using standards which detract from and distort the true picture.

Backwardness Is in the Mind

The battle against economic backwardness will be waged and won in the minds of the people. For economic take-off one must have the concept, the will and the means. The will can create the means. The means will not compensate for lack of will. The Cultural Revolution certainly got the priorities right.

All propaganda and political education is aimed at transforming the Chinese agricultural masses from individual peasants obsessed by survival into a unified community working toward a single goal.

We are not able to judge very accurately the progress which the Chinese have yet to make. Because we see China from a distance, as a single entity and as a great civilization, we tend to think that the Chinese live instinctively at a high level of historical and civic consciousness. It is not certain that they do.

The peasant is not the only one who is too narrowly obsessed with his work in the ricefield. Very early in our trip we realized how hard it was going to be to grasp the national picture, even from our vantage point with the help of our guides; China is a varied land and this variety in itself presents an obstacle to understanding the country as a whole.

Whether it was in Nanking, Shanghai, Sian or Wuhan, each time we turned our discussions to the economic or social problems that affect the whole of China—even with those who were responsible for dealing with these problems on a provincial level—we had cause to regret it. To our great astonishment, cotton experts and representatives from the Ministry of Culture are completely thrown by general questions about China. Beyond their own province, they know neither the figures nor the facts, and they deal with the problems only in the most general ideological terms.

By allowing the locals to use their own initiative, leaders of the Cultural

Revolution stressed the diversity of China. They took the risk because they believed that unity would result from a common ideology rather than uniform laws and regulations.

The sense of collectivity is halfway to development, because it is inseparable from ambition. To give several hundred million people a group identity and power over the group's destiny is to give them the consciousness of their own power and the desire to increase it and make use of it.

For the leaders of the Chinese people, both ideologues and nationalists, man has reality only as part of a plan, only in his social dimension. This view may seem shocking to us, since our liberal societies are founded on the distinction between the individual and the group, between the citizen and the state, and each is omnipotent within his or its own sphere, each armed with his or its own rights.

Unlike previous dictatorships, Maoism does not seem to deny individual conscience. In fact, it relies on and uses it, in order to support the sense of collectivity. The "external marks of respect" are not enough; obedience must be an active total commitment. The conscience interiorizes the life of the group within each of its members.

The Chinese know what energy can be created when man is taken out of himself, and they are determined to exploit it.

Propaganda, constant explanation, ideological education and the spreading of new cultural myths—however obsessive and crude they may seem to us—do have a cumulative effect; they free the conscience and teach each individual that he is responsible for the destiny of all.

In this way the Chinese expect to destroy passivity and egocentrism, which are the most serious obstacles to genuine economic development.

Furthermore, this transformation finds firm support in the spreading of "industrious industry," which will undoubtedly make it possible for an industrial mentality to form gradually among the peasantry.

Is this appeal to the creativity of the masses an illusion or hypocrisy? The word-perfect ideologies one hears might suggest the latter, but then these are very real examples of their creativity and achievements which, although imperfect, are impressive.

Can the concept of enterprise—if not of free enterprise—be instilled in an entire people? Whatever success it has and whatever its cost in terms of productivity and organization, it is certainly an attempt to get human development and economic development in step with each other. And this attempt has not been made so definitely and resolutely anywhere else in the world.

Economic development—or, in one word, industrialization—has always been an autonomous phenomenon. Rural societies near industrializing areas and the individual's privacy and liberty have suffered greatly from industry, but ultimately all reached coexistence. Nevertheless, industry has remained very much an alien element.

China wants development to spring from agrarian society and from the individual. If this really is the direction of China's planning—behind the Marxist phraseology—it is worthy of admiration. We shall see the outcome later, but we must consider the successes that already have been achieved.

We visited six provinces and met many Chinese. Everywhere the people we saw were active and alert. If they have shortcomings, they lie in the excess of their qualities: a blundering, muddle-headed activism, an excessive militancy, and an ingenuous enthusiasm. Everyone remembers that in the "Great Leap Forward" many people died; nonetheless, we saw a people whose *spirit* no longer seemed to be that of an underdeveloped people.

Navigating a Tight Course

The economy has its own laws—or, at any rate, restraints—and in the case of China the margin between success and failure is very small. Future prosperity hinges on tiny percentage variations and on how they occur.

The policy of complete independence limits recourse to foreign capital, and the underexploited foreign trade fails to create the necessary investment funds. Production capital must come from the people's labor. Investment, then, will be all the more important as private wants become less, public expenditure better controlled and productivity higher.

In a country which has suffered from chronic shortages, limiting private consumption may seem paradoxical: it was necessary to set a standard higher than that of the majority but lower than that of a minority. Unlike the Soviet Union between World Wars I and II, China has not taken huge amounts of money from the peasants in order to develop industry. Austerity will be necessary for a long time; the number of consumers would magnify the slightest rise in the standard of living dramatically and would reduce the available capital.

To limit consumption also requires control of the growth of the population. China has less need of manpower than of increasing the productivity of the manpower she already has. It is risky introducing the idea of productivity in a country where labor costs next to nothing, but only if she takes this risk will China "take off" economically.

It is fascinating to watch how she sets about it. From completely the wrong end—or so it seems. According to the innumerable almost identical speeches we heard, the major sin of the renegade Liu Shao-chi was introducing the output bonus. Apart from the ideological reasons put forth, one was purely economic: the cost of the bonuses outweighed any increase in efficiency. Ideology could do better, more cheaply.

In the same way, industrialization of the rural areas might seem to us to dissipate labor as much as the workshops do, but Chinese leaders are convinced that, on the contrary, it will control investment, guarantee low-cost operations and serve the country's needs. In addition, these small enterprises draw labor into rural areas where laborers are paid least and work hardest; we did not have the feeling that large units like the Wuhan combine created an atmosphere conducive to productivity.

The decision to transfer the cost of education from the state to the people's communes was based on the same principle: since work pays for investment, the two must be brought closer together. Education is certainly an investment—and its profits cannot be calculated. Everyone knows that education costs are heavy.

But the central problem is agricultural productivity. China cannot solve it by "manpower deflation." Her industrial development is not rapid enough to absorb a possible large-scale exodus from the rural areas. Such an exodus would improve productivity without increasing production, which is barely adequate as it is and which China quite reasonably wants to raise by some twenty percent per head. So Chinese agriculture must keep its manpower and get the most out of its land. Plans for mechanization, then, have been temporarily shelved. The solution is technical—it is called chemical fertilizer.

The Growth Spiral

No one can judge the effect of these decisions; it is not something that can be measured at a glance, even by the Chinese leaders. The economy is above all a matter of politics, and thus is not subject to rational evaluation. In addition, the Chinese have deliberately played up the role of psychological factors.

But what one can do is to judge achievements so far. China's agricultural production has survived the uncertain climate for two decades now and provides enough food for the whole population. The country has instituted an agrarian reform which—for the first time in three thousand years—has not collapsed under famine. Her economic power is comparable with that of France or West Germany, she has impressive technological achievements to her credit, and everyone enjoys a decent standard of living.

Future prosperity depends on population growth. If China does not succeed in overcoming the problem, all her efforts will be in vain. Investments will be consumed and will drop, making China once again the poorest and weakest nation on earth.

If, on the other hand, she succeeds in overcoming these difficulties, China's development will spiral; she will be able to construct a powerful industry in a few decades, and this will provide her with a platform for further population growth.

Part IV

The Price

of

Success

"Lacking an analytical approach, many of our comrades do not want to go deeply into complex matters, to analyze and study them over and over again, but like to draw simple conclusions which are either absolutely affirmative or absolutely negative."

Mao Tse-tung (1944)

"We must learn to look at problems all-sidedly, seeing the reverse as well as the obverse side of all things."

Mao Tse-tung (February 1957)

"One-sidedness means thinking in terms of absolutes, that is, a metaphysical approach to problems. In the appraisal of our work, it is one-sided to regard everything either as all positive or as all negative. . . ."

Mao Tse-tung (March 1957)

22

The Price in Terms
of Blood

The Other Side of the Coin

Could such amazing results have been achieved painlessly? Could an entire people have transformed their own situation and their place in the world—transformed themselves, in fact—without cost? It would have been the first time such a thing had ever been done.

In weighing the good and the bad effects of the Maoist regime, many Herculean achievements can be enumerated on one side—control over population and environment, abolition of the feudal system and its aftereffects, the elimination of poverty. On the other side, because human beings are fallible, there are the tragedies and the mistakes.

"When you've seen the provinces," Chou En-lai told me as he was seeing me off on the steps of the Palace of the People, "I'm sure you'll feel that all that we've done is neither totally commendable nor totally reprehensible."

How difficult it is to form a balanced view of a situation so impossible to assess! Some observers are so overwhelmed by the successes of the regime that they forget the price that is still being paid. Others see only the penalties and ignore the achievements. One must not ignore the horrors of the recent past, the deficiencies and hardships of the present, or anxieties about the future.

It is hard both to temper one's admiration for the regime with restraint and to temper one's criticism with understanding. The enormous literature on China bears this out; each episode in the revolution has been greeted with fresh enthusiasm and fresh disapproval. Those who can form a balanced judgment after listening to many conflicting views are rare and their opinions extremely valuable.

Mao himself called for a balance between condemnation and flattery: "Views inspired by pessimism and a feeling of powerlessness, and by pride and presumptiousness are equally erroneous." All his writings after 1923 urged people to look not only on the bright side, but on the dark side of things too.

For a pragmatist like Mao, success was a criterion of truth: "In general that which succeeds is right, that which fails wrong." Failure is necessary for success: "After he fails, he draws his lessons, corrects his ideas to make them correspond to the laws of the external world, and can thus turn failure into success; this is what is meant by 'failure is the mother of success.' " Failure brings the individual in touch with reality: "When we study the causes of the mistakes we have made, we find that they all arose because we departed from the actual situation at a given time and place . . ."

Mao condemned idealists who concern themselves only with theories which they never put into practice: "The most economical theory in the world is idealism or metaphysics because it enables people to say whatever they wish, regardless of objective reality, with no need for corroboration with facts." He was bemused by the awkward way they analyzed situations as though they were fixed instead of diverse, complicated and contradictory.

In order to understand the full picture, both sides of the question must be taken into account. Mao quoted Wei Cheng of the Tang dynasty: "Listen to both sides and you will be enlightened, heed only one side and you will be benighted."

To imagine—as the French "Maoists" often do—that enthusiasm for revolution, eagerness for work and group discipline can be achieved without denouncing, punishing, "reeducating," imprisoning and eventually exterminating the idle, the freethinkers, the oppositionists and the deviationists is to live in a dream world. The pleasant and unpleasant sides of a situation cannot be dissociated from each other. If a movement is to be total and single-minded, it has to include compulsory training and discipline based on reward and punishment. You do not get the one without the other, but to a certain extent the end justifies the means.

"In studying a problem," Mao said, "we must guard against . . . one-sidedness. . . . One-sidedness consists in not knowing how to look at a problem as a whole."

The Hecatomb

A look at China's past should include the darker side of the picture. For Mao's regime to triumph, there had to be a quarter of a century of civil war and a terrible slaughter—before, during and after the Liberation.

How many victims were involved in this human sacrifice?

Every time we asked the question, we got the same answer. "Tens of millions."

Rewi Alley and Edgar Snow, two foreigners who followed the revolution most closely, put the number of dead from the civil war* at about fifty million; they include the Chinese losses on both sides, but not those who died at the hands of the Japanese or as a result of the famines.

Rewi Alley's experience of China is unique. Born in New Zealand, he went to Shanghai in 1927 as an inspector of hygiene; once there, he had the idea of setting up industrial cooperatives. This attempt to decentralize the Chinese economy meant that he had friends in both camps. He traveled all over the country, often organizing his centers in the midst of guerrilla warfare. He stayed in China after 1949, perhaps the only foreigner with the status of "permanent resident." He remained there for about forty years.

"I have myself estimated," he said, "that the deaths through political executions, Kuomintang 'cleaning up' in Kiangsi, Fukien, etc. [1930–34, during five anti-communist expeditions], in man-made famines [blockades] in Hunan, Honan, etc., in 'incidents' [armed clashes or 'border warfare' before the outbreak of renewed major civil war in 1947] and following the KMT-CP breaking of armistice negotiations, then in the general [civil war] struggle subsequently, all add up to something like fifty million from the break [counterrevolution] in 1927 up until 1949."

Today Rewi Alley seems to feel that such a large number of lives were not lost in vain. Fifty million lives in order to transform China, when almost every year millions of Chinese died as a result of famine, infanticide and disease—this was "worth it." Edgar Snow has arrived at the same macabre conclusion.

These figures must, of course, be viewed with some caution. Since it is not known to the nearest hundred million how many people actually live in China now, how can the number of Chinese who died during a period of utter disorganization in the now fairly remote past be established with any certainty?

However, this figure is likely to be about right. Fifty million out of a population which at the time was about five hundred million—this is decimation.

It goes without saying that Mao and his regime were not solely or even mainly responsible. There was the sclerosis of the empire, the intervention first by the Western Powers and then by Japan, the "warlords," and the errors of the Kuomintang; all these were at least as much to blame. And life in China had become intolerable for so many people! It is impossible to decide

---

*In fact—to be more accurate—from the two civil wars, of 1927–36 and 1946–49, and the skirmishes that marked the truce period of 1937–46.

who should answer for the slaughter. After all, throughout the history of China, the fall of each dynasty was either triggered or followed by a period of murderous anarchy. The new leader cannot be justly held responsible for the victims of the troubles that brought him to power. Uprisings are often caused by the inability of the previous authorities to solve their problems, and by their cruelty.

Suffice it to say that Mao triumphed after a civil war which seems to have cost China approximately the equivalent of the population of France.

Settling Accounts and Liquidations

On top of this first hecatomb, the years following the defeat of Chiang Kai-shek's regime saw a settling of accounts which eliminated not only those who had collaborated with the occupier but also feudal lords, landowners, mandarins and representatives of the ruling classes.

Westerners who were present when the Red Army finally seized the whole of China—during 1949—saw scenes of appalling carnage in the streets of towns and villages. All "liberations" have produced similar behavior. There were grim scenes in North Vietnam in the summer of 1954, in Algeria in the summer of 1962, in Biafra in January 1970 and in East Pakistan in March and December 1971. Long years of suffering, accumulated hatreds, the cheap heroism of those who use brutality in order to make people forget their lack of initiative before the troubles—all these things create explosive situations. As far as China is concerned, the experts' assessments vary from one to three million "collaborators" or "reactionaries" killed after the "Liberation."

Another phase which has the reputation of being every bit as murderous is the one which accompanied the first revolutionary transformations of society. Here one has access to official information.

Chou En-lai said that 830,000 "enemies of the people" were "liquidated" between 1950 and 1954 during the "campaigns," in which land was confiscated and there were mass trials of landlords and round-ups of counter-revolutionaries. If this is not an underestimate, it represents sixteen people out of every ten thousand in a population that at the time numbered about five hundred million. Although it is "official," this figure—like the others—is still hypothetical. What is certain, though, is that many Chinese were victims of the triumph of communism, and that many more—possibly twenty-five times as many—died in the years of upheaval that led to it.

A Generation Bled White

One Chinese in ten. In terms of France, this would mean about five million killed in the civil war, a hundred thousand killed in the settlement of accounts when the new regime came into power, and another eighty thousand summarily executed during the years of social transformation that followed. This figure—in French terms—of five million is two and a half times the number of French killed in the First World War, and that loss drained the country so completely that it took more than a generation to recover. The Second World War cost five hundred thousand French lives—on all fronts and counting losses in the Resistance and from deportation. Proportionally, this is a tenth of the losses China suffered in the civil war.

Why should slaughter on this scale come as a surprise? The American War of Independence, the French Revolution, the War of Secession, the Russian Revolution and the Spanish Civil War produced carnage which was comparable in proportion.

No state would be thrown into such upheaval unless conditions had become intolerable for a major section of the population. Civil war, with the chain reactions it produces, is the most savage form of armed conflict. Those who support a revolution in its early stages are inevitably outstripped, dismissed as renegades, and eventually wiped out by their companions, victims of assassination, revenge, Red terror and White terror, military and people's tribunals who sit beside the guillotine and the firing squad. Violence begets more violence. At least a generation has to pass before the wounds heal.

In judging the Chinese, the fact that this bloody conflict remains vividly in their memories should be taken into consideration. There is not a village or a part of a town which did not lose dozens of its children as soldiers in the two camps and which has not known summary executions in its streets. There is not a family which has not been struck by some kind of tragedy. Perhaps there is no need to look any further for the reasons behind their remarkable docility, and their at times rather hysterical behavior; these people have lived in a state of terror for a long time, and still live with its memory.

The Chinese revolution—like the Great Wall—is built on corpses: those of innocents who were enlisted under duress, of martyrs and heroes, of landowners and "feudal lords." Carnage on this scale rules out the possibility of moderation.

The Recrudescence of Violence: The Cultural Revolution

Revolutions are a violent break with history, and even when they grow up and mature they never quite settle down. For the revolution to stay, so must violence. This is also the message of the Cultural Revolution.

It is precisely because the Party cadres had lost their heroic zeal and a bureaucratic caste had reestablished itself that blood flowed again seventeen years after the Liberation—so that the revolution could be regenerated.

A series of excessive acts, vandalism and killings began the assault on the new leading classes. From the spring of 1966 to the end of 1969 this unrest checked and disturbed the life of the country—its universities and laboratories, its public services and government, not to mention its production.

As our journey proceeded, we learned more details and more secrets. In Canton the conflict had assumed the intensity of a civil war. At the University of Peking people fought with rifles and submachine guns, and students and professors were killed. In Wuhan they fought with field guns—"not big guns," we were told, "just small ones." And in Shanghai corpses littered the streets and floated in the yellow waters of the Huang-pu.

In several towns we were told that Chou En-lai had come while the fighting was raging, had been able to land only at night, and on several occasions had narrowly missed being taken prisoner by one faction or the other.

While we were visiting a monument, one of our hosts made a discreet allusion to many different kinds of excesses committed by the Red Guards. He spoke of iconoclastic zeal in museums, ransacked pagodas, paintings in the Summer Palace covered with lime; great splashes of whitewash are still there, covering idyllic or pastoral scenes of the imperial past, which gave a false idea of the old regime. The leaders had to launch appeals for the "people's property" to be respected. These appeals were not heeded, and so all monuments and historic places were closed and guarded by the military, just like the Forbidden City, which fully deserved its name for five whole years.

Scenes of cruelty were interspersed with absurd destruction. In Peking and Shanghai the stone or wood sculptures which once decorated the façades of bourgeois houses were smashed to pieces with a hammer, as furiously as Polyeuctes set about smashing the idols. Neon signs were torn down as symbols of capitalism. Restaurant and florists' windows were broken because the establishments were considered to be dens of luxury. Fish—albeit red ones—were killed in their ponds because they distracted the casual passer-by from the revolution. Chessboards and chessmen were destroyed because they provided relaxation for the bourgeois.

Boys in the street wearing pointed shoes were seized, and the ends of their shoes were cut off; sometimes a toe went as well. Girls with long braids were forced to have them cut off. In Peking and Shanghai, ta-tzu-pao and petitions called for traffic lights to be turned upside down; red—the symbol of the forward march—could not be allowed to mean stop.

But there were more serious things. The Red Guards burst into people's houses and smashed any old piece of furniture or objet d'art that was within their reach. They led processions of suspects through the streets with placards around their necks, hoods over their heads, hands bound behind, whipping their backs with belts. Sometimes these processions ended in murder. Private individuals, afraid of being caught, delivered themselves to the *auto-da-fé;* others committed suicide. University professors, school teachers, top civil servants and leading members of the Party—hardly anyone was sure of being spared.

Most of the people we talked to remembered this period as if it had been a nightmare, and the anguish it had caused was still evident.

"For a long time I've wondered," a member of the Nanking Town Committee told me, "if it was really necessary for Chairman Mao to put the country to fire and sword in order to get rid of the traitor Liu Shao-chi. I felt there must have been many simpler ways of eliminating him. Now that the violence is over, I think that Mao was right—as he always is—but that China only barely escaped real danger."

A Revolutionary Puts His Trust in the Revolution

Everything seems to indicate that Mao and the little team that remained loyal to him instigated this street violence, at the risk of losing control over it. When Mao recommended to his followers that they "bombard the headquarters," he apparently did not wish to be taken at his word. From August 1966 on, appeals carried over all loudspeakers and printed in all the newspapers called on activists to use persuasion rather than violence, and exhorted them not to "beat their victims to death."

Questions are still being asked about this enormous four-year pogrom. In time of revolution such devastating measures seem logical and acceptable. If a revolution is afraid of such risks, it means it is afraid of itself. To be revolutionary means putting trust in the revolution, however unpredictable its progress and direction may be.

Early Mao texts condemn those who recoil in the face of revolution because they prefer security and money: "Those who, by manual or mental labor, earn more each year than they consume for their own support . . . very much want to get rich and are devout worshippers of Marshal Chao*. . . . Their mouths water copiously when they see the respect in which those small moneybags are held. People of this sort are timid . . . and also a little afraid of the revolution."

About a year before the Cultural Revolution, Mao Tse-tung exhorted communists to accept the challenges of "the bourgeoisie who are still a threat," and sharply criticized the intellectuals whose attitude went contrary to the revolution. In the Sixteen Points of August 8, 1966—which concluded the eleventh plenary session of the Party Central Committee and gave the Cultural Revolution its charter—Mao praised the "proletarian world outlook" and said people must "place their trust" in it. The masses—and

---

*Chao Kung-ming, God of Wealth in Chinese folklore.

especially the youth—would be "tempered by the struggle"; they must be mobilized, but also they must be "left a free hand."

The idea of abandoning a country to "the broad popular masses" is both admirable and terrifying. It is admirable because it reveals a profound faith in the people and a stubborn denial of the *embourgeoisement* in which revolutions usually end. And it is terrifying because it protects no one from the mob which is unleashed upon the "class enemies," because it grinds a country under the wheels of violence, and because it replaces institutional injustice with insurrectional injustice.

Violence Must Not Cease

The government faced its most difficult task in 1970—the violence they had set in motion had to be quelled and the people—above all, the youth— had to be persuaded to return quietly to work after they had become used to agitation rather than labor.

Mao was convinced that the violence had to continue. After the killings of the summer of 1966, he told an Albanian military delegation in April 1967: "The construction of socialism cannot be achieved with one, two, three or four Cultural Revolutions. There will have to be many more of them. But now we need at least ten years of consolidation. Cultural Revolutions like this one can be mounted only two or three times in a century." In Shanghai, Hsu Ching-hsien told us the same, very emphatically.

The state and the nation emerged intact from this experience, and it is clear that Mao's presence was largely responsible. Where will Cultural Revolutions end up now that he is no longer around to guide them? Will his successors dare to start others—and if they do, will they be able to keep them under control? If they don't, will they be ousted?

This is the important question. Without violence, revolution does not work, but that violence all too soon escapes the control of those who instigate it.

"No Revolution without Terror and Bloodbath"

Among Marxist intellectuals who do not know their Marxist texts very well there is a myth that Lenin refused to entrust the succession to Stalin because he felt he was too violent. Too "rude" was in fact what he wrote, in January 1923. But actually Lenin wanted to remove Stalin because he feared his propensity for bureaucratic centralization. He could hardly have denounced him for his violence. "A revolutionary," Lenin said, "must be violent. There will be no revolution without a bloodbath." A law promulgated by Kerensky introducing the death penalty for troops was repealed on the initiative of Kamenev. Lenin was beside himself with rage. "Nonsense! Nonsense! How can one make a revolution without firing squads? Do you think you will be able to deal with all your enemies by laying down your arms? What other means of repression do you have? Imprisonment? To this no one attaches any importance during a civil war when each side hopes to win."

It is an illusion to think that if Lenin had lived Russia would have been spared the Stalinist purges. He constantly maintained that revolution implies terror. "Do you really think that we shall come out victorious without any revolutionary terror?" He warned against the temptations of liberalism: "Those . . . 'revolutionaries' [who] imagine that we shall achieve our revolution in a nice way, with kindness. . . . What do they understand by 'dictatorship'? And what sort of dictatorship will that be if they themselves are ninnies?" He insisted that bloody examples be made: "If we are incapable of shooting a White Guard saboteur, then what sort of a great revolution is this?"

Trotsky admired the clarity of Lenin's teaching: ". . . Lenin at every opportunity stressed the inevitability of terror. Any signs of sentimentality, of easy-going cordiality, of softness—and there was a great surplus of all this—angered him not by themselves, but because he saw in them proof that even the elite of the working class was not fully aware of all the extraordinarily difficult tasks which could be accomplished only by means of quite extraordinary energy."

Trotsky was treated as a counterrevolutionary by Stalin not because he had condemned the killings, but because anyone who opposes a revolutionary becomes—as far as Stalin was concerned—a counterrevolutionary. But on the question of violence, Lenin, Trotsky and Stalin were in complete agreement.

In this Mao never deviated from the views of Lenin and Stalin; he took care not to join Khrushchev in the chorus of denunciations of the Stalinist excesses.

This was probably where their paths separated. True revolutionaries like Lenin and Stalin have to be cruel because they give priority to the revolution over protection of people and property. Lenin and Stalin are honored as founding fathers of the Chinese regime—alongside the two philosophers, Marx and Engels—because they were true revolutionaries, who did not hesitate before shooting. On the other hand, Khrushchev and his successors are rejected as "renegades" and "revisionists" because they give economic expansion priority over the progress of the revolution; they choose to protect people and property, rather than pursue a course of violence.

Mao was vehement about those who are naïve enough to believe that revolution can be made gently. "A revolution is not a dinner party, or writing an essay, or painting a picture, or doing embroidery. . . . A revolution is an insurrection, an act of violence by which one class overthrows another."

To understand Maoism one must take into account the suffering Mao and his family experienced. In the Hall of Honor of the Institute of the Peasant Movement in Canton, visitors are shown—in respectful silence—about half a dozen large murals. They remind you that even if Mao himself escaped being shot or ambushed, his family paid a heavy price. Mao Tse-kien, his little sister, was killed by the Kuomintang in 1929; Mao Tse-tan, his younger brother, was killed by the Kuomintang in 1935; Mao Tse-min, his other younger brother, was killed by the Kuomintang in Urumchi in 1943; his wife Yang Kai-hui, his "beautiful poplar,"* was garotted by the Kuomintang along with the communists of Changsha in 1930; Mao Chung-hsiung, his nephew, died in 1946 at the age of nineteen, shot by the Kuomintang; Mao An-ying, his eldest son, died in Korea in 1950 at the age of twenty-eight. One is bound to think of Vladimir Ilyich Ulyanov, the future Lenin, overwhelmed by the hanging of his elder brother, Alexander Ilyich, who had refused to petition for mercy after taking part in an attempt to assassinate Tsar Alexander III. A leader who has suffered so much himself has the right to make demands on his people. Mao had to keep his self-control in order to drink a toast with Chiang Kai-shek in Chungking in 1945.

But no matter how much they have suffered, individuals have the strength to continue when they believe in their cause. The knowledge that they have emerged victorious from a desperate situation gives them confidence in themselves and in their ability to continue their mission.

Throughout his life Mao repeated this axiom: "Revolutions and revolutionary wars are inevitable in class society . . . without them, it is impossible to accomplish any leap in social development and to overthrow the reactionary ruling classes and therefore impossible for the people to win political power. . . . This principle of Marxism-Leninism is valid everywhere, in China as well as in other countries."

His praise of justifiable revolution is reminiscent of Péguy's of justifiable war: "Revolutionary war is an antitoxin which not only eliminates the enemy's poison but also purges us of our own filth. Every just revolutionary war is endowed with tremendous power. . . ." The new China owes everything to the hard fighting in which she was born: "Without armed struggle neither the proletariat, nor the people, nor the Communist Party would have any standing at all in China and . . . it would be impossible for the revolution to triumph."

Mao replied to those who mock his warmongering by poking fun at the pacifists: "Some people ridicule us as advocates of the 'omnipotence of war.' Yes, we are advocates of the omnipotence of revolutionary war. . . . It is only

---

*Her surname means "poplar." Mao wrote a poem commemorating her death and that of her friend's husband; it begins, "I lost my proud poplar . . ." It can be found in the back of Stuart Schram's Pelican biography of Mao (TRANSLATOR'S NOTE).

by the power of the gun that the working class and the laboring masses can defeat the armed bourgeoisie and landlords."

This exhortation to be ready to make the supreme sacrifice was Mao's most impressive lesson: "We must thoroughly clear away all ideas among our cadres of winning easy victories through good luck, without hard and bitter struggle, without sweat and blood."

The Romantic Illusion

It is an illusion to think that any self-respecting revolution can avoid civil war, and that civil war will not bring the worst violence. Simone de Beauvoir, Jean-Paul Sartre, Maria-Antonietta Macciocchi, and Maurice Clavel seem not to have heard about the arbitrary trials, massacres and live burials. Some intellectuals are only too pleased to accept the myth that the Chinese communists are quietly satisfied with implementing a program of agrarian reforms. They should face reality. The Chinese communists are true revolutionaries and their conviction is so strong that they never flinch at death—be it their own or that of their adversaries. They won because they fought ferociously.

Mao sharply ridiculed the "liberal intellectuals" who delude themselves into thinking that they can be revolutionary and liberal at the same time: "Liberalism . . . is a corrosive which eats away unity, undermines cohesion, causes apathy and creates dissension. It robs the revolutionary ranks of compact organization and strict discipline. . . . It is an extremely bad tendency." The liberal intellectuals can be Marxists only in words: "They approve of Marxism, but are not prepared to practice it." Mao devoted one of his basic works—"Combat Liberalism" of 1937—to condemning liberalism: "Not to obey orders but to give pride of place to one's own opinions. . . . To show no regard at all for the principles of collective life but to follow one's own inclination. . . . To be among the masses and fail to conduct propaganda and agitation or speak at meetings or conduct investigations and enquiries among them . . ."

The first duty is not to underestimate the difficulties: "It must not be imagined that one fine morning all the reactionaries will go down on their knees of their own accord."

No revolution can avoid a counterrevolution. "Everything reactionary is the same; if you don't hit it, it won't fall. It is like sweeping the floor; where the broom does not reach, the dust never vanishes of itself." It is no good waiting for one's adversaries to withdraw: "The enemy will not perish by himself. Neither the Chinese reactionaries nor the aggressive forces of U.S. imperialism in China will step down from the stage of history of their own accord."

Anyone who entertains the hope that a revolution can be accomplished without repercussions is living in a fantasy world. There is no country on earth in which the landowners would allow themselves to be dispossessed by the peasants, in which the bosses would allow themselves to be driven out by their workers, and in which the bourgeois would allow themselves to be imprisoned by their servants—without having done everything possible to crush the revolt. No property owner is going to offer his neck like a lamb to the slaughter.

On the other hand, people who accept the acute sufferings inflicted by civil war do so in order to escape even worse. The barbarism of revolutionaries is only a response to the cultures they suffered. Before 1949 in the landlords' fortresses and ancestral temples it was normal to inflict the cruellest kinds of corporal punishment. In some cases the cruelty even went as far as death. People were beaten to death, drowned and buried alive. Those who were treated similarly during the civil war and after the Liberation had often been responsible for such atrocities; if they had not personally carried them out, they had allowed others to perform them. Often the peasants demanded their death because they feared that if they spared a former tyrant who had assassinated dozens of unfortunate people on his land, they might be assassinated themselves.

There can be no radical change without holocaust, and there is no holocaust without good reason—namely that life under a particular regime has become intolerable. Marx had ignored this kind of Carnot principle of revolutionary energy; he had not realized that the intensity of the suffering that causes a revolution is proportionate to the intensity of suffering it provokes in its turn. Its energy is derived from the suffering that has been experienced and inflicted. Marxists in Russia and later in China learned this truth by paying for it with their blood.

23

The Sacrifice of Freedom

Coercion

The ambiguous position of manual labor (*hsia-fang*) in China is something a visitor can never fully comprehend. For those doing it, manual labor may mean promotion or deportation; it may be something desirable or something they fear—a return to the soil or forced labor.

There is too much evidence already about the attacks on individual freedom in China for anyone to doubt that, like all totalitarian regimes, the People's Republic depends on a powerful repressive apparatus, which ranges from supervised work or "reeducation" to the death penalty, and is implemented in all manner of ways. There are "open" labor camps, but, unless he manages to get to Macao or Hong Kong, anyone who escapes has little chance of getting a casual job without being caught again; there are concentration camps surrounded by barbed wire; there are prisons with cells and prisons without them; and there are executions.

Two pitfalls must be avoided: seeing the Chinese revolutionaries as paragons, and seeing them as tyrants.

Simone de Beauvoir, Curzio Malaparte and Maria-Antonietta Macciocchi never tire of praising the dignified and humane conditions in which the prisoners live. They visited prisons in which "the cell doors remain open day and night. There are none of the usual buckets in the cells; the prisoners are free to go to the toilets. There are no bars. They come and go freely within the prison confines, and I never once saw an armed warden—and I have got a good pair of eyes."

No doubt there are some model prisons in China, but they are still prisons. Malaparte marvels naïvely at the periods of work and relaxation: "Everyone, men and women, political convicts and common law criminals, work in the textile workshops and the stocking factories. After five in the afternoon, they play football or basketball, go to the cinema or to the theatre." Perhaps these prisons without bars were where the subtlest pressure and most refined punishments were exercised.

It is quite possible—indeed we did it ourselves—to travel thousands of miles without spotting any of those camps surrounded by high walls and watchtowers from which soldiers with machine guns in their hands stare down sourly—the kind one sees in the communist countries of Eastern Europe. On the other hand, one does see thousands of men and women busy building roads, dams, railways, and big buildings, without anything leading one to suppose that their freedom was in any way restricted. The view advanced by some biased writers that China is one huge concentration camp can hardly be taken seriously.

Disquieting News

Nonetheless, there are disquieting first-hand accounts of repression.

An Italian who had lived for a long time in China before 1949 and who has visited the country since then regularly saw the son of a family with whom he had become friendly on the eve of the revolution. He inquired about sending a message to the son through a member of the foreign colony in Peking. He found out that a few days later the young man was arrested by the police and probably deported to a camp. Since then he has had no news of him—so either he has been kept incommunicado, or he is no longer alive.

Top Chinese leaders—even members of the Central Committee—have seen their wives disappear into corrective labor camps. One Chinese of our acquaintance has been without his wife since the beginning of the Cultural Revolution; she is being "corrected" and he has had no news of her for several years.

We had a number of conversations in China, and some of them did—especially after much questioning and a certain amount of cross-checking of information—cast some light on the mystery, enough at times to make us shudder.

Many families have been separated. In the factories and people's communes, we were often told that a husband and wife were working several hundred miles from one another and were unable to meet more than once a year. When we asked if they could not move closer to one another, we were told that nothing could be done. Sometimes our question was answered with strong conviction—"everyone must stay where the revolution has put him"—and at other times with a sort of resigned sadness.

Returning from a people's commune near Shanghai, we encountered a column of about forty men flanked by soldiers who were marching to the fields with their shovels over their shoulders. I asked who they were and what they were doing. I was told—with what seemed to be some embarrassment—that they were prisoners who were being sent to work in the open air, and this was healthier for them than remaining in prison. It was impossible to find out why they had become prisoners in the first place.

The "reform-through-work" camps—in which the individual is obliged to do unpaid work of a kind he would have no natural wish to do—are useful in that they make any citizen who might feel tempted to criticize the regime think again.

One of the effects of the Cultural Revolution was that the prisons and other corrective labor camps* filled up. But it also lifted a corner of the veil. Extreme Leftist movements like the *Cheng wu lien* of Hunan, which had not hesitated to "steal arms wholesale" and "exterminate the bureaucrats," used tracts and *ta-tzu-pao* to protest against the "odious oppression" to which they were subjected, especially by large numbers of their members being sent into "the repressive system" and "nightmare prisons which have not changed since the time of the emperors."

Nonetheless, people are deported en masse to the country, and even to the "virgin lands" like Mongolia and especially Sinkiang.

Can the Chinese who remember what life was like before 1949 and the intellectuals who are able to compare the Chinese system with those of other countries put up with such restricting conditions of life and thought without becoming impatient?

The Chinese Context

Would it be correct to assume, on the basis of horror stories told here and there, that this regime is satanic? In the West, such a regime would probably seem so to a large section of the population. But in China it is the continuation of an old penal tradition, and it is a way of coping with the enormous problems that have yet to be solved. A Westerner is horrified when he comes face to face with the kind of subjugation that reminds him of a George Orwell novel. The majority of Chinese are less repelled by dictatorial methods; they consider them inevitable and perhaps even fairly natural.

Traditionally, the Chinese have known strict discipline, as well as ruthlessly detailed laws, obligations, sanctions, severe penalties (including torture), and rewards, such as being cited as an example for the people to follow. "The School of Law"—in the third century B.C.—boasted a truly terrifying penal code, based on the belief that the more severe the punish-

---

*In China, where liberty is not one of the basic values, Saint-Just's principle "No liberty for the enemies of liberty" becomes "No liberty for the enemies of the people."

ments, the less often they had to be meted out. "If the punishments are heavy
and strictly applied, the people will no longer try to see how far they can go.
And in this way, the punishments themselves will disappear." This is the
theory of dissuasion. There is no more eloquent plea for the liberating power
of enslavement. . . .

What can be made of the accounts of this repressive system which we
have received from its few survivors? Their secrets are exploited in the way
which will most effectively move the Western public to pity. As publishers
admit, they are not generally spontaneous accounts; they are ghost-written
and edited by Western writers and journalists. Even those survivors who
suffered so much that they were prepared to run the risks involved in escaping
have difficulty seeing what foreigners find horrifying about their experiences.

These "accounts"—*Les Prisons de Mao, Une femme dans l'Enfer Rouge,
Mémoires d'un Garde Rouge*, and so on—ghosted though most of them may be,
are nevertheless based on actual experience. However, their importance is
exaggerated by experts in Western psychology who are intent on arousing
sorrow and pity.

Most of the authors belong to a very small section of the population—
they are either bourgeois themselves or the sons and daughters of the
bourgeoisie; many are intellectuals and Christians. The tale of Lai Ying,
which was taken down by Edward Behr, is an emotional account of some
unhappy adventures with what seems to be a genuine enough plot. Lai Ying is
a Catholic intellectual of bourgeois origin, a talented painter and teacher. She
often used to visit Hong Kong to see her relatives. She was arrested for spying
and spent years in the gruelling confines of prison cells and forced labor
camps. It should be remembered that the Catholics represent less than 0.5
percent of the population of China, and many of them are poor peasants; only
a tiny minority are in Lai Ying's social class. The communist regime, which is
a dictatorship in the name of the proletariat, has never concealed the fact that
it was tough with the isolated representatives of tiny groups which it
denounced as "privileged," as "abusers of power," or as suspects in "counterrevolutionary plots." This was certainly cruel, but it reduced their power and
their significance as individuals.*

One could make similar observations about most of the eyewitness
accounts secured by the propaganda machine of the Kuomintang and their
American allies, but there are some personal histories which do not come
through biased journalists or writers and which are unquestionably sincere.
Without doubt the most moving is the ordeal of the Belgian missionary,
Father Van Coillie. On being ordained in 1939 he was sent to China and lived
there until his arrest in July 1951. Two years of that time he had spent in
Japanese concentration camps. Van Coillie was to spend three years in a

---

*Of course, Lai Ying was not alone in prison; she found a strange sample of humanity there.

cramped Maoist prison cell along with eight Chinese—a "warlord" general; a young man whose father had been secretary to a close associate of Sun Yat-sen; a man of about sixty who had been involved in an attempt to assassinate Chou En-lai during the civil war; a former rickshaw man who had taken part in bank robberies; a former landowner; a petit bourgeois with a stammer; a Catholic who at first seemed to be helping Father Van Coillie but in the end betrayed him; and finally the head of the cell. The latter was an intelligent young man who shared the life of his companions but who was fanatically cruel to them in the hope of being allowed to go back to his house, his wife and his children as soon as possible. Under his surveillance of terror, the political and common law prisoners were subjected to the same regimen.

Exhausted after his first interrogation, Father Van Coillie returned to his cell with the hope that his companions would not yet have gone to sleep and would be sympathetic. They were indeed waiting for him, but only to carry on where his inquisitor had left off. "Why have you got handcuffs on your wrists? . . . Did you refuse to acknowledge your mistakes? . . . From now on, you're forbidden to sleep, to go to bed or to sit down," the cell chief yelled. Turning to the others, he added: "Take turns watching this hardened reactionary. Everyone must watch for an hour, and when the hour's up wake up the next man."

Day and night for weeks on end, the prisoners hurled questions at him, not giving him a moment's rest. "There's nothing more terrifying than being shouted at, scorned and cursed by the men with whom you are imprisoned. But are they still men? Confined as they are in this diabolical way, they really cannot behave otherwise. Would time make me angry too and turn me into a torturer full of abuse and jeers for other victims? Would I manage to hold out against my human weakness?"

The prisoner cannot hold out when in the end he meets—not by accident, of course—a humane, cultivated judge who is *full of concern and consideration*. Confronted by the judge, the poor unfortunate melts with gratitude and relief. He is physically exhausted, and believes he has found a friend at last; he embarks on a long series of confessions:

"Did you sometimes send letters abroad?"

"Yes."

"Did you write about communism in these letters, about the new situation in China?"

"Yes."

"Explain exactly what you wrote. Give me an example."

Van Coillie puzzled over his answer, not because he was trying to remember what he wrote, but because he wanted to invent something plausible.

"I wrote that in February 1949 the communist Eighth Army entered Peking."

The man was unable to conceal his joy: "Perfect. Now we'll analyze this information."

First, it is military, and second, Van Coillie sent it to members of his family. They certainly passed it on to other people—friends and neighbors. There is every reason to suppose that the information reached the government in Brussels—which of course is reactionary. "To sum up: you sent military information to a government which is an enemy of the people. Who other than a spy does something like that? You are an international spy."

Without drugs and without any special "treatment," just from extreme fatigue—which is a depressant—and the illusory comfort created by an expression of sympathy, the individual begins to feel ashamed of those things in which he had once taken the most pride. "When I went to prison, I made a firm promise to myself that I wouldn't give in on anything. Now, I was no longer the same man. I was like a tame animal. . . . Had I suddenly become a coward? This question had a shattering effect on me. Now, it was no longer the judge who was accusing me, but my own conscience. I began to rise up against myself."

Now and again Father Van Coillie was interrogated *respectfully* by a French-speaking agent of the judge, Louis, and he felt a growing *desire for friendship*. Until, that is, Louis gave expression to his personal feeling of revolt against the regime.

"How I would have loved to talk in confidence! But I had learned to distrust everyone. . . . Here, eyes—and ears—are everywhere. Maybe in a microphone hidden in the room. Maybe in Louis's head, deep down in his subconscious—or in mine? Any one day, our *popular awareness* having grown, he or I might risk talking. . . . I pitied Louis and he probably pitied me. But between these respective feelings of compassion a wall rose up that prevented us from bringing our feelings together. A wall of anguish, a wall of terror, of mistrust and of clichés like *popular awareness*."

Through the worst physical and mental torture, Father Van Coillie retained sufficient clarity of mind to be able to spot the basic techniques of brainwashing and to observe their ineluctable results, both in his companions and in himself—even to the point of psychosis.

Putting the "Idle" to Work

The Western intellectual is moved by the sight of Chinese intellectuals forced to do manual work; he cannot imagine being treated as a coolie himself. The People's Republic is too egalitarian to allow such distinctions; as we have seen, any Chinese—be he an intellectual or a manual worker—may be assigned manual labor.

Where does one draw the line between work which is freely undertaken—when a university professor or his student goes each year on his own initiative to work in a factory or on a farm—and what may be called "compulsory service"? The distinction, it seems, might be in the mind of the participator. There is no point in balking at it and in doing it glumly, because there is no choice. It is better to accept it with a smile, like a volunteer.

A law passed in 1957 to "transform idlers" says that any "idler" and any individual "not in regular employment" must be subjected to a "full-time regimen of training through work." The law applies equally to members of the Party who have been expelled, to the "revisionists" or "renegades," and to citizens who have been condemned for "political error." It can embrace all who have been "expelled from organizations, groups, enterprises, schools or other bodies to which they belonged and have no other means." It also covers those who "do not fall in with their working arrangements or with their transfer to other work . . . or who do not improve in spite of repeated efforts to educate them." In China justice is subject to "democratic centralism"; in other words, it is in the hands of the "top leadership," just the same as executive and legislative power. They have a very powerful means of pressure at their disposal, and it is clearly a terrifying fate for an individual to be cast out like a derelict and obliged to do forced labor.

A Circular on Deportation

Following the 1957 law, other instructions were published which made the conditions of compulsory labor even worse. The most official documents reveal that the intellectuals and young people were less than enthusiastic about Chairman Mao's imperious instruction: "Send the intellectuals into the villages and down the mines." These recalcitrant people had to be forced to do what they were told, and merciless measures were taken to make sure they did.

The campaign to send "innumerable townspeople into the mountains and onto the steppe to do manual labor" had not been a success. Either people fixed it so that they did not go, or once they had gone they escaped at the first opportunity. A circular posted on August 8, 1967 gave strict instructions concerning particularly school-leavers and students, the social group from which the Red Guards were recruited:

"*To all the provincial, town and district revolutionary committees. To all the military control commissions. To all the mass organizations in the towns and in the country.*

"Make sure without delay that the young people, intellectuals and others, are sent to work in the villages and the mines. . . . Some of them have been influenced by a handful of pro-capitalist leaders and have left the countryside. They have been back in the towns for some time. They must all return as quickly as possible. The mass organizations in the towns and the families of those who have been sent into the country must give their active backing to this revolutionary action. The revolutionary cadres must set an example by sending their own children into the country. Anyone who stays in the town will lose his residence permit. . . . The young people must not leave their place of work just as they please, in order to swap revolutionary ideas.* They can express their views about their work in the villages and down in the mines by means of wall newspapers."

This "imperative circular from the Central Committee of the Chinese Communist Party and from the Council of State"** was not published in the press; it was posted on the walls of schools and universities, and many copies of it reached the West. There can be no doubt about its authenticity. It reveals clearly which achievements of the Chinese revolution were made spontaneously and which were the result of force.

But this proves nothing. The Chinese people had never known freedom in the Western sense of the word. They would probably not have been able to achieve anything if, at the very moment when the greatest sacrifices were being demanded of them, they had thought of doing away with the restrictions to which they were accustomed. Nature does not go forward by leaps and bounds, even in periods of "great leaps forward." Just as Mao was a prisoner of the same kind of worship accorded the emperors before him, so the Chinese people themselves could not change their ethnic and cultural identity overnight; it must evolve slowly.

Religious Conflicts

Many times I asked people: "Why is your regime—like all communist regimes—against religion? What is there to fear from it? Anyone can see your success. You shouldn't be afraid of competition from a religion."

My questions usually received the same stereotyped answers:

"Freedom of worship is guaranteed by the Constitution. Those who want to practice their religion are free to do so. If there aren't more followers of the various religions, it's because the people don't want religion."

However, one intellectual from Shanghai did not attempt to dodge the question: "The Chinese revolution isn't an occupation for amateurs. It isn't addressed to one part of the individual, or to a certain section of the population. It takes possession of the whole being, of the masses in their entirety. It demands total and unreserved commitment. It is impossible to be revolutionary and religious at the same time. That would mean believing in two different religions."

---

*This refers to the first year of the Cultural Revolution, when millions of young people were continually on the move all over China.
**I.e., from the Council of Ministers, chaired by Chou En-lai.

The Chinese revolution cannot be satisfied with an occasional tribute or mere lip service. It demands whole-hearted devotion. The study of Mao Tse-tung thought is an ardent form of worship, a form of worship which has its own catechism, missal, hymns, priests and liturgical processions. One cannot worship mutually exclusive divinities.

Holy Places Put to New Uses

Everywhere we went, we asked to visit the pagodas; some were only a hundred years old, others had been standing for a thousand years. These religious places have become dead sanctuaries. Groups of children waited under the arches to accompany us. They amused themselves by racing us up and down the interminable stairs. They have taken the place of the Bonzes.

"What has become of them?" we asked.

The replies varied, but meant essentially the same thing: "The Bonzes had no work, because the people don't believe any longer in these superstitions, so they were put to work." "They are being reeducated." "They are doing periods of rectification."

We were assured that some pagodas were still being used, but it was never possible to see them. Westerners based in Peking had not seen any since 1966.

Yet Buddhism has certainly left its mark on Chinese thought and art. The monasteries had a tradition of prosperity and growth. They were involved in commerce; they owned land which was farmed by their own peasant-serfs; they lent money at high rates of interest. From time to time the emperors, tempted by this opulence and urged on by the Confucian scholars who feared this religious influence, seized the monasteries' wealth for secular purposes and reduced the Bonzes to laity. Then the process started all over again, as it did with the agrarian reforms.

Many pagodas had already been put to new uses before 1949, but there were still organized religious communities like the great Buddhist monastery of Chen-fou, the lama monastery of Peking, and the temples of Loyang. Before the Cultural Revolution diplomats could come to see the monks; it was one of their more pleasant pastimes. Since then, everything seems to have been wiped out. Two thousand years of religion, civilization and art destroyed.

On Fei Lai Feng mountain in Chekiang province, we had a glimpse of one of the great places of Buddhism. The temple of Ling Yin Si has been restored with quantities of gilt and ochre. Three gilded wooden Buddhas— one of them fifty-seven feet high—gaze down benevolently at their visitors over their expansive paunches. Opposite, four "Guardians of Heaven" roll their eyes menacingly. Everything is brand-new. Here and there stands a pagoda or a tenth-century statue which had the good luck to escape destruction and restoration. The regime fights against Buddhism, yet preserves the

masterpieces of Buddhist art and incorporates them into the "people's treasures."

The Chinese flock to this dead monastery. What are they looking for
among all these gaudy paintings? What are they expecting from this soulless
sanctuary which has neither beauty nor any sense of communion? What
history lesson booms out through the loudspeakers hidden in the trees and
the monastery courtyards? No doubt the answer is in the long inscription,
which reads: "These temples reflect the intelligence and creative spirit of the
people," although they were "conceived by the ruling classes, who influenced
the working people in order to guarantee the perpetuation of their
privileges."

Are the mosques treated any better than the pagodas? Hardly anything
is known about goings on in Chinese Turkestan. The struggle against the
Muslim religion is probably a hard one, but these areas are closed to
foreigners and there is no first-hand evidence.

In the eighteen provinces that are half-open to visitors, only two
mosques are known to exist—one in Peking and the other in Tientsin. And
these are for the use of the Muslims among the foreign community in the
capital. We were told that no Chinese had entered them since the Cultural
Revolution. In January 1972 it was reported in the press that a religious
service had been held in the Tungzu mosque in Peking on the occasion of the
Id al-Adha,* and that it was celebrated in the presence of several diplomatic
representatives from Muslim countries. "Chinese Muslims" were also said to
have taken part. Had they made the journey all the way from Sinkiang?

A Violation of Sovereignty

No other religion seems to have been eliminated as systematically as
Christianity was. It seems that not only are there no churches or chapels for
Chinese Christians, but that there are none for Western Christians either; in
fact, in this respect they are worse off than the Muslims in the diplomatic
community.

Before the Cultural Revolution, one of the Western embassies would
arrange for a priest to come clandestinely to China once a year—as a
personally invited guest; he would celebrate Mass in a catacomb-like atmosphere either at Christmas or at Easter. During the violence of the Cultural
Revolution it became apparent that however discreetly it was done, this
practice was dangerous. The "tourist" was playing with his life, or at any rate
with his liberty.

In Peking, Shanghai, Canton, and again in Sian, we asked if we could
attend mass. This request put the officials who were accompanying us in a
difficult position. They said with some embarrassment that they would make

*The Feast of the Sacrifice (of Isaac by Abraham), a very solemn Muslim festival also known as Id al-Kabir
(The Great Feast) (TRANSLATOR'S NOTE).

enquiries. Nothing was done. We reminded them several times, and in the end they practically ignored us. Our Sunday program in Peking was too full; perhaps something could be done in the provinces. The church in Shanghai was being repaired. The chapel in Sian had been ransacked by the Red Guards. And in Canton, just as we were about to leave the country, they said: "What a pity that you're not coming back to Peking. We could have arranged a religious service for you to attend." In fact, it seemed that no priest was authorized to celebrate Mass, even for a special Sunday service, and not even in the towns most open to foreigners.*

If the Chinese authorities appear to have a special fear of contact between Chinese and foreign Christians, it is because for a long time the Christian religion—particularly the Catholic confession—was a violation of sovereignty. The emperors refused to allow a group of their subjects to be drawn from their spiritual authority toward a foreign sovereign, namely the Pope. They had given the first Jesuits a warm welcome in the sixteenth and seventeenth centuries because they valued their scientific knowledge, but they became outraged when Chinese converts rejected their authority in favor of orders from the Holy See.

In the 1960s there was a nationalistic reaction against communists who followed the "Khrushchev line"; this was of the same order, since they were suspected of owing their allegiance to Moscow. They received their directives from a foreign capital, and so they were bad Chinese. One could no more accept "these servants of Soviet imperialism," "these renegades," "these revisionists in the pay of Moscow," than one could the "servants of the Vatican."

The Coup de Grâce

The Cultural Revolution stepped up the campaign against the church. Until 1966, China's priests were able to regroup behind the bishops, and it seemed that Chinese Christianity would be tolerated on the condition that it had nothing to do with the Vatican. With very few exceptions, foreign missionaries and nuns had been either driven out of the country or imprisoned. It looked as though the Chinese national church—like the Russian Orthodox Church and the Polish Catholic Church—might be about to enter a period of isolation, in which, although there would be no direct attacks on worship itself, the church would not be allowed outside allegiances.

---

*Our request did not do us any good, but it did help others. Some weeks later, the Italian deputy, Signor Colombo, asked if he could attend Mass, and he was permitted to do so. A delegation from the foreign affairs commission of the French National Assembly was also able to attend Mass. In both cases, the Mass was said by a visibly "profane" priest in the presence of a few old women who seemed to have been specially recruited. At the end of the service the priest attacked the "reactionary politics" of the Vatican, which he said was "an ally of the Kuomintang and the imperialists." The Mass was in Latin, so it would seem that the news of Vatican II had not yet reached Peking.

But the first mass demonstrations of the Cultural Revolution saw the development of a savage anti-religious campaign, conducted under the pretext of xenophobia. The few churches that remained open were broken into and ransacked; the ornaments, crosses and sacred vessels—items which distinguished their sanctuaries from ordinary assembly rooms—were pillaged or destroyed. The only remaining convent—that of the Franciscan Sisters of Mary—was broken into. The nuns were thrown out onto the street and publicly humiliated, beaten and spat on. The foreign sisters were expelled to Hong Kong. The thirty-three Chinese nuns were kept in China, and what became of them no one knows.

The vandalism did not stop there; the small Christian cemetery for foreigners was attacked; the military tombs were destroyed. Crosses were reduced to rubble. The walls of Peking were covered with photographic montages—the inspiration behind them was similar to that behind the anti-religious museums in the Soviet Union. Accusations against the Roman Catholic Church spread: orphan girls "sold as servant-mistresses to land-owners," nuns "being cruel to the orphan girls in their care," missionaries "giving their support to the European imperialists."

The history of Christians in China is a chronicle of hatred. The mobs of the Cultural Revolution carried on an old tradition. The massacre of missionaries at Tientsin in 1870 and the Boxer Uprising of 1899 were basically xenophobic; the non-Christian Chinese could not tolerate the way the Christian Chinese were so carefully protected by the missionaries. They did not disapprove of Christian charity as a principle; they felt humiliated by it because it was practiced by foreigners and because it was applied preferentially to "annexed" coreligionists. Some refused to believe in Christian mercy. Macartney had already observed that it was dangerous to take a wounded man home with you to treat him; if the man died in spite of all your efforts, you—the Good Samaritan—would immediately be held guilty of killing him. The motives of the nuns who stubbornly continued after 1949 to care for children who had been afflicted with trachoma, the terrible endemic disease of the eyes, must obviously be questionable. The missionaries were obviously trying out foreign cures on the Chinese children, and taking their eyes out to make medications from them. In the years following Mao Tse-tung's victory, the prisons filled up with missionaries, Chinese priests, nuns, and even Protestant pastors. This was one of the main reasons behind the Western countries' reluctance to recognize the new regime.

Are the Chinese Priests Any Better Off than the Foreign Priests Were?

How many ordained priests managed to escape imprisonment or deportation? Do they hold services in secret, as the first Christians did in Rome? It is hard to answer these questions.

It was estimated that in the whole of China there were three million baptized Christians. No doubt the church does survive in its own little world, but it is in the last stages of a gradual death. It would be very surprising if the faithful did not feel the need to practice their religion in spite of the risks, but it would also be surprising if a clergy whose senior members had been removed, which had no contact with the outside world and which was the object of denunciation and abuse could exert very much influence, or even survive for very long.

It is more than likely that many Chinese Catholics have tried to be both good Christians *and* good communists. In the years after the Liberation, a movement got underway to rally Christians to the revolution. There is plenty of evidence of this. As a Chinese Mother Superior said in 1956, "The people live better than ever before—that's undeniable. And it's also true that there's been an increase in alms: the faithful do not feel that there is any incompatibility between socialist China and the Catholic religion." Many Chinese Catholics acknowledged the progress that had been made by the country's economy, and only asked that they be able to maintain their religious beliefs while contributing to it.

Since then, the situation has reversed. Communism no longer needs Christian support. It is strong enough that it can do without their contribution and decimate them, punishing the Chinese clergy and the faithful for having obeyed the orders of their bishops and Cardinal Tien and for having supported Chiang Kai-shek right through to the end—and beyond.

Could this be called persecution? A Chinese priest now outside the country begged me not to use the word: "Whenever the word 'persecution' is used, it means that there are martyrs, and there aren't any in China. There is a conflict between church and state. The church—on the orders of its bishops—fought against the setting up of this state, and this state is now making it pay dearly for having done so. No, it's not persecution."

From behind the blinding glare of the interrogator's lamp, the judge told Father Van Coillie: "The sovereign people do not poison priests. We arrest only spies and enemies of the people. Now, someone like you, who has worked against the people and against the government—we no longer regard you as a priest; we regard you as a reactionary. You understand?"

Vatican Diplomacy

Would this church—which Western Christians are sorrowfully watching as it slowly disappears—have had a better chance of survival if the Holy See had recognized its national character immediately? This is a reasonable assumption, although there is no way of proving it. It is often said that problems arose over Christianity in China because congregations were answerable to Rome and maintained their See in Rome or Paris. The Chinese church, which has remained directly subordinate to the Pope, has kept its

Latin character since the sixteenth century; the Holy See did not allow it to become Chinese by incorporating Chinese culture, customs and songs into Catholic ritual. Furthermore, it developed only at the pace of colonial expansion.

When the Chinese bishops made every effort to create a Chinese national church—organizing themselves to face the communist state—Pope John XXIII, frank and open as he was, referred to a schism. Vatican diplomacy since 1949 seems to have followed that of Washington.*

Have the three million Christians in continental China been the victims of the Vatican's predilection for the Taipeh regime? Some, like Louis Wei Tsing-sing, believe they have. This Chinese priest has managed to retain contact with communist China without being disowned by the Vatican, and he believes that the Christians of China could be saved if the church would agree to give up its support for the émigrés of Taipeh and to recognize that the communists represent the people of China. Would their government stop treating the Chinese Catholics as traitors to their country if this happened? This is not certain, but such a step might give them a chance to avoid being totally wiped out.

The Beginnings of Wisdom

A Bicyclist Goes through a Red Light

A policeman on point duty at the crossroads—a soldier in green with a battered cap—blows his whistle. A bicyclist has gone through a red light; he looks around furtively and pedals on. Another whistle. The bicyclist has gone less than a yard when pedestrians leap into the road in front of him. They force him to dismount and form a hostile circle around him, waiting for the policeman to arrive. The officer says only one word, and in a more moderate tone of voice than one might have expected from the rather menacing attitude of his "assistants." He disperses the crowd and sends the bicyclist on his way. No taking down of particulars. No reprimand. The drama is resolved just as quickly as it developed. The soldier-policeman returns to his duty; he simply jots a brief note in his book.

The next morning, just as he is leaving his apartment for the textile factory where he works as a packer, the reckless bicyclist gets a visit from a member of the revolutionary committee for the block. Speaking harshly, the official reproaches him for his folly of the day before, and gives him a long

---

*Since 1965, Vatican diplomacy has become more flexible; note Pope Paul VI's speech at the United Nations and the message to Mao in 1966.

lecture. It is a serious matter to have gone through a red light. It is a serious matter not to have stopped when the policeman blew his whistle the first time. It is a serious matter to have provoked the anger of the broad popular masses who breathe the revolutionary air of Mao Tse-tung thought. It is an even more serious matter not to have realized the seriousness of what one has done.

The bicyclist is in a quandry. He is going to be late for work. Time is moving on, and he is getting later and later. He starts thinking of the trouble he will be in when he turns up late for work. When the official from the revolutionary committee finally lets him leave, our bicyclist—who was becoming more and more shamefaced as the lecture progressed—realizes that this is the beginning of a whole series of troubles. He gets to the factory half an hour late and is called over to see his foreman. He explains why he is late, and is immediately asked to go and account for his behavior to the officials of the factory revolutionary committee. He is reprimanded for being late, for the cause of his being late, for the damage he has done to the factory's production, for the shadow he has cast over the enterprise's reputation, and so on.

In the days that follow, the nightmare grows. A member of the district revolutionary committee and a Party official come and reprimand him at his apartment. He has to criticize himself in front of his workmates and neighbors.

This true story—which is like something out of Kafka—happened in Peking in 1967; it was told to me by an eyewitness. There are probably thousands of similar cases every day. The whole country is divided into zones, and everyone's identity is known and catalogued; everyone's movements are closely followed. After prisoners finish their sentence, just as tight a check is kept on them as when they were inside. Closed prison to open prison, and open prison to probation—there are only slight differences among the three. No one in China can escape from the system.

The Obligation to Inform

Every time one of our group looked a bit skeptical when he heard an official talking about the virtue of the Chinese, the story of the bicyclist came to mind.

Doesn't anyone smoke opium now? Are there really no prostitutes in China? No adultery? Do men really abstain from sexual relations until they are thirty, and women until they are twenty-five? How can we believe this?

"There is no evil in them. They are guided by the conscience of the masses. If they find themselves on the point of giving in to temptation, they know that they will soon be denounced for it."

"Denounced? How?"

"Denounced by their neighbors, by their workmates, and by the officials of the revolutionary committee in their enterprise or district."

"And those who manage not to get caught?"

"It did happen during the disorder of the Cultural Revolution, but in normal times it's quite impossible."

"Don't people collude with one another, though? Isn't there an advantage in keeping quiet about one thing so one can benefit later from something else?"

"It can happen, but there is always someone who will break his silence, and the broad popular masses will be as tough on those who have kept quiet as on the person they've been covering up for."

This is the official version. Of course, in China, as everywhere else, the most rigid rules can be bent, but it is much more difficult than in most countries. It is highly likely that the student who sleeps with his girlfriend is running serious personal risks, as are the man who is unfaithful to his wife, the prostitute who tries to resume her profession, and the family that enjoys a style of living which is above the average and beyond its means. This is the beginning of wisdom. And without any need for large numbers of policemen or an all-powerful political police as other communist countries have. In China the "conscience of the masses" takes the place of the KGB.

The practice of informing on others was a virtue long before the People's Republic of China was founded. In Athens it was known as *Menusis** and was one of the basic elements of democracy. In monastic communities every monk is obliged to report to the Superior any lapse or shortcoming he has witnessed, even indiscreetly. This obligation has been respected for centuries— especially in convents; at chapter meetings, monks who hesitate to point out their own errors are generally helped by their brothers.

Are people virtuous by nature once the constraints are lifted and there is no fear of being observed? Has a society ever existed that justified this Rousseau-like principle? It is odd that people cite the works of Mao or Freud in support of the "spontaneous nature" of instincts. Maoist society is virtuous, but the virtue is a collectivist one imposed by social pressure. And Freud, whom people like to portray as one of the fathers of the "permissive society," gave copious proof in his writings that there is no civilization without repression. "The majority of men obey orders which limit their instinctive desires only where external constraint can be felt and only to the extent that they fear it. They do not deny themselves the satisfaction of their greed, aggressiveness and sexual covetousness. They do not hesitate to harm their fellow men by lying and theft if they can do so with impunity."

The Chinese philosophers of the "School of Law"—contemporaries of

---

*The functioning of which was described by Plato in *The Laws*, as well as by Thucydides and Demosthenes, in terms perfectly appropriate to Mao's China.

Alexander the Great—said exactly the same thing: "Man is by nature bad. If one can, one must persuade him to act correctly; if not, he must be compelled to do so." By himself, he is not able to behave in a way appropriate to society. He must submit to the pressure of the group: "Men will be divided into groups, responsible one to another, and they will be obliged to denounce one another for their crimes. If they fail to, they will be punished the same as the man who commits the crime."

In fact, in classical China people were called upon to keep a check on one another's behavior and to denounce each other, much in the same way as a schoolboy is given the "responsibility" not of representing his classmates in front of the master but of "sneaking" on them for their own good.* Macartney had observed this practice when he was in China: "There is an *institution* in China which is worth noting. . . . Every tenth merchant is responsible for the behavior of nine families in the neighborhood, in those things which it is possible for him to keep an eye on." Why should the Chinese authorities abandon this tradition at the point when it has become more useful than ever? In fact, it may be the most effective—and perhaps the least hypocritical— way of keeping a rapidly changing empire of eight hundred million people on an even keel.

Those who deal cruelly with nonconformists are not troubled by their conscience—their excuse for their actions is religious in nature: these transgressors are agents of the devil, although they look like human beings. The revisionists are called dogs. And since the dogs have been systematically destroyed in China, why should anyone have any scruples about liquidating "revisionist dogs" as well? It is as if the moral conscience of the Maoist "faithful" had been inverted.

How the Chinese Suffer under This System

The Chinese system could not work without causing anguish. In Wuhan a gray-haired woman with delicate features leaned out of her window to watch us go by in the street; she had a despairing look about her. And later, in Canton, as a young woman answered my questions through an interpreter her eyes seemed to be saying: "I'd like to talk to you, but you can see I can't with this interpreter and my colleagues here listening." There are hints of such silent distress everywhere. Time and again, despite the fact that all doors were open to us (or perhaps because they were), we were confronted by silly little "secrets" and mysteries made out of nothing. The guides never said anything which could not be repeated to their superiors. But there were so many occasions when secrets and confidences seemed to pass from eye to eye.

---

*Actually, the clan system took care of most cases of wrongdoing, and so the system was not as authoritarian as it might seem.

This does not necessarily mean that the masses are hostile to the regime—a regime which has transformed their lives. Over the centuries they have become quite used to obedience and submission to a degree which virtually made them slaves. The harshness of the present system must seem to them mild compared to the feudal regime under which they suffered. But those who belong to the privileged classes—or those who have been able to make comparisons with other societies—must privately feel frustrated and impatient. And who could easily tolerate the representative of the street revolutionary committee—a kind of Party concierge—keeping his beady eye on everyone's movements, sniffing the air for a trace of opium, tracking down lovers, getting in anywhere without the slightest excuse, making a note of the fact that a Mao portrait is not hanging over someone's bed, telling the police of suspicious visitors, and bringing "help" in case of illness in the form of compulsory medicine which will cure the victim of his unhealthy ways, a blend of denunciation, "reeducation" and fanaticism.

Does the Concept of Liberty Have Any Meaning in China?

Many Chinese intellectuals consider freedom to be a Western concept, without significance for China. Sun Yat-sen summed it up in 1924: "Since this idea of liberty made its appearance in China, only scholars, by their research, have managed to understand it. If we talk about liberty to a country person or the man in the street, he will understand nothing. Liberty means something only to those who have studied abroad, or to those who take an interest in the politics of Europe and America and who hear the word all the time, or read it in books. But even they do not really know what liberty is."

One can only understand what one has experienced: does love have any meaning for someone who has never known it? The Chinese do not feel deprived in the same way a Westerner would, because they have never experienced real freedom. It is a luxury for those who already have the bare essentials for living.

Sun Yat-sen's denunciation of liberty is not without ambiguity. Twenty pages further on, the "Father of the Chinese Revolution" says somewhat paradoxically that China, rather than lacking liberty, has too much of it: "Europe made the revolution in order to conquer liberty, of which she was deprived. We, on the other hand, want to make it because we suffer from an excess of liberty."

Are these ideas contradictory? Before the revolution, China lacked unity and was incapable of resisting foreign pressure; she lived in a careless, free-and-easy style on the border of anarchy. An inorganic and uncontrollable magma, China had too much freedom, even if individual liberties were hampered by imperial, feudal and bureaucratic oppression. According to history, liberty most often was not the smooth, narrow passage between despotism and anarchy which some liberal and developed societies have managed to steer, but more often a despotism counterbalanced by anarchy, a despotism which is all the more brutal and cruel the longer it remains on a small scale and at a low level of development. To the Chinese, liberty—like Christianity or commerce—is a Western idea, and should be rejected as such. Liberty has been swept away by Chinese nationalism, which owes its success to faultless group organization. China has renounced individual liberties in order to gain group liberty. Here, too, Mao did what Sun Yat-sen preached. "In order to drive off foreign oppression, one must make a breach in individual liberty. If we applied this concept of 'liberty' to the individual, we would once again become a 'heap of sand.' It must be applied to the nation as a whole. The individual must sacrifice his liberties, while the nation must acquire total liberty."

The Chinese put up with such a repressive regime because of their patriotism. Their leaders are convinced that any relaxation of the iron discipline would increase the proportion of "individual liberties." This would weaken the nation's efforts to develop economically and to become a united, cohesive force; the nation would risk becoming a semi-colony once again, prey to exploitation by the rich countries of the world. With the subsequent impoverishment, China would lose her "collective liberty" all over again. And would individual liberties be regained?

This argument has some merit. We may think that the price is excessive. And often we have the feeling that this idea that collective and individual liberties are mutually exclusive is arbitrarily exaggerated. But is it for us to answer for China?

24

Making the Mind Conform

Putting Pressure on the Individual Conscience

"I was on the wrong path. I was behaving in a revisionist manner without realizing it. I had allowed myself to be insidiously enticed by bourgeois pleasures. But I was helped by the criticism of the masses. I underwent a difficult period of reeducation. Today, I understand my mistake."

This refrain—which we heard so often while we were in China—is one variant of the old doctrine which crops up constantly in a minor way in the history of Chinese thought: that the individual is not capable of discerning what is best for him on his own. He must follow a line which others point out. When he follows his own path, he is bound to make mistakes. As Han Fei-tzu, one of the masters of the School of Laws, said in the third century B.C.: "If one had to wait until one found a piece of wood which was naturally straight, one would wait a hundred generations and one would still not make an arrow. If one had to wait until one found a piece of wood which was naturally round, one would wait a hundred generations and one would still not make a wheel. And yet for generations now men have been climbing into chariots and hunting with bows and arrows. How has this been achieved? The art of straightening and bending wood has been applied." The art of straightening and bending minds in China stems from an age-old tradition.

"It's better to kill ideas than men," a leader of the Kiangsu Provincial Revolutionary Committee, a *bon vivant*, told me as he sat across a lavishly spread dinner table. Our fellow diners, both Chinese and French, concurred warmly. How could one disagree with such a reasonable principle?

But it was a terrible thing to say, even though he meant well. What if an individual's ideas are as important to him as life itself? These ideas may be so deeply rooted that stifling them could take all the meaning from a person's life.

It is hard to say which is dominant in this attitude—contempt for ideas or contempt for the individual. But the Chinese have not misunderstood the individual—they know he is malleable. Thus theirs is perhaps the first social regime which has demanded from everyone not only obedience, but also commitment, and has also been so successful in securing this that the need for obedience has become secondary.

Are willing slaves still slaves? In China it is hard to say how willing the people really are. We know of cases—or we guess there are cases—where enormous and continuous pressure is exerted on their consciences.

Since the "campaign to eliminate counterrevolutionaries" ended in 1954, the Chinese communists do not seem to have carried out the kind of systematic liquidation of people which Stalin continued for so many years after the establishment of the Soviet regime. In fact, as it has become more effective in guiding people's thinking, Chinese communism has spared more lives. The intellectuals in particular seem by and large to have escaped summary execution, which has most often proved to be the fate of the "landowners" and "war criminals." At first, they were "seduced" to the side of the regime, and only later were they subjected to the tough vicissitudes of the "rectification" campaigns.

Once again the Maoist regime is pushing a Chinese tradition to its logical conclusion. Today—just as two millenia ago—everyone is invited to "turn resolutely against the enemy lurking within his skull." The self-criticism session can in times of crisis be turned into an accusation session, followed by exclusion, arrest and even, at times, execution—although this seems to be very rare. Since the Sino-Soviet break in 1960, the Russians—freed from their "bad consciences" by the destalinization campaign—have not hesitated to accuse Mao of "intellectual cruelty," and they have compared his favorite resort of Hangchow with the Emperor Tiberius's Capri.

In reality Mao was the successor of the emperor, and as such became the guardian of doctrinal purity, which was preserved by a vast inquisitorial apparatus.

Brainwashing as a Matter of Course

No Chinese civil servant, worker, peasant, employee or intellectual should forget that he is in a situation of perpetual "rectification."

At the regular meetings in production units, if someone forgets to accuse himself of shortcomings, others will do it for him. Comrades who remain silent when a fault is discovered become accessories to the fault. "They help their comrade to open his eyes and see his faults and, if need be, to find the right road again," I was told by one of our Chinese companions. If he persists in his error, they pillory him until he confesses his sins:

"I realize how enormous my faults are. Thanks to you, I can see them clearly. I had allowed myself to take the easy way out and go back to former ways. Now I see how much damage I have done to our workers' community. I know what to do about it. I am going to do what I can, under the guidance of the revolutionary committee, to purify my thinking and to show myself worthy of Chairman Mao."

I have already demonstrated how collective psychotherapy is used in these sessions, but, having admired the feat of this gradual, careful "rectification," one wonders how much coercion is involved.

When Mao launched the "Hundred Flowers" campaign and called for "constructive criticism from all sides"—to provide a basis for essential reforms and to reshape group conscience on a grand scale, was it because he believed his fellow countrymen were already such good revolutionaries that spontaneity could be safely encouraged, or was his purpose to set a trap for them? There was plenty of criticism. But instead of attacking the bad revolutionaries—as a well-controlled self-criticism session would do—the criticisms were undermining the very foundations of the revolution. There had to be a speedy return to harsher measures. So it became possible to eliminate the dissident intellectuals as well as the Party members who had given free rein to this dissent.

Many of the criticisms made at the time reached the West. One is an open letter to Mao Tse-tung, published in a Hankow newspaper: "An untold number of citizens throughout the country were detained by the units where they were working (this did not happen to myself). A great many of them died because they could not endure the struggle [thought reform]. . . . I admit that in seven years . . . achievements are predominant. However . . . the intellectuals who chose to die by jumping from tall buildings, drowning in rivers, swallowing poison, cutting their throats or by other methods were innumerable . . ."

This moving document and many like it reached the West thanks to the group delirium of the "Hundred Flowers" campaign and the Cultural Revolution. They do exist. They do not fade with the passage of time. One must look hard at them and ask why—and under what kind of pressure—men chose to die.

There are several books that bear witness to this demoralization, and that give detailed descriptions of the clever techniques of "brainwashing." What is perhaps most disquieting is the realization that these are not exceptional measures taken against particularly virulent and obstinate "class enemies" but—albeit in an attenuated form—a universal, everyday phenomenon.

When he was freed, Father Van Coillie reread Arthur Koestler's *Darkness at Noon*. When he first read it, it had seemed "exaggerated, hidebound and written for propaganda purposes." This time, "when I put it down," Father Van Coillie writes, "I found that it fell far short of reality. What I discovered in the jail in Peking was worse than what Rubashov experienced in the Soviet Union, except for his own final liquidation."

The effects of brainwashing make themselves felt long after the experience itself. On the boat to Hong Kong, Father Van Coillie was still in a state of high nervous tension, although he was on his way to freedom. He did not dare tell anyone what he had suffered. When he heard a group of people speaking Russian, he rushed over to them, and said: "Are you Soviets? You are our brothers! You know, I'm a criminal. In the past I slandered you, but I was wrong. I was talking about something I knew nothing about. Since then, my eyes have been opened. . . ." Rather taken aback, the Russians let him carry on, but in the end had to tell him that they were White Russians who had left their country a long time ago . . .

Lying on his bed, Father Van Coillie started to analyze what he had said. Did he really believe it? Of course not. "My speech was prompted by a kind of anguish psychosis, and out of the habit of repeating what I had heard thousands of times. If you press the button on the robot marked 'Soviet Union,' the whole litany pours out quite automatically. More than six hundred million Chinese—from children of eight to old men of eighty—have done the same on similar occasions."

The Enormous Suffering of the Intellectuals

The only sufferings of the intellectuals we heard about were inflicted during two quite exceptional periods of Chinese history, the "Hundred Flowers" campaign and the Cultural Revolution, and of such there were many reports. The methods used by the regime are relatively humane, since the idea is to convert and not to kill. But by converting in this way one runs the risk of killing the mind.

The pressure of the group is so strong that almost all intellectuals who are subjected to it publicly repent and try to find "union with the masses"; they cannot survive isolation.

It is humiliating for Chinese intellectuals with a Western education to see themselves passed off as ignoramuses by militant communists. The purveyors of propaganda outdo the teachings of the Master and hold their "specialisms" up to ridicule. They spread tales like the one about the ear, nose and throat doctor who refused to treat a man's left ear because he was a specialist in right ears. The barefoot doctor with three months' training cures patients much better than the narrow-minded specialist. The engineer with six years' university education behind him has less insight when it comes to inventing a new technique than the worker armed with Mao Tse-tung thought. And so on. Of course, Chou En-lai and some other leaders have always seen it differently.

Intellectuals who consider their international reputation in their vocation of some importance are crushed when they are made to behave like schoolboys in front of Party cadres who seem intellectually inferior to them. It is with difficulty that they admit that the revolutionary devotion of a young peasant or a worker is higher up the scale of Maoist values than the most distinguished learning in the most abstruse discipline.

But for an intellectual the worst punishment is still to be unable to work. To be turned down for a job—often with no idea why or on whose orders—and unable to play a role or exercise any influence is desperately frustrating. In classical China, a scholar-official who was deprived of his job lost a great deal of his prestige, since he was eliminated from the social competition for a fault which was assumed to be serious; in the People's Republic, the intellectual who is rejected by the system also wonders anxiously if this enforced idleness is not the prelude to still harsher sanctions.

As a doctor told me, "Acupuncture is very necessary for relieving nervous tension. We don't use psychoanalytical cures and we don't teach Freud, but we do have a lot of nervous diseases, especially among intellectuals who are in conflict with themselves."

Clearly, our Western civilization does not have a monopoly on nervous breakdowns.

Certain of the methods are harsh and, like so many things in this country, as old as China herself. The Kuomintang often had recourse to them for "reeducating" communists. Washington has authorized publication of official correspondence proving that before 1944 the State Department was fully aware of "the existence of *thought-reform* camps in at least nine provinces of Kuomintang China." In these camps, "torture was carried out" and those who had the good fortune to escape it remained "generally broken in body and mind."

It is moreover remarkable that the West never took exception to the existence of forced labor under the Kuomintang; many foreign observers before 1949 saw peasants working in the fields, harnessed to one another like beasts of burden, with ropes tied around their necks. They walked bent over, and were shipped like galley slaves by police and soldiers. No one was at all disturbed by the existence of millions of peasant-serfs, people condemned to forced labor, and other victims of oppression under a regime which was an ally of the Western democracies.

There are similar peasants in the labor camps today, and they are there because they have not complied with the strict rules of the Maoist system. Most are still too backward to escape, and indeed to feel any sense of shock at what happens to them. They silently accept punishments every bit as severe as those inflicted on their ancestors by earlier regimes. There is only one way out of this chilly universe of camps and prisons, and that is to accept totally the will of the group, to absorb and accept Mao Tse-tung thought without question, and to increase production. So why not take this way out?

These practices—carried out both by the Kuomintang and the communists—reflect a widespread belief that goes back to well before Alexander's Asian conquests. There is no way of ensuring the survival of the people other than by making them obey: "If the head is not shaved, the scurf will return. If the boil is not lanced, it will get bigger and bigger. But while one is giving the child this treatment, he is shouting and crying—although his mother is holding him tenderly and trying to calm him. He does not understand that the small pain one is causing him will bring him a big benefit."

Confucius wanted to convince people, because he believed in the inherent good of human nature. Han Fei-tzu wanted to coerce people, because he believed human nature to be inherently evil. Mao fused these two together into a single system. Like Confucius, he appealed to the individual's conscience for total dedication and devotion, but his methods—from which there is no escape—had the harshness of Han Fei-tzu.

The Passion to Convince

The Westerner who would like to admire the impressive achievements of the regime reacts to information of "reeducation" with something approaching shock: why should the Chinese find it necessary to keep denouncing the past and to keep glorifying the present with such insistence if the truth were self-evident?

Those we spoke to had a ready answer for everything. In Shanghai, an additional interpreter was loaned to us to reinforce the cohorts already escorting us. He was as coarse and uncouth as they were gentle and refined. When we were out visiting, he would frequently grab me roughly by the arm to make me move on. When I asked a question about the operation of a factory or the way a piece of agricultural machinery had been developed—in a tone which perhaps suggested that I was not wholly persuaded of the overwhelming superiority of the Chinese system—his reaction would be vehement: I did not know such and such a quotation from Chairman Mao, or I had forgotten the conclusions of such and such a congress of the Chinese Communist Party. When the foremen's answers came through his guttural translation, it sounded as though they were arrogant enough to believe they were infallible. . . . But such dogmatism, instead of winning converts, can have the opposite effect.

Our regular interpreters were for the most part thoughtful and independent, but the officials of the revolutionary committees—and especially those in charge of "Mao Tse-tung thought propaganda"—seemed to be passionately determined to convince us of their ideas. Whenever they finished making an opening statement about something, they would ask the ritual question: "We would be happy if you would now be quite frank with us—give us your criticisms and suggestions." How was one to deal with this invitation? It was clear that the Chinese people were living better and better with every year that passed, but at the price of appalling coercion and constraint which none of the rich people of the world would tolerate. What was there to criticize? What changes in detail could we suggest? It was all very much take it or leave it.

He who is not with the regime is against it. During the civil war, if the leaders of the revolution had not remained inflexible and uncompromising they would not have had the courage to win. In their eyes, anyone who does not think the way they do is suspect. Their conviction that their country is both vulnerable and backward is too strong for them to abandon their implacable doctrine. One predictable result of an unstable system is that it produces unstable judgments.

Close Supervision

It is hard to state categorically that every member of the Party is convinced of its infallibility, or that all those who have been convinced are members of the Party; however, in a totalitarian regime militancy is a good reference guide.

In Yenan, near Mao's house, there is a board which shows the rapid growth in Party membership from one Congress to another.* When asked point-blank, the guide said that the number of members had risen to seventeen million—the figure that was made public before the Cultural Revolution.

To this Party membership one must add the members of the armed forces and police (four million), the militia and reserve troops (twenty-five million), trade unionists in industry (about twenty million), and members of non-industrial unions (about the same). There are also between 120 and 140 million children undergoing some form of education, and they will have been conditioned all the way from elementary school. There are also the members

---

*In 1921, when it was founded, there were twelve members; this was at the first congress in Shanghai. At the second congress the following year there were 195 members, and at the third congress in 1923, 420. At the fourth congress in 1925, the membership was 950, and at the fifth congress two years later it had reached 57,300. At the sixth congress the next year the figure fell to 40,000 after the massacres, particularly in Shanghai, but by 1945 and the seventh congress it had soared to 1,210,000.

of the Communist Youth movement, Red Guards and Pioneers, and the Federation of Democratic Women; even if about thirty percent is subtracted for those who belong to more than one of these categories, this leaves a figure in the region of 200 million. *About one Chinese in four—and one man in two between the ages of fourteen and forty—belongs to one of the various organizations which are directly under communist influence, and so is constantly being called on to support the regime.*

Even though the Party and the trade unions were badly shaken by the Cultural Revolution, all the activists in the mass organizations—through which the Party acts—are still called on to build socialism; they are like soldiers of Mao. In addition, the candidates for Party membership, who are at a "probationary" stage, are probably very large in number. So all in all it seems that Mao and his government can count on the support of half of all able-bodied Chinese, activists at various different levels and each recruiting the next.

Young people make up an important part of the population; more than three hundred million Chinese are under the age of twenty. And it is to them that the regime addresses itself first of all. "Politics first," but also "Youth first"—these are the main aims. Those who regret the passing of the old regime are too few, too swamped by the masses and too densely surrounded by suspicion and threats to constitute an opposition.

The members of the Party, the army and the various mass organizations are at one and the same time both conditioned and conditioners of others. They are trained to conform, and repeat what they have been taught with all the more conviction. They have never read any newspapers other than the *People's Daily*, the provincial paper and possibly their enterprise newspaper—reading matter which is just about as critical of the regime as parish magazines of the local church. They have never heard any ideological argument which was not "controlled" by a political commissar, a member of a "Mao thought propaganda team" or some other guardian angel whose job it is to keep a watch over "the line." No information gets to them which has not been filtered through the New China News Agency, Hsinhua.* If they happen to pick up news in Chinese broadcast from Taiwan, Hong Kong and Tokyo, it is so remote from their universe that it simply encounters a solid wall of incomprehension, or a reaction of fear. Unorthodox news and ideas that get through now and again must at all costs be kept from the people.

Can the fourteen- to twenty-year-old Red Guards and the eight- to fourteen-year-old little Red Guards possibly escape the magical and apparently irresistible attraction of the Mao cult? Open and outward-going as they

---

*The top leaders—and even the middle ranks in the Party—are actually very well informed about what is going on both in China and in the world outside. They read secret bulletins which are very different from the official propaganda.

are at this stage in their lives, are they capable of resisting when they are called on to "give their hearts," when they are made to utter the ritual oaths in which they say, "Our hearts beat only for Chairman Mao, light of our lives"?

The sharpest and liveliest adults, who might tend to dismiss this kind of propaganda as infantile, are well aware of the risks they would be running if they did. The intellectuals are asked to remember that they must *learn* from the workers and peasants and not *teach* them.

It is often hard for a Westerner to suppress a smile when confronted with the rather puerile emulation campaigns—the honors board at the factory gates, the note of commendation giving official recognition for hard work, the photographs of the best workers published on the wall newspaper, the red scarf tied around the necks of the most zealous, the red flag which only top-echelon workers have the right to fly on top of their machine-tools.

The system makes use of all the various branches of popular psychology. Eight hundred million people are not directed, but persuaded—not ordered, but fashioned. The way China is organized is rather like a telephone network with an infinite number of lines, all of them radiating from a central point which is ruled by a single will. The individual is caught in this network, and it is only with the greatest difficulty that he could escape all the stimuli and promptings he receives, since there are hardly any other possibilities open to him.

The Apparent Destruction of the Spirit of Criticism

Comparison and criticism are not without their disadvantages. They make individuals vulnerable; once the things people have grown to accept and depend on break down, they no longer know what to cling to.

Even before the Cultural Revolution, China's embassies in the West were taking strict measures to prevent the few Chinese students who were at that time studying abroad from making contact with local people and local groups. At the start of the Cultural Revolution they were all recalled.

Behind the Bamboo Curtain—even more than behind the Iron Curtain—ignorance and misconception about the rest of the world are so total that even in the universities people can be made to believe and accept the most amazing simplifications and distortions. After seeing a film based on *Oliver Twist*, students at Peita University appeared to believe that Dickens's novel painted a typical picture of present-day English society. They greeted statements that things had not changed much since Dickens's day with arrogance—perhaps arrogance to order.

There is little difference between the indoctrination of the Chinese people by the Maoist regime, that of the Soviet people by Stalinism, and that of the German people by Nazism. The techniques used in all three are closely related: a single party, an organized youth movement, a leader cult, the regulation of opinion, and a general system of remote-control command. Anyone who has seen the Hitler Jugend, the Komsomol and the Red Guards on the march and has heard Nazi, Soviet and Chinese loudspeakers blaring in the streets cannot avoid making comparisons. In the years 1934 to 1938 distinguished Frenchmen admired Hitler for having inspired a badly governed Germany, breaking down under unemployment and inflation, with new life and a new sense of purpose. He saw to it that everyone had a "square meal."

However, even if the methods have certain things in common, the aims are different. At least, they are at present. The Brown Shirts said the Aryans would rule over the other races, conquer the world and destroy the Jews. The Chinese leaders have set themselves the goal of delivering their people from poverty, feudal slavery and foreign domination. Skeptics will say that they are simply waiting to conquer the world for Mao Tse-tung thought and to return to the sinocentric universe which was suspended in 1839.

The Effects of Regimentation

How do the Chinese people live under a regime which, although it may appear to use persuasion, is actually subjugating them?

In China, even more than in other countries, one can only go by appearances and guesswork. Judging from the serene expressions of the adults and the cheerful, beaming faces of the young, they appear to be withstanding the removal of their individuality as easily as the body withstands the removal of the appendix. Be they workers, peasants, shopkeepers or laboratory assistants, men and women under the age of forty are healthy and unpretentious, rather monotonous and seemingly asexual, doing their exercises in the streets at dawn, bicycling around in the hundreds, marching past by the thousands, working harder than ever—following the right line, that is, thinking Mao Tse-tung thought. To all appearances they are not suffering at all, but are enjoying the simple pleasures of an austere life.

The discovery that there is no alternative to the present system encourages resignation. The Kuomintang are held in too much contempt for anyone to believe their return to power is possible. As for Western-style democracy, no one is going to believe that such a system would be capable of gaining control over such a vast population and overcoming its inertia. For a Chinese who loves his country, or who simply wants to live in the least unpleasant way possible, there is *no* other solution in sight but to make the best of it—to put up with the present regime and find one's own equilibrium in it. Thinking Chinese are perhaps not too enthusiastic, but even they are more inclined to adapt without illusions than to rebel without hope.

Westerners who have employed Chinese servants cannot speak too highly of their gifts as both actors and directors. One valet used to dress in rags the last week of every month until the mistress of the house realized that he needed an advance, but not for anything in the world would he demean himself by asking her; as soon as he got the advance, he would put on his ordinary clothes again. This went on every month.

During the Cultural Revolution, the Chinese who worked as domestic servants for Western diplomats used to demonstrate with clenched fists outside the embassies where they were employed. The following day, they would gaily explain that they had had "obligations" to fulfill outside and that there would be more of them to come. These "obligations" varied, but they were planned; in the morning the Yugoslav Embassy, in the afternoon the British Embassy. Of course, the demonstration was a spontaneous movement of the "broad popular masses."

The most brilliant of the directors was surely Mao himself. He was able to get eight hundred million Chinese to play their own roles so well that they no longer realize that it is all an act.

The Duty to Distrust

Not surprisingly, the Chinese practice of denouncing one another's faults is applied also in relations with foreigners. Every Chinese citizen knows that a personal encounter with a foreigner becomes reprehensible if it takes place outside the tight circle of official relations; and any clandestine dialogue is a matter for the most severe punishment. These contacts—or at least the suspicion that they have taken place—are often responsible for people being arrested.

It is not merely language and race barriers that make contact with the Chinese so difficult. They rarely go beyond an amiable smile—and when they do, it is often to order—because they are wary of establishing close relationships under the ever-present surveillance to which they are subjected.

When all is said and done, surely distrust of the foreigner is justified, since the Chinese people are surrounded by enemies and live with a constant obsession about espionage? Who can deny that the U-2 spy planes stationed in Japan and, in recent times, the spy satellites have flown all over Chinese territory, taking millions of photographs? Who can deny that the CIA has set up an espionage network in Hong Kong and Macao, with tentacles stretching into China itself? Who can deny that Kuomintang spies often land in southern China from the islands along the coast, and that they are brought across in nationalist vessels under the protective cover of American naval units?

A "snoop" cannot conceal what he is up to. He is a potential spy. He is recognized immediately, even among a crowd of several thousand pouring out of a theatre or sports stadium. The attitude of passers-by is still ambiguous; they can turn in a split second from cheers to anger.

To accept a gift from a foreigner would be to acknowledge that relations with him had taken a personal turn. It would also be to confess a desire for possessions in a system that teaches disinterest in property. "Don't give me anything for Christmas," the wife of a Western diplomat was told by her Chinese teacher on the eve of the Cultural Revolution. After 1966 it became quite impossible for a private citizen in China to receive a Westerner in his home.

A French mission which arrived in China in July 1970 laden with Sèvres porcelain vases took them home again without unpacking them; they had been given to understand that they would not be accepted. We did manage to give presents when we arrived in Peking and again when we said farewell in Canton—silver and bronze medals engraved with the emblem of the National Assembly. But the gifts were made anonymously and we were forewarned that none of the people we handed them to would keep the medals for themselves; they would be passed on to the organization to which they belonged, either the Permanent Committee of the People's Assembly or the Protocol Section of the Ministry of Foreign Affairs. Of course, it is just the same with religious communities; the only way of expressing gratitude to the nun who has nursed you to health is to offer flowers for the chapel. But the monks and nuns have chosen their vocation themselves; no one has taken the vow of poverty in their name.

A Chinese who reacts to something spontaneously suppresses it very promptly, for reasons which are almost always impossible to pinpoint. A university teacher who had had a number of useful conversations with a certain Western diplomat suddenly pretended not to recognize him. A guide who had no doubt been reprimanded by his superiors for having been too friendly with the foreigner he was accompanying was completely unresponsive when he passed him in the street; but in the one glance he gave him, he concentrated all the warmth and friendship he was obliged to hide.

Still no Westerner has been able to get to know a Chinese intimately. Behind their impenetrable silence and their ambiguous smile is *terra incognita*. The Westerner who thinks he *knows* this hidden land instantly arouses my suspicions. The conformism of the Chinese who come into contact with foreign visitors is disconcerting and misleading. One cannot assess instantly what is hidden behind this façade.

After all, how else—apart from voluntary isolation—can people protect themselves from the havoc wrought when two very different civilizations clash? Sheltered as she was from the rest of the world, China had fallen behind in economic and technological development and was able to catch up only at the cost of revolution. In order to ensure the success of this revolution, China had to intensify her isolation, and by remaining isolated she runs the risk of seeing her backwardness return.

In the Soviet Union perceptive theorists like Liberman, Trapeznikov and Sakharov have realized the mortal danger for the economy of the somewhat rarefied atmosphere in which it has confined itself. But the remedies they propose—competition and profit—cannot be applied to a system based on radically opposite principles. Will China be able to escape from the vicious circles in which all the other communist nations have become caught, and which so far none of them have managed to escape?

25

The Fugitives of
Hong Kong and Macao

A nosebleed poses no immediate threat to the human body, but if it keeps coming back it may be a symptom of something more disturbing. People's China suffers from something rather similar—something which is not very well known in the West and is unsuspected even by the majority of those who make a professional study of contemporary society.

Every month thousands of workers, intellectuals, cadres and technical men "choose freedom" by secretly crossing the border into Hong Kong.* There they find jobs paying five to ten times as much, as well as an atmosphere of freedom, the attraction of which Western intellectuals often forget, because they already enjoy it.

The figures, and the way they have increased, are a matter of concern to the Chinese authorities. At the end of the Second World War the population of Hong Kong was 600,000; by the time the People's Republic was proclaimed in 1949, the exodus caused by the civil war had pushed it up to 1,700,000. Some of this increase, of course, was due to the natural growth of the existing population, and some to the immigration of "Overseas Chinese" from places like Indonesia, but by far the most important factor was the arrival of refugees from China.

---

*I shall be concerned here only with those who go to Hong Kong, since they are the ones I have had a chance to study, but one could say much the same of those who make for the Portuguese colony of Macao or the little offshore islands under the control of the Taipeh government.

The influx of these people—which, over a period of twenty-four years, averaged more than fifty thousand a year—varies according to the internal situation in China. Very large numbers arrived in the years after the Liberation, and then the level gradually dropped off until 1960. It picked up again in 1961 and particularly in 1962, after the bad harvests and the failure of the "Great Leap Forward." Then it dropped off again until 1966 and the bloody start of the Cultural Revolution; in the next few years it was back to a trickle—11,000 in 1967; 14,000 in 1968; 7,000 in 1969; and 8,000 in 1970.*

Suddenly in 1971 the flow resumed. The year before refugees had been arriving at the rate of 650 a month, but by April 1971 the figure was up to 1,500, and in May to 3,000; then until the summer of 1972 they were coming over at the rate of 4,000 a month, the highest level since 1962.

Of course, these estimates are only approximate, and they represent fewer than seven emigrants per year per hundred thousand Chinese, whereas the corresponding figures for Italian, British and German emigrants in the United States are thirty-five, forty and fifty, respectively. But the numbers are not negligible and they are interesting. Is it a mild illness or a sign of something more serious?

Not Immigrants, but Fugitives

Edgar Snow has gone to great pains to establish that this movement of Chinese out of the country harks back to an old tradition. For the inhabitants of Kwangtung province—all 50,000,000 of them—Hong Kong and the Kowloon peninsula are not foreign territory; they are simply an extension of Cantonese land which had been theirs before the Opium War. Back in ancient times, those who lived in the very densely populated villages of the Three Rivers used to spill over onto and around the Kowloon peninsula in their sampans. Children and slave girls were exported there as a kind of security, and even when they were very old they were still sending money home. The Canton delta was the Sicily of China. When Kwangtung province is hit by drought or flood, the natural reaction of the people is to move to the British colony, almost all of whose inhabitants are of Cantonese origin, rather than move north, where their dialect is not understood and where they have difficulty getting used to the cold climate.

---

*These figures come from the British authorities in Hong Kong. Most of the refugees take great care to arrive unnoticed; their friends and relatives who are already in the crown colony put them up and find them work. These estimates were obtained by multiplying by five the number of refugees whose arrival is actually registered by the British police.

Is Snow's argument wholly convincing? This is not immigration, but a dangerous flight. Why is there this permanent influx which, instead of slackening, has grown since the disturbances of the Cultural Revolution died down? The refugees no longer die of famine; indeed, more often than not they are not even undernourished. If they are hungry when they arrive, it is because they have been waiting for at least a day for the right moment to try to get across the border. Ideology does not seem to be the reason for the flight any more than malnutrition. They have no belief other than communism. Only rarely do they have anything critical to say about Chairman Mao. None of them try to get to Taiwan; none of them are interested in Chiang Kai-shek. The Kuomintang tries hard to win them over through its emissaries, but they resist. So, what is it?

In Peril of Their Lives

Many more try to flee than actually succeed. In May 1962 the communist authorities in Kwangtung province suddenly opened the doors to anyone who wanted to go to Hong Kong. The news spread like wildfire. Hordes of immigrants swept into the colony, trampling over the barbed wire and completely overwhelming the British border guards. About seventy thousand refugees arrived in a matter of a few days; eventually, after Whitehall protested to the government in Peking, the flood was stemmed. The majority of the refugees were sent back some days later. The Chinese guards let them through and persuaded them to go back home. Did Peking want to test how many Chinese wanted to leave, or did they want to test how hospitable the Western world would be to the poor, the hungry and the unskilled? Did they want to kill the desire of the people living in the border areas to leave by showing them, once and for all, that "capitalism didn't want them"? Or did they want a temporary solution to the food shortage caused by the bad harvest of 1961, which was felt most savagely in the early spring?

This short, intense hemorrhage was just one rather worrying indication of the desire on the part of many Chinese to leave their country. From this it is reasonable to conclude that millions would immigrate if they could.

This is borne out by another even more significant fact, namely that the government has since adopted the very opposite policy: since 1962 the Chinese authorities have made it virtually impossible to cross the border. Now fugitives risk their lives to reach Hong Kong.

The barbed wire and watchtowers that one sees from the train on the way from Canton to Hong Kong are guarded by troops. Hardly anyone manages to get across; now and again one hears gunshots. Cases have been reported of Chinese getting through by hiding in trucks carrying cabbages or pigs; they run a terrible risk of being caught. Some slip aboard ferryboats, the "snake boats." But these are just a few isolated cases.

Almost all the defectors who get across do so at night by swimming one of the two bays on either side of the colony, Deep Bay in the Northwest and Mir's Bay in the Northeast. At its narrowest the crossing is a mile, but there are strong currents; in addition, the Chinese navy has laid wire netting across both bays, and they are patrolled by armed junks. In the winter of 1970–71, several hundred fugitives died of the cold. One morning in November 1970, about sixty corpses were found washed up on the beaches of Hong Kong. Those who managed to force their way through the barrier often tore their arms and legs on the oyster beds, and their blood attracted the sharks. To get over so many obstacles, you have to be something of an athlete. The fugitives are often boys and girls of between eighteen and twenty-five who have spent months following in Chairman Mao's footsteps, training in lakes and swimming pools before embarking on their adventure. The Great Helmsman probably did not foresee this indirect consequence of his celebrated swim.

Inadequate Countermeasures

Since the Cultural Revolution, the Chinese authorities have once again stepped up their efforts to discourage escape attempts. A campaign has been waged since 1970 in the areas adjacent to Hong Kong and Macao to put the population on their guard against the dangerous and fatal fascination of these cities, which are sinister examples of capitalist decay and colonialist decadence. A great deal was made of the dramatic deaths of the fugitives in the winter of 1970–71. Very harsh punishments are inflicted on those who fail in an escape attempt and on those who help them. Local peasants are trained to help patrols track down escapees.

It was rumored in Hong Kong that police dogs had found groups of young people hiding behind rocks on the way to the coast; they were shot without trial. It is very likely that the Chinese authorities made quite sure that the report was spread widely on the mainland. Those who are not killed on the spot are imprisoned or sent away for "corrective" treatment. People who have tried to escape often end up in forced labor camps.

Even so, in spite of the danger of death and the strong likelihood of being captured, the number of refugees is not only not dropping—it is increasing. Why is this, when the Chinese are being fed better and better, their standard of living has improved markedly, and the political and social climate has settled down after the wild days of the Cultural Revolution?

The fugitives who are officially accounted for by the Colony authorities are immediately interviewed by private or public organizations like the

United Nations refugee service, the Social Welfare Department, International Social Service and the International Rescue Committee. They are discreetly encouraged to tell about their lives in the People's Republic, and these interviews have become one of the best sources of information about the attitudes and thinking of young people in China. The majority are peasants and workers, but a certain number are intellectuals, students, technical people and former Red Guards who have become disillusioned.

Disturbing Evidence

The morale of many of the young townspeople who are sent "back to the land" seems to be bad. With their intellectual abilities, they are humiliated when they are relegated to the rank of rice-planters. They feel they are losing face, and this is even more serious in China than in other countries. Some confess that they had hopes of being given positions of authority during their stint in the country, or perhaps responsibilities in the local Party machines—things which would stand them in good stead when they returned to the towns or tried to go to the university. In fact, the peasant cadres mistrusted them and let them do only the very simplest jobs. They felt they would have to work as peasants forever and would never be able to take up their studies again or return to the towns. So they fled from a regime which did not recognize their merits. They were lucky to be sent to Kwangtung province, because the authorities—in an attempt to reduce the number of defections—cut down on the number of young people sent to the coastal areas. It is difficult enough to escape when you live near the border, but it is virtually impossible when you don't; a person who is not conforming to the rules is quickly spotted, particularly because his residence permit—which he is always being asked to produce—is not in order.

Some technical people frankly confess that they were attracted by the high salaries paid in Hong Kong. Most simply say that what drew them was the rumor circulating among young people in China that an individual is welcomed in Hong Kong, finds work easily, lives better than in China, and is free of fear. In fact, the British authorities, who are now less embarrassed by these arrivals than they were in the first few years of the People's Republic, are very pleased to have them; young technicians and qualified workers are just what is needed for an expanding economy. The colony is receiving highly motivated young people who are keen to work and whom China has trained and educated, so it is all to the advantage of Hong Kong.

The situation of the refugees in Hong Kong is hardly comparable with that of the refugees from East Germany, Poland or Czechoslovakia, who crossed barbed wire at the risk of their lives. It does not seem right to compare them with the traditional émigrés from poor countries either. These people are not like the bourgeois and the intellectuals who left China after 1949, having lost both their fortunes and their positions. They are not exiles from poverty—they are young people, often of the most humble origin, but full of health and vitality.

Although they have not known any other regime and do not lack the basic necessities of life, they seem unable to put up with the social pressure, the absence of any prospects of personal promotion, and the political and religious intolerance. They have a hazy picture of another type of society in which they hope to improve their lot.

The actual rate of immigration—one Chinese leaves each year for every fifteen thousand who stay behind—is negligible statistically, but it represents much more in human terms. We should not attach to the refugees the excessive importance given them by the China watchers who lie in wait for their arrival, pen in hand, ready to rewrite their adventures for readers in the United States, Japan and Taiwan. We should not, however, overlook their disturbing testimony.

It is also unsettling that Lin Piao and his eight companions tried to flee to Moscow, the Mecca of a "revisionist" ideology which Mao's appointed successor had himself condemned with such passion during the Cultural Revolution.

26

The Precariousness of the Regime

On the day the first banquet was to be given in our honor—by the People's Assembly in the Palace of the People—I asked the chief of protocol at the Ministry of Foreign Affairs to whom I should make my toast: Mao? Lin Piao? Chou En-lai? He replied: "Chairman Mao and Prime Minister Chou En-lai, naturally. And Kuo Mo-jo as well, if you like. But, Lin Piao—no, that's not necessary." It was July 16, 1971, the day it was announced that President Nixon would be making a visit to Peking. I did not take any special notice of this remark at the time. It was exactly a year later that the leadership confirmed that Mao's "closest companion-in-arms" had been eliminated. And this news was given only to foreign visitors*; the Chinese people had to work it out for themselves from the fact that the "appointed successor" was no longer referred to—as if he had never existed. Unless, of course, there were rumors as well, and this is difficult to know in the West, since our understanding of the way Chinese public opinion is formed and develops is almost nil.

The Palace Revolutions: Continual Secret Conflicts

This episode reveals two fundamental characteristics of the Chinese political regime: the permanent conflicts between the leaders and the fact that the way they develop and are resolved always remains a mystery.

---

*The French Foreign Minister, Mr. Maurice Schumann, and the Prime Minister of Ceylon, Mrs. Bandaranaike.

Marx said of China—the "typical Oriental empire"—that she was characterized by "the immobility of the social structure and the continual instability of the personnel in the political superstructure." In that case, China has remained ever since the most typical of the Oriental empires: her social structure still seeks to achieve a certain degree of immobility through uniformity and the political personnel are still continually on the move.

It was normal practice in the past for the Emperor to have his ministers' heads cut off in the presence of the Court.* After dark seraglio intrigues, which went on "behind a curtain," each courtier was turned into a witness. The hazardous power game, although it was restricted to a select few, ended up as a public performance. Nowadays, the silence rule is even more implacable: the worst adversaries respect it, right through to the end; even the vanquished and the victims do not appeal to the people's judgment or to the judgment of history. Silence falls on the palace revolutions. In Peking the Tarpeian Rock is in the Capitol.

The chronicle of eliminations, following one upon another, is a real thriller, even if it is hidden behind a smokescreen. As in all the other communist regimes, the purge is a product of the system and a condition for its survival. The rule, which binds everyone within the Party, is that *ideology reigns:* ideology cannot permit purely personal conflicts—in other words, in normal language, leaders struggling for power. *Tendencies*, which are given all sorts of vague names like "deviationism," "Leftism," "revisionism," are condemned, to enable *men* to be eliminated. Then one can dispense with actually naming the "criminals"; they fade away as individuals, behind their "crimes," which survive them. A few who escape being killed become living symbols of their own stigmas—men like Marshal Peng Teh-huai and the President of the Republic, Liu Shao-chi. Others are suddenly and inexplicably released from their disgrace.**

The Risk of the Regime Destroying Itself

Is this permanent confusion over the difference between conflicts of ideas and conflicts between people a strength or a weakness of the Maoist system?

It is a great strength, because the government can always give the masses, and even the numerous semi-initiates (cadres, militants and propagandists), the illusion of unity and solidity—and this certainly helps to

---

*Unless the ministers were granted "the mercy of suicide" in the intimacy of their homes or prisons.
**An example is Teng Hsiao-ping, who was dismissed during the Cultural Revolution and who regained his post as Deputy Prime Minister in the spring of 1973.

bring that unity and solidity about. By using imprecise and interchangeable words, the impression that the leaders are following the "general line" can always be created. No matter that the leaders are tearing each other to pieces and forcing one another out of positions of power and influence: the dogma remains intact. The principle of the infallibility of power is preserved; indeed, it is even extended—retrospectively, if necessary, by rewriting history—to all Mao's actions and statements. This is enormously reassuring, amid so many upheavals. It provides a shield from all dangers.

But it is also a weakness of the system. Personal conflicts and factional struggles seem to get worse, precisely because this camouflage is so effective. The leaders are probably poisoned by the ideological atmosphere in which they live: any divergence of view becomes a struggle between truth and heresy. Rare indeed are leaders like Chou En-lai who are sufficiently masters of their own mind not to allow themselves to be led away by their own language or to be confined by the dogmatism it produces.

It is said that Lin Piao "conspired" against Mao Tse-tung and even "planned to assassinate him," either by "shelling the villa in Shanghai where the Chairman was living, or by using mortars to destroy the train in which he was traveling." These methods of assassinating Mao were worthy of a feudal court. No doubt Lin thought he would be able either to cover up the attempt on Mao or, after a few months' indoctrination, to present this accident of the revolution as a historical necessity—or, better still, to reveal the accident only after it could be seen as such.*

It is possible that he refused to go on following a chief with whom he had become identified to the point where he was his sole confidant and heir. A companion-in-arms who is trusted above all others must feel that there is no other way out to make such an extreme decision.

In any case, the machinations took a long time; it took a whole year of propaganda before the ignominious death of Mao's "best disciple" could be revealed to the masses. By then it was no longer an event that was being reported, and it was no shock to the people; it had become a lesson from which everyone was to draw a moral. But a year was needed. Mao himself started drawing the moral from the Lin Piao affair in the summer of 1971; in great secrecy, he personally warned a tiny circle of leaders. He traveled the country, telling the top Party leaders in the provinces of the deviationism to which Lin Piao had succumbed and of the plot he had hatched. Then, over the next twelve months, the news spread cautiously from door to door, from one circle to the next, until everyone had been properly informed.

---

*If Lin Piao really wanted a rapprochement with Moscow, why would he have supported the Leftists and tried to push the Cultural Revolution—which was more than anything else a struggle against Soviet-style "revisionism"—to its absolute limits? There seems to be something wrong with this line of argument. Will anyone ever know what really happened?

So, the strength of the system is that it absorbs its conflicts; its weakness is that it increases their number.

What if the plot had not been uncovered? What if it had succeeded? What if Lin Piao had ascended the throne, just like the pretenders of old who succeeded their dead emperor after dark struggles with the rival blood princes? It might have been the perfect crime, and Chinese policies would have been different. There would have been no normalization of relations with the United States; there might have been a rapprochement with the Soviet Union. There would have been no Thermidorian reaction; there probably would have been a new outbreak of the Cultural Revolution. Leftists would not have been eliminated; in fact, they would very likely have been triumphant. There would have been no move toward peace in the world; the atmosphere of detente would have given way to hostility.

Gerontocracy: A Revolution That Devours Men

During the summer of 1971 we had the impression that China had emerged from the crisis of the Cultural Revolution. Yet the Chinese leaders were struggling with a new crisis which we knew nothing about. Would this crisis be the last? For want of participants? Maybe. The crises of the "Great Leap Forward" and the Cultural Revolution decimated the political figures who had emerged during the Liberation; no new blood had been brought in, and the personalities who remained were getting old. We could not then anticipate the chaos that would follow Mao's death.

Chou En-lai, an astonishingly youthful septuagenarian, seemed when we met to be preoccupied by the problem of age. He was struck by the youthfulness of our delegation. "Almost all of you were born in the twenties," he said, looking at a list he had in his hands. "Two members of the Standing Committee of our National People's Congress are over ninety. Because of their age, they haven't been able to come here to meet you. One, Vice-Chairman Ho Hsiang-ning, was in the Tung Meng Hui with Sun Yat-sen. The other, Chang Shih-chao, who's ninety-one, has just written a book of over a million characters."

Although they were lively, these old men were still old men. Chou, who was born in 1898, was one of the youngest of the top leaders. The generation of the Long March has either been decimated by the enemy or has torn itself to pieces over the years; it has not been replaced. While we were in China we did meet many officials who were in their early forties, but between the old men and this generation several age groups have been lost.

Chou expressed regret that he would not be around to celebrate the second centenary of the "Great French Revolution" and said he envied us, for we probably would be. He smiled, but behind his smile lay a certain anxiety.

The deeper we went into the provinces, the more we were struck by the enormous generation gap between the top dignitaries of the Chinese regime and the local cadres.

The members of the Standing Committee of the National People's Congress—whom we met during our stay—were a row of small, frail old men who were mostly rather hard of hearing. Was this octogenarian chorus presented to us to show us that scholars and highly civilized men had rallied to the regime or that the Cultural Revolution had, contrary to expectations, respected these valuable relics of the past? They seemed to be floating weightless, social misfits deaf to all the rumors buzzing around them. We first met them when we arrived at Peking airport, standing in a long line under a burning sun; the second time was the following week at the same place. This time it was raining hard, but there they were standing in exactly the same order, seeing us off on our flight to Sian and Yenan. One of them, Pei Shih-chang, the deputy for Hangchow, followed us on board the Ilyushin; he was to accompany us throughout the journey, friendly, smiling, but almost always silent.

On the other hand, both in Peking and in the provinces, we were welcomed by young men with energetic handshakes—vivid examples of the practical producer generation. And most of the military people, intellectuals, enterprise heads, cadres and workers' and peasants' officials belong to this category.*

There are no national and provincial leaders between these two generations. The Cultural Revolution violently attacked the cadres and thereby highlighted the fact that they were no longer there. No doubt this was the reason why so many of them reappeared once the Cultural Revolution had died down. But who can confidently claim that the succession is guaranteed?

If the combatants are fewer in number, will they in fact be less ruthless? What the temporary ending of the Cultural Revolution has brought to light is the coexistence of different forces. The conflicts between individuals conceal the opposition of real power centers—the army, the Party and the administration. There is no point in attempting to describe their relations past, present and future; suffice it to say that the chessboard is in a complex state and the pieces are now movable.

The Colossus with a Skull of Clay

Like any totalitarian system, the Maoist political system seems at one and the same time to be both fragile and all-powerful. It has the body of an

---

*Typical of this generation were Yao Wen-yuan and Hsu Ching-hsien, the Party leaders in Shanghai, both men in their forties.

athlete and a good brain, but it has a vulnerable head. The Chinese colossus has a skull of clay.

How will the septuagenarian and octogenarian generations of the Long March be succeeded by the generation of men and women in their forties, who have escaped the massacres and purges of the revolution? How will the heirs of the revolution respond when China's accession to the status of consumer society brings temptations and tensions from which she was protected by her state of penury? Of course, this is not something that is going to happen tomorrow.

Chou En-lai was the one person who always found the way out of the various conflicts which have from time to time threatened the revolution. Because he was a solitary person, he was able to scheme and maneuver between all the factions and power centers—not only in order to survive himself, but also in order to neutralize them and get them to cooperate with one another. Now that this master fixer has disappeared from the stage, how will things work out? How will the various forces be restrained from going to the limit in their confrontations?

As far as Mao is concerned, one can assume that since his main power was always spiritual, this will continue after his death. No doubt his successors will be able to govern—at least at first—only through him and by appearing to be the obedient disciples of a master who will be praised even more highly than he was during his lifetime. Mao has bequeathed to the Chinese a living synthesis between Marxism-Leninism, Confucianism, Taoism, Sun Yat-senism and the deepest of popular traditions, and they will be able to continue deriving their thoughts and actions from this—"for two thousand years," Kuo Mo-jo told me, "as long as they nourish their thought on Confucius."

But can one be so certain of this? Because they all subscribed to this ideal and deified being that was Mao Tse-tung, the Chinese felt they had some value. But now that Mao is dead, will they feel that they died with him? Will they realize that they are not gods, but poor naked wretches? The depressive state of melancholy which could overwhelm the entire people is a frightening prospect.

Can *demaoization* be ruled out? Not immediately, but some years from now. Even if Maoism survives Mao as Marxism survived Marx, there is a strong possibility that some of the things that will be done in Mao's name will make him turn in his grave. Sacred texts, unless they tell a story, like those of the Jews and the Christians, either cause discord or stifle initiative—or do both. Where Mao Tse-tung's thinking is vulnerable is in its doctrinal purpose. But now that Mao is no longer around to interpret himself, there is a very strong risk that his heirs will hurl their own interpretations in each other's faces. If Gaullism was able to survive de Gaulle, it was because de Gaulle did not lay down a doctrine; instead, he defined certain great principles which he then demonstrated by applying them. If one were to reduce

Maoism to its basic inspiration—nationalism, populism, agrarianism, permanent revolutionary tension—its chances of survival would be great, because one could scarcely be Chinese without in this sense being a Maoist. But there is still plenty of room left for tactical differences, and in the atmosphere of dogma that surrounds any communist regime these differences and divergences tend to turn into fierce opposition.

Could these conflicts be limited to the Chinese? The Russians have been following the evolution of Chinese communism closely, and one can be sure that they were awaiting the death of Mao—just as they are awaiting the deaths of Tito and Enver Hoxha—in order to try to reestablish the unity of the "socialist camp." They have the means at their disposal to act, and they are not hiding their cards. Mr. Fedoseyev, a member of the Central Committee of the Communist Party of the Soviet Union, wrote in *Pravda* in December 1971: "A large number of China's communists stand on the positions of socialism. The genuine communists have suffered a temporary setback in the struggle against Maoism, but they have not laid down their arms."

Let us imagine that once his plot had been uncovered, Lin Piao had actually managed to get to Moscow, that his Trident had not crashed—or been shot down—in Mongolia. In this event, it is quite possible that the Russians might have encouraged the formation of a government-in-exile centered around Lin, rather like the one Prince Sihanouk set up in Peking after he was ousted from power in Cambodia. Then when Mao had departed from the scene, a simple reversal of the majority in the Central Committee could have brought the Lin Piao group back to lead the Communist Party and the Empire.

There is nothing weaker than a strong regime: it is always at the mercy of conspirators. Its existence does not depend on the legitimate votes of its citizens, but on obscure, haphazard seraglio intrigues.

The Question of the Future

The China I saw during one summer—and which I have attempted to describe in this book—maintains an extraordinary, delicate and utterly unstable balance between revolutionary order and revolutionary movement. It is a sprawling organization with tentacles stretching in every conceivable direction, but it has the passionate intensity of the group spirit. With a little more organization it would become a bureaucracy; with a little more intensity it would become activist, with all the violence of the Red Guards and "rebel-revolutionaries." A little more authority would kill the spirit which justifies its existence; a few more revolutionary tensions and there would be anarchy in everyday life.

Because this balance is difficult to keep and because anarchy cannot be tolerated for long, the odds are on the side of bureaucracy. And it does not matter much who controls it—whether it is the Party, the army, the administration or a combination of all three, the collective heirs to the "celestial bureaucracy," the thousand-year mandarinate.

But the evolution may take other forms. The Cultural Revolution has shown that the troubles which beset national leadership leave a good deal of freedom of action at regional and local levels. The sheer size of the country can result in natural diversity or in compromises between the various regional differences; either way the risks are great for China's unity and independence.

Mao himself never seemed to display much optimism about the possibility of keeping the balance. "Alone in the autumn cold," he wrote in one of the poems of his youth.* The romantic illusion became the reality of old age. "Youth could negate the revolution and do bad things," he told Edgar Snow in January 1965, and the French Ambassador, Lucien Paye, the same year. He appeared preoccupied with the revolutionary quality and faith of those who are to continue the revolution.

What we saw does not seem to justify this pessimism. If Jewish children born in the kibbutzim turn away from the austere way of life of their parents, it is because Israeli society provides other models for them to follow. In China, is it likely that the young will lose their enthusiasm for long?

On the other hand, it is hard to believe that the vast mass of adult Chinese will be able to continue for very long in a state of tension. Of course, they have no way of making comparisons or being jealous of others. But Maoism has surely carried a very long way what Freud called the "idealistic misconception of human nature." And we may sooner or later see a violent explosion of instinctive impulses which have been pent up too firmly for too long.

China wants to be a convent—with personal subservience, group dignity and obligatory poverty. And it seemed to us that in many respects she was getting close to this. Just a slight shift, resulting from a new compromise between the appetite for pleasure and bureaucracy, which has itself been brought about by a lowering of revolutionary tension, in turn caused by the ending of Mao's charismatic power—and the impassioned pursuit of group dignity would immediately be in question. There would perhaps be fewer hardships, but they would be felt all the more keenly as they became less burdensome. And personal subservience would remain total. The threshold of suffering would suddenly drop. The magic of the Great Acupuncturist would no longer work.

There are other theories. If "the return of the repressed," which Freud said was a likely outcome of a period of excessively brutal and prolonged constraint, threatened China with national catastrophe, the very danger itself

---

*The first line of the poem "Ch'angsha," written in 1926 (TRANSLATOR'S NOTE).

could give rise to another Mao. For this kind of explosion would do great harm to the health and independence of China, a country condemned for a long time to underdevelopment and poverty. Turning her back on the "monastic" model and allowing "human nature" to take over would be the ideal way for progress to be slowed down and for China once again to become a colony—the exploited prey—of others. A second Mao would see the dangers. If he is alive and grown up—as is likely—he is seeing them right now. He will launch a campaign to avoid them. Like the first Mao, and like the Christians, he will say that it is true human nature to strive for brotherhood and justice, not to yield to the ego. And he will be followed by farsighted Chinese, who, like Chou En-lai, see how precarious an overpopulated China is in a hostile world; idealism and geopolitical realism will come together to revive the enthusiastic devotion to self-sacrifice on behalf of group dignity.

In the words of an anonymous Chinese Oscar Wilde, "It is dangerous to make prophecies, especially when they concern the future." The very precariousness of a political leadership which is so concentrated, so small, so old, so much a prey to the temptation of dogmatism, and so ready to tear itself apart under the protection of its immense capacity for secrecy means that almost anything is possible—except going back. The revolution will follow one of its various courses, or several, one after the other, but one cannot see it being wiped out. For a long time to come the pattern of the revolution will be militarization, bureaucratization, sclerosis, decay and sudden outburst.

When Mao died, the incarnation of the "ideal self" of the masses disappeared with him. And the people, who were intoxicated at seeing the end of a thousand-year lethargy, are suddenly confronting a new reality. But just at the point when it seems that China is awakening, it may turn out to be an illusion. Where is the dream? Where is the awakening? It is an ambiguous question, and one to which there is no answer.

27

A Perpetual State of Revolution

As time passes, some answers to the questions in our enquiry—and to others about the circumstances in People's China—will emerge, but they will be sketchy. Some of our conjectures may prove false, others will be confirmed. In any event, the revolution—which is now a quarter of a century old—does not seem to be bogged down by bureaucracy, rigidified, or in the process of breaking up. In fact, it seems to be enjoying a new lease on life; more intensely than ever, the country dwells in a state of perpetual revolution.

By 1970 the Cultural Revolution was over and the main driving forces behind it, Chen Po-ta and Lin Piao, had been eliminated. Madame Mao seemed to be out and the "Leftists" had been denounced. The moderates appeared to have won. The course of history had slowed down. Then, suddenly, came the anti-Confucius campaign—to reinvigorate a revolution which was becoming drowsy.

"The Year of the Tiger" Returns

Do day-to-day events have any long-range meaning in China? Analyses of the Chinese situation at a given moment quickly lose their value, since events change abruptly at a precipitous speed. One day you learn that an important figure in the Party apparatus has been removed from office, so you draw various conclusions from this—and then a few days later he reappears. The whole theory collapses.* The Western observer has what is really an ontological difficulty following a situation which is so hard to grasp.

Since our visit, things have been happening fast and the news has been changing all the time. Since the deaths of Chou and Mao, there are various signs that big and important developments are being prepared or are underway. There is talk of a new Cultural Revolution, of a new stage in the Chinese revolution. We can only judge from the isolated incidents and the occasional facts reported by the news agencies, newspapers and visitors.

Let us, for example, take the events that made the news during 1974. Why was there an attack on a philosopher who lived six centuries before Christ? Why was Western classical music suddenly disparaged? Why did they choose to occupy little-known islands? Why was the great film director Michelangelo Antonioni so violently attacked? Why did giant posters go up all over China, announcing, with drums and cymbals, a "people's war?" What can the global significance of all these disparate items of news really be?

At the beginning of the year, the Chinese press was continually saying that there were going to be great events and perilous conflicts and that people should prepare themselves for them. A quasi-official alert was declared. The older Chinese must have feared the return of "The Year of the Tiger"; according to popular belief, it returns every twelve years to bring great misfortunes to the masses. Each time, it has been a signal for cataclysm or violence. 1914: the First World War, the direct consequence of which for China was the occupation of Shantung by the Japanese. 1926: the start of the civil war, and Chiang Kai-shek's assault on the northern warlords. 1938: the Japanese seize the North and West of China. 1950: the outbreak of the Korean War and the systematic elimination of the "enemies of the people" and other opponents in the wake of the victory over Chiang Kai-shek. 1962: the sudden halting of the "Great Leap Forward," and, after three years of famine, the relaunching of the class struggle. 1974: had the Year of the Tiger returned?

It is true that People's China tries to suppress this old superstition, which now holds sway mainly over Chinese exiles in Taiwan, Singapore and Hong Kong. The regime makes every effort to eliminate it, as it does all vestiges of the past, but since it is still attacked it is clearly very persistent. Newspapers in Hong Kong and Taipeh referred to it, so it is very likely that it had some echo in mainland China—a sign of tensions the observer has some difficulty interpreting.

---

*This is what happened, for example, with Li Teh-sheng, the military leader who was transferred and whose attendance at and absence from official ceremonies in April 1974 led to a series of contradictory reports.

The Pekinologist is in a position similar to that of the jigsaw puzzler who is missing a number of pieces and does not know the pictures, or the scientist who is trying to reconstitute a lost species with a few pieces of a skeleton. The chances of error are great. But how can one avoid making mistakes? Experts compare their knowledge and try to come to an agreement; they exchange their interpretations of the evidence and try to work out a common conclusion. It is a question of trying one's luck, humbly but persistently.

Signs for the Investigator

It is like a police inquiry; the evidence and the various pointers, incomplete and contradictory though they are, are gathered and fitted to make the most logical overall picture. There will be no final chapter or definitive explanation, since life is richer than fiction—and there are always new episodes. At best, one can try to put together the most probable overall view and then, setting aside details, get to the essence of the matter—the spirit that moves People's China.

As far as the Year of the Tiger is concerned, this observer-investigator had eight factors from which he worked out his interpretation. With careful consideration, it is possible to spot the one unchanging element among the many that are changing all the time.

1. The Anti-Confucius Campaign

On December 4, 1973 the Peking newspaper *Enlightenments* carried a strange self-criticism by the Chinese philosopher Feng Yu-lan, a historian of philosophy and a well-known expert on Confucius. This dramatically revealed to the world a campaign against the most revered sage of Chinese antiquity which has been growing in intensity ever since. Confucius—who was born 2,525 years ago—was pilloried, and a general order issued: the masses were called on to wage a "people's war" against the philosophy of the old master. Special shelves were set aside in bookshops for anti-Confucius publications, which had been printed in a great hurry. Work groups were once again set up in production units; workers and peasants were taught to refute Confucius, a writer whom most of them were reading for the first time.

After Stalin's death, Soviet leaders who had lived in fear for thirty years dispelled their terror by launching the destalinization campaign. But it seems astounding that 2,500 years after the death of the Sage of Sages, a deconfucianization campaign should have been launched. Is the possible gain worth a national campaign?

2. Changes in the Military High Command

Seven of the eleven regional military commanders were transferred in a matter of a few days; the People's Liberation Army lost its political commissar; Lin Piao had still not been replaced as Defense Minister—or, if it comes to that, as Dauphin. Did these military roundabouts and the continuing vacuum at the top of the High Command mean that tensions were emerging between the military and the civilian population? Or that the political arm had asserted its superiority, that the Party was commanding the guns?

3. War over the Paracels

The Paracels became famous overnight. By invading them and sinking some South Vietnamese warships in the process, China asserted her presence in the South China Sea. Were these few uninhabited little islands, which France had incorporated into Indochina in 1925, worth a naval battle? Had they expected to find oil there? In any event, the affair concerned all countries bordering on the China Sea—North Vietnam, Taiwan, the Philippines, Malaysia and Japan. The question was really one of strategic balance in the region.

4. Sino-Soviet Quarrels

On January 15, 1974, a Chinese called Li Hung-shu was arrested and his confession declaimed: he was a Soviet spy trained in one of the special camps, and he had been caught in the act of passing secret information to five members of the Soviet Embassy, who were immediately expelled from the country. In reprisal, the Soviet government expelled one Chinese diplomat. The two countries once again started hurling accusations at each other, reviving a feud that had been smoldering since 1960. Were they trying to rally the country for national defense?

5. Western Classical Music Condemned

Beethoven and Mozart were called "reactionary" and Schubert was branded a *petit-bourgeois*. The Orchestre de Paris, which was following three other Western orchestras on a tour of China, had to cancel at the last moment. Had Madame Mao—who had apparently sponsored these tours—been discredited?

6. Antonioni and Jean Yanne on the Index

The famous Italian film director Michelangelo Antonioni, who had shot his film *Chung Kuo—China* with the agreement and support of the authorities, was very severely criticized. He was accused of having systematically disparaged China, of having aimed his camera at an old woman's bandaged feet, thereby insulting the dignity of a victim of the old society, of having shown old workshops while neglecting to show modern factories. Antonioni, whom some people in the West accused of complaisance toward China, was a bloody reactionary. As for Jean Yanne, his film *Les Chinois à Paris* was seen as an intolerable affront to the Chinese nation, and in China itself was responsible for launching a xenophobic movement. It looked as though the door was about to close again.

7. *The Purged Returning to Purge*

Was a new Cultural Revolution about to be launched with the help of those who had been purged by the first one and who had just been rehabilitated—people like Teng Hsiao-ping, the former General Secretary of the Party, who was spectacularly reelected to the Central Committee in August 1973 after having been, alongside Liu Shao-chi, one of the principal victims of the Red Guards? This seemed decidedly contradictory. Were the "enemies of the people," who had been eliminated by the first Cultural Revolution, actually going to become the driving force of the second? And who would be the victims?

8. *The Campaign against Aging Cadres*

Red Flag violently criticized certain Party cadres. "There are still some responsible officials whose minds are covered with the dust of the *petite bourgeoisie*," and who, "once they reach high positions, form factions." Was this the sign that the young were making a push against the old? Was Wang Hung-wen, the young No. 3 in the Party apparatus, already on the horizon, or were other "young wolves" thinking of pushing him out?

There are so many indicators and so many questions; there is no clear-cut answer to any of them. The constellation is certainly not the same from one year to the next, but amid all these variables, one can at least make out the constants.

A Westerner Discovers Chinese Amour-propre

Many of the incidents reported in the pages of the Chinese press show how strong the feeling of national dignity still is. The furor caused by the films of Michelangelo Antonioni and Jean Yanne tell a lot about the touchy pride of the Chinese.

One might have expected Antonioni—whom no one could think of as a man of the Right—to be looked upon with approval by the Chinese, but *People's Daily* carried a review denouncing his film as "a grave anti-Chinese incident and an impudent provocation against the Chinese people." Antonioni was accused of defamation—of intentionally distorting reality. The *Jen-min jih-pao* writer gave an example of what he meant. He said that when Antonioni had dealt with Shanghai and its importance as a big industrial town, he had not shown the new shipyard where 10,000-ton cargo ships are being built; all he had shown were "small boats in the distance . . . various odd shots of rudimentary equipment and processes being undertaken by hand." There was nothing in the film about China in the third quarter of the twentieth century, the China of which the Chinese people were proud—and this was taken as an insult.

The Chinese can be surprisingly thin-skinned. It is difficult to believe that by fixing his lens on diverse groups rather than giving a general picture postcard view of Tien An Men Square, Antonioni had "made a deliberate choice that he would present China as a bustling marketplace teeming with people," and had therefore willfully insulted the country and the people. Equally, by choosing low-level lighting, by showing "the waters of the Huang-pu covered in thick fog and the streets of Peking as reflecting a gray light," was Antonioni really trying to "give an impression of misery, desolation, sadness and coldness"? But this is the impression the Chinese reviewer had, or perhaps the impression imposed on him from above. In both cases, the impressions are very significant. They are indicative less of an exacerbated touchiness than of a desire to be recognized and valued on their own terms. China's achievements are worthy of recognition, and as far as the Chinese are concerned they are so evident that justice should be done to them. The Chinese revolution is now a fact which has to be reckoned with. So it is a "scandalous omission" if "throughout this film there is not a single new machine, tractor or decent school to be seen." The writer's exasperation is similar to the feelings we would have if we saw a documentary on France in which the natives all wore Basque berets or Breton coiffes, ate frogs' legs and drank aperitifs outside cafés.

To tell the truth, this reaction from the Chinese might have been expected, and is every bit as revealing as a psychoanalysis.*

The exceptional beauty of the film and the instructive nature of this incident make it worth pushing the investigation further. It points up the basic lack of understanding between Westerners and Chinese. Antonioni

---

*I went to see this Antonioni film and as I came out of the cinema I was asked for my opinion of it—I said I had the most serious reservations about the systematic way revolutionary achievements had been passed over in silence.

seems to have felt quite sincerely that he had made a film in praise of China; the Chinese, on the other hand, saw his film as an act of aggression.

Can the Revolution Be Treated as a Marginal Issue?

Chung Kuo—China presents the Chinese as seen—almost at leisure—by a man with the talent of seeing and letting others see; this is enough in itself to make it something of an event. Yet one cannot see the film without apprehension.

China is so very foreign to us (intrinsically, and because it has for a long time deliberately kept itself that way) that those who give us a glimpse of it have an almost unlimited power. Antonioni's personal bias is formidable, and in this case it is—dare we say—the subject of the film that interests us more than its creator.

Antonioni did not use China as a pretext for anything; he did not choose some facet which satisfied a current concern of his, as he did with the London of *Blow Up* and the United States of *Zabriskie Point*. In his film about China he presents his audience with the raw article, but in a refined form.

The country could hardly be shown better. The pictures are constantly convincing, powerful and beautiful. Truth of course is relative, and one is seeing China through the eyes of a Westerner—one who is amused as well as fascinated by what he sees. He is always kindly disposed to his subject and aware of the limitations of his view of it—beginning with the limitations placed on him by his hosts. As a Westerner, he has a tender affection for people and always puts the reality of the individual before ideologies and social structures. One comes out of the film liking the Chinese, although it is as un-Chinese as could be.

Antonioni's truth is also of course that of an artist, a lover of color and gesture, on whom the humblest of appearances make an impression. China appears as a kaleidoscope of beauty—pictures of Soochow, the Venice of China, faces of children and old people, the peaceful majesty of the Huang-ho, the mysterious elegance of the bicyclist who takes his hands off the handlebars to do exercises, the harmony of the wrestlers going through their movements in detail, the bright colors of the food in the Peking covered market. Also, the long sequence of a Caesarean operation in which the serenity of the mother—who is under acupuncture but awake, smiling and chatting with the surgeons between mouthfuls of pineapple—contrasts with the cruel and bloody cut of the surgeon's knife: here, beauty triumphs over horror.

In contrast to the pleasure the film gives the eye, the soundtrack is disappointing; it is often weak and sometimes inaccurate.

But there is something else that is much more serious. The commentary should show some understanding. It is astonishing that it spurns the explanations offered by the Chinese themselves and the self-evident explanations—and there is hardly any society which is more aware of its own efforts to change or which shows more respect for the myths it has built up for itself. It is a pretty remarkable feat to introduce the country in the space of two hours without mentioning the name of Chairman Mao more than a couple of times, without referring to the worship of him which makes the sacrifices demanded of the people tolerable, without saying a word about the Cultural Revolution and without even mentioning the role of the Party. It is also a challenge and a provocation to present-day China.

Such bias is questionable, because in Chinese society it is purpose and intentions that count above all—that mold actions and the instructions and the judgments that are then passed on them. Antonioni gives an admirable account of the serenity of the Chinese (liberty produces risks and hence anxieties, and the Chinese do not know liberty), but he does not convey the intense atmosphere that makes China the only country in which the word revolution is more than a word, more than a mere pretext.

Instead of giving his own explanation or quoting the Chinese themselves—probably because in his eyes their explanations would create a screen between the truth and our judgment—Antonioni puts the revolution, so to speak, in parentheses and contents himself with seeing how these people live, smile and look at life, giving his audience the opportunity to judge the society the Chinese have made for themselves through these details.

It is impossible to make a clear judgment of Chinese reality after seeing this film. A column of workers or peasants marching to work in step to a whistle, smiling faces shouting slogans, nonchalance on the march—what does all this tell us? The joy of collaboration in a group? The relativity of regimentation? Or is it nothing more nor less than atavistic behavior? To each his own truth. Antonioni does not commit himself. He shows us ducks being force-fed by machines; are they symbols of the Chinese people or simply the objects of a rather cruel sense of fun? Puppet musicians singing "The East Is Red": irony or simply beauty?

Lack of communication is Antonioni's favorite subject. His film vividly conveys the sense of foreignness that overwhelms the Western visitor and it enables the audience to penetrate the far-flung depths of the country and its people, but it does not understand the revolution. Antonioni gave the Chinese the impression that he was denying their national revolution, both as a revolution and as something national.

As a matter of fact, it is difficult for a non-Chinese to present China to other non-Chinese without irritating the Chinese themselves. The furor aroused by Antonioni's film was really due to wounded pride on the part of a people who, although they have broken with their past, still prefer to fall back on it when faced with a challenge from a foreigner. Only a Chinese has the right to judge China.

The Yellow Peril Insult

With the film *Les Chinois à Paris*, the Chinese found themselves in front of another distorting mirror. They reacted very badly to a caricature that was closer to satirical farce than to a comedy of manners or a character comedy. The problem was different, for this was historical fiction and not reportage. In the film, the Chinese have invaded Europe; Paris is being occupied, and all the old occupation characters reappear—the collaborators, the profiteers and the resistance workers. For his material the director drew heavily on the experience of the German occupation of 1940–44, and this served as his model for Paris under Chinese occupation in the year 2000 or so.

The director—a Frenchman—used the Chinese revolution as a pretext for ingenious variations on the eternal theme of relations between the occupier and the occupied. The Chinese government might have done better to refrain from commenting, but it decided to make its reaction public. "The Chinese People's Army is ridiculed and slandered. . . . The parallel between socialist China and fascist Germany is intolerable." Here once again China felt it was being defamed; it was somehow as if the state of tension in which the Chinese lived prevented them from having a sense of humor about it.

The French press—reacting in the normal Western way—saw the Chinese protest primarily as an attack on freedom of expression. Here they failed to understand that the Chinese feel that their revolution, if not beyond challenge from within, is certainly beyond ridicule from outside. The Chinese revolution demands respect because an entire people have devoted their lives to it. The Chinese feel they have the right to respect, and lack of understanding seems scandalous to them; they see it as proof of systematic opposition. The Chinese revolution—in which so much love and willpower have been invested—does not tolerate being unloved.

One cannot deny that the Chinese are sensitive on such matters, but then all people are. Frenchmen are quite ready to laugh when another Frenchman makes fun of them, but they do not accept it so easily from a foreigner. There is more to it, though, for the Chinese have special reasons for being so sensitive. They are aware that they belong to the oldest civilization in the world, and that for one hundred and thirty-five years they have been invaded, colonized and governed by others. All Chinese remember having been unrecognized as a nation; how could they possibly not have a deep national pride?

Moreover, the revival of the old myth of the Yellow Peril could only offend them. Contrary to what we in the West sometimes think, the Chinese sense of superiority stems from being a people that has never sought to conquer the world. In four thousand years of history, they have never ventured beyond the natural boundaries of their civilization, and to apply the term "Yellow Peril" to them is wholly misleading and somewhat grotesque. In 1900, as he was reviewing his troops before they left for China, Kaiser Wilhelm II said: "Peking must be razed to the ground. The whole of Europe is fighting Asia and you are going to protect her from the Yellow Peril. No mercy, no prisoners." It was really Europe fighting against Asia; the poor Chinese were utterly incapable of being a peril to anyone—in fact, they were incapable even of defending themselves when the soldiers arrived from Europe.

As regards "Yellow Peril," China has herself been a victim of it more than any Western country. The first "Yellow Peril" was the Huns, and the Chinese had to build the Great Wall to keep them out. Then there were the Mongols, who invaded and ruled China for a hundred years. The third "Yellow Peril" was the Manchus, who subjugated China for three hundred years. And the fourth was the Japanese, who attacked and occupied part of China. As Chou En-lai said to me, "There is not a single Chinese soldier stationed on foreign territory . . . you can't say the same of every country." The pacificism of the Chinese and the trials and afflictions they have suffered have earned them the right to take jokes like *Les Chinois à Paris* badly.

The Campaign against Imported Music

It is no doubt patriotic backlash that caused the attacks on Western music and the cancellation of tours by the great European orchestras. *People's Daily* carried a violent denunciation of Schubert's *Unfinished Symphony*, which the paper said was a typical work by one of those "*petit-bourgeois* intellectuals who were aware that they were in a political and economic impasse but who did not have the courage to fight, and displayed melancholia, hesitation, pessimism, despair and the desire to escape from social reality." To a Chinese revolutionary, such historical analysis was putting in their rightful place works which were going to be presented as universal masterpieces for the naïve admiration of the Chinese people. Other editorials condemned revisionists "of the Liu Shao-chi type" who wanted "to glorify Western techniques" and to "separate" composers from "the workers, peasants and soldiers" or from "proletarian politics." Once again it is the same reaction of national pride.

Traditional Chinese opera is attacked just as much as Western music. As a way of ridiculing those who still hankered nostalgically after the old Chinese music, *People's Daily* quoted the following anti-Confucian anecdote: Confucius is brought a new type of wine cup. It does not have the traditional shape. Old Confucius examines it suspiciously and mutters grumpily: "This isn't a wine cup, a real wine cup!" Between "Western *petit-bourgeois*" music and old Chinese feudal music there is room for a modern and revolutionary art—an art that is modern *because* it is revolutionary. "Artistic form must be changed when the content changes," says *Red Flag*. The Cultural Revolution opened the way for a new culture which the Chinese revolutionaries will be able to create themselves.

The Rehabilitation of a Tyrant

Undoubtedly more significant even than the attacks on Confucius is the rehabilitation of the builder of the Great Wall, Chin Shih Huang-ti. He put into practice the totalitarian precepts of the School of Laws, the movement which was opposed to the Confucian School. Between 246 and 221 B.C. he united China at the cost of an inexpiable war with the six other princes who ruled over the territory. The emperor, unmoved by the suffering and slaughter, had built up a centralized and authoritarian regime by the sword, and had earned the lasting hatred of the intellectuals for having ordered the burning of all books and for having buried alive those scholars who refused to submit; if some Confucian chroniclers can be believed, he cut off their hands and feet before burying them.

It is odd that present-day political officials with power over the editorial committees of the big Party organs and enough influence to direct a press campaign consider it necessary to pillory a philosopher who died several years before Socrates was born and whose serene figure had served as a model for hundreds of thousands of Chinese over twenty-five centuries. But it is even odder that these same officials should praise a tyrant who lived at the time when Rome was still young and who had been detested by scholars for twenty-two centuries. Did this ostracism on the one hand and this return to favor on the other mark the replacement of persuasion by coercion and self-administration by autocracy? The praising of Chin Shih Huang-ti could be interpreted as a plea for authoritarian centralization and the abolition of the privileges that had hitherto been accorded the local authorities, whose behavior recalled the Confucian attitudes that were being condemned.

The glorification of Chin Shih Huang-ti—who had always been portrayed as a bloodthirsty despot, at least in the Confucian version of history—took place no doubt because, like Mao, he had brought together a China that was powerless to remain a nation.* The campaign against Confucius must be a reminder that, in order to survive, a nation must sometimes sacrifice individuals and place the "broad masses" of manual workers before or *above* the mandarins, scholars and bureaucrats of Confucian society—whom it must sometimes crush like a steamroller.

There Always Has to Be an Enemy

One can see more clearly than ever in these campaigns the determination to provide the Chinese nation with modernized but profoundly national bases. When Chou En-lai said at a banquet, "Social imperialism—that is to say, the Soviets—and those foreigners who are relentlessly hostile to the Chinese people are attacking our campaign. That shows that our action is correct," he was interrupted by a burst of applause from the Chinese guests.

Mao always viewed China as a nation confronted by its adversaries—the Japanese, the Americans and then the Soviets. Today, the Americans are still considered adversaries, but less dangerous by reason simply of their retreats; but the Soviets are even more dangerous, one is told, since they do not look as though they are retreating. It is essential to denounce them while building up images of their strength—this way the Chinese nation builds itself up.

There is still tension between the Soviet Union and China, even though one must not attach too much importance to the various incidents that keep recurring. The expulsion of Russian "spy-diplomats" in January 1974 and the well-publicized arrest of the Soviet agent Liu Hung-shu are merely one episode in the war between the world's secret services. Affairs of this kind are certainly not unique to China. They crop up fairly regularly in the Western democracies without ever creating too much of a stir; they are just symptoms of a state of rivalry that has become accepted as natural. The main Sino-Soviet dispute, though, is of a different kind. Every so often as temperatures rise, troops amass along the common border. In 1969 the American journalist Harrison Salisbury came back from a trip to Siberia and announced that war between the Soviet Union and China was imminent. Five years later, British experts were reckoning that troop concentrations had reached such a level that the explosion could not be far off. Although many observers do not believe that either protagonist would take the risk of starting a war, China—

---

*No doubt this glorification is also aimed at developing the theme of "the struggle between two lines" and replying to Lin Piao's accusation in the "Outline of Project 571" that Mao was "an even worse tyrant than Chin Shih Huang-ti"; Lin, in Confucian terms, had been the perfect sage.

alert as ever on the frontiers of the Empire—"still thinks" of her northern border, even if, in the famous phrase, she "never talks about it."

A Few Small Islands as Symbols of the Integrity of the Empire

When the government in Peking sent troops to occupy the forgotten Paracel islands, was it after—as was unanimously and dogmatically asserted in the Western press—the possibility of oil from the sea? This is a thoroughly Western interpretation of the action—bearing the marks of rationality, economism and concern for short-term advantage. Is it to be believed? The Chinese revolution is irrational, at least in terms of our logic; it places economics second and politics "at the command posts"; and it is not concerned with the present, but with the mainstream of history.

The explanation offered by the Western press is rather like saying of Péguy that he left for the front on the eve of the Battle of the Marne because he wanted to increase the sales of his books. This was certainly one consequence of his death at Villeroy. It is not impossible that one day the Chinese will get oil from the sea around the Paracels, but are they in such a hurry to embark on offshore exploration—which is both costly and chancy—when their own territory has numerous unexploited oil resources? What if they were simply seeking to establish their presence in the China Sea? To show, by occupying islands that long ago were Chinese, that they were taking upon themselves the legacy of the Middle Kingdom, against the two Vietnams, the Philippines, Malaysia and Japan, and to galvanize their army and navy into action to show them how indispensable they are to the safety of the country? What if in order to recover a position that had been held by their ancestors they were craftily seizing a place and a moment where neither the Russians nor the Americans—both preoccupied by the aftermath of the Yom Kippur War—could react?

Advancing the Wheel of History

Chou En-lai has said: "Lin Piao and Confucius were both reactionaries who tried to roll back the wheel of history," a comparison and an expression that are equally revealing. The news from China after the end of 1973 raised this probability—that every effort was being made to revive the flickering revolutionary flame.

The Party organs *People's Daily* and *Red Flag* denounced "the unhealthy practices at work within the organisms of State" in terms which looked very much like an attack on the government. They raised a hue and cry about the "abuses of power" by "elderly cadres." They complained about seniority being the sole criterion for promotion in the Party and in government. They protested by implication the "recuperation" of personalities who had been eliminated by the Cultural Revolution—one of the most prominent being Teng Hsiao-ping, the former General Secretary of the Party and for a long time a close associate of Liu Shao-chi. They criticized the return to "material incentives" and the "pragmatic management of enterprises." Big-character wall posters—the famous *ta-tzu-pao* of the Cultural Revolution—were pasted all over the streets again, extolling fidelity to the Maoist ideal.

For the first time since 1968 *People's Daily* recalled the occasion in 1966 when Mao had received the Red Guards. The Party's theoretical review, *Red Flag*, did not shrink from defending and justifying revolutionary violence. A new slogan appeared which was a rather strange invitation to responsible officials to go "against the stream," an incitement that was very like the principle set out by Mao in 1966, which said that "one must know how to rebel." In fact, there was a resurgence of a revolutionary style closely related to that which was evident during the first year of the Cultural Revolution. Confucius was reproached for having come out in favor of the return to power of personalities who had been rightly ousted; the allegory is clear enough.

Among many other signs are the letters that were published in the newspapers. *People's Daily* carried a letter from a young soldier who publicly criticized himself, saying that he had entered the university "by the back door," through the influence of his father who was a veteran of the Long March. The young man was asking to return to his unit and let someone better qualified have his place. The letter was prefaced by a short note written in a style which led some people to think it may have been written by Mao; it was reminiscent of May 1966, when Mao wrote his own *ta-tzu-pao*. Once again the "base," the "broad popular masses," were making clear their desire to maintain the revolutionary spirit.

Leadership of the Cultural Revolution had almost slipped from Mao's grasp; he had gotten it back in the nick of time. No doubt he had learned from this experience, for in 1974 he took on less dangerous adversaries. Liu Shao-chi and the Party cadres who were the victims of the first movement Mao launched had reacted vigorously, and it had taken at least two years to eliminate them. This counterrevolution had nearly plunged China into civil war. In 1974 Mao relaunched the revolution, because he felt that if it did not advance it would retreat. He launched it against two dead men, whom there was no reason to believe anyone would come forward to defend. Confucius, who had been dead for two and a half thousand years, and Lin Piao, who had been dead for just two and a half years, provided targets sufficiently distant for there to be no fear of the attack rebounding and yet close enough for the campaign launched against them to be capable of mobilizing the masses.

Were twenty-five centuries not time enough for Confucius to become harmless? Who was the real target behind him? Just Lin Piao, the dead man whose elimination had been essential? Or the hydra of capitalism and revisionism?

Certainly one can find many Confucian formulas in the writings of Mao. The *new man* the Maoist revolution seeks to create is—from one point of view—a restoration of the ancient man of whom Confucius provided the model. But at the same time the teachings of the old Master were being tenaciously denounced* as incompatible with the historical necessity of the class struggle.

Confucius is reproached for defending "benevolence" and thereby having helped for two thousand years to maintain feudalism, the domination of the many by the few. "Be benevolent and the people will obey," Confucius wrote. One can take people in and lull them to sleep with "benevolence," and this was why there had to be action. A society does not advance by "benevolence" or "respect for rites" but by a ceaseless class struggle. *The revolution must continue or wither away. It is either permanent, or it is not a revolution at all.*

Unlike other revolutions in history—especially the two biggest, the French revolution and the Russian revolution—the Chinese revolution does not seem to be running out of steam. On the contrary, it still arouses a kind of popular enthusiasm. The masses are still ready for action, and they derive new energy from Mao Tse-tung thought, which is the driving force behind a society which has discovered perpetual motion.

This is undoubtedly the most important thing; too realistic an interpretation—one which explains developments in terms of ambition—is not sufficient. We have seen that just like the other communist regimes, the Chinese regime cannot do without purges, and it presents them in an ideological form. It is rather as if we in France wanted to attack the Prime Minister and instead of mentioning his name we launched a campaign against Descartes (and even Descartes is eight times nearer our own times than Confucius). Behind this camouflage, the clashes between the factions get fiercer.

Observers are often wrong about who is in and who is out of favor at Court. In fact, some observers—particularly in Moscow—had thought that Chou En-lai was being criticized for being too clever and too much the peacemaker, for having been able to quell the Cultural Revolution. But there were other signs that showed that the Prime Minister was imperturbably pursuing his policies of pacification within and opening out to the West. In

---

*For example, in "The Orientation of the Youth Movement" of May 4, 1939 (*Selected Works*, Volume 2, pp. 241–48), Mao makes fun of Confucius for not knowing how to plow the fields or grow vegetables. The man and his teachings are often targets of Mao's jibes.

August 1973, Chou—who, with Wang Hung-wen, had made one of the only two big speeches at the Tenth Party Congress—was the first to give notice that the Cultural Revolution was going to be relaunched.*

But another subtler interpretation which is compatible with the rumors coming out of Moscow should not be altogether ruled out. It is said that Chou En-lai—who was widely regarded as a pure product of the Confucian mandarin society—was at first the target of the anti-Confucius campaign, which had been launched by circles close to Mao, and possibly with the support of Mao himself. Then, using his consummate skill in seizing situations and turning them upside down, Chou took control of the campaign and set himself at its head. In the third phase, he stated that the campaign was aimed *simultaneously* at Confucius and Lin Piao. Then, he diverted it so it was aimed *essentially* at Lin Piao and *secondarily* at Confucius. Thanks to these rapid shifts of accent, he had once again changed the course of history.

It has also been suggested that Madame Mao—known in Taiwan as "the actress Chiang Ching"—was involved. It was she who had allowed the piano into China and it was she who personally received visiting Western orchestras. Schubert and Beethoven banished and the Orchestre de Paris tour canceled—surely these developments were repudiations of Madame Mao's actions?

Madame Mao has certainly played an important role in Chinese politics, but was there any need for all this turmoil in order to reduce her influence? Judging from the ranking order of the Political Bureau, she had been downgraded at the Tenth Congress. Nevertheless, she had withstood the purges that eliminated her companions in the Cultural Revolution struggle, Chen Po-ta and Lin Piao. Surely her position was strong enough that she could withstand other purges? Especially since—as the development of this new campaign showed—people continued to seek shelter behind the figure of Mao in any discussion involving ideas. The Chinese press kept assuring its readers that Chairman Mao was *personally* directing the attacks on Confucius, and whether or not this was correct, it is certain that Mao's personal prestige continued to be the sole guarantee for the success of any campaign to win over public opinion.

The Chinese Crisis of the European Mind

Many signs that have appeared simultaneously indicate a revival of Chinese nationalism. There is the glorification of the builder of the Great Wall, the irritation felt when "bourgeois" culture penetrates China from the

---

*At a banquet on February 24, 1974 Chou En-lai let it be understood that he was taking direction of the movement.

West, the wounded pride caused by indiscreet film cameras, the expulsion of spy-diplomats, and the assertion of Chinese sovereignty by the seizure of deserted rocks in the sea. There are also many good reasons for Westerners to remain restrained and maintain a discreet reserve in the face of such profoundly Chinese reactions. The Chinese regard this new "people's war" as their own affair—just as they did the first "Cultural Revolution." They are a people who have enjoyed forty centuries of glorious civilization and one century of humiliation, so it is hardly surprising that they should consider any Western interference—even intellectual interference—a new attempt at a break-in.

But by a strange reversal—possibly the most surprising there has been in a century which has seen the direction of history change so many times—people in the West are beginning to feel that they are the victims of an interference by the Chinese which is so subtle that it is being brought about without a "break-in."

China, on the whole, seems like a monastic community of eight hundred million people who, without realizing they are doing it, are observing the three vows, practicing equality in work, sobriety, unselfishness, devotion to the public good and selflessness. And all this seems to be achieved by continuous indoctrination, pious incantation willingly and knowingly entered into, and collective idolatry—in fact, by a few very simple techniques. One cannot help being struck by the close affinity with Christian asceticism. The Chinese seem to be mortifying their own flesh, rather as monks do, by fasting, self-deprivation, vigils, working until they drop, controlling their covetous desires, stifling their passions, repressing their concupiscence—all through keeping a constant watch on one another and doing a penance meticulously worked out so as to make their desires submissive and their will incapable of resisting the orders they receive. What if the lofty ambitions and far-reaching effects of the Chinese revolution entailed a collective conversion which, like the Christian conversion, inverts the meaning of the words "liberation" and "alienation"?

What a paradox! The evangelized West has become a consumer, a pleasure-seeker and a lover of the erotic, keen for profit and yet at the same time wasteful, individualistic and anarchic. Non-evangelized China, on the other hand, a country which has been hard on evangelists, shows us that she rejects and denounces this frenzy, that she professes the ascetic virtues, that she cultivates the spirit of poverty, chastity and obedience, and that she is giving birth to an austere and communal breed of human beings. A nation which is officially materialistic is giving a remarkable lesson in indifference to material goods to countries which, in spite of two thousand years of spiritualistic civilization, betray the closest attachment to these same material goods.

The paradox no doubt explains, at least partially, why we are going through what Paul Hazard might have called a *Chinese crisis of the European consciousness.* * The books, accounts and studies of China which are pouring out in quick succession are indicative of more than curiosity; the fascination with China is becoming so intense now that it must be a sign of real uneasiness. Previously, it was mainly a question of gaining more knowledge and understanding of the most populous and mysterious of states. Now, as was the case to a much lesser extent in the eighteenth century, China serves as a reference point in an anxious questioning by the West of its own values. China has become an example, and the West has to adopt a definite position toward it. It is as if the West feels itself being insidiously invaded by a feeling of guilt about having lost a purity and an absolute—which the Chinese have been able to find. Today, as we watch the way the Chinese live, we are asking questions about ourselves.

---

*The reference is to the author of a study of the revolution in European thought at the end of the seventeenth century and beginning of the eighteenth century, *La Crise de la conscience européenne*, first published in Paris in 1935 and translated by J. Lewis May in the Penguin Books edition as *The European Mind, 1680–1715* (TRANSLATOR'S NOTE).

28

The Awakening of China:
A "Model" or a "Miracle"?

In the first half of the twentieth century China saw the various plans it tried to implement fail one after another, until the day when the conditions were right for the only remaining one to succeed—the only one, it seems, that was suitable. The leaders of the Empire before 1911, then the leaders of the Republic, Yuan Shih-kai, Sun Yat-sen, Chiang Kai-shek and Mao Tse-tung, were united on one essential point: China could be governed only by a dictatorial and nationalist regime.

There was nothing more urgent than to get China—which had collapsed beneath the weight of the Western Powers—on its feet again. Strict supervision of the population was essential. Those Chinese who had been educated in the West or who had studied European and American history felt most acutely the severe underdevelopment of their country and the total disintegration that threatened it. The time that had been lost since the nineteenth century—especially in relation to Japan—ruled out more gradual solutions.

It is significant that the three governments which were ruling in China before the final triumph of communism—the communist government of Yenan, the nationalist government of Chungking, and the "collaborationist" government of Nanking—were all led by successors of Sun Yat-sen. Mao Tse-tung, Chiang Kai-shek and Wang Ching-wei—who had all emerged from the same Cantonese seraglio—were agreed on the aim: a nationalist revolution. They differed only on how to achieve it. Should the system use the support of the Japanese in order to throw out the Western invaders, that of the Westerners in order to drive out the Japanese, or that of the partisans in the mountains in order to get rid of them both?

Many Western observers have expressed their surprise that the Chinese people rallied to a totalitarian rather than a capitalist regime, albeit a corrupt one. "The choice between Chiang Kai-shek and Mao Tse-tung was the choice between corruption and tyranny; the surprising thing is that so many Chinese chose the latter." In reality, at the end of the Second World War the Chinese did not feel that they could choose between liberty and slavery. In any case, they could not escape some form of despotism. But the visible collusion between the Kuomintang and a pleasure-seeking minority of landowners and bankers with foreign links contrasted vividly with the austerity of the Red Army; the people had only two possible options: generalized corruption or a struggle for purity. In other words, they could accept decay through fear of the revolution, or reject it through acceptance of the revolution and its attendant violence.

People will ask: "How can you logically say that there was no solution for China other than communism, without yourself believing in the doctrine?" It is a question of historical observation, not ideological belief. I am not saying—in the abstract or in absolute terms—that Maoist-type communism is the only practical path for a feudal and underdeveloped country such as China to follow. I am simply saying that in 1949, after the collapse of the Kuomintang, the only group capable of taking China in hand, uniting the country, and liberating her from her past was the Party of resistance to the Japanese, the Party of the guerrillas who were fighting the feudal lords, and the Party of the pioneers who had actually brought about Liberation in the province of Shensi. This was the only group which was ready to step in.

People's China is always condemned for denying individual rights, but does this concept have any meaning in such a historical context? And if so, what meaning? Criticisms of this kind are based on Western values, not on Chinese values. Just as happiness is relative, so is liberty. The revolution has given the Chinese a collective liberty of which they were deprived when their country was a dismembered vassal state; it has also given them some individual liberties of which many people are unaware. It has "liberated" the peasants from the landowners, the hungry from famine, the debtors from the usurers, sons from the despotism of their fathers, women from the tyranny of their husbands, civil servants from the prevarications of their bosses, the people from poverty. The irresistible force that pushed the masses to join in the campaign being led by the Red Army was the hope of liberation; no one can say that this hope has been wholly frustrated.

Most Chinese are aware that their new destiny as a group holds more promise than before. When they talk about the "Liberation," for the majority of them—in spite of certain appearances—it is a reality. It took the West several centuries to reach its present level of development; China is doing it in just a few decades. The effort demanded of them is so superhuman and the redeeming role of suffering so cruel that the Chinese cannot but feel that they are emerging from the shadows into the light. They know that their sacrifices are providing their country with the shortest route from the Middle Ages to modern times.

Mao was anxious to ensure that China would enjoy the greatest degree of harmony. He reestablished a balance within society by giving the manual workers security and dignity; this could only be to the detriment of the intellectuals and the bourgeois and also to a very large number of artisans, traders and employees who were among the relatively privileged classes of society. Westernized China was merely a fringe—albeit a massive one—composed of the privileged who had survived the fall of the old regime and had formed again under the new. By giving priority to rural expansion, Mao reestablished a biological balance in a nation which was disintegrating; this has been to the detriment of the townspeople. By getting everyone back to the starting line, he gave equal opportunities to all, handicapping those who would have made the best showing in the race.

One must expect the victims of such a leveling process to resent its harshness and to try to escape it. Is this a reason for ignoring the fact that a new society is being built in accordance with a coherent overall plan?

It is a question that is meaningless, like wondering whether China's economy would have grown as fast, or even faster, under Chiang Kai-shek's regime. Economic progress is just one aspect of the problem. The Chinese communists reckoned that the need for independence was far more urgent than the need for prosperity. Better for China the fate of the raw-boned wolf, who is free to move about, than that of the well-fed dog wearing a collar; moreover, it is by no means certain that China would have achieved greater prosperity even if she had sacrificed some of her independence.

Of the changes that have convulsed China, the most profound is the change in her behavior toward other countries. She has solved her problems *herself*. She has become a nuclear power on her own. She has joined the United Nations in spite of American and Soviet hostility. This is much more important than if she had during this period increased her annual per capita income by a few dollars—assuming this would have been possible.

From Utopia to Reality

Some Western idealists dream of reconciling collectivism and liberalism. Others believe that a marriage between Marxism and Christianity is both possible and desirable.

Would it have been possible to find a way of profiting from the achievements of communism without suffering its constraints? Of establishing the dictatorship of the exploited without liquidating the exploiters? Of achieving absolute equality without the deprivation of liberties?

Sun Yat-sen had already succumbed to this temptation to reconcile everything. He accepted Marx's views on social evolution, but rejected violent transformation. He wanted state socialism without class struggle. The struggle which should be waged should not oppose one class and another, but "the people as a whole against poverty." The Kuomintang had taken over this theory: Marxism, yes, but without the dictatorship of the proletariat.

Others wonder whether, once the dictatorship of the proletariat is established and the former ruling classes are liquidated, there might not be a return to a more liberal regime. Unfortunately, experience shows that trying to introduce liberties into a system which excludes them is like trying to square the circle. Ever since 1917 every attempt to liberalize a communist regime has been followed by a period in which the controls were reimposed.

In People's China it has happened at least three times, not always on the same scale but certainly with the same kind of results: in 1956 and 1957, when the "Hundred Flowers" campaign loosened tongues; in May 1962, when the people living near the border with Hong Kong were given the freedom to leave; and between 1966 and 1969, when the Cultural Revolution all but swept the lot away. Each time the regime loosened the reins, the horse bolted.

These historical facts have been obscured by the half-digested Marxism spouted—usually without understanding—by so many intellectuals, teachers, journalists and even priests. Their generosity of spirit leads them to forget that "the class struggle is not a fancy dress ball."

If a Marxist society accepted political pluralism, freedom of expression and freedom of conscience, it would be engulfed in untenable contradictions. Each type of society creates its own universe in which everything is interdependent.

In Hankow in 1927, Borodin—in conversation with Anna Louise Strong—likened the Leftist intellectuals faced with the military power of Wuhan to "a rabbit confronted by a cobra, trembling, knowing that he is going to be eaten and yet rooted to the spot, hypnotized." This comparison is as valid as ever. Faced with a Party which is perfectly organized for the conquest of power, the "intellectuals' great hearts" have, in Borodin's view, always been doomed to "the fate of the rabbit."

The intellectual's habit of analyzing things tends to lead to some of the details being forgotten, and it is almost always those details which change everything and which only a global view—even if it is blurry—can make out.

The dictatorship of the proletariat is essentially totalitarian. Any "royal path" is narrow. Anything worthwhile has to be paid for. China's success has something of the miraculous about it. But it is a miracle that is hard to bear, and a miracle that is restricted to China.

A miracle? The Chinese leaders do not like this expression. According to Marxist doctrine, there is no such thing. Everything is inevitable. There is no part for freedom to play—not even with leaders, for, however great they may be, they are mere playthings in the hands of history.

However, the more one studies the development of the Chinese Revolution from 1911 to 1949, the more one is struck by the extraordinary coincidence of factors from which the regime has profited. Let us think just how many fortuitous circumstances came together to make its success:

an empire which had for thousands of years prided itself on being the center of the universe had this pride wounded unbearably by foreign domination;

a vast, overpopulated territory was in the dark ages of illiteracy and feudalism;

a poor proletariat which was no longer able to feed itself had reached such a state of despair that it no longer feared violence;

the traditional ideology which until then had explained everything and had never been held in question had collapsed;

a man of genius was able to embody the aspirations of his country.

If one modified just one of the factors in the equation, it would change it completely. For example, if the Chinese were crammed into a small country—like Taiwan, Singapore or Hong Kong—communism would not be the only solution. The equation would also change if the territory and population density were much as they are now, but the Chinese were either a more apathetic or a more religious race—in India, for example, the expectations aroused so far by communism have not been sufficient to mobilize the nation.

Even if there was a certain *fatality* about it, one must admit that it was dependent on the combination of a large number of circumstances. In the struggle against Japan, China lost a lot of blood, but she found the national solution to her national problems—a solution which sprang from the coming together of an unequaled people, extreme circumstances and an exceptional man.

The Model Nation

By educating the Chinese masses, the "Great Teacher" managed to give them a higher opinion of themselves. He addressed himself to their energy, which he kept high, and their spirit, which he protected from humiliation, rather than to their bodies, which he had removed from the stranglehold of poverty. He ensured China her military, diplomatic and economic independence. He gave renewed significance to the traditional values by adapting them to the contemporary context.

Once they recovered their self-respect, the Chinese could allow themselves the modesty and humility of the proud. At the time of the "Great Leap Forward," the Chinese still had the arrogance that results from wounded pride. Romantic optimism was no doubt necessary in order to galvanize the masses: they were told that they were going to catch up with Britain in ten years. Now, China's successes are so striking that it is her backwardness that is constantly being emphasized, although the gap is already being narrowed.

If China is now after so many years beginning to open up to the outside world, it is no doubt because she has acquired the openness of mind of those who are successful. Regained self-confidence enables one to have a certain confidence in others, even if this double confidence is still fragile enough that it can be revoked at any moment.

Untransposable Experiences

It is hard not to believe in ethnic realities when you see how the Chinese live and when you study their past. The rapid changes in their history in the past half-century and the new organization which the revolution has given them seem to have had very little effect on the human context within which they move. Marx has not replaced Montesquieu. Three factors are still as important as ever. They are *race,* or rather ethnic group, *environment,* and actual historical *moment*. Race encompasses the customs passed on from one generation to the next, the collective attitude of mind, a people's memory embedded as it is in a common subconscious—in short, the indestructible cultural matrix of which certain morphological or anatomical characteristics are merely the outward and visible signs. The environment includes the geographical environment, the level of development, size and the physical and social climate. And the moment comprises the contingencies and men able to turn them to advantage.

Even if the internationalist pretensions of Marxism have usually led Maoist ideology to play down China's special peculiarities, everything in the thought and actions of Mao echoes them. The Chinese people have inherited not only "the most brilliant civilization," but also the civilization "which is famous throughout the world for its endurance in misfortune and its passion for work." Many Chinese think—and not without good reason—that their people are superior to others, simply by virtue of the fact that they are efficient, disciplined and hard-working. "We built the People's Congress Palace in nine months"; "we have developed the nuclear bomb"; "we have built the great bridge over the Yangtse which the Russians and Americans said was impossible." The Chinese people are admirable, passionate and patient, ambitious and modest, proud and obedient; they have enormous stamina and never give in, yet they are always ready to laugh and joke. They have a very civilized degree of courtesy, no matter how humble their social milieu.

Given these special characteristics, can the model which the Chinese have made for China be transposed just as it is for a people in a different geographical situation with different historical conditions? Only a people with similar ethnic character, similar circumstances, and as great a personality to lead them could try the experiment. No people fill the bill but the Chinese between 1921 and 1972.

A Model for the Chinese

The Chinese model is a model for the Chinese. Even that is a great deal —a living model which brings together people in all conditions from all provinces. It is a model which respects and at the same time breaks with tradition, a model which is always being reformed, a model through which Mao found new solutions to problems without real precedents.

If there is one omission in Marx's analysis, it is that of human attitudes. For Marx there is no difference between economic agents engaged in the same production process. Marxist theoreticians behave rather like the imperious woman who visits her hairdresser and points her finger at a model in a style book, saying: "Give me that one"; it is impossible to persuade her that her hair and the shape of her face do not lend themselves to it.

This kind of utopia has always inspired revolutionary thought. All men are not exactly the same. It is fine to proclaim equality and to try to bring about equal rights and equal opportunities, but to suppose that all men are born with the same talents and all people have the same abilities is idiotic. Men are different; people are unique; experiences are untransposable. Both prophetic racism, such as that of a Gobineau, a Houston Stewart Chamberlain or a Hitler, and a kind of primary anti-racism have led either to exaggerating or to minimizing the difficulties which come into conflict when societies draw closer together—but never to ironing them out.

Here and there ethnologists are trying to shake the conventional idea that to acknowledge the plurality of the races is to approve of the gas ovens. Claude Lévi-Strauss created something of a scandal when he dared to confess at a conference that, having completely mastered his science, he had finally come to the conclusion that the races did exist. "The more I see the East, the more I distrust the demagogy in internationalism," explained one famous anthropologist in a letter he had not dared to publish during his lifetime.

To be aware that one is different, to accept differences, and not to claim the right to impose one's way on others or to copy others requires a degree of wisdom to which one can hardly hope to aspire.

Arguing in the abstract, one leaves aside the deep-rooted motivations behind the successes of the Chinese revolution. The Maoist system excels in getting its energy from group incentives. Trying to apply the same rules to other societies—or even trying to keep what is attractive in the Chinese model and discard what is offensive—is like trying to transplant a shrub without its compost and its roots.

Those who see the Chinese model as a way of delivering themselves from injustice and suffering must realize that they will not save themselves by using imported recipes. The Chinese model does not even solve the difficulties of the Chinese; it has some virtue for them only because they make it an act of continuous creation and a demand upon themselves. As the Mother Superior of Georges Bernanos's Carmelites would have said, "It is not the rules that keep us, but we who keep the rules."

With these reservations, the Chinese revolution is undoubtedly the most extraordinary experiment of modern times—and perhaps of all time— as well as the most exciting to watch. It is virtually impossible to conduct laboratory-type experiments in the social sciences, but the human laboratory of China is an inexhaustible object of study.

Beyond the Cultural Revolution and the stunned reactions it provoked, beyond the spectacular diplomatic meetings, and beyond the rivalries for power, China has embarked on the most radical revolutionary adventure any society has ever known. Transformations which would seem incredible to us have become possible in China.

"I am most grateful to China," said Teilhard. "By her immensity, her enormous size, she helped expand my thought and raise it to a global height." If he could return there now, perhaps he might add: "By her passionate will to create a more just universe and to change man, by the courage with which she bears sacrifices which would seem intolerable to us, by the challenge she sets before us."

APPENDIXES

CHRONOLOGY OF THE CHINESE REPUBLIC AND REVOLUTION (1911–1965)

The Bourgeois Republic (1911–1927)

October 10, 1911
Revolution in Wuchang. Installation of a revolutionary government. The revolt spreads rapidly; in fifty days, fourteen of the eighteen provinces declare their independence from the Manchus.

January 1, 1912
Chinese republic set up in Nanking. Sun Yat-sen—back from the United States—becomes President of the Republic. Gregorian calendar adopted. Prince Regent Chun calls in General Yuan Shih-kai, who claims full power.

February 12, 1912
General Yuan secures the abdication of the child-emperor.

February 15, 1912
Sun Yat-sen resigns; Yuan succeeds him. Sun Yat-sen goes into opposition and sets up his own party, the Kuomintang, the national party of the people, with the program "government of the people, by the people, for the people"; it wins a majority in the elections.

April 8, 1913
Parliament meets in Peking. Faced with opposition there, Yuan Shih-kai dissolves Parliament and bans the Kuomintang. Sun Yat-sen takes refuge in Japan.

1914

Japan declares war on Germany and seizes German concessions and property in China, particularly in Shantung.

January 18, 1915

Japan presents Peking with "Twenty-one Demands" and seeks to make China a Japanese protectorate. Yuan negotiates in vain. An anti-Japanese movement develops throughout the country.

1915–March 23, 1916

Yuan Shih-kai proclaims himself emperor. There is opposition from the republicans and a revolt of the generals. Yuan is driven out, after a reign that had lasted less than 100 days. He dies in June 1916.

1916

Beginning of the anarchic period of the warlords. A nominal government exists in Peking. Sun Yat-sen has established a republic in Canton. Military chiefs ruling the various states are in continual conflict with one another.

1918–1919

175,000 Chinese workers are sent to France to help the Allies; four hundred students go too, among them Chou En-lai and Chen Yi. Mao Tse-tung accompanies them to Shanghai.

1919

May Fourth Movement

First big demonstration of nationalism—Peking university students and then people in other towns demonstrate violently against the provisions of the Treaty of Versailles, which transferred the Germans' rights in the province of Shantung to Japan. Students', merchants' and workers' strikes. Some intellectuals who are hostile toward the Western Powers turn to Soviet Russia, which renounces the czarist regime's acquisitions in China (but not the territorial conquests in Siberia and the maritime provinces).

1921

At the Washington conference, the Great Powers demand that Japan withdraw from Shantung.

July 1, 1921

Chinese Communist Party founded in Shanghai; twelve people attend the first congress, at least six of whom were later to leave: Chang Kuo-tao, Chen Kung-po, Chen Tan-chiu, Chen Wang-tao, Chou Fo-hai, Ho Shu-heng, Li Han-chun, Li Ta, Liu Jen-ching, Mao Tse-tung, Pao Hiu-sheng, Tung Pi-wu and Chen Tu-hsiu. The real founder of the Party—and future "renegade"—

Chen Tu-hsiu is elected General Secretary, and Mao Tse-tung is elected Secretary of the Communist Party in Hunan.

1921–1922
Communist cells and sections of the Chinese Communist Party are set up in France (the official date is July 1922), Belgium and Germany.

1923–1927
First Common Front between the Kuomintang and the Communist Party, resulting from the agreement between Sun Yat-sen and Lenin's representative Joffe, who promises Soviet aid (Joint Declaration of January 26, 1923). The communists are admitted as members of the Kuomintang.

1923
Third Congress of the Communist Party (Canton); Mao Tse-tung becomes a member of the Central Committee and head of the organization bureau.

1924
Soviet Republic of (Outer) Mongolia proclaimed.

1925
"May Thirtieth Movement": a vast campaign of anti-foreign agitation and strikes. Death of Sun Yat-sen. Chiang Kai-shek—with the support of the Soviet advisers—succeeds him as head of the Kuomintang. Mao organizes the peasants in Hunan and writes "Analysis of the Classes in Chinese Society."

1925–1926
"Coup of March 20, 1926"
Chung-shan gunboat incident near Canton: Chiang Kai-shek strikes out against communists. Back in Canton, Mao becomes director of the Peasant Movement Training Institute, with the tacit agreement of the Kuomintang. In 1924 the Chinese Communist Party had 300 members; by 1927 it has 57,900.

The First Civil War (1927–1936)

1927
In his "Report on an Investigation of the Peasant Movement in Hunan," Mao declares that the peasants are "the main force of the revolution." This is rejected by the Central Committee of the Chinese Communist Party. Mao is thrown out of the Political Bureau.

April

Chiang Kai-shek launches an offensive against the communists in the big cities. Communists are crushed in Shanghai. The Party goes underground.

1928

Chiang Kai-shek enters Peking. Military dictatorship throughout China. Mao Tse-tung and Chu Teh, who have found refuge in the mountains of Hunan and Kiangsi, form the first "Red Army" and set up a local soviet.

1929

Britain gives China some of her concessions. Mao and Chu Teh proclaim a "Soviet Government" in Kiangsi.

1930

Agreement between France and China under which China recognizes France's rights in Indochina in exchange for her concessions. Conflict between Mao and the head of the Political Bureau, Li Li-san, over peasant and urban insurrection. Chiang Kai-shek's new offensive against the communists; Mao's wife and sister are executed. New communist setbacks in their offensive against towns in central China (Changsha, Wuhan, Nanchang).

1931

Japan invades Manchuria and sets up the Manchukuo. First All-China Congress of Soviets meets in Juichin: Mao is appointed President of the First Government of the Chinese Soviet Republic (in Kiangsi), and Chu Teh is appointed commander-in-chief.

1933

The Japanese occupy part of Hopeh province.

October 1934–October 1935

The Red Army of Kiangsi—threatened with encirclement by the troops of Chiang Kai-shek—undertakes the Long March with Mao and Chu Teh at its head; 8,000 miles were covered in a year, and the March ended—after many lengthy detours—in the Paoan region in North Shensi.

1935–1936

Other Red Armies embark on other Long Marches to rejoin Mao and his group.

December 1936

"Anti-Japanese Soviet" government installed in Yenan under the presidency of Mao.

Common Front between the Kuomintang and the Communist Party against Japan (1937–1947)

December 1936
The Sian Incident. Chiang Kai-shek—a prisoner of his subordinate, Marshal Chang Hsueh-liang—is persuaded by Chou En-lai to promise that he will stop fighting the communists and turn against the Japanese.

1937
The Japanese invade Northern China and the Shanghai region.

1940
Chiang Kai-shek and his government—who have been driven back into Szechwan—establish the seat of the central government in its main town, Chungking.

1940–1941
The agreement between the communists and Chiang Kai-shek breaks down.

1942
Communist Party "rectification" movement; among others, the pro-Soviet members are among those who are "remolded."

1943
Liu Shao-chi praises Mao for having "created a Chinese form of Marxism." According to Chou En-lai, the Communist Party has 800,000 members.

1945
The Seventh Congress of the Party announces that there are 1,200,000 members. Treaty of Alliance between the Russians and Chiang Kai-shek. After the defeat of Japan, the Red Army occupies Northern China and Manchuria until the arrival of the Nanking troops supported by the United States.

Second Civil War between Communists and Nationalists (1947–1949)

The communists continue to back up their military action with active propaganda among the peasant masses (the themes: nationalism and agrarian reform). The Russians maintain their official support for Chiang Kai-shek.

1948
Marshal Lin Piao defeats Chiang Kai-shek's troops in Manchuria.

January 1949
The Red Army occupies Peking.

1949
Chiang Kai-shek—his troops routed—withdraws to Taiwan.

Founding of the People's Republic of China (1949–1957)

1949–1952
New institutions set up: the "New Democracy"
The communists set about eliminating their opponents and beginning the ideological transformation of the masses.

October 1, 1949
Official Proclamation of the Republic. Mao becomes Chairman.

1950
Sino-Soviet Treaty of Alliance. Korean War: under Soviet pressure, the Chinese send "People's Volunteers." Taiwan passes under the military protection of the United States. Agrarian reform.

1953–1957
Economic construction gets underway.

1953
Korean armistice. Death of Stalin.

1954
Khrushchev's first visit to Peking.

1956–1957
"Hundred Flowers" period:
In an attempt to rally the intellectuals, the Party promises them more liberal treatment. Mao launches a "Party rectification" movement. Its purpose: to get rid of the shortcomings of "sectarianism, bureaucratism and subjectivism" through criticism and self-criticism. The movement degenerates in a few weeks into an explosion of discontent. It is followed by a period of harsh repression and retrogression. Hundreds of thousands of intellectuals are sent to forced labor in the country.

Economic Acceleration and Uncertainty (1958–1965)

1958
Second Five-Year Plan. Year of the "Great Leap Forward" (which aimed to achieve the objectives of the Five-Year Plan in two years). Creation of people's communes. Khrushchev withdraws unconditional nuclear support from China. China refuses to place herself under Soviet military command.

1959–1962
Period of serious economic difficulties.

1959
Mao Tse-tung hands over the Chairmanship of the Republic to Liu Shao-chi, but remains Chairman of the Party.

August
Eighth plenum of the Chinese Communist Party Central Committee is held in Lushan. Confrontation between "Rightists" and "Leftists." Marshal Peng Teh-huai, the Minister of National Defense, is disgraced.

July 1960
Moscow recalls all Soviet advisers and technicians. The Chinese openly call Khrushchev a "revisionist."

1961
Chou En-lai walks out of the Twenty-Second Congress of the Communist Party of the Soviet Union in Moscow when Khrushchev denounces the Albanian party. The three harvests of 1959, 1960 and 1961 have been bad ones. Famine.

September 1962
Tenth plenum of the Party Central Committee in Lushan. Ideological hardening: the "socialist education movement" is launched to raise the revolutionary spirit of the intellectuals and peasants. The cult of Mao Tse-tung thought develops. Ideological reorientation of the army by Lin Piao.

1963–1965
Economic convalescence.

1963
Peking strengthens its ideological campaign toward the revolutionary movements in the Third World. Chou En-lai visits Africa.

January 1964
On the initiative of General de Gaulle, France and China decide to exchange ambassadors. The Sino-Soviet rift deepens.

CHRONOLOGY OF THE CULTURAL REVOLUTION AND ITS "THERMIDORIAN REACTION" (1966–1973)

The complex nature of the events which marked the Cultural Revolution— from November 1965 to April 1969—defies any attempt at real classification. The way I have chosen to present them below is no less arbitrary than any other, and its aim is to catalogue the main ideas and events in as logical a way as possible.

The Preliminary Offensive (November 1965–August 1966)

Summer 1964
Festival of Peking Opera.

November 10, 1965–April 1966
Reaction to Wu Han's allegory:
On Mao's instigation, the Shanghai press violently criticizes the writer, historian and Deputy Mayor of Peking, Wu Han, for his allegorical play denouncing the misdeeds of autocratic rule, *Hai Jui dismissed from office*—a transparent allusion to the elimination of Marshal Peng Teh-huai, who had dared to criticize Mao at the Lushan plenum in 1959 over the "Great Leap Forward." Peng Chen, the Mayor of Peking and a member of the Political Bureau, tries to stem the flood of criticism of Wu Han; in February he publishes his Outline Report on the "Current Academic Discussion."

April–May 1966
Mao instigates agitation in the universities:
The attacks are against Teng To, the former editor-in-chief of the *People's Daily*, and the Peking press, which is controlled by the Mayor, Peng Chen.

May 16
A Central Committee circular, attributed to Mao, announces the revocation of Peng Chen's February Report and gives the current discussions a new

dimension: the proletarian struggle must spread from the artistic and literary arena to the political, and must turn its attention to the representatives of bourgeois revisionism who have edged their way into the Party, the government and the army.

May 25
The dispute takes root in the universities: the "first national Marxist-Leninist *ta-tzu-pao*," at Peita University, violently criticizes the Rector, Lu Ping, and the two men responsible for university affairs in the municipality of Peking—all three of them friends of Peng Chen.

June–July 1966
Preparations for the big offensive:
The Party leaders who were the targets of the May Sixteenth Circular—especially the President of the Republic, Liu Shao-chi, and the General Secretary of the Central Committee, Teng Hsiao-ping—try to tap and direct the intellectual agitation, particularly by setting up "work groups." Peita University passes under the control of the future Red Guards. University courses are suspended. Mao Tse-tung returns to Peking after a voluntary absence of nearly two months intended to allow the enemies of the current movement to reveal themselves; he resumes leadership of the Central Committee.

The Difficult Start (August 1966–December 1966)

August 1–12, 1966
The "Sixteen-Point Decision" gives the
green light to the Cultural Revolution:
The August Eighth Resolution of the eleventh plenum of the Central Committee—known as "the Sixteen Points"—officially launches the Cultural Revolution. The "work groups" are condemned. Cultural Revolution groups are set up instead. The masses are hurled into the attack on revisionist elements in the Party. Lin Piao becomes Vice-Chairman of the Party, replacing Liu Shao-chi, who is dropped to eighth place in the Political Bureau. Chou En-lai stays third.

August–November 1966
The Red Guards' assault on the Party bureaucracy:
Several hundred thousand Red Guards march past in Tien An Men Square on August 18, in the presence of Mao. They make journeys all over the country, purging the Party cadres in the towns and destroying vestiges of the feudal past (monuments and works of art). The movement starts reaching the

factories and the managers, and then extends to the peasant class. Liu Shao-chi is forced to make a public self-criticism on October 23. But Leftist excesses and divisions appear within the Red Guard movement; the Party apparatus is paralyzed.

Great Tribulations (January 1967–September 1967)

January–February 1967
The working class joins in:
The movement spreads to the whole working class, especially in Shanghai, where the struggles are very violent. On February 5 the Shanghai Commune is set up; it has a Leftist character and takes as its model the Paris Commune. Anarchy is dealt with either by direct intervention from the army—as was the case in several towns—or by "great alliances" which bring together representatives of the masses, the cadres and the army.

March–August 1967
Anarchy reaches its height:
There are more and more bloody clashes in all parts of the country. Real armed insurrections in Wuhan and Canton. The revolutionary committees have difficulty setting themselves up; the Leftists start attacking Chou En-lai. Splits appear at all levels. Liu Shao-chi makes another public self-criticism.

September 1967
The army's hour:
Chou En-lai does his utmost to restore order; the army is given very broad charge of maintaining production and sorting out local problems.

Mao's Victory (September 1967–October 1968)

September 1967–January 1968
Mao Tse-tung thought becomes the instrument of the anti-bureaucratic struggle:
Mao returns to Peking from the provinces and strikes simultaneously at the Left and the Right. He gives Chou En-lai his full support. An attempt is made to set up revolutionary committees more speedily. On October 1 Lin Piao announces periods of Mao Tse-tung thought study.

February–July 1968
A moment's remission for the bureaucratic opposition:
The Liu Shao-chi line tries to reestablish itself, with the help of the errors of

the Leftists. Mao launches an appeal for the defense of the revolutionary committees.

July–October 1968
Fall of Liu Shao-chi:
The revolutionary committees are installed throughout the country and form a tighter and tighter network. The twelfth plenum of the Central Committee is held from October 13 to 31; Liu Shao-chi is dismissed and expelled from the Party. Mao Tse-tung has won his case, without letting Leftist extremism get the better of him.

The Thermidorian Reaction—The Return to Order (October 1968–Spring 1973)

While preparations are underway for the Ninth Congress of the Chinese Communist Party, a whole series of reforms begins to affect economic, administrative and university life. The Ninth Congress takes place between April 1 and 23, 1969. It elects a new Central Committee and adopts new statutes. Also in 1969 there are clashes on the border between China and the Soviet Union. Throughout 1970, China nurses her wounds, while Leftists keep a number of strong positions, among them the second place in the hierarchy, held by Marshal Lin Piao.

July 1971
Announcement of the outcome of secret negotiations about President Nixon's visit to China. This new orientation of Chinese diplomacy brings internal tensions in its wake: the Leftist opposition comes into the open, and leads to the elimination and disappearance of Lin Piao (September 13, 1971).

October 25–26, 1971
China admitted to the United Nations.

January 1972
People's Daily editorial on January 1 deals with China's social and economic situation. Death of Marshal Chen Yi.

February 1972
President Nixon's visit to Peking.

July 1972
Maurice Schumann visits China—to be followed by Herr Walter Scheel (October), Sir Alec Douglas-Home (November) and Signor Medici (January

1972). China insists on the need for Europe to unite politically to counter the designs of the U.S.S.R.

Summer 1972
Official announcement of the elimination of Lin Piao.

September 1972
The Japanese Prime Minister, Kakuei Tanaka, visits Peking.

February 1973
The United States Secretary of State, Henry Kissinger, visits Peking: agreement to set up "liaison offices" in Peking and Washington, embassies in all but name. Paris: international conference on Vietnam. The first big conference in which China has taken part since the 1961–62 conference on Laos.

March 1973
With the establishment of diplomatic relations between China and Spain, all European countries—with the exception of Ireland, Portugal and the Vatican—have official links with Peking. China now has diplomatic relations with eighty-eight countries.

January 8, 1976
Premier Chou En-lai dies.

September 9, 1976
Chairman Mao Tse-tung dies. The end of an era.

October 14, 1976
Hua Kuo-Feng succeeds Mao Tse-tung as Chairman of the Chinese Communist Party, and is also named Chairman of the Military Commission and Prime Minister. This constitutes an unprecedented combination of positions in the government, the army and the Party—a combination which no Chinese leader, including Mao, has ever before held.

WHAT IS THE GROSS NATIONAL PRODUCT OF PEOPLE'S CHINA?

The World Bank estimated China's G.N.P. for 1968 at 58 billion dollars (*Trends in Developing Countries*, 1971); the per capita G.N.P. works out at 83 dollars on an estimated population of 730 million. In the same year France's

G.N.P. was 105 billion dollars, a per capita rate of 2,406 dollars. On the basis of these figures, then, the average Chinese is twenty-five times poorer than the average Frenchman, fourteen times poorer than the average Japanese and five times poorer than the average citizen of Uruguay. There are a number of reasons to doubt the validity of these figures and comparisons:

(1) They are not based on certain and quantified information. The most recent Chinese statistics are from ten years ago.

(2) The evaluation in dollars is based on exchange rates, which are in turn based on international trade—that is, the value of the products and services which constitute this trade. These prices are plainly higher than the real prices within the country; this is particularly true of agricultural products in underdeveloped countries. The corrective factor which has to be used is particularly high in the case of China, a country that has a policy of very low prices for all basic consumer products. In other words, the comparison of production in terms of dollars is not a comparison of buying power but of living standards. The World Bank itself says that a correction of this kind, made in 1959, reduced the difference between the per capita G.N.P. of the United States and India from 30:1 to 12:1.

(3) The per capita estimate depends on an estimate of the population; the population of China is not known to the nearest 100 million, so this gives a margin of error of about 14 percent.

(4) Furthermore, per capita comparisons must take into account the mean factor. With equal per capita production, there will be many more poor people in a country with a wide income range than in a country like China, which has a very narrow one.

Since these figures were worked out, China has supplied some information about her production. In 1970, Chou En-lai said, industrial production was on the order of 90 billion dollars and agricultural production on the order of 30 billion dollars, for a total of 120 billion dollars. This is about double the World Bank's estimate for 1968. On January 1, 1972 the New China News Agency quoted the Prime Minister as saying that in 1971 production was up ten percent from 1970, so this would make it 132 billion dollars. The corresponding figure for Japan in 1969 was 125 billion dollars.

Chou En-lai did not give the detailed figures on which his figures were based. Taking the G.N.P. in 1971 as 132 billion dollars, the per capita estimate works out to between 170 and 193 dollars, depending on the population; the most likely estimate of the population in 1971 is 750 million, which would put the per capita income at about 180 dollars.

This figure seems very likely to be right. With 180 dollars, the average Chinese in 1971 would find himself on a par with the average Formosan ten years before or the average Brazilian in 1953.

Furthermore, for ideological reasons this estimate fails to account for an entire sector of the economy: the services.

To compare China with Western countries, one would have to try to determine the value added by administration and commerce.

Without the figures, let us proceed by analogy: In India, the services sector represents 26 percent of the G.N.P., which breaks down as follows:

Commerce   10.4%

Other services   15.5%
(of which administration makes up 4.5%)

If one takes into account this 26 percent, the Chinese national product rises to 170 billion dollars for the year 1971. And even this figure does not take into account an enormous sector of public works (like irrigation and air raid defenses) undertaken voluntarily, or at least free of charge, by the peasants and workers. If one adds this factor, the per capita income is on the order of 225 dollars, equal to that of Japan in 1915, less than half that of Italy in 1930 and that of Spain in 1955.

With a per capita income of 225 dollars the communist Chinese would be only six years behind the Chinese of Taiwan. True, the latter climbed to 320 dollars in 1971. Nevertheless, without economic aid—Soviet aid, which has been costly, lasted only ten years and was completely broken off in 1960—and in spite of the jolts of the "Great Leap" and the Cultural Revolution, People's China does not seem so far from reaching the standard of living on Taiwan, an island which has enjoyed considerable aid from the United States.

Furthermore, People's China would have overtaken by far Pakistan, India and Indonesia, all countries which stood above her in 1949 in terms of per capita income.

BIBLIOGRAPHY

ANON., *China*, Nagel Guides, Paris 1967.

BACKHOUSE, E., and BLAND, J. O. P., *Les Empereurs mandchous, Mémoires de la Cour de Pékin*, Preface by H. Maspero, Paris 1934.

BALASZ, ETIENNE, *La Bureaucratie céleste*, Paris 1968.

BARY, W. T. DE, CHAN, W. T., and WATSON, B., *Sources of Chinese Tradition*, New York 1960.

BEAUVOIR, SIMONE DE, *La Longue Marche*, Paris 1957.

BERNARD-MAITRE, FATHER HENRI, *Sagesse chinoise et philosophie chrétienne*, Hien-hien 1935.

BETTELHEIM, CHARLES, "Chine et U.R.S.S.: deux modèles d'industrialisation," *Les Temps Modernes*, August–September 1970.

BETTELHEIM, CHARLES, CHARRIERE, JACQUES, and MARCHISIO, HÉLÈNE, *La Construction du socialisme en Chine*, Paris 1965.

BETTELHEIM, CHARLES, *Révolution culturelle et organisation industrielle en Chine*, Paris 1973.

BIANCO, LUCIEN, *Les Origines de la Révolution chinoise*, Paris 1967.

BODARD, LUCIEN, *Mao*, Paris 1970.

BRINE, LINDSAY, *The Taiping Rebellion*, London 1962.

BUCK, PEARL, *La Chine comme je la vois*, Paris 1971.

CHANDRASEKHAR, *China's Population*, Hong Kong 1960.

CHEN PO-TA, *Notes on Mao Tse-tung's Report on an Investigation of the Peasant Movement in Hunan*, Peking 1966.

CHESNEAUX, JEAN, *Les Syndicats chinois*, Paris-Hague 1965.
CHIANG KAI-SHEK, *Destin de la Chine*, with an introduction and commentary by P. Jaffe, Paris 1949.
CHOU EN-LAI, *A Great Decade*, Peking 1959.
CHOW TSE-TUNG, *The May Fourth Movement, Intellectual Revolution in Modern China*, Cambridge 1960.
CREEL, H. G., *La Pensée chinoise de Confucius à Mao Tse-tung*, Paris 1962.
DELEYNE, JEAN, *L'Economie chinoise*, Paris 1971.
DUFAY, FATHER FRANÇOIS, *L'Etoile contre la Croix*, Paris 1955.
DU HALDE, FATHER P. J-B., S. J., *Description géographique, historique, chronologique, politique et physique de l'Empire de Chine*, Paris 1735.
DUMONT, RENÉ, *La Chine surpeuplée, Tiers Monde affamé*, Paris 1965.
ELIA, PASCAL M. D', *Le Triple Démisme de Suen Wen*, Shanghai 1929, translated, annotated and with a commentary by Pascal M. d'Elia.
ESMEIN, JEAN, *La Révolution culturelle chinoise*, Paris 1970.
ETIEMBLE, *Le Nouveau singe pèlerin*, Paris 1958.
ETIEMBLE, *Connaissons-nous la Chine?* Paris 1964.
ETIENNE, GILBERT, *La Voie chinoise*, Paris 1962.
FAIRBANK, JOHN K., and TENG SSU-YU, *China's Response to the West (1838–1923)*, Cambridge, Mass., 1954.
FAURE, EDGAR, *Le Serpent et la tortue: les problèmes de la Chine populaire*, Paris 1957.
FAURE, LUCIE, *Journal d'un voyage en Chine*, Paris 1958.
GERNET, JACQUES, *La Vie quotidienne en Chine à la veille de l'invasion mongole*, Paris 1959; *La Chine ancienne*, Paris 1964.
GIGON, FERNAND, *Et Mao prit le pouvoir*, Paris 1970.
GITTINGS, JOHN, *The Role of the Chinese Army*, Oxford 1968.
GOSSET, PIERRE and RENEE, *Chine rouge, an VII*, Paris 1958.
GROUSSET, RENE, *Histoire de la Chine*, Paris 1962.
GROUSSET, RENE, and DENIKER, GEORGE, *La Face de l'Asie*, Paris 1962.
GUILLAIN, ROBERT, *Six cent millions de Chinois*, Paris 1956; *Dans trente ans, la Chine*, Paris 1965.
GUILLERMAZ, JACQUES, *La Chine populaire*, Paris 1959; *A History of the Chinese Communist Party, 1921–1949*, translated by Anne Destenay, London 1972; *Histoire du Parti Communiste Chinois*, Volume 2, Paris 1972.
HALDANE, CHARLOTTE, *The Last Great Empress of China*, London 1965.
HAN SUYIN, *China in the Year 2001*, Harmondsworth 1970.
HUDELOT, CLAUDE, *La Longue Marche*, Paris 1971.
ISAACS, HAROLD, *The Tragedy of the Chinese Revolution*, Stanford 1962.
KAROL, K. S., *La Chine de Mao*, Paris 1966.
KAZANTZAKIS, NIKOS, *Chine-Japon*, Paris 1938–1971.
KEIM, JEAN A., *Petite histoire de la grande Chine*, Paris 1966.

KHRUSHCHEV, NIKITA SERGEYEVICH, *Khrushchev Remembers*, translated by Strobe Talbott and with an introduction, commentary and notes by Edward Crankshaw, London 1971.

LAI YING, *Les Prisons de Mao*, told to Edward Behr, French text by Jacky le Corre, Paris 1970.

LEYS, SIMON, *Les Habits neufs du Président Mao*, Paris 1971.

MACARTNEY, LORD, *Journey to China and Tartary*, 12 volumes.

MACCIOCCHI, MARIA-ANTONIETTA, *De la Chine*, Paris 1971.

MALAPARTE, CURZIO, *En Russie et en Chine*, translated from the Italian by M. Arnaud, Paris 1959.

MAO TSE-TUNG, *Selected Works* in four volumes, Peking 1967–9.

MAO TSE-TUNG, *Quotations from Chairman Mao Tse-tung*, Peking 1966.

MENDE, TIBOR, *China and Her Shadow*, London 1960.

MENDES-FRANCE, PIERRE, *Dialogues avec l'Asie d'aujourd'hui*, Paris 1972.

MEHNERT, KLAUS, *Peking and Moscow*, London 1963; *Pékin et la nouvelle gauche*, translated from the German by Georgette Chatenet, Paris 1971.

MERAY, TIBOR, *La rupture Moscou-Pekin*, Paris 1966.

MICHAUX, HENRI, *Un Barbare en Asie*, Paris 1945.

MORAVIA, ALBERTO, *La Révolution culturelle de Mao*, translated from the Italian by Jean-Louis Faivre d'Arcier, Paris 1968.

MYRDAL, JAN, *Report from a Chinese Village*, London 1965.

PELISSIER, ROGER, *De la Révolution chinoise*, Paris 1967.

RIVIERE, CLAUDE, *En Chine avec Teilhard 1938–1944*, Paris 1968.

ROTHSCHILD, ROBERT, *La Chute de Chiang Kai-shek*, Paris 1972.

SAUVY, ALFRED, *De Malthus à Mao Tse-tung*, Paris 1958.

SCHRAM, STUART, *Mao Tse-tung*, Harmondsworth 1967.

SCHRAM, STUART, and CARRERE D'ENCAUSSE, HÉLÈNE, *Le Marxisme et l'Asie*, Paris 1965.

STAMPAR, A., *The North-western Provinces and Their Possibilities of Development*, Nanking 1934.

SNOW, EDGAR, *Red Star over China*, London 1937; *Red China Today: The Other Side of the River*, London 1963, Harmondsworth 1970.

STRONG, ANNA LOUISE, *China's Millions*, New York 1935.

TAWNEY, R. H., *Land and Labour in China*, London 1932.

TEILHARD DE CHARDIN, PIERRE, *Letters from a Traveller*, London 1973.

TROTSKY, LEV DAVIDOVICH, *On Lenin, Notes towards a Biography*, London 1971.

VAN COILLIE, DRIES, *J'ai subi le lavage de cerveau*, Paris 1964.

VERCORS, *Les Pas dans le sable*, Paris 1954.

WIEGER, R. P. LÉON, *Le Feu aux poudres*, Hien-hien 1925.

WEI TSING-SING, LOUISE, *Le Saint-Siège et la Chine*, Paris 1971.

Index

399